DISMANTLING THE **BIG** BANG

GOD'S UNIVERSE REDISCOVERED

DISMANTLING THE BIG BANG

GOD'S UNIVERSE REDISCOVERED

ALEX WILLIAMS

First printing: July 2005
Second printing: June 2006

ISBN-13: 978-0-89051-437-5
ISBN-10: 0-89051-437-2
Library of Congress Control Number: 2005925567

Unless otherwise noted, Scripture is from the Revised Standard Version of the Bible.

Cover by Left Coast Design, Portland, Oregon

Printed in the United States of America

Please visit our website for other great titles:
www.masterbooks.net

For information regarding author interviews,
please contact the publicity department at (870) 438-5288.

Master
Books

A Division of New Leaf Publishing Group

ACKNOWLEDGMENTS

We are extremely grateful to Dr. Carl Wieland for initiating the project, and for his inspiration and skill in editing the text, to Barbara Williams for reading and commenting on the first draft, to Dr. Russell Humphreys for discussion on cosmological issues, to Doug Fletcher for discussion of theological issues, to Dr. Jason Lisle for reviewing the completed manuscript, and to Kym Holwerda for stylistic and proof corrections. Alex Chapman inspired the idea of the scoreboard.

CONTENTS

A BRIEF OVERVIEW...13

    Four Reasons to Reject the Big-Bang Theory 13

    Four Reasons to Accept Six-Day Creation 14

    Four Reasons to Avoid Compromise 16

INTRODUCTION 19

CHAPTER 1 — FROM THE BACKYARD TO THE BIG BANG —
A BRIEF HISTORY OF COSMOLOGY 21

    Backyard Cosmology 21

    Timekeeping and Navigation 22

    The Shape of Things 23

    Wanderers and Houses 24

    Spirit Universe 25

    Scientific Cosmology — The Classical Period 27

    Jewish Cosmology 29

    The Middle Ages..32

    The Renaissance...34

    What Are Stars Made Of? 38

    How Far Are the Stars? 38

    What's in It, Anyway? 42

    The New Physics and the Universe Within 44

    Nuclear Physics 47

    The Big Bang 47

    Slide Back into Metaphysics...49

CHAPTER 2 — SCIENCE, WORLD VIEWS,
AND COSMOLOGICAL MODELS 53

    The Juggernaut Scenario 53

    The Juggernaut Fallacy..54

    The Foundation of Thought 55

    First Choices in Physics and Metaphysics 56

    Assumptions Influence Conclusions...58

    World Views 61

        The Naturalistic World View 61

        The Biblical World View 63

        Idolatry...64

Further Limitations of Science 65
   "Facts" May Not Be Universally True 66
   "Right" Theories Can Be Wrong.....................................66
   Human Frailty and Scientific Objectivity.......................67
   The Scientific Method 68
   Tricks of the Mind 70
   Science and Faith 71
   The Parsimonious Monk 72
The Anthropic Principle 72
Intelligent Design 75
A Necessary and Sufficient Universe..77

CHAPTER 3 — TOOLS FOR EXPLAINING THE UNIVERSE 81
Chance 82
   Chance Is Not a Force 83
   Chance Is Not Alone 83
   Gambling Costs Money 84
   Possible and Impossible Events 86
Necessity...87
   Quantum Mechanics 87
   The Four Forces of Physics 89
The Achievements of Gravity 91
   Orbits..91
   Spheres 94
   Nuclear Fusion 95
   Singularities and Black Holes..96
   Avoiding the Primordial Singularity 100
Rotation and Turbulence...102
Dimensions...103
A Global Trend in Science..105
The Laws of Thermodynamics 106
   The Equilibrium Universe 106
The Geometry of Space...108
The Cosmological Constant..110

CHAPTER 4 — THE BIG-BANG MODEL...............................115
Stage A — The Primordial Singularity 118
Stage B — Inflation 121
Stage C — From Energy to Matter 124

Stage D — Decoupling and the CMBR..127
Stage E — Origin of the Galaxies...128
   Gravitational Collapse and Galaxy Formation..............................130
   Galaxy Distribution and the Cosmological Principle.......................132
   The Dark Matter Problem 136
Stage E — Origin of Stars..140
   What Is a Star?...140
   Star Populations..143
   Gas Cloud Dynamics..143
   "Star Forming" Regions..147
   Binaries and Clusters 148
   Summary of Star Formation...150
Stage F — Origin of Planets..151
   The Rocky Planets 151
   The Gas Giants and Ice Planets 154
   Origin of Moons...155
   Origin of Meteorites and Asteroids 157
   Origin of Life..158
Summary of the Big-Bang Model..161

CHAPTER 5 — TIME SCALES..163
What Is "Age"?...164
Age and World Views..166
Age Within the Biblical World View 167
   Functional Creation and the Appearance of Age 168
   Non-relativistic Models...174
   Relativistic Time Dilation 176
Time Indicators in the Cosmos 185
   The Clock Problem 185
   The Age of the Earth 187
   Creationist Views of Earth Age Indicators..............................189
   The Age of the Solar System 198
   The Age of the Universe 199
Summary of Time Scales...203

CHAPTER 6 — THE BIBLICAL MODEL 205
What Is the Universe? 205
The Seven Cs of Thelein History 207
Principles of Biblical Interpretation 207

Jesus' View of Genesis 210
   Why the Intensity? 213
Moses' View of Genesis 214
   Who Is Yahweh? 216
Who Are the Israelites? 217
The Garden of Eden, the Fall, and God's Great Plan of Redemption 218
The Six Days of Genesis Creation 224
God's Method and Timing of Creation 233
   Irreducible Complexity 234
The Super-Alien Galaxy Collector 237
Summary of the Biblical Model 252

CHAPTER 7 — THE SCOREBOARD 259
   Causality 260
   Individual and Common Scores 261

CHAPTER 8 — FUTURE TRENDS IN COSMOLOGY 265
   Summary of Future Trends 269

EPILOGUE — THE CHOICE 271

APPENDIX A: SOME OTHER COSMOLOGICAL MODELS 273
   Brief Overviews 273
   The Arpian Universe 275
      Quasars 276
   The Quasi-Steady State Model 283
      Redshift and Quasars 285
      The QSS and the Big Bang 286
   Carmeli's Cosmological General Relativity 289
   Van Flandern's Meta Model 291
   Summary of Other Cosmological Models 294

APPENDIX B: THEOLOGICAL ISSUES 295
   The Consequences of Compromise 295
   Doctrinal Collapse 296
      Destroying the Gospel 297
      Sin 298
      Dishonoring God 300
      Idolatry 304
      Retreat into Deism 304
      Undermining the Authority of the Written Word of God 306

Biblical Inerrancy 306

The Source of Deception 308

Thelein History — A Stronghold of Faith 309

APPENDIX C: THE SCOREBOARD TABLES 313

Big-Bang Theory 313

The Biblical Model 317

The Common Scoreboard 321

APPENDIX D: AN OPEN LETTER TO THE
    SCIENTIFIC COMMUNITY 327

INDEX 331

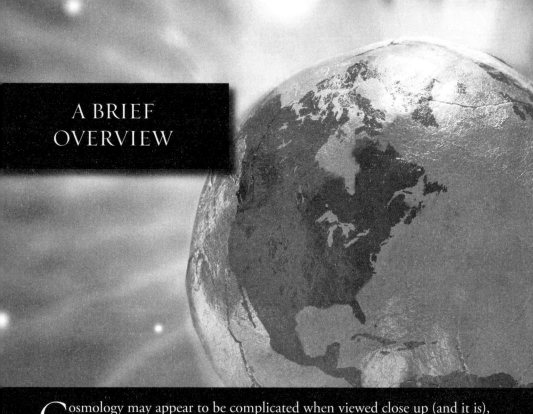

A BRIEF OVERVIEW

Cosmology may appear to be complicated when viewed close up (and it is), but it is easy to understand when viewed from a distance. In this book we have endeavored to give you an easy bird's-eye view — and, in the following few paragraphs, an even easier summary.

Four Reasons to Reject the Big-Bang Theory

It doesn't work.

The universe consists of galaxies, stars, planets, and people, but even when given the credit of every possible doubt, the big-bang theory only produces an expanding cloud of gas. Expanding clouds of gas do not spontaneously reverse their expansion and collapse into the kinds of objects that we observe in the real universe around us today.

The theory lacks a credible and consistent mechanism.

Big-bang theory is based on the laws of physics but those laws cannot explain the important components of the model. The big-bang universe begins in a singularity (all matter, energy, space, and time crushed into a point of infinite density) and there is no known mechanism to start the universe expanding out of the singularity — the equations in the theory only work *after* the expansion has begun.

It then requires a hypothetical period of stupendous inflation to stop the universe from recollapsing. It further requires incredible fine tuning to maintain stability. Its mechanism for turning primordial energy into matter would produce equal amounts of matter and anti-matter but our universe is made only of matter. It has to violate physical laws and appeal to unknown forces (dark energy) and substances (dark matter) to explain what we observe.

Chemical evolution of life (eventually leading to intelligent life, an essential ingredient of any evolutionary cosmology) is clearly excluded by the evidence.

There are basically only two kinds of objects under consideration in cosmology — the *matter* of its substance and the *mind* that contemplates it. Big-bang theory starts with matter (or rather its energy equivalent), and so it must derive the life and mind of the cosmologist by some step-wise process involving at its outset the self-organization of non-living matter. None of the major steps in that supposed chemical evolutionary process can be reproduced in the laboratory (under simulated naturalistic conditions) because the laws of chemistry prevent them. Appeals to chance do not work because chance cannot accomplish what the laws of nature do not allow.

Science cannot produce any final answers on the subject of origins.

Science works in the *present*, by observation and experiment; it has no direct access to the past. We cannot directly observe the past, we cannot revisit it in a time machine, nor can we repeat it (as an experiment would require), so anything scientists say about the past has to be based on extrapolation from *present-day* observations. These extrapolations have, in turn, to be based on assumptions. Those assumptions are necessarily constructed within the framework of a *belief system* about the nature of the universe and how it came to be the way it is. Christians therefore need to study the universe within a Christian (i.e., biblical) belief system, and not think they must rely on the beliefs of atheistic naturalism. The purpose of this book is to help Christians do just that.

FOUR REASONS TO ACCEPT SIX-DAY CREATION

Genesis 1 clearly states that God created the universe in six ordinary-length days.

While the word "day" has a variety of possible meanings, the meaning intended by an author is always specified by the *context*. The context in Genesis 1 is "evening and morning, one day." The author clearly intended the word to mean an ordinary-length day. The Ten Commandments, which God wrote down with His own finger in stone, confirm this conclusion. The Fourth Commandment says that the Israelites were to observe the Sabbath as a memorial to the fact that God created the universe in six days.

Jesus was totally committed to the authority of the Scriptures, particularly the writings of Moses (which begin with Genesis), and He said that we must be too.

Jesus said that if we did not believe what Moses wrote we could not believe what He said, because Moses wrote about Him. Jesus claimed to *be* the God whom Moses wrote about, and He claimed that the writings of Moses provided the foundation for His incarnation, atonement and resurrection. Jesus made it a condition of Christian discipleship that we believe what He says.

The honor and glory of God are revealed in His work of creation.

God defines himself throughout the Bible as the Creator. His honor and glory are shown forth in His work of creation, so it is logically absurd for Christians to worship God as Creator, but then to refuse to believe what He says on the subject of creation.

The Atonement depends upon Genesis creation.

According to Genesis, man was created to live with God forever. There was no suffering, no accidents, and no death. Death entered the world only after the Fall, as the penalty for man's sin. God's plan of redemption involved several important steps. First, He delayed the penalty of death to give man *time* to repent. Then he withdrew some of His upholding power to give man a small taste of what life without God is like — this is called "the Curse," and it is the explanation for human suffering and the decay of the universe. God did this to give man a *reason* to repent; otherwise, he could have continued forever in his fallen state. Then God cast Adam and Eve out of the paradise of Eden, to block their access to the Tree of Life so that they would not continue to live forever in their alienated state and would eventually die. Then God provided a sacrifice to die in their place and pay the penalty of sin for them. At first, this was an animal sacrifice, but the true sacrifice was God himself. God the Son, Jesus Christ, died in our place to pay the penalty for our sin, so that in Him we might become the righteousness of God. Once the penalty had been paid, death could no longer hold Him, and Jesus rose from the dead. However, evolution is based on the idea that death is a natural part of life and it was in the world for millions of years before man ever existed. Even long-age creationist views that reject biological evolution must accept that death was around for eons before man sinned, but if death is indeed a natural part of life then it cannot be the penalty for sin — it's only natural, after all. If we accept "billions of years of earth history," then death existed before sin, and the story about Christ dying to pay the penalty for our sins becomes meaningless.

Four Reasons to Avoid Compromise

The number one reason for compromise — the time scale — is no longer a stumbling block.

Up until the time that geologists first began to speculate about the world being millions of years old, Christians generally believed in the biblical time scale. When Darwin's theory of evolution was married up with the long ages of uniformitarian (slow-and-gradual) geology, large numbers of Christians rejected the biblical time scale and adopted the evolutionary one, but recent research has shown that the evolutionary time scale is a "house of cards." Long-age dating methods are all crucially dependent upon long-age naturalistic assumptions, and the assumptions you begin with determine the conclusions you come to. When the scientific evidence is interpreted within the biblical world view, using biblical assumptions, the evidence is consistent with the biblical time scale. While the vastness of the cosmos requires a time scale of billions of years, relativity theory shows that time is not a constant, and during the creation week it's possible that only one day may have passed on earth while billions of years passed in the cosmos. The biblical model is consistent with the evidence on a wide range of time scales, and provides better explanations than does the big-bang theory.

Compromise destroys the internal consistency of the Bible.

The method, timing, and purpose of God's work of creation are inextricably interconnected and cannot be separated without doing violence to all three.

(a) God spoke the universe into existence out of nothing. He also holds it in existence by that same word of power. If, however, parts of the universe did not come into existence until billions of years after God commanded them to do so, it destroys the logical connection between the cause and the effect. Consider an example. If Lazarus had not come out of the tomb when Jesus called him to come out, but came out five years later, could we say that Jesus raised him from the dead? Of course not — the connection between cause and effect is lost if too much time intervenes between the two.

(b) Much of the creation shows evidence of irreducible complexity, a principle of design that requires the assembly of all the parts at one time in order for the system to work. If some parts had to wait around for millions of years before the other parts turned up, the ravages of time would have degraded and/or dispersed them and they would not work.

(c) God's stated reason for creating the universe in six days was to give man a convenient time scale to commemorate and celebrate His person and work of creation. If this time scale is expanded to billions of years, it makes nonsense of the Fourth Commandment.

Compromise positions do not earn respect among non-Christians.

A common motivation for Christian compromise on six-day creation is the fear of ridicule from evolutionists. This is understandable — no one wants to be thought a fool. However, this reason is not likely to gain much favor with the One who called us to follow Him on the way of the Cross. As it turns out, it gains no respect in the secular community either. Even the most casual reader can see that Genesis says God created the universe in six solar days. When Christians try to deny this, they damage their own credibility.

Compromise positions are neither good science nor good theology.

Secular scientists are becoming more and more strident in their calls to restrict scientific explanations to naturalistic causes. While the motivation of many is primarily to exclude the Creator, there is some rationale behind their thinking, in that only naturalistic causes are open to observation and experiment. Big-bang cosmology is a useful scientific theory (even though it is demonstrably wrong) because it proposes a naturalistic cause, which is, in principle at least, open to experimental testing, albeit indirectly. If supernatural creation events are inserted into the big-bang scenario (as some theistic evolutionists and "progressive creationists" do), then the power of the naturalistic explanation is overturned. On the other hand, we argue that supernatural causes should not be excluded from science, because their *effects* and *consequences* can be observed and tested. Thus, the biblical model can be (again indirectly) tested. First, we read what God says He did in creating the universe, and then we look for the effects and consequences to see if they are consistent with the revealed explanations. However, if the biblical account is changed to fit the naturalistic model (all compromise positions do this), then the value of the revealed account is destroyed because it no longer says what the author intended it to say. Compromise positions are therefore neither good science nor good theology.

INTRODUCTION

Most people today believe — because they have been taught it is so — that physics can explain the origin of the universe. Some people say that this is the way "God did it," but since God is not necessary in such a physical explanation, then His involvement (and even His existence) soon becomes irrelevant.

This modern scientific myth is a house of cards, built not upon the evidence but upon the *assumptions* of naturalism — the idea that matter is all there is. When the actual evidence is examined (as distinct from scientific *interpretations* of the evidence), we find that physics can explain something of the history of the universe, but not its origin. Nor indeed can it explain the origin of the important objects within the universe. The difference between history and origin is immense. Science, it turns out, can provide *no* final answers to questions of origin. Science works via observation and experiment in the present, but the unique originating events of the past cannot be directly observed, nor can they be repeated in an experiment. Without a time machine, science is largely blind to the past, having only the relics of it in the present day to speculate about. Those speculations are always developed within a *world view* — a belief system about where the world came from and how it came to be the way it is. Questions of origin therefore ultimately come down to a comparison of world views — how we *think* about the universe.

The purpose of this book is threefold. First, we aim to moderate the extremes of naturalistic thinking. The late Dr. Carl Sagan once wrote that the big-bang theory appeared to be so successful in explaining the origin of the universe that it left "nothing for a Creator to do."[1] In this book we will demonstrate that big-bang cosmology is not at all successful in explaining the origin of the universe. It is an interesting theory, but it simply doesn't work in practice. We believe that Dr. Sagan is now aware of his error.

Our second aim is to moderate the extremes of Christian unbelief. Many years ago, one of us had the difficult task of confronting a Christian colleague about an adulterous relationship. When it came time for "The Bible says you shall not commit adultery," the reply came, "The Bible also says that God created the universe in six days, and you don't believe that do you?" At the time, we did not have access to the modern creationist literature, and had nothing further to say. The point of this story is that if you don't believe the first page of the Bible, then you have little reason to believe the rest of it. Our churches and theological colleges today are laced throughout with Christian unbelievers, all because they think that six-day creation is not theologically and scientifically defensible. This is not the case. Theologically, six-day creation is so important that God wrote it down with His own finger in stone in the Fourth Commandment, and scientifically, it makes perfect sense when understood within the biblical world view.

That leads to our third objective, to stimulate exploration of the biblical world view at its foundation in cosmology. We hope that this book might inspire young Christians to take up the challenge to think biblically in every area of their lives and to explore God's marvelous creation by seeking to think about it in the way that God thinks about it. That, we contend, is the only way to understand it correctly.

We have opportunities today to glorify God and to enlighten, edify, and encourage His people in ways that none before us have ever had. Let us use those opportunities while we may, and be found still at work when the Master comes to take us home.

---

1. Carl Sagan, introduction to *A Brief History of Time: From the Big Bang to Black Hole*, by Stephen Hawking (London: Bantam Press, 1988).

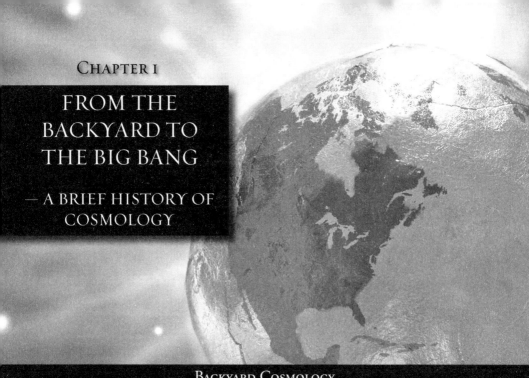

CHAPTER 1

FROM THE BACKYARD TO THE BIG BANG

— A BRIEF HISTORY OF COSMOLOGY

BACKYARD COSMOLOGY

Early cosmology was easy. All you had to do was to look at the night sky. Well, you had to look at it for a long time, and you had to look at it night after night all year round. But before television there was nothing much else to do at night anyway, and before streetlights and cities it was also much easier to see the night sky and its blaze of glorious starlight.

We can be sure that someone did manage to stay up all night and notice that the stars went the same way as the sun and the moon. They all disappeared over the western horizon, following one another like a flock of sheep. Because they all followed the same path night after night it would soon become obvious that the heavenly bodies were traveling in circles around the earth.

The earliest cosmologies therefore represented the earth as the center of the universe, with the sun, moon, and stars turning in circles around it. Despite our sophisticated modern knowledge, this model still works perfectly well in everyday life. Scientific bodies such as meteorological offices, maritime service organizations, and the world's time-keeping authorities all refer to "sunrise" and "sunset" times and "moonrise" and "moonset" times, and they predict tides and moon phases and other phenomena associated with the heavens from the point of view of a stationary earth and a moving sky.

TIMEKEEPING AND NAVIGATION

From the earliest times, the celestial bodies have served as timekeepers. Many ancient cultures erected large stone structures, some of which survive today, that enabled them to obtain fixed reference points for the calculation of the progress of the seasons. One such place is Stonehenge in England.

Because the sun played such an important role in timekeeping, some ancient cultures, notably among native Americans, used a "compass" with four cardinal points marked by the position of the sun at sunrise on winter solstice

Stonehenge — At midsummer dawn, the sun rises directly over the "heel" stone in the background of the picture.

(the shortest day of the year), sunset on winter solstice, sunrise on summer solstice (the longest day of the year) and sunset on summer solstice.

The stars also provided a means of navigating, particularly at night and at sea. In Genesis 1:14, when God was creating the stars, He said, "Let them be for signs and for seasons and for days and years." We will consider their role as timekeepers shortly, but one obvious meaning of "signs" is that they point toward something. This can have a prophetic directional sense for the future, as we shall look at later, but it can also have a geographic directional sense for the present. In the northern hemisphere, for example, the famous "Pole Star" shows the way to the north pole, and in the southern hemisphere the famous "Southern Cross" shows the way to the south celestial pole (which falls approximately where the long axis meets the bisector of the two pointers).

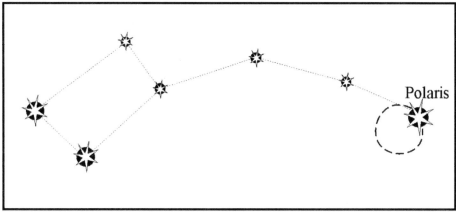

The constellation Ursa Minor. The north celestial pole lies within the dashed circle. The bright star Polaris, or Pole Star, shows night travelers where it is.

THE SHAPE OF THINGS

There is a common myth that ancient peoples thought the earth was flat. Some may have thought so, but most others certainly did not. Seafarers plied the Mediterranean from very early times and they would all have known that ships disappear over the horizon and yet do not fall off the edge. Even the shortest journey, such as from the coast of Lebanon to the island of Cyprus for example, a distance of about 95 miles (150 km), would have been sufficient to yield this insight. Aristotle (384–322 B.C.) reasoned as follows: "Earth's shape must necessarily be spherical. For every portion of earth has weight until it reaches the center, and the jostling of parts . . . would bring about . . . convergence . . . [and] if an equal amount is added on every side the extremity of the mass will be everywhere equidistant from its center, i.e., the figure will be spherical." He also noted that the changing star positions with latitude pointed to a spherical earth. In his view, the diameter was "of no great size" and he quoted an un-named mathematician's estimate of 400,000 stades (about 64,000 km).[1] Others figured out that a lunar eclipse is caused by the shadow of the earth falling across the face of the moon, and they noticed that the earth's shadow was always exactly circular in shape, regardless of the orientation of the earth at the time of the eclipse. If the earth had been round and flat, it would have cast circular shadows only when an eclipse occurred near midnight. For eclipses that occurred near sunrise or sunset, the sun's rays would strike a flat earth obliquely, and would produce an elliptical shadow, not a circular one. The only shape that always casts a circular shadow is a sphere.

Eratosthenes (276–196 B.C.), the director of the great library at Alexandria, in Egypt, measured the circumference of the earth with somewhat greater accuracy.[2] One day he read that in the southern Egyptian town of Syene, near the first cataract of the Nile River, at noon on June 21, vertical sticks cast no shadow on the ground, temple columns cast no shadows, and a reflection of the sun could be seen in the water at the bottom of a deep well. The sun was apparently directly overhead. He was thereby inspired to test whether the same thing happened at Alexandria. However, on June 21 his sticks at Alexandria did cast a shadow. The difference, he thought, might have something to do with the curvature of the earth. So he calculated the angle that would account for the difference in shadow lengths and then hired a man to pace out the distance between Alexandria and Syene. The distance was about 800km and the angle was about seven degrees. Seven degrees is about 1/50 of the circumference of a circle, so 50 x 800 = 40,000 kilometers. Our best estimate of the earth's circumference today is 40,074 kilometers. Not bad!

WANDERERS AND HOUSES

Another observation that was made early on is that some stars are fixed and some stars move. Some move detectably from one night to the next, while others move on longer time scales of weeks, months, or years. These moving stars were called "wanderers" by the Greeks, and their word for wanderer is now our word "planet."

------

1. Dennis R. Danielson, *The Book of the Cosmos* (Cambridge, MA: Helix Books, 2000), p. 41–42.
2. Carl Sagan, *Cosmos* (London: Macdonald & Co., 1980), p. 14–15. The apparent accuracy of this estimate is rather fortuitous, given the uncertainties in the measurement methods that he used.

The early timekeepers also noticed that the sun, moon and stars all followed roughly the same path through the sky; what we call today the "plane of the ecliptic." Furthermore, they noticed that the annual cycle of the seasons corresponded with a complementary cycle of fixed stars. Identifiable groups of fixed stars ("constellations" — such as Orion or the Pleiades) would move slightly each night and complete one whole circuit of the heavens in concert with the progress of the sun through the seasons. So they divided the background stars into 12 "houses," which we now call the "signs of the zodiac,"and they plotted the movements of the sun, moon, and planets through these "houses" as a way of describing the progress of the seasons. Later time-keepers moved on to the use of calendars instead of star charts but those who practice astrology still use this method of timekeeping today.

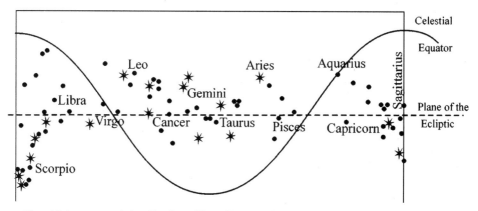

The 12 houses of the Zodiac. The "Plane of the Ecliptic" is the path taken by the sun, moon, and planets. The "Celestial Equator" varies because the earth is tilted at an angle of 23 degrees to the ecliptic.

SPIRIT UNIVERSE

It is only in modern times that many people have chosen to see the universe as a purely physical entity. All ancient cultures viewed the universe as embracing a spiritual dimension as well as a physical one. The denizens of the spirit world included the spirits of dead ancestors, nature spirits, and creator spirits or gods. Many cultures believed in a supreme Creator or Great Spirit.

The biblical world view includes a spirit realm that is beyond time and space, the dwelling place of the Creator God who is a spirit being (John 4:24). The physical world is described as having been spoken into existence by the Creator (Gen. 1) and as being held in existence by that same creative word (Heb. 1:3; Col. 1:17). The physical is thus a product of the spiritual, and depends upon it for its continuing existence. In the spirit universe there are also innumerable angels, personal spirit beings created to be servants of humanity in God's great work of redemption (Heb. 1:14). Some of these spirit beings (Satan and his followers) rebelled against God and were cast out of heaven down to the earth (Rev. 12:7–11), where they are called demons and are the enemies of mankind.

In some cultures it was thought that the sun, moon, stars, and planets all moved through the sky by the action of spirit beings. Ancient people from northern Europe, for example, represented the sun as being carried through the sky by a spirit horse.

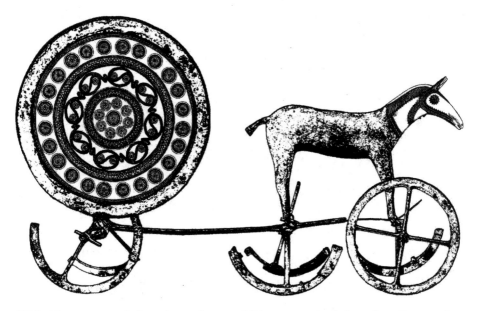

Gilded bronze sun being drawn by a spirit horse and carriage in a Bronze Age sculpture from Denmark, with reconstructed detail.

Bible authors sometimes personified the heavenly bodies. For example:

> . . . the sun . . . comes forth like a bridegroom leaving his chamber, and like a strong man runs its course with joy (Ps. 19:4–5).

They were warned against attributing any divinity to the heavenly bodies that might induce them to worship, such as their pagan neighbors did (Deut. 4:19). Sometimes certain persons were identified with stars — Jesus is called "bright morning star" (Rev. 22:16) and Satan is called "Day Star, son of Dawn" (Isa. 14:12) — but this is simply a metaphorical use of language.

Sometimes stars are associated with the angels (Job 38:7; Isa. 14:13; Rev. 1:20; 12:4), but the sense is that of heavenly exaltation which both stars and angels enjoy, as compared to mankind, who are made a little lower than the angels (Ps. 8:5;NIV). At no time does the Bible suggest that the heavenly bodies are moved by spirit beings.

One of the great achievements of scientific cosmology was to show that spirit beings are not necessary to explain the movements of the heavenly bodies — just gravity and the laws of motion are sufficient. Atheists trumpet this advance as a fatal blow to theism, but biblical creationists see it simply as an advance in our understanding of how the world works. In fact, the "laws" of science imply a lawgiver. Scientific laws are a description of the way God normatively works within this physical universe. The very notion of a lawful, consistent Creator God was in fact a major impetus to the rise of modern science. It gave a reason to expect, and thus look for, the consistent lawful way in which the world operates.

Scientific Cosmology —
The Classical Period

The beginning of what we might call "scientific" cosmology arose when people began to try to explain what they saw in the heavens using causes that they were familiar with on earth. Interestingly, the great thinkers who contributed new insights into scientific cosmology all included elements that were wrong. The lesson for us today, we believe, is that we are also probably including elements that are wrong. None of us has all the relevant information, therefore as our knowledge grows some ideas will be proved right and some wrong.

Pythagoras (580–500 B.C.) was one of the earliest writers to formally develop the idea that the earth was a sphere, and that it was rotating on its axis. This accounted nicely for the circular movements of the heavenly bodies. However, he also falsely believed that the earth was orbiting a central, unseen fire (not the sun) and that the earth, moon, sun, and the five known planets (Mercury, Venus, Mars, Jupiter and Saturn) were all arranged according to a musical scale and produced what he called "the harmony of the spheres."

Plato (427–367 B.C.) was one of the most creative and influential philosophers of the classical period and had a great impact upon subsequent Western thought. He promoted Pythagoras' ideas of circular motions but he held to a stationary earth. He also erroneously taught that Mercury and Venus rotate from west to east rather than east to west, as did the sun, moon, and other planets. In fact, the planets do sometimes appear to go backward (i.e., from west to east). This "retrograde motion," as it is called, is today explained as the result of the planets orbiting the sun at different rates to the earth and thus sometimes appearing to move backward against the background of the distant stars.

The retrograde motion of Mars.

Eudoxus (408– 355 B.C.), a younger contemporary of Plato, addressed the problem of retrograde motion by suggesting that each planet orbited the earth in a system of spheres within spheres. By using 33 such spheres, he was able to account for the apparent motion of the five planets.

Aristotle (384–322 B.C.), a student of Plato and tutor to Alexander the Great, was one of the greatest of the classical scholars and he contributed to many different fields of knowledge. In his study of cosmology, he set out to construct an actual physical model of Eudoxus' spheres, but he found that he required 55 spheres to get it to work.

Aristarchus (310–250 B.C.) came up with the brilliant idea that the earth was a planet and that all the planets revolved in circular orbits about the sun. This vastly simplified Aristotle's complicated model. But alas, the great Aristotle continued to rule the world of ideas long after his death, and Aristarchus' idea lay dormant for another 1,800 years.

Ptolemy (A.D. 120–180) was the last great astronomer of classical times. His book, called the *Almagest*, which has come down to us via Arabic scholars, has been an important source for much of our knowledge of ancient science. One problem that Aristotle's model did not address was the variation in the brightness of planets such as Mars. Ptolemy imagined the earth as the center of the universe, and the sun orbited the earth, while the planets orbited the sun in circular orbits. By representing the orbits as wheels, he found that he could explain the observed orbits of the planets using 39 wheels within wheels. In this "epicycle" model the variations in planetary brightness resulted from varying distances between them and earth.

With the decline and fall of the Roman Empire in the 4th and 5th centuries A.D. there were no new insights into scientific cosmology for the next thousand years. Ptolemy's epicycle model later became (fatally for some) embedded in the doctrine of the Roman church.

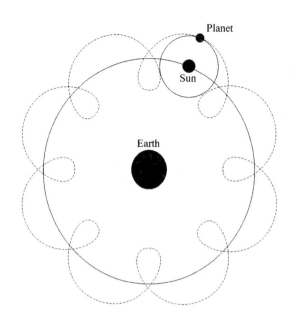

Planet

Sun

Earth

Ptolemy's epicycle theory — planet orbits the sun as it orbits the earth, thus explaining retrograde motion and varying brightness.

Jewish Cosmology

During the classical period, the Jews developed a rich literary tradition, of which the Dead Sea Scrolls are an abundant sample, unique among ancient literature. Having been conquered by the Greeks in the 4th century B.C. and been subjected to their policy of Hellenization — the universal teaching of Greek language and culture — they were well acquainted with the challenge of Greek thinking. In many areas they adopted the new Greek ideas, but when it came to cosmology they remained very conservative.

The Torah (the writings of Moses) was very clear on the issue of creation. Indeed, it stands as a monument of rationality amidst a sea of mythology, as we will see. The first book of the Torah, Genesis, begins as follows:

> In the beginning God created the heaven and the earth.

God is simply assumed to exist, without question. Then God created everything in the universe by speaking it into existence (and the New Testament adds that He holds it in existence by that same powerful word — Heb. 1:3). When it comes to the heavenly bodies, they likewise are attributed to God's direct acts of creation:

> And God said, "Let there be lights in the firmament of the heavens to separate the day from the night; and let them be for signs and for seasons and for days and years, and let them be lights in the firmament of the heavens to give light upon the earth." And it was so. And God made the two great lights, the greater light to rule the day, and the lesser light to rule the night; he made the stars also. And God set them in the firmament of the heavens to give light upon the earth, to

rule over the day and over the night, and to separate the light from the darkness. And God saw that it was good (Gen 1:14–18).

Some scholars have suggested that the Genesis account of creation was derived from the "earlier" Babylonian creation story in the *Enuma Elish*. The absurdity of this claim can be seen when we compare the majestic rationality of the Genesis story with the obviously mythical plot of the *Enuma Elish*:

> The assembly of the gods was overturned by Tiamat and her consort Kingu. The gods were forced to call upon a young, strong god, Marduk, to regain their position. Marduk and Tiamat engaged in combat and Marduk killed her. Marduk then created the world from the body of Tiamat and he created man from earth and the blood of Kingu. The purpose of human life was to serve the gods so that they might live an easy life. And Marduk was elevated to the position of king over all the gods.[3]

This story assumes the existence of multiple gods, none of which transcends human-like frailty. It gives evil (rebellion and war) a primordial position and the creation is made out of pre-existing material. In contrast, the Genesis story depicts one God, transcendent over all, creating all things out of nothing by His spoken word. His creation reflects the perfect goodness of His own being (Gen. 1:4, 10, 12, 18, 21, 25, 31). Evil entered the world only through the rebellion of God's creatures.

In regard to the time scale, Genesis describes God's work of creation to have occurred over a period of six ordinary-length days, marked by the phrase "evening and morning" for days that are counted from one to six. The word "day" is defined as the period of light that alternates with the darkness, which He called "night," and also as one complete day/night cycle, so there cannot be any confusion over what the author intended the word to mean (Gen. 1:5). Furthermore, the idea of creation in six ordinary-length days is affirmed in the Ten Commandments. God commanded the Israelites (and wrote it down with His own finger in stone!) to observe the Sabbath as a perpetual memorial to the fact that God created the universe in six days (Exod. 20:11; 31:17–18; 32:16). It would be impossible to interpolate millions of years here because man could not work for six multi-million-year periods and then rest for one! Furthermore, mankind was created on day 6, so the history of the universe is coincidental

---

3. Ninian Smart and Richard D. Hecht, editors, *Sacred Texts of the World — A Universal Anthology* (Bath, UK: Macmillan Reference Books, 1984), p. 6–9.

with the history of man. The genealogies given in Genesis 5, 10, and elsewhere in the Bible, ending up with Jesus in Luke 3:23–38, add up to a creation date around 4000 B.C.

שֵׁשֶׁת־יָמִים

Hebrew text from the Ten Commandments, saying "in six days."

Other religious narratives are generally timeless in their stories of origin, so the Bible's clear location of the originating events in historical time, verified by the lists of the descendants of the first humans, is quite remarkable. The Hindu *Suryasiddhanta* calendar, for example, purports to give an age of the earth equivalent to 1,972,947,099 B.C., but this is based on astronomical calculation, not on history.[4] Events of Hindu history cannot be located in time and space beyond about the second millenium B.C. The Han Chinese believe in cycles of destruction and re-creation every 23,639,040 years,[5] but once again there is no connection with actual Chinese history, which only goes back a few thousand years.

Many modern liberal scholars, both Jews and Christians, in attempting to harmonize the Bible with modern science, try to make out that Jewish scholars in the classical period did not interpret Genesis to mean that God created the universe in six ordinary-length days. However, the evidence is clearly against them. The earliest manuscript evidence we have is the Dead Sea Scrolls and they assumed a straightforward reading of the creation texts in Genesis 1–3.[6]

The literature of orthodox Judaism was contained in three types of writings — the Bible, the Mishnah, and the Talmud. The Jewish Bible is our Old Testament — the Protestant Bible is based on the Hebrew manuscript (the Masoretic text) and the Catholic Bible adds some extra elements that were contained in the Greek manuscript (the Septuagint), but both agree on the writings of Moses (the Torah or Pentateuch), which include the creation accounts. The Mishnah was the "Oral Law" and was handed down with the written Law (the Bible) as a supplement to it. The Talmud was a collection of scholarly commentary on, and interpretation of, the Mishnah.

---

4. U. Aswathanarayana, *Principles of Nuclear Geology* (Rotterdam: A.A. Balkema, 1985), p. 228.

5. Lawrence Badash, "The Age of the Earth Debate," *Scientific American* (August 1989): p. 78.

6. L.H. Schiffman and J.C. VanderKam, *Encyclopedia of the Dead Sea Scrolls* (Oxford University Press, 2000), Vol. 1, p. 155.

The Mishnah addressed 63 subjects in 523 chapters and its main purpose was to assist the faithful to understand and apply the law of Moses in their daily life. The subject of origins was not included in the list of 63. The Mishnah urged the avoidance of all metaphysical speculation and specifically prohibited cosmogonical speculation ("cosmogony" deals with the origin of the cosmos).[7] The rabbis (Jewish teachers) took the Genesis account at face value and did not enter into speculation about it.

Their attitude is well illustrated by a difference of opinion that arose between the two leading rabbis in the time of Jesus — Shammai and Hillel. Shammai argued that the intention of God during creation was developed during the night and His acts of creation were carried out by day, but Hillel argued that both the intention and the act took place by day. The argument was settled in the following century by rabbi Simeon who said: "The intention was both by day and by night while the fulfillment was with the waning of the sun."[8] This clearly illustrates three important points: (1) these rabbis accepted the Genesis account as fully authoritative, (2) they allowed themselves to speculate only upon the most trivial of cosmogonical issues, and (3) they worked strictly within the literal-day framework.

If any doubt should remain on this question, we need only refer to the Jewish calendar. The year A.D. 2003 is, in Orthodox Jewish reckoning, the year A.M. 5764. The "A.M." stands for *anno mundi* and means "the year of the world." Jews count the years since creation. According to their calendar, creation took place in the year 3761 B.C.

THE MIDDLE AGES

It is common among secular histories of scientific cosmology to represent the Middle Ages, or medieval period, as a time during which the Church suppressed free thinking about the universe. This is not true. Two profound changes came over the Western world that directly caused the lack of progress in scientific cosmology.

First was the fall of the Roman Empire. The social and economic structures that had supported the learning of Greek and Roman times collapsed. In the chaos that followed, people had to be more concerned about survival than about learning for its own sake. There were no longer any schools where young people could be trained and inspired to break new intellectual ground. Only in

---

7. *Encyclopedia Judaica* (Philadelphia, PA: Coronet Books Inc, 1994) Vol. 5, p. 1063.
8. Ibid.

the Christian monasteries did learning survive, so in fact rather than suppressing learning, the Church preserved and promoted it.

The second great change was that Christianity became widespread throughout the known world, and Christian cosmology so thoroughly eclipsed Greek and Roman cosmology that these latter died out almost completely. The Greeks had studied the *creation* and the Romans had followed in their footsteps, but the Christians had encountered the *Creator*. For a thousand years, the best minds of the Western world were wholly consumed with understanding the incredible events that had occurred in the land of the Jews. Jesus of Nazareth had claimed to be the Creator incarnate and had proved it by multitudinous miracles and by rising from the dead.

Not only had the Christians encountered the Creator, but they brought with them a religion that was intellectually engaging. The religion of Greek and Roman times was based on myths and legends that did not inspire philosophical inquiry, but Jesus was a real person who could be located in time and space and who brought with Him a rich heritage of prophetic and historical literature. A complete and satisfying cosmology was available in the early chapters of Genesis, so there was no urgency about further observational study of the heavens. The most obvious subject for any learned person to pursue in these times was the study of the Creator and the prophetic literature that had prepared the way for His incarnation.

Heavenly Signs

In biblical cosmology, one of the functions of the heavenly bodies is as "signs" or portents of God's intervention in earthly affairs. For example, a star guided the Magi to the birthplace of Jesus (Matt. 2:1–11) and several heavenly signs are mentioned in association with end times (Acts 2:19–20).

When Halley's Comet appeared in A.D. 1066 it was taken as a portent of the Norman victory in England. The event was subsequently immortalized in the famous Bayeaux Tapestry, commissioned by William the Conqueror's wife, Queen Matilde. A section of the tapestry depicting the comet is shown below.

When economic and social conditions did begin to improve once again, to the point where people could pursue learning in a wider field, it was the Christians who were in the forefront. Christians started the first universities in Europe. Copernicus, who spearheaded the cosmological revolution, was a Polish Catholic priest who dedicated his work to the pope. Galileo, the person most quoted as having been persecuted by the church, was a devout Catholic. Galileo's altercation with the church was not a matter of science against the Bible, as is often portrayed, it was about his own personal arrogance, the envy of his colleagues and the politics of an evil pope (Urban VIII). He was not accused of criticizing the Bible, but of disobeying a papal decree.[9]

Giordano Bruno, a contemporary of Galileo, was less careful of his own fate and was burned at the stake for heresy. He is often represented as a martyr to cosmology for promoting Copernicus' views, but he was not a competent astronomer. His heresy — which included belief in an infinite universe that left no room for God — was the product of a wild imagination and a fascination with Hermetic alchemy (Egyptian magic). It was not the result of astronomical observation.

Even so, any fair-minded historian would have to admit that the church which killed Bruno and confronted Galileo was a grossly corrupted version of the Church founded by Jesus.

After the Reformation in the 16th century, much of the church's corruption was corrected and many Christians in the Reformed traditions became prominent leaders in the new age of science. Virtually every branch of modern-day science was pioneered by Christians who embraced a creationist world view, and their scientific endeavors were often inspired by their biblical faith. Because the world was created by an intelligent designer, they believed that it would yield to understanding by intelligent inquiry.

The Renaissance

As western Europe gradually became more prosperous and more politically stable, learning for its own sake began to re-emerge in a more organized form. During the 12th century, Christian universities were established in Paris, France, and at Oxford and Cambridge in England. Their initial focus was theology, law, medicine, and the arts, but as study of the classical authors grew, they inspired a re-emergence of cosmology.

---

9. T. Schirrmacher, "The Galileo Affair: History or Heroic Hagiography?" *TJ* 14(1):91–100 (2000).

The Calendar Problem

Time-keeping consists of three natural units — the *day* (one rotation of the earth on its axis), the *month* (one circuit of the moon around the earth), and the *year* (one circuit of the earth around the sun). Lunar calendars were widely used in the earliest times. The interval between one new moon and the next is 29.53 days and there are 12 lunar cycles in a solar year. But the match is not exact — the lunar year is 354 days long, which is 11½ days shorter than the solar year. To correct this confusion, the first Roman

Julius Caesar, first Roman emperor.

emperor, Julius Caesar, in 45 B.C., following the advice of the Greek astronomer Sosigenes, standardized the calendar across his empire to a solar year of 365 days, with an extra "leap day" every fourth year. This "Julian calendar" remained in use for the next 1,500 years.

The problem popped up again during the Renaissance, and fueled a renewed interest in cosmology. The Julian year, it turned out, was 11 minutes and 14 seconds longer than the solar year. This may not seem to be much of a difference, but over a period of 1,500 years it accumulated to the point where the spring equinox was 10 days too early. So in 1582, Pope Gregory XIII issued a decree dropping 10 days from the calendar and he instituted a new system, called the *Gregorian calendar*, in which century years divisible by 400 should be leap years but other century years should be common years. Thus, 1600 and 2000 were leap years but 1700, 1800, and 1900 were common years. This calendar is the one we use today.

Nicholas Copernicus (1473–1543), a Polish priest, revived Aristarchus' idea that the earth orbited the sun. He retained the idea of circular orbits and so had to retain some of Ptolemy's epicycles, but the result was a very much simplified system. The idea was very controversial when Copernicus published it in 1543, and by 1616 the Catholic church placed his book on their forbidden reading list, although it was taken off the list again shortly after, following some minor revisions.

Tycho Brahe (1546–1601), a Danish astronomer, carried out very accurate observations and discovered that comets were much more distant than the moon and that they followed highly elongated orbits. This discovery challenged the notion held by the classical authors that the heavens were "perfect" and therefore followed perfect geometric shapes — in this case the circle.

Johannes Kepler (1571–1630), Brahe's assistant, applied the non-circular model to planetary orbits and discovered that they followed elliptical orbits. Indeed, the accuracy of his master's observations allowed him to calculate

Comets move in elliptical orbits.

what have since become known as *Kepler's laws of planetary motion*. These included the idea that as the planet comes close to the sun, its orbital speed increases, and then decreases as it moves away. This change in velocity follows a regular and predictable geometric pattern.

Kepler's laws mark a very important turning point in science in general and cosmology in particular. Classical scholars had used geometrical models to explain the motion of heavenly bodies but they did not know about algebra. During the Middle Ages, Arabic scholars developed an understanding of algebra, drawing on sources from India as well as Greece and Rome. During the 12th century, these Arabic works were translated into Latin (the language of scholarship at the time) and European scholars made further advances in the 16th century. Kepler's work marked the beginning of the use of algebra as a tool in cosmology. This was a powerful new combination. By matching astronomical observations against algebraic models, and distinguishing between what is explained and what is left over, new ideas could now be generated for making new observations and/or modifying the algebraic models. The synergy between these two lies at the heart of all modern advances in cosmology and in many other areas of science generally.

Galileo Galilei (1564–1642), an Italian physicist, was the first astronomer to use a telescope. This allowed a better view of the planets, but the stars remained just pinpoints of light. Galileo correctly concluded that the stars must be very much farther away than the planets. Since the time of Copernicus, the idea of the earth not being the center of the universe had grown in popularity and Galileo defended it. He discovered four moons orbiting Jupiter and this provided a model for the idea of a "solar system" in miniature. He also

Galileo's telescope

observed that Venus went through phases just like our moon, which showed that it must orbit the sun. He also discovered sunspots and this further discredited the old Greek idea that the heavens were perfect and immutable.

Sir Isaac Newton (1642–1727), possibly the greatest mathematician and physical scientist of all time, was born in England the year that Galileo died. He contributed to cosmology in four important areas: (1) he discovered the law of gravity; (2) in order to do his calculations of gravity he invented the branch of mathematics called calculus (independently of the German mathematician Gottfried Wilhelm Leibniz); (3) he developed the laws of motion; and (4) he improved the telescope by moving from a lens-based system to a mirror-based reflecting system which gave true color and allowed larger telescopes to be built. Newton's laws of motion and gravity beautifully explained Kepler's laws of planetary orbits and thereby solved the age-old problem of how the heavenly bodies move. The old idea that spirit beings moved the heavenly bodies was no longer necessary.

Sir William Herschel (1738–1822) was born in Germany but moved to England as a young man. Originally a musician, he studied astronomy in his spare time and eventually built the largest reflecting telescopes of his day. With them he discovered a sixth planet, Uranus, and also "milky nebulosities," which he considered to

Newton's reflecting telescope. The mirror is at the rear and the eyepiece near the front.

be other "island universes." Other astronomers ignored his views on this latter subject, but by the 20th century Herschel's ideas were vindicated — we now call them *galaxies* (from the Greek word for milk).

Following Herschel's achievements in telescope technology, attention moved beyond the solar system to "outer space" and the most urgent question became that of the distance scale. How far away were the stars? Before an answer came to that question another astonishing breakthrough occurred. Scientists stumbled onto a method for analyzing the composition of stars!

WHAT ARE STARS MADE OF?

The masters of Renaissance astronomy had come to the conclusion that the planets (that is, the "wanderers" in the solar system) were bodies like the earth, which orbited the sun. That meant the planets were perhaps of similar composition to the earth. This was the first step in our beginning to understand what the universe is made of, but the stars remained remote pinpoints of light that yielded no clue as to what they might be made of.

The breakthrough came via a revolution in our understanding of light. Sir Isaac Newton found that a glass prism could split light up into the colors of the rainbow. What appeared to be white light on one side came out as many different colors on the other side. This *spectrum* of colors was seen as only a novelty at first, but later researchers began to study it in more detail and with better optical equipment, using a device called a *spectroscope*.

ultraviolet   infrared

An electromagnetic spectrum with absorption bands identifying the elements present in the source.

Eventually, with more precise equipment, they began to see lines within the spectrum. These lines remained a riddle until 1861, when two German scientists, Kirchoff and Bunsen (of Bunsen burner fame) discovered that various elements, when heated in a flame, produced distinctive colors — and these colors were associated with distinctive absorption and emission lines in the spectrum of light they emitted. When they turned their spectroscope to the sun they found similar lines — Fraunhofer lines — a number of the same elements they had examined in the laboratory also appeared to be present in the light coming from the sun. So the sun must be made of some of the same elements that we find here on earth. When they turned their spectroscope onto starlight, they found a similar picture — the stars were remarkably like our own sun!

HOW FAR ARE THE STARS?

If the stars are suns just like our sun, then they must be very far away, because even the most powerful telescopes showed them only as pinpoints of light. Early measurements of the distance to the nearby stars used the parallax method of triangulation.

The method works like this. If you study the same stars at a six-month time interval, you get to see them from two different positions in the earth's orbit around the sun. Stars that are close to our sun will appear in slightly different

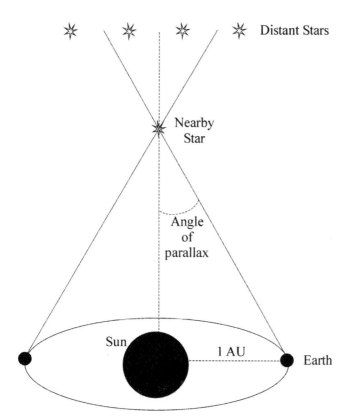

Distant Stars

Parallax method

By comparing the position of a nearby star relative to the position of distant stars at a six-month interval, the angle of parallax can be measured and the distance calculated in units of the earth's distance from the sun (1 Astronomical Unit, AU).

parts of the sky relative to the more distant background of stars, which will appear in approximately the same place at the different times. The angle of this movement is called the "angle of parallax." The distance from the earth to the sun is called one astronomical unit (AU), and it provides the base of a right-angled triangle with a line perpendicular to it from the sun to the nearby star. Using this baseline distance and the angle of parallax, the distance to the nearby star can be calculated using elementary trigonometry.

Another unit of distance, the *parsec*, was also introduced with this method. One parsec is a distance of one *arc second* that a star is displaced by parallax. (A complete circle consists of 360 degrees, each degree consists of 60 arc minutes and each minute consists of 60 arc seconds, so one arc second is the angle in the sky corresponding to $1/360*60*60=1/1,296,000$ of a complete circle.) One parsec is equal to 207,270 AU.

The first parallax measurement was made by German astronomer and mathematician Friedrich Bessel (of *Bessel function* fame) in 1837. He found that the star 61 Cygni was about 523,000 astronomical units away from the earth. Now the average value of the AU is about 149 million km, so 61 Cygni is about 78 million million km from earth. Such distances were staggeringly incomprehensible, and that was just among the nearby stars!

Astronomers continued to apply Bessel's parallax method and were able to push the distance scale out to about 850 million million km, after which the angles became too small to measure accurately.

About this time another unit of cosmic distance, the "light-year," was also devised. The speed of light in a vacuum was accurately measured in 1879 by Albert Michelson, the first American citizen to earn a Nobel Prize. He found that it travels at about 300,000 km/sec. The "light-year" is thus the distance that light will travel (in a vacuum) in a year. The light-year works out to be 9,461 billion km, which corresponds to 63,580 AU and about 0.3 parsecs.

The earth-based parallax method could only go out as far as about 90 light-years, but even at these incredible distances there were countless stars that remained pinpoints of unmoving light, so they must be even farther from earth. In searching for a new method of distance measurement, astronomers began to use properties of the stars themselves such as apparent size, color, and luminosity.

Enter Harlow Shapley, the man who mapped our galaxy. Working at the Mount Wilson Observatory in California between 1914 and 1921, Shapley got the idea that newly discovered variable stars called "Cepheid variables" could be used as "standard candles." These stars vary in brightness over a period of days or weeks and do so in a very precise pattern. Henrietta Leavitt, a rare (and talented) female astronomer, discovered a relationship between the period of variation and the average brightness of these stars. Since brightness is related to distance, Shapley was able to map the distribution and distance of the Cepheid variables and thus produce the first spatial map of our galaxy, the Milky Way. The result was mind-boggling.

Shapley found that the Milky Way was a large, flat, spiral disk about 100,000 light-years across. Our solar system is nowhere near the center — indeed we now know that life would be impossible if we were too near the center. Instead, we are about 26,000 light-years from the center, in one of the spiral arms. We are far enough away from everything else so that we can get a magnificent view of the galaxy without having to suffer the ill-effects of the gravitational and radiation powerhouse that drives it.

Shapley believed that he was the first man to see the edge of the cosmos. He believed that the galaxy *was* the universe and nothing lay beyond it. But others were not so sure. What about the "milky nebulosities" that had so far defied resolution? Shapley believed they were gas clouds within the Milky Way.

What the Milky Way might look like from above. It is a spiral galaxy and the earth and our solar system are out in one of the spiral arms.

Telescopes got bigger and science moved on. In 1920, Edwin Hubble was appointed to the new 100-inch Hooker telescope at Mount Wilson and he began to study the nebula known as Andromeda. By pushing to the limit the telescope and the photographic techniques used to capture images (and by the patience of one man pursuing a dream), Hubble got to the point where, in 1923, he claimed to have resolved the Andromeda nebula into what appeared to be dense swarms of ordinary stars. Shapley was unimpressed — the "stars" were probably just artifacts of the photographic emulsion!

So Hubble now began to compare the photographic plates with one another. In 1924, he found what he was looking for — a pinpoint of light that became brighter, then faded, then became brighter again. He had found a Cepheid variable star! Like a beacon, flashing across the unimaginable immenseness of space, Hubble read the message — "I'm a star . . . I'm a star . . . I'm a star." If there was one star in Andromeda, then the "nebulosity" probably represented billions more of the same — all of them so far away that he could barely see them, even with the new giant telescope.

Hubble then applied Shapley's distance scale for Cepheid variables. Andromeda was an inconceivable distance away — at least one million light-years! More was yet to come. Telescopes got even bigger and we now know that there are hundreds of millions of galaxies out there, some of them billions of light-years away.

WHAT'S IN IT, ANYWAY?

The size of the universe was not the only thing that beggared the imagination of the new generation of astronomers; knowledge of its content, too, exploded.

Throughout the history of cosmology so far, only visible light had been used in the study of the heavens, but the part of the electromagnetic spectrum visible to the human eye is only a small window. Electromagnetic radiation can exist in many different forms, depending on the wavelength — the distance between the peaks of the waves. The names we give to them, in order of increasing wavelength, are: gamma rays, X-rays, ultraviolet, visible light, infrared and radio waves.

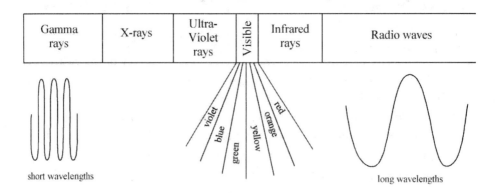

The electromagnetic spectrum, showing the position and size of the window visible to the human eye.

In 1927, transatlantic radio communication was established between America and Europe, but it suffered from a great deal of static interference. Carl Jansky, an employee of Bell Telephone, was assigned the task of tracing the source of the static. He constructed a large mobile radio antenna and moved it around in circles in a New Jersey potato field to find out which direction the static was coming from. He soon learned that thunderstorms were a major

source of static, but there was also a persistent hissing that continued during fine weather. It seemed to be strongest at a certain point in the sky. Jansky obtained a star chart. The noise was coming from the center of the Milky Way. Could there be a gigantic thunderstorm at the center of the galaxy? Subsequent investigations suggest that there might indeed be something very much like this.

After World War II, radio telescopes like this one at Jodrell Bank in Cheshire, England, opened up a whole new radio universe.

Jansky's work led to a whole new field of radioastronomy — drawing maps of the universe based on radio waves rather than visible light. We now also have gamma ray maps, X-ray maps, ultraviolet maps, and infrared maps of the sky. Sometimes the images match up with visible light sources, and sometimes they don't. The result is a vastly more complex universe than anyone ever imagined.

The majority of astronomers responded to the discovery of the vastness of the universe by reflecting on how insignificant that seemed to make the earth and mankind. As Professor Carl Sagan put it, we are "lost somewhere between immensity and eternity." That is only the viewpoint of someone who, like Sagan did, believes that the physical universe is "all that is or ever was or ever will be."[10] For someone who believes that the cosmos is the work of a Creator, the discovery of the immenseness and complexity of the universe points

---

10. Sagan, *Cosmos*, p. 4.

unerringly to the super-immensity and super-complexity of the Creator who made it, and who is therefore bigger and wiser than all of it put together!

THE NEW PHYSICS AND THE UNIVERSE WITHIN

While Shapley and Hubble were applying Newton's classical physics to the apparently ever-larger size of the universe, a dramatic revolution was taking place within physics itself. Albert Einstein, with his special and general theories of relativity, showed that Newton's physics did not work at high speeds or near large gravitational fields. Newton assumed that space and time were fixed quantities — but Einstein postulated that they were relative to the position and motion of the observer. Time slows down at high speed, and space bends in the presence of gravitational fields. Yet both these things could happen to you without you being aware of it — because it depends on where you are. Surprisingly, the only thing that turned out to be absolute was the speed of light, regardless of the motion of the source or the observer. Space and time — called "spacetime" by Minkowski, who described it with a mathematical measure called a metric — are inextricably part of one another and they can be squashed and stretched. The speed of light (in a vacuum) is constant, irrespective of the motion of either the source or the observer. This sounds weird but it has been experimentally confirmed many times.

Other tests of relativity have also vindicated it. Relativity theory predicts, for example, that when a beam of light passes close to a massive object such as a star, the dent in spacetime would cause the light beam to bend. This prediction was loudly proclaimed to have been confirmed during a solar eclipse in 1919. Astronomers plotted the position of a star as it passed close to the sun and found that, just as Einstein predicted, the proximity of the sun made the star appear to move in the sky — the light beam had been bent as it passed around

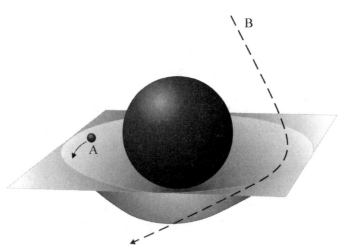

Gravity as a dent in spacetime. Satellite A rolls around the dent. Light ray B bends as it passes by.

the "dent" in spacetime! As it turned out, the technology they used was not precise enough to gain the necessary resolution. However, subsequent experiments have confirmed the effect with much greater accuracy. Also, his prediction that time would slow down in the presence of a strong gravitational field has been confirmed in subsequent experiments.

At the subatomic scale a whole new and weird universe was uncovered. Einstein came up with his famous equation $E=mc^2$, where E=energy, m=mass, and c=the speed of light. One of its consequences was that energy and matter were interconvertible. Since the speed of light is a very large number (about 300,000 km per second), this meant that previously unimaginable amounts of energy could be released from just a few grams of matter if only the nuclear forces that hold the atoms together could be "unlatched." He was proven dramatically (though unhappily) correct once again through the development of the atomic bomb.

The atomic bomb demonstrated that Einstein was right. Matter can be converted into energy, with devastating consequences!

German physicist Max Planck found that energy cannot be emitted or absorbed by matter in a continuous form, but only in discrete packets that are all the same size, which he called "*quanta*" (singular, *quantum*). New Zealander Sir Ernest Rutherford probed the structure of atoms with the radioactive particles newly discovered by Polish-born French Nobel laureate Marie Curie. To everyone's surprise, atoms turned out to be mostly empty space. They consisted of a positively charged central nucleus with a set of negatively charged electrons moving around it at some distance, almost like a miniature solar system. Danish physicist Niels Bohr proposed that the electrons orbited in a set of discrete concentric shells at a fixed distance from the nucleus. Talk about empty space! The volume of the nucleus, the heaviest part of the atom, is only a thousand million millionth of the volume of the whole atom. That means atoms are about 99.9999999999999 percent empty space!

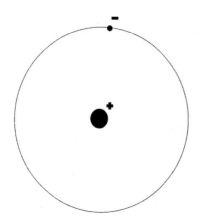

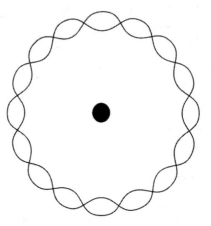

A hydrogen atom (not to scale) contains one positively charged proton in its nucleus and one negatively charged electron in its outer shell. It is mostly empty space.

The electron is also a wave. It can appear as a particle, but you cannot tell exactly where until you measure it. And you cannot exactly measure both its location and momentum simultaneously.

The emission and absorption of energy from an atom occurred in such a way that the "jumps" between shells corresponded to Planck's quanta. Light rays were found to be made up of quanta of light energy called *photons*, yet paradoxically, light also exhibited the characteristics of a continuous wave. So does light consist of discrete photons or continuous waves? The answer seems to be, "It depends on what you are looking for" — if you look for waves you find waves, but if you look for particles you find particles. Another weird property of photons is that they have no "rest mass" — if you could stop them moving they would have no mass! Because they travel at the speed of light, Einstein's theory suggests that they are timeless.

Researchers also came up against a limit to their observations of subatomic structure in what is called Heisenberg's uncertainty principle. This principle says that you cannot at the same time exactly determine both the position and momentum (mass multiplied by velocity) of a subatomic particle. You can find out exactly where it is but not its momentum, or you can measure exactly its momentum but not where it is (within certain limits of course). Thus began a whole new, but strangely uncertain, world of subatomic physics called *quantum mechanics.*

NUCLEAR PHYSICS

In the post–World War II period, following the development of the atomic bomb, nuclear physics took off. The atom was probed with ever-higher-energy particles in specially designed particle accelerators, and hosts of new particles and antiparticles were discovered. For every particle, so they discovered, there is an antiparticle. When the two come together they annihilate each other, giving off a prodigious amount of energy in the process (remember $E=mc^2$). To their surprise, they found that not only could particles be destroyed — they could also be created! Einstein's equation can be rearranged to produce mass from energy, thus $m=E/c^2$. If the energy is high enough, then new particles can be produced. The curious thing is that whenever a new particle appears in this high-energy environment, its antiparticle also appears. If you produce an electron, then an anti-electron (called a *positron*) will also appear; if you produce a proton (the positively charged particle in the nucleus) then an antiproton will also appear, and so on.

It was not long before the inevitable happened — the astrophysicists and the nuclear physicists got together. The result was a theory of the universe that began at the subatomic level. The big-bang theory was born!

THE BIG BANG

When Einstein first developed his theories of relativity he believed, like most of his contemporaries, that the universe was static. The universe was today, he believed, the way it had always been, but a different solution to his equations, developed by Alexander Friedmann, seemed to indicate that the universe exists in a dynamic form — either expanding or collapsing. To return the universe to its "proper" static form, Einstein fudged the mathematics by adding a "cosmological constant."

Meanwhile, other people were pushing the boundaries of observation, and Einstein was about to get the surprise of his life. Edwin Hubble was quietly exploring his new-found world of galaxies. Having established that galaxies were indeed clusters of billions of stars, just like the Milky Way, he then examined the constituents in the light coming from them using a spectroscope. A curious pattern emerged. The light from most galaxies was redshifted. This means that the absorption line in the spectrum for, say, hydrogen was not where it should be — it was shifted toward the red end of the spectrum. That is, the wavelength had been stretched out (the blue end of the spectrum corresponds with shorter wavelengths).

Now there is a well-known phenomenon in physics called the "Doppler effect," in which wave energy is shifted to a longer or shorter wavelength because the source is moving in relation to the observer. If you are standing on the roadside, for example, and you hear a motorcycle coming, you will notice that when it passes you the pitch of the engine noise will suddenly become lower. This is because the approaching vehicle is causing the waves of sound to move past you more quickly than if it were stationary, and so the frequency of the sound (the pitch) appears to be higher. Then, when the vehicle passes and is moving away from you, it causes the sound waves to reach you more slowly and so the frequency of the sound appears to be lower.

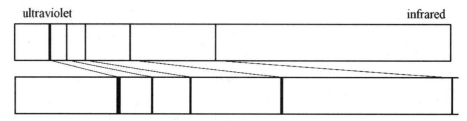

ultraviolet   infrared

Red shift. The top spectrum is from a nearby galaxy and the lower spectrum is from a distant galaxy. The spectral lines in the light from the distant galaxy are shifted toward the red end of its spectrum, and they are broadened.

Could the redshifts which Hubble observed in the light from galaxies be Doppler shifts? Could the galaxies be moving away from us?

Hubble continued his work and catalogued the redshifts for the 25 most distant galaxies, which he published in 1929. He found that there was a strong correlation with distance — the farther away the galaxy, the higher the redshift! If they were indeed Doppler shifts, then the galaxies were receding at incredible speeds never imagined before, and the farthermost galaxies were receding faster than the closer ones.

Strangely, Einstein was unaware of Hubble's expansion, and Hubble was unaware of Einstein's fudge. It was a Belgian priest, Abbé Georges-Henri Lemaître, who brought the two together. Lemaître reasoned that if the universe is expanding then there must have been a time when the expansion began. He imagined reversing Hubble's expansion, back to a point where all the space, time, and matter of the universe was in the same place — a single point or *singularity*, as it is called. To escape from this singularity, he thought, the universe must have exploded (thus "big-bang," a name later coined in derision) and the expansion we see today must be the result of this original "explosion." He pictured our present universe as the "ashes and smoke of bright but very rapid fireworks." When Einstein heard about Hubble's discovery, and Lemaître's interpretation of it, he immediately accepted it and promptly discarded his fudged "cosmological constant," calling it the biggest blunder of his career.

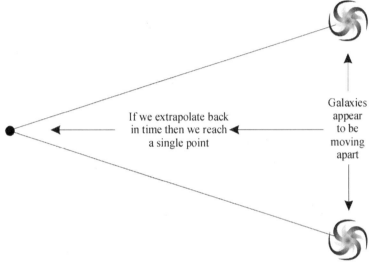

The basic principle of the big-bang model.

SLIDE BACK INTO METAPHYSICS

Lemaître's idea was just an idea. Unless it could be tested experimentally or observationally, it would be of little use. Indeed, it was a disturbing idea, for it took cosmology out of the realm of physics and put it back into the realm of metaphysics. All the laws of physics would break down in the supposed singularity and any explanation would have to appeal to forces beyond physics. "Beyond physics" could mean either "new, unknown physics" or it could mean the supernatural or miraculous. The whole endeavor of modern science had been an attempt to explain the world in terms of the natural, not the supernatural!

George Gamow, a refugee from Stalinist Russia, was one of the first nuclear physicists to venture into cosmology. He suggested that the big bang would have been a vast thermonuclear explosion. As such, it would have released enormous amounts of heat energy that should still be dimly perceptible throughout the whole universe.[11] The instruments of the time were not sensitive enough to detect it, however, so the idea remained dormant.

In 1965, two Americans, Arno Penzias and Robert Wilson, published some startling results. They had found throughout the universe a very low level of microwave radiation. Microwaves are the shortest waves within the radio frequency band. Everywhere they pointed their antenna they found them. Having gone to great lengths to eliminate all known sources of interference, they were forced to conclude that it must be the leftover radiation from the original big bang.

The microwave horn antenna used by Penzias and Wilson.

Penzias and Wilson were awarded the Nobel Prize, and to this day their Cosmic Microwave Background Radiation (CMBR), as it is called, in addition to the expanding-universe interpretation of redshifts, provides the primary evidence for the big-bang theory.

When Hubble's rate of expansion is taken back to the singularity, the age of the universe appears to be about 15 billion years. The most distant galaxies

---

11. Gamow is generally cited as the originator of this idea but a recent book by his collaborators at the time, Ralph Alpher and Robert Herman, claims that they were the originators. See A.R. Liddle, "Spotlight on cosmology: the old and the new," Astronomy and Geophysics 43(5):30–31: 2002.

yet observed, at the time of writing, are believed to be about 13 billion light-years away — assuming Hubble was correct (we will look further at this issue shortly). One might hope that one day we may see the big bang itself, but according to the theory, we already have — the CMBR is it!

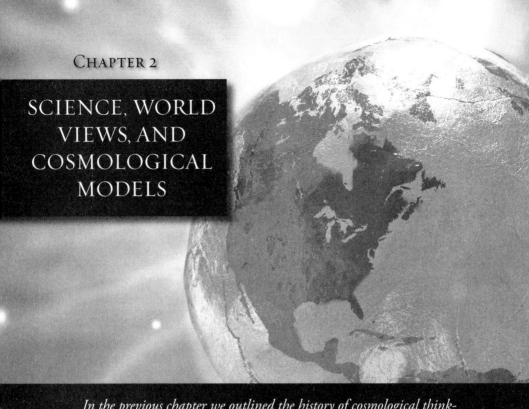

CHAPTER 2

SCIENCE, WORLD VIEWS, AND COSMOLOGICAL MODELS

In the previous chapter we outlined the history of cosmological think-ing that led to the big-bang theory, and in chapter 4 we will critically evaluate the big-bang model to see how well it explains the universe. In order to do this we need to have a basic understanding of what science is, how scientific theories are developed, and how our belief system influences these processes.

THE JUGGERNAUT SCENARIO

Some writers present big-bang cosmology as if it is a great juggernaut of scientific achievement that moves inexorably forward and crushes all op-position in its path. This view has been promoted by atheistic humanists, such as the late Professor Carl Sagan, by theistic evolutionists (who would appear to be in the majority), and by progressive creationists, such as Dr. Hugh Ross and his colleagues.

Professor Sagan was keen to present big-bang cosmology in this light be-cause it gave scientific respectability to his atheism. He did not *want* God to be in his universe, and big-bang cosmology appeared to provide a good excuse to remove Him. Yet it is easy to show up his error, as we will illustrate shortly.

Theistic evolutionists are generally those who take the easy road of com-promise. They accept big-bang cosmology and add God to it.

Progressive creationists present big-bang cosmology as the only possible explanation for two apparent reasons. One is that they do not want to upset their evolutionist colleagues by making "offensive" claims about a young earth.[1] The other is that astronomy is producing some remarkable evidences of intelligent design and they are keen to use the science for ideological purposes in evangelism.[2]

The big-bang juggernaut crushes the steady state model.

Why do we take exception to these points of view? We have both scientific and theological reasons. Scientifically, we reject big-bang cosmology because it falls short of a satisfactory explanation of origins — and is, as we shall see, demonstrably wrong anyway. Theologically, we reject big-bang cosmology because it ignores the explicit eyewitness account from the Creator that He created the universe in six ordinary-length days, in the time of Adam, just several thousand years ago. These two reasons are really just one — as scientists, the Bible provides us with crucial eyewitness evidence on the question of origins and it would be irresponsible of us to ignore it.

THE JUGGERNAUT FALLACY

The juggernaut scenario is based on the erroneous assumption that there are only two possible scientific models of cosmic origins — the big-bang model and the steady state model (the idea that the universe has always been much the same as we see it today). Since recent scientific advances appear to have discredited the steady state model, these writers conclude that there is no other possible explanation for the origin of the universe — it must therefore have begun with the big bang.

To understand why we consider this view to be erroneous, consider the following quote from evolutionist Professor Joseph Silk, head of astrophysics at Oxford University:

---

1. Hugh Ross, *Creation and Time* (Colorado Springs, CO: NavPress, 1994), p. 72.
2. In *The Creator and the Cosmos* (Colorado Springs, CO: NavPress, 2001), p. 45, Dr. Ross says that "the big bang is the most exquisitely designed entity known to man," and he claims it involves fine-tuning far beyond any machine ever made by man.

Because there is essentially no direct and unambiguous experimental consequence of our assumptions about the first seconds in the big bang, we may question the model of a simple, uniform and isotropic big bang. Surely, the metaphysical conjecture continues, a highly irregular and chaotic beginning seems the most likely of the infinite set of possible models of the early universe. The one constraint is that such models must eventually decay to a uniform state of expansion to provide an adequate description of the currently observed universe.[3]

In big-bang theory the foundation for everything else that happens in all the history of the universe is set during the period referred to as the first few seconds. Of this period, Silk says there is an "infinite set of possible models of the early universe," among which "there is essentially no direct and unambiguous experimental consequence" that could be used to distinguish between them. Any particular model is the result of a "metaphysical conjecture" and he illustrates the point by saying we could equally well start with a simple uniform model or a highly chaotic model. It doesn't matter which model we choose as long as we can get it to eventually turn into the universe that we see around us.

What is a *"metaphysical conjecture"*? A *conjecture*, according to the dictionary, is "the formation of conclusions from incomplete evidence; guess." *Metaphysics* is "the branch of philosophy that deals with first principles, especially of being and knowing." So a metaphysical conjecture about what happened in the beginning is a philosophical guess. One guess, it seems, is as good as another, so long as it leads to the right end result.

Let us hasten to add that we are not in any way critical of Professor Silk or his colleagues for basing their work on metaphysical conjectures. Indeed, the whole point of this book is to illustrate the fact that *all* scientific study of origins is crucially dependent upon assumptions as to what happened in the beginning. In the absence of a reliable revelation, this means it is dependent on (educated) guesswork. To understand this better, we need to look at the foundation of thought itself.

The Foundation of Thought

All thinking about the remote past has to start with *assumptions*. We were not there to observe the beginning of the universe so we cannot be sure what happened. The past is unique, so we cannot repeat it in an experiment. Even if we should come up with a reasonable explanation of what *might* have happened,

---

3. Joseph Silk, *The Big Bang*, 3rd ed. (New York, NY: Freeman, 2001), p. 130–131.

we could never be sure that it *did* happen like that. The only way we could know for sure is if we could visit the past in a time machine and observe it for ourselves. No one has ever invented a time machine. Some theoreticians have toyed with the idea but with little prospect of success.[4] We suspect that no one will ever invent one in the future, either, because if they ever did then everyone would want one and they would come back to visit us — we would be flooded with "time tourists." In the absence of such time tourists, the best we can ever do is to begin with metaphysical conjectures and see how reasonable they are, given the evidence of our present-day observations.

Even our metaphysical conjectures are severely limited, because we don't know everything, and even our imagination of what *might* have happened in the past is limited by our own experience. We cannot even be sure where the beginning is in any particular line of reasoning. Any starting point that we do choose will have to face questions such as, "What happened before that?" or challenges such as, "Perhaps it wasn't like that."

All good scientific investigation of the past will therefore begin by stating what the basic assumptions (metaphysical conjectures) are and will keep an open mind to the possibility that they could be wrong. People who want to think logically about the past need to examine how their understanding is built upon their starting assumptions. If contradictions occur then you need to trace your chain of reasoning back to see where you might have made a mistake. An obvious place for a mistake will always be somewhere in your starting assumptions.

FIRST CHOICES IN PHYSICS AND METAPHYSICS

The question of your starting point for thinking about the universe goes right to the heart of who you are as a person. This may sound surprising, but

---

4. Paul C.W. Davies, *How to Build a Time Machine* (Melbourne, Victoria, Australia: Penguin), 2001.

we believe that if you ignore this point then you risk self-delusion (in the name of "science").

Consider, then: Why are you studying the universe? What do you hope to gain by it? We would like to suggest that the great endeavor of all science is to explain the world in terms of causes that we can understand *so that we can then manipulate them to our own advantage*. The term "our own advantage" may include simply our own enjoyment of life and the world around us, or it may include gaining power and control over our world (and sadly in some cases, the world of others). We further suggest that there are basically only two starting points — self or God.

If you begin with yourself then *you* get to choose where you start. You may be surprised how many different cosmologies there are in the world, invented by the man and woman in the street who decide for themselves where the world came from and where it is going. Such diverse cosmologies may survive in the minds of the masses, but far fewer can survive the tests of scientific scrutiny. The serious inquirer will soon discover that his own choices are limited by his personal knowledge, wisdom, and experience and these are not up to the task. Something more is needed.

Where do we turn for this "something more"? The "respectable," "scientific" answer is to begin with matter and energy and the laws of physics. These things can be observed and tested in the laboratory and we can use the scientific method on them to weed out the fanciful theories from the useful ones.

What about the God-honoring creationist who wants to begin his cosmology with God? He cannot observe God at work in creation, nor can he bring God into the laboratory and carry out experiments on Him. Does this mean that God is useless as a scientific starting point? Not at all! The God of the Bible has told us *how* and *when* and *why* He created the universe, so we can begin with God's Word as the starting point for our cosmology.

The fact that God cannot be brought into the laboratory and made the subject of observation and experimental testing places a limitation on materialistic science that has profound implications for cosmology. It means that if God really did create the universe, then a materialist could never establish that fact by the scientific method. Science may point in that direction, but it can never go "all the way" there. It also has profound implications for atheism. Atheists are keen to use God's absence from scientific explanations of the universe as a justification for their atheism, but in fact it is nothing of the kind — it is simply the result of this fundamental limitation of the scientific method!

So for materialistic physicists, the starting "something" in their thinking has to be matter or energy — things that can be studied in the laboratory. In the case of the big-bang theory, they assume the existence of all the matter and energy of the universe, and all of space and time, wrapped up into an infinitesimally small point. From this "singularity," as it is called, the whole universe sprang forth. The energy was converted into matter and the matter condensed into stars and galaxies.

This is physics, you might say, not metaphysics. Well, no, it isn't physics, because no one has ever observed such a thing. The laws of physics break down in a singularity, so physicists simply do not know what can or cannot happen in such a state (this will be explained in more detail shortly). So materialistic physicists, in striving to be good scientists, are forced into the realm of metaphysics, because there is nowhere else they can go to find a starting assumption for their cosmology.

The creationist position is, we believe, rather more rational. Instead of starting with physics and being forced back into metaphysics against our will, we *begin* with metaphysics. We begin with God, and then we derive our cosmology from what God *tells us* He did in the beginning. Instead of blindly following the materialist constraints of the scientific method that cannot, by definition, study God, we make a choice to begin with God.

This is the choice that you, our readers, are also faced with. This is the choice that we want to help you make, based on your own understanding of how science works. The choice is whether to begin with God, or without Him. It's your call.

ASSUMPTIONS INFLUENCE CONCLUSIONS

When scientists study questions of origin they do not draw their conclusions in a void, unaffected by outside influences. Quite the opposite! The assumptions they begin with powerfully influence the conclusions at which they arrive.

To give a simple illustration, consider an ordinary drinking glass that is half full of water. Is it really half full? Or is it half empty? If it is *assumed* to have been full to start with then it is now half empty, but if one *assumes* it was empty to start with then it is now half full. Here we see the necessary connection between the starting assumption and the conclusion. The evidence is the same in both cases (the water in the

Is the glass half full or half empty?

glass), but entirely different conclusions are reached depending on the starting assumptions.

So it is with our reasoning about the universe. We need to keep our starting assumptions in mind as we carefully weigh the evidence. If we lose sight of our starting assumptions, then we risk thinking that our conclusion has come purely from the evidence, when in fact it is a logical consequence of our starting assumptions.

This illustration leads us to two possible starting assumptions: (1) the universe is a random system of matter and energy in the process of ordering itself, as evolutionists[5] say; or (2) it is a once-perfect, created universe now in the process of decay, as the Bible says. Which does the evidence best support? In the next few chapters we will help you to answer this question in a way that keeps in view the connections between assumptions, evidence, and conclusions.

Here is a real-life example of confusion between assumptions and conclusions. The theoretical astrophysicist, Professor Stephen Hawking of Cambridge University, in his best-selling book *A Brief History of Time*,[6] claimed that his big-bang theory was "in agreement with all the observational evidence that we have today." In the introduction to that book, one of America's leading astrophysicists of the day, the late Professor Carl Sagan of Cornell University, said, "This book is also about God . . . or perhaps about the absence of God . . . a universe with no edge in space and no beginning or end in time, and nothing for a Creator to do."

Now the casual reader might reasonably conclude from this that Hawking's big-bang theory explained the origin of the universe. In Hawking's own words, it agreed with all the evidence (i.e., it explained everything), and Professor Sagan clearly understood this to be Hawking's meaning as he said it left nothing for a Creator to do — it had all been explained with physics!

Surprisingly, this is not the case. A few sentences after Professor Hawking claimed that his big-bang theory had explained all the evidence, he admitted that among the few remaining unanswered questions was the question of the origin of the stars and galaxies.

----

5. When we refer to evolutionists throughout this book, the term encompasses all naturalistic theorists from big-bang cosmologists to biological evolutionists. There is no clear distinction between them because any naturalistic theory of biological evolution must be built upon a naturalistic theory of cosmic origin.

6. Stephen Hawking, *A Brief History of Time — From the Big Bang to Black Holes* (London: Bantam Press, 1988), p. 121.

Now in the universe where *we* live, if you take away the stars and galaxies there is in effect no universe left to explain.[7] Professor Hawking claimed to have explained *everything* (his theory agreed with *all* the observational evidence) and Professor Sagan took this to mean that Hawking had left nothing for the Creator to do, but in fact the essential substance of the universe — the stars and galaxies — remained unexplained. How could the world's leading scientists possibly get it so wrong?

The answer is that the assumptions they started with determined the conclusions they came to.

Professor Hawking is a theoretician and the universe he is concerned with is the universe inside his own head, not the stars and the galaxies of the real universe. He began with a problem in his head and he solved it in his head to his own satisfaction.

Professor Sagan, however, was a practical astronomer, a pioneer in the SETI program (Search for Extra-Terrestrial Intelligence), and consultant to the NASA Mars landing program, so he was very aware of the real universe. The reason that he came to the "no God" conclusion was because that is what he started with. He made it very clear elsewhere in his prolific writing that he had no time for God. Hawking's work gave him an opportunity to promote that point of view, even though he had to quote selectively in order to do so.

This illustrates how self-delusion can creep into a "scientific" study of the universe. Everyone has a bias of some kind that influences their starting assumptions, and therefore their conclusions. The only honest thing to do

---

7. In a later section — The Necessary and Sufficient Universe — we will show that the stars and galaxies are the fundamental objects in the universe that any theory of cosmology needs to explain.

with bias is to acknowledge it, and observe *how* it influences our conclusions.

There is a very important distinction to be made between an ordinary person who has a biased opinion about something and a scientist who (inescapably) has a bias in his starting assumptions. The scientific journey gives the scientist an opportunity to examine and test the consequences of his bias, and if the consequences conflict with the observations about the universe then he has an opportunity to change his assumptions — that is, to change his bias. In contrast, the person who simply has a biased opinion may never see a reason to change their mind on the subject.

This is what we want to help you do in this book — to understand what your starting assumptions are regarding the origin of the universe, then to embark on the scientific journey to see what the consequences are. You can then return to your starting assumptions and decide whether they match what you see in the universe. We believe that when you do so, you shall return to where you started from, enriched and encouraged in your faith, and better equipped to share it with others. You will also understand that materialists, starting with materialistic assumptions, will inevitably end up with materialistic conclusions. Unless, of course, we can persuade them of their error and convince them to change their starting assumptions. If you, the reader, are a materialist, we invite you to "try on for size" a different starting assumption, and to go along the journey with us for a while and see how things "fit."

World Views

Starting assumptions are not the sole property of cosmologists. Every culture has its starting assumptions. These have to do with what cultural anthropologists call our *"world view"* — which is basically our story about where the world came from and how it got to be the way it is. So cosmology is simply the application of the scientific method to what everybody does in their own head anyway. Cultural world views come in many and varied forms which we will not attempt to cover here. The two that we are most concerned with in this book are the world view underlying the big bang and the world view of the Bible.

The Naturalistic World View

The world view that underpins big-bang cosmology is naturalistic materialism. It tries to explain the world without God, using only matter, chance, and the forces of nature. This seems scientifically quite respectable, because God cannot be studied in the laboratory, whereas matter, chance, and the laws of nature can.[8]

Atheists champion the naturalistic world view because it "appears" to support their atheism. For them the ideal universe would be one that is infinite in both time and space, and random in its organization. No beginning is needed, and thus no beginner. If chance and the laws of physics can explain the universe, then no designer is needed, but the big-bang model actually poses a problem for them, because it points to a beginning, and perhaps therefore to a beginner. (This is why, as we indicated earlier, progressive creationists feel it is a useful tool for them in defending the notion of God. But more on that later.) There have consequently been attempts to remove the beginning by suggesting a cyclic universe that expands and collapses and expands and collapses and so on. However, there is no evidence for this — it is just a trick with words to avoid an embarrassing conclusion. In fact, it does not solve the problem for the atheist, because each successive cycle would, like a bouncing ball, lose a little energy available for the next "rebound." So there can be no infinite series of rebounds.

A more sophisticated way to escape the implications of a universe that looks as if it had a beginning is to postulate that ours is only one of an infinite series of universes that appear like bubbles on a sea of foam, each one with different laws of physics. There is then a "natural selection" process, so that only those universes "fit" to produce stars and galaxies (and, continuing the evolutionary story-telling, ultimately intelligent life) will be the ones that are studied by intelligent beings like ourselves. This is also meant to explain away the observation that conditions in the universe are "fine-tuned" for our existence. If they weren't, the argument goes, we wouldn't be here to observe this universe. This accumulating evidence for fine-tuning, which points toward a Designer, will be considered further in following chapters.

A major contradiction within the atheist world view is the rationality of the scientific method and the structure that it reveals in the universe. Science works in the most spectacular way, as evidenced by the fantastic equipment (e.g., spacecraft, telescopes, computers) that cosmologists can use these days to study the cosmos. It is revealing a marvelously structured universe that can be understood in terms of natural laws of physics and mathematics. How could such a rational and highly structured universe appear out of nowhere by

---

8. While God cannot be studied in the laboratory we can certainly study the consequences of God's stated actions as given in the creation accounts in Scripture. The impression that the naturalistic world view has superior scientific respectability is therefore only superficial.

mindless chance? This "rationality paradox" has no real solution in the naturalistic world view.

The Biblical World View

The Bible presents a world view of God, the eternally self-existing one, who created all things. The manner in which He created is crucial to the integrity of the story. He created all things by calling them into existence (Gen. 1) out of nothing (Heb. 11:3). He spoke, and they appeared (Ps. 33:6– 9). Not only did He create all things by His spoken word, but He also upholds all things by that same word (Heb. 1:3; Col. 1:17). By the same word, the world of old was judged by a world-destroying flood in the time of Noah and "by the same word the heavens and earth that now exist have been stored up for fire, being kept until the day of judgment and destruction of ungodly men" (2 Pet. 3:7). That same Word, incarnate, is Jesus Christ, the Alpha and the Omega, the first and the last, the beginning, and the end (John 1:1–3; Rev. 22:13).

The biblical world view solves the "rationality paradox" because God is a rational being. He is able, by definition, to create a structured universe. He is able to create man to be like himself, with similar rational abilities to understand and appreciate what He has done.

There is also another world within the biblical framework, the world of fallen man. The ruler of this world is a liar and the father of lies (John 8:44; 12:31; 14:30; 16:11; 1 John 5:19). Anyone searching for truth in this world is therefore more likely to encounter a lie. The most powerful lies, of course, are those that are mostly true. Just a little bit of deception can go a long way. According to Paul, the ascendancy of the lie is actually a judgment from God upon the disobedience of mankind (2 Thess. 2:9–12).

This may come as a shock to Christians who are aware that God is good and true, but He gave dominion over His creation to man (Gen. 1:26–28) and man ceded it to the devil by believing the devil rather than believing God (Gen. 3:1–6; Rom. 6:16). The devil is ruler of this world only as usurper. According to the Bible, the only way to escape the rule of the liar is to repent of believing his lies and return to believing what God says.

The original sin of man was that Adam and Eve did not believe what God said.[9] We suffer from the same problem today — we do not believe what God

---

9. Their manifest sin was disobedience — they did what God told them not to do. Eve expressed a nominal belief in what God said (Gen. 3:2–3) but it was the devil's suggested course of action that she followed. We need to be aware of this potentially fatal trap of nominal belief.

says. If we are to regain our dominion, under God, we need to return to believing what He says.

What did God say that Adam and Eve failed to believe? In the Garden of Eden, God told Adam, in essence, that "the penalty for sin is death" (Gen. 2:17). Adam did not believe this, and many Christians today persist in not believing God on this foundational issue (they have swallowed the evolutionary view that death is a natural part of life). This is the starting point for our biblical view of cosmology — to believe what God says. Some of the important theological implications of this position are outlined in appendix B.

Idolatry

We showed in an earlier section that science can point us toward God, but it cannot take us there. That is a journey that we have to make on our own. We have a choice regarding the kind of God that we seek. What kind of God do you want? A God of your own making? Or the God who has revealed himself in Jesus Christ?

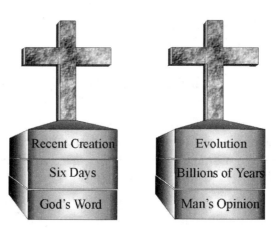

At which altar do you worship?

If you want a God of your own making, then you can start from anywhere you like and make it up as you go along. If you want the God who has revealed himself in Jesus Christ, then you need to begin with what Jesus Christ said. This will be your world view and it will provide the starting point for the assumptions that you will require to make sense of the data of cosmology.

If you decide for yourself what God did (or did not do) during creation, then you are setting yourself up as the authority in the matter, and the God you invoke is a man-made god. Idolatry is the worship of a man-made god. So beware!

FURTHER LIMITATIONS OF SCIENCE

We have already seen that our starting assumptions in cosmology can strongly influence our conclusions, independently of the evidence, but there are also numerous other limitations to the way science works — when it is applied to the unobservable past. For example, we are finite beings who don't know everything and we never have all the relevant information on the subject in hand. To illustrate this point, consider the classic crime novel by Agatha Christie, *Murder on the Orient Express.*

A wealthy gentleman is found dead in his cabin on the train, stabbed many times. As the investigation unfolds, no less than 13 suspects are found to be on the train, all with a possible motive for the murder. The story follows the attempts of detective Hercule Poirot to eliminate suspects and identify the killer. As possible scenarios are investigated, new information arises and causes a new round of speculation. Not until the end do we discover that 12 of the suspects did it conjointly.

This example was chosen because it has interesting mathematical permutations. Throughout most of the story, Poirot had the idea that only one killer was involved. Had he allowed himself to think that more than one killer might have been involved then the possibilities were enormously complex. There were 13 possible choices of suspects if the people acted independently, there were 78 possible combinations of suspects if they acted in pairs, there were 286 possible combinations of suspects if they acted in threes, and so on (don't worry about the mathematics). There is a total of 8,191 possible ways of choosing all possible combinations of suspects. In fact, only one of these 8,191 combinations was correct, and 8,191 is only the number of combinations of possible subsets of the 13 suspects; it does not include the number of different ways that they might have carried out the murder.

Three points come out of this illustration. First, our study of the past (in this case the murder) is limited by our imagination (Poirot initially considered that only one person was guilty). Second, there is an enormous number of possible ways that the world could be configured in any situation, and if you don't have all the relevant information you cannot hope to come to the right conclusion. Third, Poirot had the crucial advantage that all the suspects were alive and present and were able to confess, and thereby corroborate (or refute) any theory. If all the suspects were dead or missing then no one would ever have been able to know for sure who did it.

Now apply these points to the study of cosmology. First, we are limited in our imagination of what *might* have happened at the beginning of the universe.

None of the current forces of physics are creative — they are all conserving forces (this will be explained in the next chapter), so the creative forces that were at work are beyond our experience. Second, we do not have all the relevant information on the subject. Third, the only witness was the Creator.

Given these limitations it is only reasonable to conclude that any theory of cosmology will be likewise limited. The correct scenario can only be the one that is corroborated by *the* single living witness.

"Facts" May Not Be Universally True

Science is usually thought of as being based on observable "facts," but these "facts" may not be universally true throughout space and time. For example, Darwin's theory of the origin of species by means of natural selection is based on the apparent "fact" that death is a natural and universal part of life. We can verify this "fact" by observation — everything eventually dies, but the Bible tells us that death is not a natural part of life, because we were originally created to live forever, and animals ate only plants and there were no diseases or other malicious agents to cause death. Death has not always been a part of life — it came into the world only as the result of man's sin (Rom. 5:12, citing Gen. 1–3). As earlier stated, the only way we could verify this statement would be to go back in a time machine and check it out, but we don't have a time machine, so we have to choose what we will believe — the Bible or the assumption of uniformity, i.e., that there was no drastic change in the order of things.

Likewise, the big-bang theory is based on the observed "fact" of universal cosmic expansion. We agree that the universe may well be expanding at present (or at least has expanded in the past), but we cannot presume from this that cosmic expansion has operated right from the beginning. The Bible suggests that the original creation was relatively static and that cosmic expansion occurred at some later stage (creation day 4, see our young solar system model in chapter 6, *The Biblical Model*). The universal expansion assumed in big-bang theory leads to the conclusion that the primordial universe was in a singularity (we will deal with this shortly). This is disastrous for their theory because a singularity is a thermodynamic dead end and does not explain the origin of the universe.

The lesson to be learned here is that supposedly observable "facts" can be "contaminated" by interpretations that arise from ideology, not from observation.

"Right" Theories Can Be Wrong

Most cosmologists today believe that the big-bang theory is the correct theory of cosmic origins because, as pointed out at the beginning of this chapter, what they perceive to be the only alternative theory — the steady state model — is clearly wrong. Consider the following scenario.

Imagine two archaeologists debating the history of a human skeleton that was found at a place that one of them thinks may have been the site of a battle during the American Civil War. The other is convinced from historical records that no such battle took place at the site. To check the Civil War theory, they examine the skeleton for wounds that might be indicative of battle. They thus look for bullet holes, sword cuts, bayonet impacts, and club-type injuries. Suppose they find a sword cut — a deep, clean cut that could only have come from the heavy blow of a very sharp blade. This would appear to support the Civil War theory, as such cuts would be unlikely to occur in more domestic settings. The other concedes that the historical records were wrong on this occasion and that this was indeed the site of a Civil War battle.

Even though the evidence clearly supports the Civil War theory, both archaeologists are still wrong. The sword cut was not a sword cut at all. It was the result of a blow from a machete. This was, in fact, the site of a slave uprising on a plantation.

The methods used by the two archaeologists were not faulty. Their reasoning was not faulty. They did not have all the relevant information, and their imagination did not supply the missing possibility. Being "right," on issues dealing with the past, is not necessarily enough!

Human Frailty and Scientific Objectivity

All cosmologies begin from the position that man is here as the observer and he needs to explain the world and his own place in it. As we have seen, the limitations of man's perceptions, man's imagination, man's knowledge, man's rational abilities, and, finally, the limitations of man's moral character should put us all on guard concerning the possibility of deception or error. The great claim of science is that it provides a means of gaining knowledge objectively, independent of such human weakness. This is generally true of science dealing with the present, but it is not so in the science which deals with the past.

The sort of science which deals with present-day events (how the world works, sometimes called "operational science") is based on observation and experiment. If a particular theory is wrong, then subsequent experiments and observations can (eventually) peel away the layers of falsehood and reveal the underlying truth. The past cannot be repeated in an experiment, nor can it be directly observed, so we cannot directly test our theories in these ways. So the scientific study of the past (sometimes called "historical [or forensic] science" or "origins science") is severely hampered in its ability to sort out truth from error.[10]

Astronomers *claim* that they can observe the past, but this is not strictly true. The starlight they observe is coming to them *from* the past, but they are doing the observations in the present, not in the past. The light they observe arrived just a moment ago in their telescope. They are not observing the world as it *was* billions of years ago, they are observing the light environment as it *is* on planet earth right now. In order to get from the present light environment on earth to the light environment of distant galaxies billions of light-years away requires the application of assumptions about what happened to the beam of light as it traveled through the vast gulf of distance and time in between. Astronomers can certainly observe light that carries information about the past, but in order to correctly interpret that information they must make assumptions about what happened in the past.

We therefore need to make a clear distinction between what people see, what they think, what they think they see, and what they report that they see. We would hope that all four of these things would be consistent, but the story about Professor Hawking and Professor Sagan demonstrates that they may not be, even among the most talented scientists on the planet. Even if all these things are consistent, they still may not be correct.

The Scientific Method

What is science anyway? We have said that it is based on observation and experiment, but what do we *do* with our observations and experiments? Philosopher of science Karl Popper claimed that the ideal of science is the process of "conjecture and refutation." In this process we make certain conjectures

---

10. Experiments and observations are obviously a part of historical science, but only in a much more indirect and limited way.

(guesses, but not blind guesses; they are usually informed by our observations) and then by experiment and/or further observation we try to refute them. Those conjectures that are successfully refuted can be discarded and those that survive all attempts at refutation can be considered useful theories that perhaps reflect some aspect of underlying reality. He pointed out that science cannot prove anything to be absolutely true because the next observation might prove it false. However, we can prove that something is false, so like the sculptor who chips away all the stone that he doesn't want, we can chip away the ignorance and falsehood and eventually reveal the truth underneath.

This ideal process sounds nice but it suffers from at least two major difficulties. First, Thomas Kuhn pointed out that people tend to formulate their ideas within the context of a ruling "paradigm." A paradigm is a framework of thinking about a particular subject. No individual scientist can investigate everything, so he has to take a lot on trust from others. The ideas that he accepts on trust from others constitute the paradigm within which he carries out his work. While a paradigm is useful for structuring thought and communicating ideas, it is only an approximation to the truth, and a time will come when it no longer helps but hinders further progress. At such a time (it is hoped) some independent thinker from outside the paradigm will lead the people into a new and better paradigm. In reality, the independent thinkers tend to be ostracized and denied research funding. Paradigm change generally only happens when the champions of the former view die out. But the system does work — at least for operational science, dealing with the present.

The "science of the past," as we have pointed out already, suffers from many, many more problems. This brings us to the second difficulty with Popper's ideal. Theories about the past are generally so fuzzy and flexible that a simple process of refutation is hard to achieve. What one person might consider a clear refutation will be seen by another as simply a minor unsolved problem. No one can revisit the past to obtain a definitive solution, so the proponents of different views continue to persist in their own little coteries, largely ignoring the others. It is usually the mass media that then decides the popular view.

One of the major outcomes of this situation is that researchers will tend to try to refute conjectures *within* their favored paradigm, but they will rarely (and for most people, never) try to refute the paradigm itself. The ruling paradigm of Western cosmology today is the big-bang theory, mostly interpreted via a naturalistic, materialistic mindset. Conjectures within this framework will be subjected to experimental testing, but the framework itself will not be. Readers beware!

Tricks of the Mind

Carnegie Observatories astronomer Dr. Allan Sandage once called cosmology "the search for two numbers" — one the Hubble constant, telling how fast the universe is expanding, and the other the cosmic deceleration parameter, telling how fast the expansion is slowing.[11] Not every cosmologist might agree with this summary, but let's put it in a more understandable context.

Imagine you are standing in your backyard enjoying your garden in the sunshine, and a ball flies over your head and crashes through your greenhouse. You yell out in the direction of the boys playing next door, "Where did that ball come from?" A freckled face pops over the fence and says, "It was traveling at 50 meters per second and was decelerating at a rate of 10 meters per second per second." Would you be satisfied with the answer? If you had physical measurements taken and found that the boy's words were technically correct, would you then be satisfied? Of course not. You would want to know who did it and therefore who is going to pay for the broken glass, and you would want some assurance from the perpetrator that it would not happen again.

Neither should we be satisfied with a cosmology that tells us the universe is expanding at a particular rate and decelerating at a particular rate. These quantities are parameters (variables) in the big-bang *model* of the universe — they are not the universe itself. Cosmology is the study of the *universe*. Models can certainly help us to understand the universe but only if we realize that they are models, and not the universe itself. Dr. Sandage appears to have lost sight of the universe and has mistaken his big-bang model for the real thing. The importance of this will be illustrated in appendix A, *Some Other Cosmological Models,* where we will see that it is possible to view the *observational* evidence in such a way that Dr. Sandage's model-dependent summary is totally irrelevant.

How is it possible that an extremely intelligent, well-educated and highly experienced scientist could get so far off the track and not know it? Here is a suggestion.

When your main goal in life is blocked, you engage in some other activity that brings you the satisfaction you would rather have had from achieving your main goal. Psychologists call it "displacement behavior." Displacement behavior appears to be common in cosmology. Cosmologists would love to be able to explain the origin of the stars and galaxies, of planets and of life. They find

---

11. John G. Hartnett, "Cosmologists Can't Agree and Are Still in Doubt," *TJ* 16(3):21 (2002).

themselves thwarted (as we shall see shortly) and so they occupy themselves with other matters. These other matters are then reported as being the main issues in cosmology, and the impression is created that the main issues are being addressed and satisfactorily answered, but it is an illusion.

Science and Faith

Many people think of science and faith as two different kinds of human endeavor, but they are not. Faith is just as important within science as it is in ordinary life. Faith plays just as big a role in the life of an atheist as it does in the life of a theist. The objects of faith may differ, but the activity of putting faith in numerous things is common to all.

What is faith? "Faith is the assurance of things hoped for, the conviction of things not seen" (Heb. 11:1). According to the dictionary, it is "strong belief in something without evidence or proof." When you sit on a chair you are putting your faith in it to hold you. You could obtain proof by testing its integrity before you sit on it but to save time and energy you simply trust that it will hold you without requiring any evidence or proof. You sit on chairs numerous times every day so you have good reason to trust this one.

When a scientist comes up with a promising new conjecture about his field of study he invests a great deal of time, effort, and resources in testing it. He expends all this effort by *faith* — faith that it is a worthwhile conjecture that may reap rewards for him. If he *believed* it was a waste of time he would not proceed with it.

Some years ago a prominent Australian vertebrate palaeontologist made a major discovery of vertebrate fossils in a limestone deposit. To expose the fossils, they dissolved away the limestone in an acid bath. Periodically, they would throw out the debris in the acid bath, believing it to be just rubbish. To their surprise, one day a colleague discovered some most extraordinary, beautifully preserved insect fossils in the "rubbish." As a vertebrate specialist he had looked for large bones and teeth, not for tiny insects. The "rubbish" he once threw out, *believing* that it was useless, he now scours thoroughly in the *belief* that he may find something new.

When you put your money in the bank you *trust* the institution to keep it safe for you. You don't *know* that it will — banks sometimes collapse — but you have reasonable grounds for *believing* that it will keep your money safe. When you drive your car you *trust* that it will get you safely to your destination. You don't *know* that it will, but you have reasonable grounds for *believing* that it will — you have it regularly serviced and keep it topped up with fuel.

Everyone exercises faith in numerous things and persons everyday. We all trust in something or someone when it comes to explaining the origin and destiny of the universe. In this book we are asking you to examine where you are placing your faith in regard to these important questions. Who are you going to believe? Certain scientists who weren't there and don't know what happened in the beginning and who have no certain foreknowledge of the future? Or the Creator who was there and knows exactly what happened in the beginning and exactly what He is going to do at the end?

The Parsimonious Monk

Since faith plays such an important part in the science of the past we need some guidelines regarding how many different faith assumptions we can tolerate. The minimum possible number of assumptions is one — so it is only fair on any theory of origins to allow at least one unprovable assumption. How many more can we reasonably allow?

William of Occam (sometimes spelled "Ockham"), a British Franciscan monk who studied and taught at Oxford University in the 14th century, put forward a very reasonable solution to this problem. It has come to be known as "Occam's Razor." This principle says that assumptions should not be multiplied without necessity. In practical terms, it means that if explanation **A** requires 3 assumptions, and explanation **B** requires 5 assumptions, then explanation **A** is preferred on the grounds of economy. A word that is widely used in modern scientific circles for this same idea is "parsimony."

So if we follow the principle of parsimony, then when we come to comparing big-bang theory with the Bible, we can simply add up the number of unprovable assumptions required for each scenario and the one with the smallest number "wins." We will do just that in chapter 7, *The Scoreboard.*

THE ANTHROPIC PRINCIPLE

The purpose of cosmology is to explain the universe — what it is made of and where it came from. To do this we have to reconstruct it, in theory, from some given starting conditions. What possible starting conditions could produce a universe like the one we observe about us? To answer this question we need to know what the universe looks like on the largest scales. This apparently innocent question leads to some surprising and challenging ideas.

As we learned in the history chapter, the geocentric model, in which the earth was the center of the universe, was overturned by the work of Copernicus and Galileo, who discovered that the earth orbited around the sun. Even this heliocentric (sun-centered) model was overturned by the later discovery that the solar system orbited around the center of the Milky Way galaxy, and that there were billions of other galaxies in the universe. The general view nowadays is that earth is an insignificant "pale blue dot" (in the words of Carl Sagan) in the middle of "nowhere." More formally, cosmologists say that (on a large enough scale) the universe looks much the same as we see it from any and every point within it. It has no center and no edge,[12] and we do not occupy a privileged position within it. This is called the cosmological principle, and we shall deal with some of its implications in chapter 4 on the big-bang model.

In 1948, Hermann Bondi, Thomas Gold, and Fred Hoyle applied this kind of reasoning to time as well as space. They proposed that the universe also looked the same through all points in time, an idea known as the perfect cosmological principle. From this they derived the steady state theory. To accommodate the observed expansion of the universe, they proposed that matter was continually being created in minute, undetectable amounts in interstellar space. Their original theory was generally abandoned after the discovery in 1964 of the cosmic microwave background radiation, but a revised version has been proposed, the quasi-steady state theory, and is discussed in appendix A, *Some Other Cosmological Models*.

In 1961, Robert Dicke of Princeton University came up with a line of reasoning that is completely contrary to the perfect cosmological principle. Instead of our time being no different to any other time in the universe's history, he found that we view the universe from a very special, and therefore privileged, time. Paul Dirac had discovered 30 years previously that there was a curious coincidence in three numbers that describe the fundamental structure of the universe. The value of the gravitational coupling constant was about 10^{-40}, the Hubble age in atomic units was 10^{40}, and the number of heavy atomic particles (protons and neutrons) in the universe was about 10^{80}. When Dicke looked into the reasons why these very large numbers should appear to be so evenly related he found that they only became so at our present point in history (on the evolutionary time scale). In the (remote) past and future they would not coincide so remarkably. We are therefore observing the universe at a very special period in history!

So would the universe always have looked special? Or does it just "look" special at the present time because of the present "coincidence" of the cosmic numbers? If it has always looked special, then perhaps it was designed to be that way. If it just happens to "look" special at the present time and not at

---

12. This does not contradict the notion that it is finite, however.

other times, then perhaps the "appearance of design" is an illusory result of chance. Unfortunately for the atheists, even the big-bang scenario implies that it has *always* looked special.

Professor Hawking and his Cambridge colleague C.B. Collins found that the big bang must have produced a rate of expansion, right from the beginning, that exactly balanced the inward pull of gravity. If the rate of cosmic expansion had been different by as little as one part in a hundred thousand million million, then galaxy formation and subsequent human life could not have developed (according to evolutionary reasoning).[13] The more that scientists study this question, the more evidence they find that even the existence of human life (regardless whether the world evolved from a big bang or was specially created) is delicately dependent upon the exact structure of the physical universe. Not just gravity, but all four fundamental forces of physics are finely tuned to produce the right conditions, as are the structure of atoms, the unique structures of the water molecule, and the carbon-based molecules in cells, even the position of the earth in relation to the sun and moon, and numerous other things. All have to be more or less exactly as they are or human life would be impossible. However we look at it, the universe appears as if it is designed for human life.

This presents materialists with a problem. They cannot accept the design argument, so there must be some other explanation. This is how they get around it: the appearance of design could arise from only two possible sources — prior conditions (e.g., those chosen by a cosmic designer) or subsequent conditions (the actual development of human life). They cannot accept the former so they must accept the latter. Thus, the universe "looks" as if it was designed, because if it wasn't we would not be here to observe it. It is nothing more than observer bias. This is called the anthropic principle (*anthropos* is the Greek word for man).

How do they explain the uniqueness of the universe? Since there is only one universe and it looks designed for human life (and always has looked that way), there is no room for a chance explanation. Only if there were many universes, of which this just happens by chance to be one that contains human observers, could one invoke a chance explanation, and so they do. They invoke either a "multiverse" — a set containing many different universes where the laws of physics and the starting conditions on each are different to ours,

---

13. Stephen Hawking, *The Theory of Everything* (Beverley Hills, CA: New Millenium Press, 2002), p.104.

or "multiple universes," of which ours is just one universe of the many, with a chance combination resulting in human observers.

Creationists would say that the universe *looks* like it was designed for human life because God's Word tells us it *was* designed for human life. Furthermore, there is only *one* universe that we can observe, so that rules out the multitudinous universes required by the appeal to chance.

This leads us to the two cosmological world views that really matter, the *atheistic materialist* world view, which says that matter/energy is all that exists, and the universe appears to be designed only because of observer bias, and the *theistic* world view, which says that the universe appears to be designed because it *was* designed by God, the cosmic Designer. Both these world views come from metaphysics, not from physics. If we are to find out who is right, we need to identify those things in the realm of physics which might point to the correct metaphysical world view. The answer, we believe, lies in the logic of intelligent design.

INTELLIGENT DESIGN

Scientists since Darwin's time have generally excluded the concept of intelligent design from their studies of the natural world. It has only been in the last decade that intelligent design has re-emerged as a topic for serious scientific study. William Dembski has pointed out that there are only three kinds of causes that we can call upon to explain the world around us — chance, necessity (the laws of nature), and intelligent design.[14]

For example, we can explain the clouds in the sky in terms of the physics and chemistry of water vapor forming into cloud droplets, the random diffusion of gas molecules, and the thermodynamics of air mass movements. No appeal to design is necessary. However, an airplane that flies through the clouds cannot be explained in terms of the physics and chemistry of aluminum, plastic, steel, copper, and silicon, nor of any random or necessary combinations of these things. We have to appeal to intelligent design.

We use these three kinds of explanations every day to explain the world around us, yet scientists generally reject the use of design when it comes to the question of origin. This leads to some curious contradictions. A work of art can be attributed to intelligent design by an artist, but we cannot apply the same

---

14. William A. Dembski, *The Design Inference: Eliminating Chance through Small Probabilities* (Cambridge, UK: Cambridge University Press, 1998); William A. Dembski and James M. Kushiner, editors, *Signs of Intelligence: Understanding Intelligent Design* (Grand Rapids, MI: Brazos Press, 2001).

explanation to the artist himself. Consequently, an archaeologist is allowed to speculate about the intelligent origin of ochre markings on a cave wall, but is forbidden to speculate about the intelligent origin of the bones that he finds on the cave floor.[15] Likewise, an astronomer is allowed to speculate about a possible intelligent source for the radio signals that he receives from a star, but is forbidden to speculate about the possible intelligent origin of the star.

We believe that this is absurd. If scientists use design in their everyday life to explain the world around them, then they have no excuse for excluding it, in principle, from their explanations of origins.

This modern disdain for design largely began, as we said, with Darwin. He claimed to have discovered a mechanism — natural selection — that could explain the *appearance* of design in living things. So widespread was Darwin's success that the appeal to design was quietly deleted from *all other fields of science* as well, but even if Darwin had been correct in the field of biology, there would have been no grounds for extending the principle beyond biology. Natural selection only works among organisms that are able to reproduce themselves and pass their (naturally selected) characteristics on to their offspring. Reproduction of this kind does not occur outside the realm of biology, so the principle of natural selection cannot logically be applied outside of biology either.

Even within biology, Darwin was wrong in seeing natural selection as ousting design. Natural selection can only select from organisms that *already exist*. The genetic and reproductive structure of life must already be in place and fully functional before natural selection can even begin to work, so it *fails* to explain the design apparent in living organisms. Neither does it create any new genetic information, but can only "cull" from information that is already present. So on its own it cannot explain the progressive development of life that is alleged to have happened, with its associated increase in genetic information.[16]

This is another example of the corruption of human thought in this fallen world. Tragically, Professor Hawking invoked Darwin's notion of natural selection to assure himself that the process of evolution would eventually lead mankind to a correct understanding of the universe![17]

---

15. This is meant in the ultimate sense, of course; i.e., the creature belonging to the bones was not directly, individually created, but its originating ancestor was.
16. Mutations have not been seen to add new information either — Carl Wieland, "Beetle Bloopers," *Creation* 19(3):30 (June–August 1997); Carl Wieland, "Muddy Waters: Clarifying the Confusion about Natural Selection," *Creation* 23(3):26–29 (June–August 2001).
17. Stephen Hawking, *A Brief History of Time: From the Big Bang to Black Holes* (London: Bantam Press, 1988), p. 12–13.

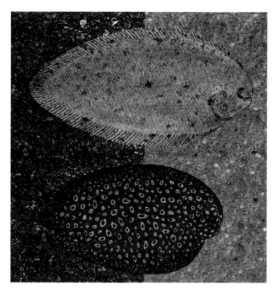

Natural selection can favor these differently colored flat fish (flounder and sole) against different backgrounds, but it can only operate on organisms that already exist and can reproduce themselves in different forms.

A Necessary and Sufficient Universe

In the following chapters, we will examine the universe and some of the objects in it and evaluate explanations which are based on chance and the laws of nature. If we can explain the universe in terms of chance and the laws of nature, then we have no reason to appeal to intelligent design. If we *cannot* explain the origin of the universe in these terms then we are faced with two alternatives — either the explanation lies in physics that we have not yet discovered, or it lies in intelligent design. Neither of these alternatives will bring any joy to atheists, because the former they cannot appeal to (we haven't discovered it yet) and the latter they don't like.

How much universe do we need to explain? The more we look, the more we see. The more sophisticated the instruments, the more complex the information we receive. The catalog of weird and wonderful objects in the universe is continually expanding with no sign of an end anywhere. Where do we draw the line? We shall use the logic of cause and effect as our guide.

It may seem trivial, but a foundational issue in science is that the world works by a process of cause and effect. If something happens, then something else must have caused it to happen. Events don't happen in isolation. Even miracles have causes.[18] Governments and industry spend billions of dollars every year on science in order to explain the world in terms of causes that we can understand so that we can then manipulate those things to our own advantage.

To provide an adequate explanation of something that is unknown in terms of what is known, the description must satisfy two requirements of cause

---

18. Supernatural ones, by definition.

and effect. First, the cause must be *necessary* to produce the effect. Second, the cause must be *sufficient* to produce the effect.

A *necessary* cause is one that must be present for the observed effect to occur. Gravity, for example, is necessary for a cloud of gas to collapse into a star. A cloud of gas will not collapse if gravity is not present.

However, though gravity is present in all clouds of gas, not all clouds of gas will collapse into a star. Small clouds of gas will simply dissipate into space. If the cloud of gas is too big it will collapse into a black hole (if it has sufficient initial density). It is only gas clouds of a certain size that are able to collapse and form a star. So while gravity is *necessary* for star formation, it is not, in itself, *sufficient* for star formation.

Even a gas cloud with the mass of our sun is not sufficient to collapse into a sun-sized star. The pressure within this gas cloud is far too great and the force of gravity is far too weak to make it collapse. Something more is needed — something that can overcome the gas pressure and allow gravity to take over. Astrophysicists typically invoke dramatic cooling and/or a shock wave of some kind, perhaps from a nearby supernova, to overcome the pressure problem.

So a necessary *and* sufficient cause for gas cloud collapse into a star is a gas cloud of the right size, plus gravity, plus an extra push from something that will overcome the pressure. None of these causes alone can produce the star. All of them must work together.

So let us now consider what a "necessary and sufficient universe" might look like. The *necessary* universe must contain man. Without mankind there is no scientific discipline of cosmology and no need to find cosmological explanations. To sustain human life, we require a planet just like the earth that is cool enough to live on but close enough to a star to keep warm, provide energy, and avoid the hazards of deep space. It needs to rotate on its axis so that heat inputs are evenly distributed around the globe. It needs a magnetic field to protect us from cosmic rays and the solar wind; an atmosphere to provide gas and water cycling; and the list goes on and on.

The *sufficient* universe will depend upon your point of view. The Bible says that God wanted the heavenly bodies to provide markers of times and seasons and to give light on earth. From that perspective, we need a moon as well as the sun, and we need stars at night, and perhaps other planets to assist in the marking of times and seasons. In short, a solar system like ours and a galaxy would provide a sufficient universe. The great astronomer Harlow Shapley was satisfied with that much, so we are in respectable company. Let us hasten to add that we in no way wish to detract from the enormity and amazing diversity of the universe — we simply want to lay down a minimum definition of a universe so that we do not make impossibly tedious demands of any explanation for its origin.

In the next chapter we will look in more detail at the tools available to physicists for explaining the origin of the universe — that is, the tools of *chance* and the *laws of physics*. If big-bang theory can explain the origin of our galaxy and our solar system, using chance and the laws of physics, there will be no place left for an appeal to intelligent design (except perhaps a very abstract notion of design within the laws of physics themselves, with nothing else for a designer to do from that point on).

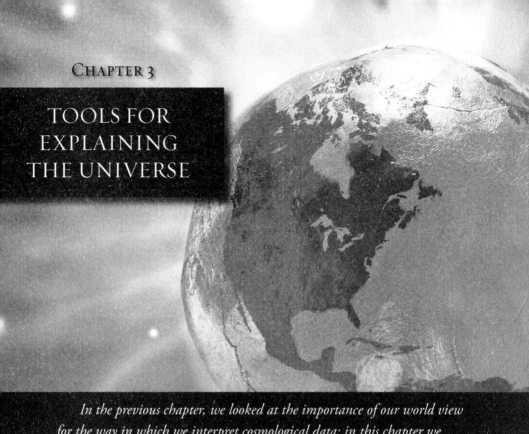

CHAPTER 3

TOOLS FOR EXPLAINING THE UNIVERSE

In the previous chapter, we looked at the importance of our world view for the way in which we interpret cosmological data; in this chapter we shall examine the tools available in physics for explaining the origin and history of the universe.

What does it mean to explain something?

Many years ago, one of us (A.W.) went trekking with a colleague in the mountains of Papua New Guinea. Our guide deserted us and we found ourselves alone on a narrow track, halfway up the side of a precipitous mountain, at night, in the pouring rain. After a while the rain stopped and, in the stillness that followed, the most terrifying noise I have ever heard pierced shrilly through the blackness from across the valley. It was so foreign to my experience that it took my subconscious mind a while to register that this was a terrifying noise and that I should therefore be terrified. Before I could marshal my "fight or flight" response, my colleague calmly said, "These crickets make a lot of noise, don't they!"

I hastily agreed. I needed some explanation, and "cricket" sounded fine to me. Crickets make piercing noises. Insects in this part of the world grow to enormous sizes. That horrible sound could well be coming from an enormous cricket. I held firmly onto the "cricket" theory and refused to think about it any more. The alternative was too awful to contemplate — some *unknown* horror.

To this day I have no idea what made that noise but the story illustrates what it means to "explain" something. We describe the unknown in terms of the known. I knew that crickets make piercing noises and I knew that insects in New Guinea grew to enormous sizes. I did not know what was making the noise, but the "very large cricket" theory was a reasonable explanation — and I badly needed *some* explanation.

Likewise, when we come to cosmology, a scientific explanation of the origin of the universe will need to describe the unknown (the origin of the universe, which is beyond the reach of our observation) in terms of the known — chance and necessity (the forces of nature). As pointed out in the previous chapter, if chance and necessity cannot explain something, then we might reasonably invoke intelligent design. In the following sections we will consider what chance can explain, what necessity can explain, and then see what is left over.

CHANCE

Chance is probably one of the most abused concepts in all of cosmology (and origins science generally). The most extreme abuse scenario goes something like this: (a) anything is possible, even if it might be very improbable; (b) the universe is so vast and has been around for so long that even the most improbable events become likely (or even certain); (c) therefore, the most improbable events are likely to have occurred somewhere at some time. This scenario is false and misleading because all events in the material world are subject to the laws of physics. Chance cannot violate the laws of physics. Miracles may violate the laws of physics, but chance cannot.

A less extreme, but no less erroneous, example is found in all evolutionary scenarios. The naturalistic materialist world view only allows chance and necessity as explanations for the world around us so their explanations follow this set pattern: (a) an explanation built upon necessity is developed; (b) any remaining "holes" are plugged with chance. Because "chance" is such a nebulous and inscrutable concept, the general public assumes that someone has worked it out in a satisfactory manner somewhere and they swallow it. However, as we will show, it is alarming how much ignorance and bluff can be concealed in the word "chance."

The systematic study of chance is carried out in the mathematical discipline of statistics. According to the principles of statistics there are four major faults in these common misuses of chance.

Chance Is Not a Force

First, chance is seen as some sort of "force" that can do things independently of necessity. This is not true. Chance is not a force. We can illustrate the principle by using gas molecules. Gas molecules may be said to move at random (i.e., by chance) but, in fact, they don't. All objects in the macroscopic universe (above the quantum level) move according to Newton's laws of motion — which we will deal with shortly. They move in straight lines unless some force diverts them. In a liter of gas on earth at standard temperature and pressure there are so many molecules rushing around that they bump into one another and bounce all over the place, giving the appearance of random motion. In fact, all their movements occur strictly according to Newton's laws. It would be a tedious process to describe all the individual movements in terms of Newton's laws and it is generally sufficient, and more convenient, to describe the whole system in statistical terms.

So when we come to explanations based on chance and necessity, we are actually only talking about two aspects of the same thing. On the one hand, "necessity" is the *certain* result of the laws of physics, and, on the other hand, "chance" is the *possible* result of the laws of physics. In both cases the only underlying causes that can be appealed to are the laws of physics. Chance does not add anything extra, it only provides a way of deciding whether unlikely physical events might become likely under certain circumstances.

Chance Is Not Alone

The second abuse of chance is to represent it as a single variable. The probability that an event will occur is usually denoted as "p,"and the value of p can range from zero (meaning that it won't happen) to one (meaning that it is certain to happen). In problems to which statistics are usually applied, the value of p generally lies between 0 and 1 and the task is to decide which of the two extremes is most likely, that is, whether an event is more likely to happen or not happen.

Chance is *not* a single-valued quantity, it is a *two*-variable quantity, as expressed in the equation $p+q=1$, where "q" is the probability that the event will *not* happen. The smaller the value of p, the larger the value of q. If it is unlikely that the event *will* happen, then it is likely that the event *won't* happen.

The abuse here can be seen in arguments like the following "rogue gas" scenario. "There exists . . . a probability of a little less than 1 chance in 10^{80} that the hot air molecules arising from the flames on a gas stove, instead of dissipating throughout the room, could bunch together inside a small volume element, move toward you, and burn a hole through your chest and into your heart."[1] The implied logic here is as follows: (a) gas molecules move at random; (b) a possible random combination is that they could be all in the same place moving in the same direction. This scenario suffers from two faults, one of which is that it ignores the value of q, the probability that the event won't occur (the other fault will be considered below).

If you consult any textbook on statistics you might be surprised to find that, in the tables of probability given in the back of the book, values of p are usually given at three levels of significance: $p = 0.05$, $p = 0.01$ and $p = 0.001$. An extra value of $p = 0.0005$, may be given to cater for what are called "one-tailed" tests, but smaller values are never given. The reason is that as p gets smaller, q becomes larger, and you quickly reach the situation where the event is overwhelmingly more likely not to happen and the cost/benefit ratio of real life problems would demand that you not pursue the matter. Theoretical cosmologists might pursue smaller values of p because it costs them nothing to write down numbers on paper, but in the real world, cost is usually a controlling factor (more on cost issues shortly).

Now you might say that the probability of anyone winning the lottery is about 1 chance in a million, but someone wins the lottery every week. This is true. The reason is that the probability of *someone* winning the lottery is $p=1$. The event is *certain* because *someone's* number will come out in the draw, but the probability that *you* will win the lottery is $p=0.000001$. Even if you buy a lottery ticket every week for a whole lifetime the probability that you will win in the last week of your life will still be $p=0.000001$. The probability that you will win *sometime* during your life will improve if you buy a ticket every week, but the odds will remain the same in any particular week. So why do people buy lottery tickets? The reason is that the *cost* is thought to be small compared to the *benefit* of a big win. The outcome, however, is very predictable — the average person will never get a big win in the lottery.

Gambling Costs Money

This issue of cost leads us to the third common abuse of chance — isolating it from the real world so that it is no longer subject to the laws of physics. A typical example is the extreme case mentioned earlier: the argument that the probability p of an event **A** is very small, however, the universe is so vast and has been around for so long that even the most unlikely events become

---

1. Hugh Ross, *The Creator and the Cosmos* (Colorado Springs, CO: NavPress, 2001), p. 253.

probable (some people extend the argument and say that the event becomes *certain*). The implication here is that all possible permutations of the universe are equally likely, but this is not true. All interactions in the real world occur only in a limited space, so not all permutations of the universe are equally likely. All interactions in the real world use up energy, so as time goes by use-able energy is continually depleted. As a result, long periods of time do not necessarily lead to increased likelihood; they will, on average, lead to *decreased* likelihood that anything at all will happen.

We could illustrate the principle by using casino gambling. Everyone knows that the odds are structured to favor the "house." Because it costs you something each time you play, the longer you play, the more money you spend, and the less likely you are to come out ahead. The only way to make money is to pull out as soon as you get a big win. Of course you will only make money if the "big win" comes early in the process — if it does not come until very late in the process then you will likely have already spent more than you won and will still be behind.

In cosmological terms, the parallel situation is that in any particular part of the universe there will only ever be a finite amount of energy and a finite number of particles available for interaction. Any accomplishments of chance will have to come early in the process, while there is still enough useable energy

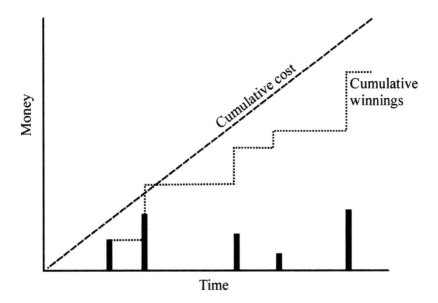

The cost of gambling. Black bars indicate wins. The only way to make a profit is to get a big win early on; the longer you play, the further you get behind.

available and the particles are still in a position to interact. Invoking vast amounts of time may be counterproductive, because it simply ensures that the energy will be used up and the particles will be either dispersed or gravitationally bound into their most probable configurations.

So what *can* chance accomplish in cosmology? Could it create the "rogue gas" scenario mentioned above? If it could, then perhaps that might explain star and planet formation.

Well, no, it couldn't. The "rogue gas" scenario suffers from chance being separated from the laws of physics. As we pointed out above, the logic of the "rogue gas" scenario depends upon gas molecules moving at random — but they do not move at random, they obey the laws of motion. Gas molecules move in straight lines unless something diverts them. If, by chance, a vacant space in the room should open up, you can be sure that nearby gas molecules will quickly fly into it because there will be no other gas molecules there to deflect them. This process will ensure that any concentration of gas molecules will quickly disperse until all parts of the room are equally filled (on average) with gas molecules.

Possible and Impossible Events

This leads to the fourth common abuse of chance. Chance can only be applied to events that *can* happen — chance cannot magically make things happen that are physically impossible. All the techniques of statistics are based upon distributions of real life events. There is a special branch of statistics devoted to estimating the likelihood of extreme events like floods and earthquakes, and in all cases the methods depend upon estimates derived from real life measurements. In the "rogue gas" scenario, chance was wrongly used to falsely imply that an impossible event was possible. Because gas molecules move according to the laws of motion (and not at random) and there are countless zillions of them in the gas volume referred to, then we can confidently conclude that they could not all congregate in one small area and move in the same direction at the same time. The probability of this event is zero, because physics does not allow it to happen. Dr. Ross assigned it a probability of 1 chance in 10^{80}, thereby falsely implying that p is greater than zero and the event is possible.

We will revisit chance again later, but for the present the most important conclusion is that chance cannot accomplish anything independently of the laws of physics. All that chance (statistics) can do is give us some tools for thinking about physical scenarios that are not certain to happen but that might possibly happen. Chance cannot be used to bring impossible events into the realm of the possible.

Necessity

Modern science is an enormous field of endeavor and we cannot possibly cover all that is known about "necessity" in a book of this kind. We will therefore restrict ourselves to just those aspects of physics that have a direct bearing on the explanation of the origin of matter, galaxies, stars, planets, and moons. Here is a brief overview of what we will cover:

- Quantum mechanics — matter can be produced from energy in the laboratory, so cosmologists believe that it could have been produced from energy in the early stages of the big bang.
- The four fundamental forces — all matter is held together by gravity, electromagnetism, and the strong and weak nuclear forces.
- Gravity — this is the only force that acts over cosmic distances. Gravity can explain orbits, spheres, the triggering of nuclear fusion, singularities, and black holes.
- Rotation and turbulence — fluid motions can sometimes become chaotic.
- Dimensions — we are used to the three spatial dimensions of length, breadth, and height, but relativity theory added time to the list and physicists think there may be more. Perhaps the world is made of "strings" or "branes."
- The laws of thermodynamics — these describe the properties and limitations of energy. They have profound implications for cosmology.
- The geometry of space — your house may be "square" and made with nice right angles at every corner and parallel edges to every wall, but your universe could be curved, flat, or saddle-shaped. The precise shape will point to either a "big crunch" or a "big chill" if projected into the far distant future.
- The cosmological constant — Einstein invented it, then threw it away, but it has come back to haunt cosmologists in the most embarrassing way.

Quantum Mechanics

One of the great achievements of physics in the late 20th century, so it is claimed, is the unification of the smallest scale (subatomic particles) with the largest scale (the stars and galaxies) in the big-bang theory. The very earliest stages of the big bang are completely explained, so it is claimed, by the standard model of particle physics. This is the elaborate theory that has emerged from particle accelerators smashing atoms in the laboratory at ever higher and higher energies. The high-energy environment of the early big-bang universe is thought to have been like the high-energy environment inside the particle accelerators, and so the standard model derived from smashing atoms has been applied to the origin of the whole universe. We see no reason to disagree with this line of argument, given the other assumptions of the big-bang theory (i.e., we don't agree with it, but we accept that it is logically consistent with the assumptions). A high-energy environment in a laboratory probably *is* very similar to a high-energy environment in an early big-bang universe. The energies achieved in the laboratory are still nowhere near to those achieved in the early stages of the alleged big bang, but the principle of comparison should be valid.

We do not need to understand much about quantum mechanics for our present purpose, apart from two things. First, the fact that energy can, indeed, be converted into matter. Einstein's idea that energy and matter are interchangeable (remember $E=mc^2$?) is now well established experimentally. The details of what happens depend only upon the temperature. The big bang supposedly began very hot, so there was plenty of energy about for creating matter. Energy produces matter by the process of quantum pair production.

One of the things we noted earlier was that when particles of matter are created in the laboratory they always appear in matter/antimatter pairs. If we get an electron, we also get an anti-electron (called a positron). If we get a proton, we also get an antiproton. If we get a neutrino, we also get an antineutrino, and so on. Just as energy can produce matter by this quantum pair production method, so when the matter and antimatter particles come together again they annihilate one another and revert back to pure energy. This has profound and unwelcome implications for big-bang theory, but we will wait until the next chapter to see why. For the present, all we need to note is that energy can produce matter if the temperature is high enough.

The second thing we need to know about quantum mechanics is that quantum events usually occur in discrete jumps rather than smooth transitions. That is, a matter/antimatter pair will either appear fully formed or not appear at all — they do not begin small and grow larger. Now quantum mechanics is usually concerned only about very small things, like photons of light and electrons. If, as big-bang theory contends, the universe was once very small, then perhaps a quantum event can explain its origin — maybe it just popped into existence like a matter/antimatter pair. This idea is being explored in the hunt for a theory of quantum gravity, but there are several objections to applying the idea to the whole universe. One of these is that quantum events are occurring all the time, so if a universe can just pop into existence once by this process, why don't we see it happening again and again? We will also meet other objections to this idea as we go along.

The Four Forces of Physics

We have already been introduced to some of the forces of physics. *Gravity* was the first to be described, by Sir Isaac Newton in 1687. It explained the movement of the heavenly bodies without having to resort to spirit beings such as the spirit horse and chariot illustrated in the chapter on history. Electricity and magnetism were next. They were intensively studied in the 18th and 19th centuries and found to be produced by the same fundamental force, which is now called the *electromagnetic* force. It was not until the 20th century that the other two forces were discovered — the *strong* and *weak nuclear* forces. The strong nuclear force holds the protons and neutrons together in the atomic nucleus, and the weak nuclear force holds neutrons together — a neutron is produced when a proton (positively charged) grabs an electron (negatively charged), the electrical charges cancel out, and it becomes a neutral particle (that's why it is called a neutron).

These are the only four fundamental forces in physics. Everything that physics can explain can be explained in terms of gravity, electromagnetism, and strong and weak nuclear forces. Four is too many for some physicists and they are trying to find an underlying theory that could explain all four in terms of just one. Such a theory has been dubbed a "theory of everything," or TOE, but so far it has eluded even the most brilliant minds.

What are these forces? That is a rather profound question that we will consider further in the section on theology. For the present, we will simply focus on what these forces do, and the distance scales over which they operate.

Gravity holds things together with a force proportional to their masses, and inversely proportional to the squared distance between them.[2] That means the greater the masses, the stronger the force, but the greater the distance between them, the weaker the force. Gravity still works at enormous distances, however. For example, it holds our solar system and our galaxy together (our galaxy is about 100,000 light-years across). It also appears to hold groups of galaxies together on scales of millions of light-years.

---

2. Newton's law of gravity states that the gravitational force F = M1 (the mass of one body) x M2 (the mass of the other) x G (a constant) divided by r^2 (r = the distance between the two bodies).

Electromagnetic force involves electricity and magnetism. The electric part is the attraction between positively and negatively charged particles (protons and electrons, respectively). Protons are firmly stuck in the nuclei of atoms, but electrons can move about. If electrons can be persuaded to flow through a conducting material (by a battery or generator, for example) we call it an "electric current." Magnetism is produced in "fields" — areas of influence — that surround a flow of electric current.[3] Electricity can flow through large objects such as the earth and the atmosphere (e.g., lightning) but it cannot flow through the vacuum of space, so it is limited to planetary and stellar scales (including clouds of ionized gas). However, magnetic fields can exist in the vacuum of space. If we could see them with our eyes then when we looked at our solar system we would see enormous magnetic fields associated with the sun and with our largest planet, Jupiter, for example.

The strong nuclear force is about 100 times stronger than the electromagnetic force, but it only works over very tiny distances. The nuclei of atoms consist of positively charged protons and neutral neutrons. Similar electrical charges always repel one another and if the strong nuclear force did not exist then atomic nuclei with more than one proton would spontaneously disintegrate as the protons repelled each other. The strong nuclear force overcomes the electromagnetic repulsion between the protons and binds them together to form a stable nucleus. The strong force cannot be felt outside the nucleus. This is fortunate for us, otherwise the infinitely variable molecular structure of life would collapse.

The weak nuclear force holds the electron and proton together in a neutron and it likewise is restricted in scale to the atomic nucleus and in most cases cannot be felt outside it (radioactive decay by beta emission is one exception).

In summary, the two nuclear forces hold atoms together, the electromagnetic force holds molecules together, and gravity holds solar systems and galaxies together. Notice that none of these forces *creates* anything new. All of them simply hold things together. Indeed, the first law of thermodynamics says that energy/matter cannot be created or destroyed — it can be transformed from one form to another, but it cannot be created or destroyed. So you can see that, right here at the foundation, physics has no tools for creating a universe. All it

---

3. Individual electrons can behave like tiny magnets and so atoms can have magnetic fields. In certain types of materials, such as metallic iron, the atoms can be made to line up in such a way that their tiny magnetic fields add together to produce a "permanent" magnet.

has is tools for *transforming* what already exists and *holding it together*. This has profound implications for cosmology that are often overlooked.

Because gravity is the only force that regularly acts at cosmic scales, our investigation of explanatory models will look at what gravity can and cannot achieve. Afterward, we will look at whether electromagnetism can usefully supplement gravity to make up any shortfalls.

The Achievements of Gravity

Sir Isaac Newton said that gravity was an attractive force between every particle in the universe, the strength of which is proportional to the combined mass of the particles divided by the squared distance between them. Although Albert Einstein's theory of relativity modified our views of gravity, Newton's formulation is still appropriate for most of what we will be considering here.

So what does gravity do to the universe so that we could look at it and say, "Yes, that object was formed by gravity," or "No, that object could not have been formed by gravity"?

Orbits

The first success of gravity in explaining the universe was Newton's explanation of the orbits of the planets and other heavenly bodies. This explanation required a combination of gravity and the laws of motion. Newton formulated three laws of motion.

1. A body at rest will remain at rest (and a body that is moving will keep moving in the same direction and at the same speed) unless acted on by unbalanced forces.

2. When a force is applied to a body it will accelerate its motion in the direction of the force.

3. For every action there is an equal and opposite reaction.

Let us imagine that the sun is a body at rest (it is actually moving in relation to the galaxy, but we can ignore that for the present). According to Newton's first law of motion it will remain at rest. Now assume that the planet Mars is moving. Once again, according to the same law, it will continue to move in the direction it is heading unless a force acts upon it. This property is called "inertia."

At this point you might object to this law of motion. On earth, things that are moving tend to slow down and stop — they don't keep going. That is because of the combined effects of friction and gravity. If we drop a lump

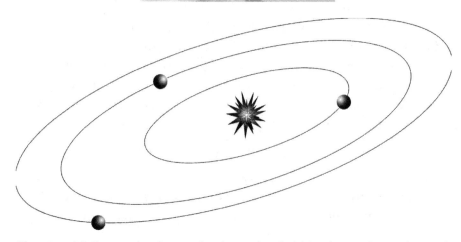

Planets orbit the sun in almost circular paths, held by the sun's gravity, and moving according to Newton's laws.

of lead it will fall to the earth and stop. The force of gravity pulled it down, but the solid earth allowed no further movement. If we bowl a ball along the grass, gravity will pull it downward and the friction of the grass will dissipate its energy and eventually bring it to a halt. On earth, motion stops because the forces of gravity and friction dissipate the energy. Friction occurs when objects bump into one another and they are diverted or deformed and energy is lost as heat. In the vacuum of space there is nothing to bump into so there is no friction — planets and other heavenly objects just keep going. The spacecraft *Pioneer 10* has been traveling out beyond the solar system for over 30 years now and it just keeps on going — it doesn't need any rocket fuel to keep it going, just Newton's first law of motion. It does still feel a tiny effect of the sun's gravity but not enough to stop it.

If the planet Mars was out there with *Pioneer 10* it would just keep going also, but it's not, it is much closer to the sun and is more strongly influenced by the sun's gravity. So there are two motion components at work on the planet Mars — the first law of motion pushes it in a straight line in the direction it is traveling, and the sun's gravity is pulling it in a straight line toward the sun. But didn't Einstein say that gravity is a curved dent in spacetime? So how come it is now acting in straight lines? A simple answer is that Newton's law of gravity works perfectly well at the velocities we are talking about here. Einstein's relativity theory only produces a different result if planetary motion is observed over centuries or if an object passes very close to the sun.

The net result of these two forces is that they balance one another into a near-circular orbit.[4] The motion component (the inertia) pushes the planet ever in a straight line, but the gravity component pulls it inward. If Mars' motion greatly slowed down, the gravity component would dominate over the motion component and Mars would be sucked into the sun. Likewise, if the sun switched off its gravity, Mars would head off into outer space like a stone out of a sling. As it is, a perfect balance is maintained and Mars keeps going round and round the sun, just like all the other planets, in predictable orbits.

Other heavenly bodies, such as comets, also behave in a similar way. They follow very elongated paths, but the forces of motion and gravity still provide the balance that creates the elliptical geometry of their movement. However, when comets come close to the sun they heat up and a significant proportion of their mass is evaporated and blown away by the solar wind. As a result, the loss of mass causes the motion component to be reduced and so gravity begins to win the struggle. Eventually, the comet will either break up or be sucked into the sun (or both).

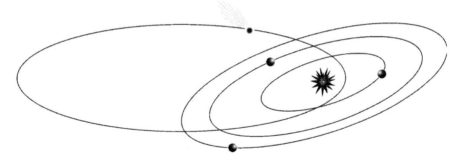

Comets orbit the sun in long, elliptical paths, many
not returning for hundreds of years.

This is one line of evidence that creationists have used to point to a young solar system. If the solar system is really billions of years old, then all the comets should have disappeared long ago. Halley's comet, for example, orbits the sun every 76 years and it loses about 1 percent of its mass each time. It could not survive more than, at maximum, about 1,000 circuits of the sun (=76,000 years) before it died, so it cannot be billions of years old.

---

4. Each orbit does not perfectly coincide with the preceding one. The orbits "precess," which means over time they describe the shape of a rosette. This precession was successfully explained by Einstein's general theory on gravity.

To get around this problem, evolutionists say there must be a cloud of comets beyond the outer reaches of the solar system. They call this the Oort cloud, after the Dutch astronomer who proposed the idea. To get this reservoir of comets to resupply the solar system they say that when our solar system passes through the disk of the Milky Way, close encounters with nearby stars dislodge a new batch of comets into near-solar orbits. This is called an ad hoc explanation. It was made up just for this purpose. There is no evidence that Oort's cloud exists.

So here is the first thing that gravity does. It produces orbits among the heavenly bodies. Everything in the galaxy orbits something else. Our planets orbit our sun, and our solar system orbits the center of the galaxy, out in one of its spiral arms. All of this can be explained by gravity and the laws of motion. No spirit horses and carriages are necessary.

Spheres

Because gravity is an attractive force between all particles in the universe it does not have any preferred direction and therefore it acts equally in all

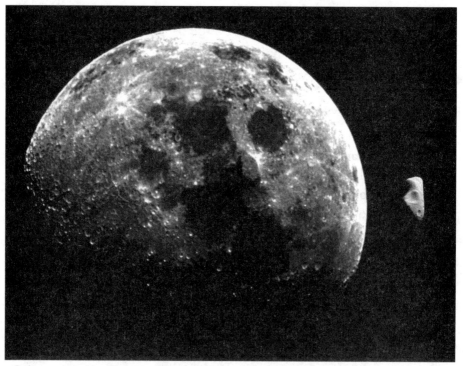

Our moon is large enough for gravity to pull its matter into a sphere, but the asteroid (on the right) is too small. The asteroid retains its original shape and may be a fragment from a broken planet.

directions. The result of this is that, in the absence of other forces, gravity will gather particles equally in all directions and the net result will be a sphere. Thus, the earth is a sphere, the moon is a sphere, the sun is a sphere, and all the known planets are spheres. Because these bodies also rotate, there is a slight deviation from a perfect sphere because of the outward pressure of the centrifugal force at the equator, but we can ignore that for the present. The sphericity of these bodies tells us that they are large enough so that their gravity can overcome all other forces and pull them into the ideal shape.

Objects much smaller than planets, for example, the smaller moons, are, however, not necessarily spherical. Small moons, asteroids and comets, for example, are too small for their gravity to pull them into a sphere.

Nuclear Fusion

Why do stars shine? Before the discovery of nuclear fusion it was thought that gravitational contraction produced enough heat to make them shine. Recent research has confirmed that there is indeed a sufficient nuclear reaction going on in the heart of our sun to explain its power output.[5]

Stars are universally made up of giant balls of gas. There are traces of numerous other elements but hydrogen gas is the most abundant. When such a ball of gas is large enough (and dense enough) the force of gravity will pull it together with such power that the gas will heat up to temperatures so high that the hydrogen atoms begin to fuse together to form helium. This is also the reaction at the heart of a hydrogen bomb. The gravitational force in a star is so great that it manages to contain the explosive reaction and the energy is converted to heat. As a result of this continual nuclear reaction, the star becomes so hot that it radiates energy like a light bulb.

Gravitational compression alone *could* explain the enormous heat and light output of a star but it would die out and grow cold before long; it could not survive for billions of years. Some years ago measurements of the sun's diameter did suggest that it was shrinking, and there were not enough neutrinos coming from the sun to justify the nuclear fusion theory. Creationists therefore suggested that perhaps stars were powered by gravity and not by nuclear fusion and were therefore much younger than evolutionists were saying. But the evidence has moved on. The shrinking trend was found to be cyclic and the lack of neutrinos was accounted for, so the evidence today does appear to favor nuclear fusion. So here

---

5. Robert Newton, " 'Missing' Neutrinos Found! No Longer an 'Age' Indicator," *TJ* 16(3):123-125 (2002).

is another lesson about science and faith — don't base your doctrine on science, because the interpretations change as new evidence comes to light.

Singularities and Black Holes

Newton's law of gravity says that the strength of its force is proportional to the combined mass of the interacting bodies, divided by the square of the distance between them (this is called the "inverse square law"). Let's explore what happens when we have large masses separated by only small distances. Say object **A** has a mass of one sun (the mass of our sun is used as the unit of mass measurement in cosmology), particle **B** (the same size as particle **A**) has a mass of ten suns, and the two "particles" are very widely separated. The strength of gravity on the surface of **B** will be ten times that on the surface of **A,** because **B** has ten times the mass of **A**. Whereas if we bring **A** and **B** ten times closer together than they were before, the strength of the gravitational attraction *between* **A** and **B** will now be 100 times more powerful than what it was previously. The reason for this is that the force of gravity is proportional to the mass divided by the *squared* distance between them.

As a result, when you have large masses in small spaces, the force of gravity can very quickly become enormous. Physicists believe that in very large stars the internal pressure is so great that it drives the nuclear reactions in the core much more quickly than in smaller stars. The star can use up all its nuclear fuel and no longer have enough heat to resist the enormous gravitational force. When this happens, the core of the star will collapse, creating a violent explosion called a "supernova," but collapse into what?

Well, for stars about the size of our sun, there is not enough mass to produce a supernova, and when all its nuclear fuel is exhausted it will become a "red giant" and then a "white dwarf" and then fade from sight when it cools down. Larger stars that are about ten solar masses or so, would produce a supernova explosion, and the end result would be a "neutron star." Gravity would be so strong that the electrons in atoms would be squashed into their companion protons to produce neutrons and the whole mass would become as dense as an ordinary atomic nucleus. A spoonful of neutron star stuff would weigh about a billion tons! The star itself would be just a few miles across and spinning at an incredible rate — many times per second.

For stars of about 50 solar masses or more, it is believed a "black hole" would form. A black hole is the condition where gravity is so strong that even light rays cannot escape. The limit which light can reach before being sucked back in is called the "event horizon," so called because no events inside this boundary can be seen from outside. So a black hole is a spherical region of space within which nothing can ever be seen by outside observers. If you were to shine a light onto it, no reflected light could come back to you to show you what is there, because the light would be sucked into the black hole. So may other nearby objects, depending on their speed and direction. The enormous gravitational field would suck in everything in the near vicinity that it can.

At the center of our galaxy there is a lot of violent activity that physicists generally interpret as being the result of the reaction of matter that is near a black hole, some even being sucked into it. There are stars near the center of the galaxy that orbit so quickly that only a very massive central body could explain it. There are also about 300 or so additional objects within our galaxy that astronomers suggest may be candidates for black holes.

A black hole is just our description of what we see on the outside. What is the state of the matter on the inside? This question was very disturbing to the physicists who pondered it early last century. In 1932, L.D. Landau concluded that above a certain size, stars would be unstable and "there exists in the whole quantum theory no cause preventing the system from collapsing to a point."[6]

In 1935, Sir Arthur Eddington realized that black holes were the inevitable fate of large stars, but he disliked the concept, saying, "I think that there should be a law of nature to prevent the star from behaving in this absurd way."[7] Eddington's reputation was so forceful that no one looked further into the matter for another 30 years. It was not until the 1960s that the name "black hole" was coined by J.A. Wheeler, and a fuller description of the phenomenon was developed.

Yet while we can discuss the issue of black holes fairly freely, the idea that matter collapses to "a point" — technically called a "singularity" — remains rather obscure. What is it like? Is it a lump of matter? Or does gravity squeeze it into "nothing?" We don't know — "the ultimate fate of collapsing matter, once it has crossed the black hole surface, is not known."[8] No one has ever seen one close up (nor would anyone want to!). Even though they are thought to exist at the center of most galaxies, we have never visited such a place and would be quickly destroyed if we did.

Singularities are weird. In his book devoted to this subject, *The Analysis of Space-Time Singularities*, Professor C.J.S. Clarke of the University of

---

6. Stuart L. Shapiro and Saul A. Teukolsky, *Black Holes, White Dwarfs and Neutron Stars: The Physics of Compact Objects* (New York: John Wiley & Sons, 1983), p. 337.
7. Ibid.
8. Ibid., p.335.

Southampton tried to approach the problem by a process of "eliminating false singularities." He said:

> The central aim of this book is the development of the results and techniques needed to determine when it is possible to extend a space-time through an "apparent singularity." . . . Having achieved this, we shall obtain a characterization of a "genuine singularity" as a place where such an extension is not possible. . . . I had at one stage hoped that there would be a single, simple criterion for when such an extension cannot be constructed, which would then lay down once and for all what a genuine singularity is. But it seems this is not to be had: instead one has a variety of possible tools and concepts for constructing extensions, and when these fail one declares the spacetime to be singular on pragmatic grounds. . . . It is perhaps one of the disappointments of the subject . . . that no final satisfactory statement emerges of what a singularity really is like.[9]

What about Eddington's idea that a force of some kind must prevent the collapse? Well, when Einstein's equations are applied to such a scenario it turns out that the energy of any such force has an equivalent mass, which then exerts an equivalent gravitational attraction, which then adds to the rate of collapse rather than opposing it. There appears to be no escape from the idea of indefinite collapse, however disturbing the concept may be.[10]

The condition of matter before the big bang is supposed to have been in a singularity — all the matter, energy, space, and time of the universe squashed into "nothing" (attempts to get around this idea will be dealt with shortly). We have no reason to believe that such a singularity would have been any different to the singularity inside the supposed black hole at the center of our galaxy. If there had been only one such singularity — the one before the big bang — then its uniqueness would put it beyond scientific investigation. Science can only study things that happen more than once. If there are many such singularities, of which the primordial one is just like any other (except that the others have event horizons around them and so we call them "black holes"), then we can begin a scientific study of singularities. Indeed, this kind of singularity would appear to be a fifth state of matter. Matter of the more familiar kind can exist in four states — solid, liquid, gas, and plasma (plasma is formed when gas

9. C.J.S. Clarke, *The Analysis of Space-Time Singularities* (Cambridge, UK: Cambridge University Press, 1993), p. xi, 152.
10. An interesting alternative theory of gravity (Van Flandern's meta model) which avoids singularities is given in appendix A.

molecules have electrons stripped from them by heat or electricity). What we know about a singularity suggests that it is a fifth state.

Now there is not a great deal we can say about singularities because we don't have one to study in the laboratory, but there are at least four things we *can* say about them:

- The matter does not "go away." The "nothing" is not really nothing, it is simply a state of matter that we cannot investigate. Its gravitational influence on surrounding matter remains, even though its usual physical manifestation has "disappeared."

- Physicists generally say that the laws of physics break down in a singularity, but this may not be entirely true. Gravity remains the same (as far as we know). The atomic structure that allows the electromagnetic and nuclear forces to act may have been destroyed but the source of the gravitational force — whatever it is — remains intact and appears to be unaffected. (They may also be electrically charged and have spin.)

- A singularity is a thermodynamic dead end. Other states of matter are interconvertible depending upon the temperature and pressure — solid can convert to liquid and back to solid, liquid can convert to gas and back to liquid, etc. Once matter is crushed into a singularity it cannot return to the other states.

- A singularity is an extremely stable state, at least in its more massive versions. Hawking radiation[11] may lead to the evaporation of "mini" black holes, but as yet no "mini" black holes have been discovered. The rate of evaporation is inversely proportional to mass. Singularities of a few solar masses or more are extremely stable over billion-year time scales.

While these properties may not seem like much, they have profound implications for cosmology. The big-bang theory begins with a singularity. That means it begins in a thermodynamic dead end. It contains the mass of the whole universe as well as spacetime itself.

The relationship between spacetime and gravity at extremely small scales is not well understood since general relativity no longer applies at near-singularity

---

11. Shapiro and Teukolsky, *Black Holes, White Dwarfs and Neutron Stars: The Physics of Compact Objects*, p.366. Hawking radiation is thought to occur when virtual particle pairs are separated at an event horizon, with one being sucked into the black hole and the other being ejected into space. Since the putative primordial singularity did not have an event horizon it could not have evaporated by this mechanism.

scales. That is why the equations underlying big-bang theory begin to work only *after* the expansion out of the singularity has commenced. This is an extremely important point in understanding big-bang theory, and we will return to it in the next chapter.

Avoiding the Primordial Singularity

When the first cosmological models were derived from Einstein's relativity theory in the early 20th century, physicists did not immediately foresee all of their implications. The prediction that large masses could collapse into a singularity, for example, was not something that they worried about. Indeed, Sir Arthur Eddington held the view in the 1930s that the idea of a singularity was "absurd" and he hoped that future discoveries would explain it away. It did not go away, however, and today singularities are seen as an inescapable part of general relativity.

One attempt at avoiding the singularity at the beginning of the big-bang model was based on the cosmological principle, which says that the universe looks much the same as we see it from any and every position within it. That is, there are no special regions such as a center or an edge. Since there is no center, the force of gravity would be everywhere smoothly distributed and there would be no gravity gradient to cause a gravitational collapse. As an illustration, when a balloon is inflated, the rubber is evenly stretched at all positions. Only if the balloon has a weak spot or is punctured does the rubber collapse. In a similar manner, if the big-bang universe had no "weak spots" and it were not to be "punctured" by a center, then it would remain in an uncollapsed state. However, the early universe needs to have small irregularities in it that can later produce the galaxies, so the perfect smoothness required to avoid collapse into a singularity is incompatible with the existence of the galaxies. These irregularities act like "weak spots" and "punctures" in the balloon analogy, and collapse occurs irrespective of whether there is a center or not.

As it turns out, however, the singularity can occur even if there are no "weak spots" or "punctures" and the mass/energy density remains perfectly smooth. Astrophysicists Zel'dovich and Novikov[12] illustrated this point using the geometrical concept of "world lines." A "world line" is the trajectory that any particle takes throughout its history in spacetime. That is, its movements in space and its movements in time together describe its world line. The laws of conservation in physics say that the world lines of photons or

---

12. Y.B. Zel'dovich and I.D. Novikov, *Relativistic Astrophysics Vol.2: The Structure and Evolution of the Universe* (Chicago, IL: University of Chicago Press, 1983), chapter 23.

particles in a stable universe continue indefinitely — matter and energy can be interchanged, but not created or destroyed. A singularity can now be defined geometrically as a point at which such a world line *does* come to an end. As we wind back the expansion of the universe, both space and time begin to warp as the matter/energy density increases. If we trace out the world lines of this universe, we find that eventually light rays converge, trajectories intersect, accelerations become infinite, and spacetime becomes infinitely wrapped up in itself. For any particle or photon, theorists say, there is at least one world line that cannot be continued without bound into the past — in a singularity, there is nowhere left in space or time for it to go.

This same point can be illustrated using the Friedmann equation (which we shall meet in the next chapter) that forms the basis of all big-bang models. It takes into account only the matter within a shell of arbitrary radius surrounding any point in space.[13] The gravitational potential within this shell depends only upon the density of matter within it. If the density exceeds a certain critical value, that region would collapse to form a singularity. Zel'dovich and Novikov state: "According to the Friedmann model, the expansion of the universe begins from a singularity . . . deviations from the Friedmann model at the beginning of the expansion do not permit one to avoid the singularity," and they cite Hawking and Penrose's general proof of this theorem in 1970. This applies to both finite universe models — where the singularity exists in a point of infinite density — and infinite universe models — where the singularity is infinite in extent.

So how do big-bang theorists get the universe out of its primordial singularity? Carl Sagan called it "the biggest mystery we know."[14] It is simply assumed that space was expanding right from the beginning and the substance of the universe "went along for the ride," and was thereby carried out of the singular state. No one can explain how, so they place their hope for an explanation in quantum gravity. The early big-bang universe would have been subject to quantum fluctuations, so perhaps quantum fluctuations allowed it to jump out of the grip of gravity, but we don't yet have a workable theory of quantum gravity so we have no idea what it may, or may not, be capable of explaining. At this stage it is still in the realm of speculation.

At this juncture we should note that the singularity we are talking about here is not a black hole. There is no event horizon around it, such as there is

---

13. Joseph Silk, *The Big Bang,* 3rd ed. (New York: Freeman & Co., 2001), p. 96.
14. Carl Sagan, *Cosmos,* (London: Macdonald & Co, 1980), p. 246.

around a black hole singularity, because there are no spatial dimensions left within which it could develop. We call this a "naked singularity." The crucial difference between the primordial naked singularity and a black hole, according to big-bang theory, is that while the expansion of space today is not strong enough to disrupt a black hole, the expansion of space in the early universe is supposed to have been strong enough to disrupt the primordial singularity.

Another suggested explanation was that the universe might "bounce." The current expansion would be an "up" phase that would be followed by a "down" phase of collapse, which would then "bounce" into another "up" phase of expansion. There are several problems with this idea. First, there is no known physical mechanism that could produce the "bounce." Second, the "bouncing" could not go on indefinitely because each cycle would dissipate some of the useable energy until none was left — just like a rubber ball loses energy with each bounce. Third, a "roughness" problem would intervene after the first cycle — the "lumpy" galaxies produced in the expansion phase would ensure the formation of one or more singularities during the subsequent collapse phase.

To illustrate the forces involved in this problem, recall how much matter is required to produce a singularity. Professor Hawking has predicted the existence of "mini black holes," but at present no one has found any likely candidates. In our earlier discussion on the fate of collapsing stars we saw that you don't need a universe (or even a galaxy) full of matter to produce a singularity — it only requires the amount of matter contained in a single large star! Since the universe contains about ten billion trillion stars, then we can be at least ten billion trillion times as certain that the putative primordial big-bang universe would have begun in a singularity.

It is therefore not surprising that, in his section entitled "Avoiding the Singularity," Professor Silk says, "we can say definitely that, subject to certain reasonable assumptions, a [primordial] singularity is unavoidable."[15] Professor Hawking takes the same view: "There must have been a [primordial] singularity provided only that general relativity is correct and that the universe contains as much matter as we observe."[16]

ROTATION AND TURBULENCE

One of the many fascinating things about objects in our universe is that all of them appear to be rotating. If we apply Newton's laws to this problem, we

15. Silk, *The Big Bang*, p. 397.
16. Stephen Hawking, *The Theory of Everything* (Beverly Hills, CA: New Millenium Press, 2002), p. 42.

quickly realize that this motion must have a cause, since motion only occurs if a force acts upon an object. The big bang cannot have produced any net rotational motion, because the explosion originated from a point and nothing was restricting it so it must have acted equally in all directions. The most that the big bang can explain is the outward movement of matter equally in all directions.

If two objects collide off-center, then each body could impart to the other some rotational impulse and get it turning. However, this explanation cannot be applied to the early big-bang universe because the only objects present are gas molecules and they are all moving away from one another. We will explore this issue further in the next chapter.

When gas molecules are confined, however, such as in the earth's atmosphere, and we apply Newton's laws of motion, a much more complex pattern emerges. The combination of numerous accelerations, decelerations, deflections, and off-center impacts results in turbulence. Weather patterns in the atmospheres of earth and other planets frequently show turbulence. Sometimes the turbulent forces can become organized in a way that focuses their energies in the same direction and hurricanes and tornadoes can result. Such turbulent behavior can also be observed in the atmospheres of planets like Jupiter and Saturn and in the giant clouds of gas and dust in the spiral arms of our galaxy.

Dimensions

We live in a world of three spatial dimensions and one time dimension. The spatial dimensions are length, breadth, and width, and the time dimension is one way, leading inexorably from the past to the future — it does not go backward.

Classical physics treated forces such as gravity as if they acted upon particles that were single *dimensionless* points in space. Much of the mathematics of quantum mechanics also treats the subatomic particles as single *dimensionless* points in space. What is a dimensionless point?

Imagine that we have two perpendicular lines that cross one another. The point at which they intersect will be a square bounded by the width of the lines, but ideal lines have only the dimension of length — they have no width. Imagine now that we draw those lines with an ever-thinner drawing instrument. Conceptually, we would eventually reach a stage where the lines existed with the dimension of length but with no width. The point at which they intersect would now be a *dimensionless* point.

A *line*, in contrast, has the dimension of length. It is a *one-dimensional* object. A *plane* has dimensions of length and breadth so it is a *two-dimensional* object. A

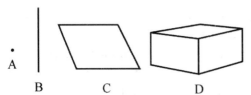

Dimensions. Point A has no dimension; line B has dimension of length; plane C has length and breadth; solid D has length, breadth, and depth. We live in a world of three spatial and one time dimension.

house brick has dimensions of length, breadth, and width, so it is a *three-dimensional* object. If we see the brick enduring through time, then it also is a *four-dimensional* object, with dimensions of length, breadth, width, and time.

Now some people have begun to think that maybe elementary particles are not dimensionless points. Maybe they are, in fact, lines having one dimension. This idea has led to what is called "string theory," in which the lines are called "strings." Some very interesting results have come out of this approach, but it has required lots of new dimensions — 10 dimensions if we include both forces and matter, or 26 dimensions if we only deal with forces. Where are all these extra dimensions? Well, they are said to have functioned in important ways in the early universe but are now wrapped up so tightly that we no longer notice them.

A further development of this principle says that perhaps our subatomic particles are not lines but planes, having two (or perhaps more) dimensions. These multidimensional objects are called "branes" (a two-dimensional brane would be a membrane) and the general idea is called "m-theory." A recent development in m-theory is the suggestion that perhaps the universe that we live in is a brane that has a companion brane universe very nearby. Wobbles in these branes (or perhaps a collision between two branes — called "the Big Crash") have been suggested to cause them to interact at points which correspond to creative events in our world, such as the big bang. Structure within our companion brane universe has perhaps influenced the structuring in our brane, such as in star and galaxy formation.

Now at this point your mind is probably spinning and you have lost all sense of understanding. Don't panic. You are not alone. One simple way of coping with this complexity is to refer back to our definition of what it means to *explain* something.

To explain something means to describe the unknown in terms of the known. Remember our wild night on the mountainside? Crickets make piercing noises; insects grow very large in the tropics; that terrifying noise might reasonably be coming from a very large cricket. That constitutes an explanation of the unknown in terms of the known.

Cosmologists endeavor to explain the unknown — in their case, the origin of the universe. In so doing, string theorists have developed 10- or 26-dimensional models to explain our four-dimensional universe. So they have *not* explained the unknown in terms of the known. They have appealed to further unknowns (dimensions that we don't know about) to explain the existing unknown (the origin of the universe) so it does not qualify (at this stage) as an explanation. If they turn out to be correct and one day we discover that there *are* strings and 26 dimensions, that will mean that the universe is unimaginably more complex than it appears to be now. Twenty-six is much larger than 4, so it is going to be much more difficult to explain the origin of a 26-dimensional universe than it would be to explain the origin of a 4-dimensional universe!

In a similar way, m-theorists now find themselves with two universes to explain when previously they only had one.

So don't let the complexity of cosmology fool you. In reality it points to the fact that cosmologists *cannot* explain the origin of the universe in terms of what they know. That is why they have to appeal to things that they *don't* know. Having said this, however, we hasten to point out that such activity is quite legitimate in science — scientists use their imagination to come up with new theories, but until those theories are tested they remain little more than imagination.

A Global Trend in Science

At this point it is worth reflecting on a global trend that is emerging in all areas of science. In cosmology we find that the more that astronomers look into space, the more they find — layer upon layer of complexity. The more that mathematicians examine their equations, the more mathematics they discover. The deeper that particle physicists delve into the structure of the atom, the more structure they find. In biology, the more that the living cell is studied, the more they are finding — layer upon layer of complexity. The more that ecologists study the web of life on earth, the more interactions, the more dependencies and the more connectedness they find. The more the human person is studied, the more complex we find the interactions to be between mind and body and between cells and organs within the body.

No one is reaching a point where they can say, "We now know it all." We believe that this points to the unfathomable depths of the Creator. A materialist universe, on the other hand, would presumably have some kind of baseline of matter from which all else is built — but this is not what we are finding.

THE LAWS OF THERMODYNAMICS

When steam engines were being developed in the 18th and 19th centuries, much effort was devoted to understanding heat and energy transfer. As a result, two laws of thermodynamics (from the Greek therme = heat) were formulated and have since been found to be generally applicable to all forms of energy and not just to heat energy. The **first law of thermodynamics** states that energy cannot be created or destroyed — it can be transformed into matter and converted from heat to electricity or to mechanical energy and back again but the total amount of energy always remains constant. The **second law of thermodynamics** says that, in the absence of any interference, the energy in a system will always tend toward its most probable distribution — a hot cup of coffee left to stand will always get colder, it won't get hotter. The most probable distribution is the one with the least energy available for useful work,[17] and with the most "random" (or "disordered") arrangement permitted by the constraints of the system.

These two laws of thermodynamics have profound implications for cosmology. The big-bang theory obeys the first law and has to assume that all the energy of the universe already existed in the beginning. The big bang has no power to create energy and thus no explanation of where it came from. The second law places enormous restrictions upon possible evolutionary scenarios. Some of these can be illustrated in the "equilibrium universe."

The Equilibrium Universe

Before we move on to explanations of the real universe, let's consider the concept of the "equilibrium universe." Equilibrium in physics is the condition where energy is distributed into its most probable form throughout the available space. When you make yourself a cup of coffee you create a non-equilibrium situation — the coffee is much hotter than the surrounding environment. If you leave the coffee long enough, its heat will dissipate through the cup and into the air and eventually the coffee will be the same temperature as the cup, the table, and the surrounding air. The system has reached thermal (heat) equilibrium.

The universe is a very *non-equilibrium* place. The stars are very hot and the rest of the universe is very cold. We live on a warm planet only because we are at a just-right distance from a star — much farther out and we would freeze, much farther in and we would fry.

---

17. While the cup of coffee was hot, the temperature difference between it and the room could have been used to derive work, but not after it has reached room temperature.

We can conclude from this non-equilibrium condition that the universe is therefore not infinitely old. If it were infinitely old then the heat would have become evenly (and randomly) distributed throughout and everything would be cold and dark.

Now the second law of thermodynamics says that the tendency of any system is always (on average — there may be localized exceptions) toward equilibrium, so we can reasonably ask: "How did our universe get so far away from equilibrium?" This is an important challenge for any naturalistic cosmology, because if we take the present-day universe in its non-equilibrium state, and wind its history back through time, we get a universe that is further and further away from equilibrium. That is, the universe becomes more structured as you go back in time. This is not convenient for atheists because it points to a highly structured universe in the beginning. This is generally acknowledged by big-bang theorists to be an unexplained problem.[18]

The biblical model, however, is consistent with the second law. It has the Creator doing the ordering work of creation at the beginning, after which entropy increases according to the second law.

Let us also consider the *final* equilibrium. The Bible says that God will ultimately destroy the present creation and make a new one. However, just for the exercise, let us consider its possible fate based solely upon the laws of physics.

If the universe contains enough matter for the force of gravity to eventually dominate over the apparent expansion, then it will collapse again in what is sometimes called the "big crunch." The laws of physics, as we know them, predict that the equilibrium condition of the big crunch will be a singularity. The force of gravity will be so great that nothing will escape its grasp, not even light. We could perhaps add that it will be a spherical singularity, because gravity has no preferred direction and therefore produces spheres. but no one would be around to notice its shape, and we would not be able to see it anyway as there would be no lighted background against which we could see its associated black hole.

The other possible fate of the universe in such a discussion is that it does not contain enough matter to force recollapse and so it will go on forever expanding. Eventually, the stars all die and it reaches what is called "heat death"

---

18. L. Dyson, M. Kleban, and L. Susskind, "Disturbing Implications of a Cosmological Constant," <http://arxiv.org/PS_cache/hep-th/pdf/0208/0208013.pdf>, August 15, 2002. The authors admit that neither string theory nor quantum gravity can explain the initial low entropy state, so they suggest some "unknown agent" must have done it.

(what we might call the "big chill"). In this equilibrium condition there will be four different kinds of objects, according to our current laws of physics. There will be dispersed gas molecules, dust particles and angular-shaped rock debris that did not end up as part of any larger structures. There will be spherical bodies of matter that were drawn together by gravity and molded into this distinctive shape. There will be black holes — bodies of matter that were so large that gravity dominated all else.

There will be no electrical activity. All electrons will have settled down to rest in balance with the protons. With no electrical activity there will be no magnetic fields. The nuclear forces will continue to bind up their charges at the subatomic scale without disturbing the macroscopic world. All will be silent.

If we push further forward into the absolutely remotest future some theorists have suggested that even the protons will decay, the black holes will evaporate and all that will remain is low energy photons and some ghostly particles such as neutrinos.

A variation of the big chill scenario, called the "big rip," takes into account an unknown kind of antigravity force that might currently be accelerating the universe's expansion. If this "phantom energy" actually exists, then it could increase in magnitude over time until it rips everything apart.

Now these end-time scenarios are rather gloomy, but they do tell us something very important. They tell us what gravity is capable of, and, if you remember, gravity is the only force that cosmologists can call on to explain the large-scale structure of the universe.

The Geometry of Space

Cosmologists describe the geometry of space — on the largest scale — in terms of the density of matter within it. A dense (or "closed") universe would produce the big crunch scenario that defines a geometry positively curved in on itself like a sphere. Parallel lines in a positively curved space would eventually meet one another, like the lines of longitude on a globe of the earth that meet at the poles.

On the other hand, a sparse (or "open") universe would produce the big chill scenario that defines a geometry with negative curvature. This is a difficult concept to imagine, but a slice through the 3-D space can be represented by a 2-D "saddle"-shaped surface which diverges to infinity at the edges. Parallel lines in negatively curved space diverge indefinitely from one another.

Balanced precariously in between the big crunch and the big chill is a possible "flat" universe where the curvature is zero. In "flat" space, parallel lines always remain the same distance apart.

The latest evidence points toward a flat universe[19] and this poses a considerable challenge for the big-bang scenario. The big-bang expansion is generally represented to have been a rather random affair. That is, the force behind the expansion would be expected to be either above or below the critical value for flatness — we should be surprised if it exactly matched that particular critical value.

To illustrate the problem, consider this story from Albert Facey's autobiography *A Fortunate Life*.[20] As an Australian soldier at Gallipoli in 1915 he was at one time assigned to take eight Turkish prisoners down to Headquarters for questioning. They had to walk in single file through a network of trenches so there was one Australian soldier in the lead, followed by one prisoner, followed by another soldier and another prisoner and so on. During the journey a shrapnel shell landed just next to them. Now if they had all been killed that would not have been unusual, or if just the few people nearest the shell had been killed that likewise would not have been unusual, but when this shell hit it took out the first, second, third and fourth prisoner and left all the Australian soldiers untouched. Facey called it a "miracle" because explosions are not usually so precise — they are usually destructive in a very general sense, which is why they make good weapons of war!

In a similar manner, if the big bang had been so ferocious that it blew everything apart forever (the big chill scenario) we would not be surprised. Or, if it had not been ferocious enough to blow everything apart and the universe collapsed in on itself again (the big crunch scenario) we would likewise not be surprised. If the "explosion" was so precise as to leave the universe in perfect balance at the time when humans happen to have developed the technology to observe and measure it, then an evolutionist would have to be suspicious. To an evolutionist, a flat universe looks uncomfortably like someone *designed its origin* and/or *controlled its history*.[21]

---

19. P. De Bernadis, et al., "A Flat Universe from High-resolution Maps of the Cosmic Microwave Background Radiation," *Nature* 404:955–959 (2000).
20. Albert B. Facey, *A Fortunate Life* (Melbourne, Victoria, Australia: Penguin Books, 1981), p. 272–273.
21. This argument is valid only within the materialistic framework. We are not suggesting that evidence like this points to God having used the big bang as His method of creation.

In 1981, when Alan Guth published his inflationary version of big-bang theory, he explained it this way. A typical closed universe would reach its maximum size and collapse again in just a fraction of a second. On the other hand, an open universe would rapidly disperse and nothing of interest would develop within it. To get a universe that looks like the one we see, and for it to endure as long as it has (on their time scale) the initial rate of cosmic expansion would have to be fine tuned to within one part in ten million trillion trillion trillion trillion of the critical value.[22]

THE COSMOLOGICAL CONSTANT

You may remember that Albert Einstein first introduced the cosmological constant by fudging his mathematics to allow the universe to remain static when his equations were telling him that it had to be either collapsing or expanding. Subsequently, when Hubble discovered that the universe was expanding, Einstein said "away with the cosmological constant," but it has never gone away. The situation was rather more complicated than Einstein expected. The value of the constant has become dramatically smaller — and it would probably be fair to say that most cosmologists would like it to disappear altogether — but its very minuteness has now become a problem bigger than any other in modern cosmology.

So what does this modern version of the cosmological constant mean? Well the "shape" of space that we talked about in the previous section is ultimately determined by the density of the matter and energy in the universe. A dense universe will have a gravitational field strong enough to produce the big crunch scenario and space will thus be positively curved. The gravitational field in a sparse universe will be too weak to cause collapse — it will head towards the big chill scenario and space will be negatively curved. Now when astronomers add up all the visible matter and energy in the universe it comes to very much less than the critical value. We know that there must be some "dark matter" out there — not every object in the universe emits light, like the stars do. There may also be some "dark energy." According to Einstein, energy has an equivalent mass and thus a gravitational influence on its surroundings. The modern cosmological constant is related to this "dark energy" — the energy density of the vacuum, that is, the more the vacuum energy, the bigger the cosmological constant should be.

---

22. Alan H. Guth, "Inflationary Universe: A Possible Solution to the Horizon and Flatness Problems," *Physical Review D* 23(2):347–356 (1981).

We mentioned earlier that because of Heisenberg's uncertainty principle we cannot say that the vacuum of space is empty — it may contain "virtual particles" that pop in and out of existence without us noticing. When you integrate the contribution from these tiny "ghosts" over the whole universe you come up with a very huge amount of "nothing" (or what appears to us to be nothing). Indeed, the latest measurements suggest that the vacuum energy may contribute between 60 and 70 percent of the whole (depending how we define the "whole" and what turns out to be in it).

Now Einstein's original reason for incorporating the cosmological constant was to stop the universe from collapsing under the force of gravity. It was designed to give an outward "push" against the inward "pull" of gravity. Most of that job has now been taken over by Hubble's discovery that the universe is expanding. The new cosmological constant also does the same kind of thing, however now its allowable value must be very, very small. A large value would cause large redshifts and spatial distortion in nearby objects. Since astronomical observations indicate that space looks "normal" out to very large distances, then we are forced to conclude that the value of the cosmological constant must be very small indeed.

So what's the problem? The problem is that the theoretical estimates suggest that the value should be quite large, while the observational evidence indicates that the value is very small. One commentator has described it this way: "Few theoretical estimates in the history of physics made on the basis of what seemed reasonable assumptions have ever been so inaccurate."[23]

The scale of this problem is so great that no other problem in cosmology comes anywhere near it. It is so embarrassing and so challenging that you can read whole books on cosmology without encountering a single mention of it. Nowhere in Professor Stephen Hawking's popular books does he spell out the nature of this problem. It's as if he does not want to acknowledge that it even exists, but he can't avoid it (if you know what to look for). In one of his latest books,[24] for example, he presents a graph of three different kinds of data that all point to a value for the vacuum energy density of between 60 percent and 70 percent of the critical value. There is no possibility whatsoever, given that the three types of data are independent of one another (supernovae, globular clusters and CMBR), that the value could

23. Larry Abbott, "The Mystery of the Cosmological Constant," *Scientific American*, 258(5):82–88 (May 1988).
24. Stephen Hawking, *The Universe in a Nutshell* (London: Bantam Press, 2001), p. 98.

be zero. Yet nowhere does he acknowledge the implications of this for the value of the cosmological constant. Toward the end of his book he says that the cosmological constant "may or may not exist in nature."[25] By failing to acknowledge the problem and by suggesting that it may not even exist he is grossly misrepresenting the real picture.

Another example is Professor Joseph Silk, head of astrophysics at Oxford University, whose textbook on the big bang is now in its 3rd edition. He makes a few very brief references to the "fine-tuning problem" but omits any explanation of its extraordinary implications. In an introductory section entitled "Issues in Modern Cosmology," he says (at the end), "One final topic deserves brief mention, if only because of the passions that it arouses among cosmologists — the *cosmological constant*."[26] Then he simply states the historical issue about Einstein — he does not mention why it continues to be a problem today!

So here we have the leading cosmologists at the world's oldest and most distinguished universities — Oxford and Cambridge — both choosing to keep this problem in the shadows.

Others are not so inclined, however. Professor Steven Weinberg is probably the most eminent cosmologist in North America. His biography includes a Nobel Prize in Physics, the National Medal of Science, the Heinemann Prize in Mathematical Physics, the Cresson Medal of the Franklin Institute, the Madison Medal of Princeton University, and the Oppenheimer Prize. He holds honorary doctoral degrees from a dozen universities and is an elected member of the National Academy of Science, the Royal Society of London, and the American Academy of Arts and Sciences. His book entitled *The First Three Minutes* was a pioneering bestseller in big-bang cosmology.

In May 1988, Professor Weinberg gave the Morris Loeb Lectures in Physics at Harvard University under the title "The Cosmological Constant Problem."[27] It is a highly mathematical treatise, but in a section called "The Problem" he explains it very clearly in lay terms. The discrepancy between the observed and predicted values for the energy density of the vacuum is greater than 118 orders of magnitude — in scientific notation, 10^{118}, which is a 1 followed by 118 zeros. To understand the significance of this problem

25. Ibid., p.139.
26. Joseph Silk, *The Big Bang*, 3rd ed. (New York: Freeman & Co., 2001), p. 23.
27. Steven Weinberg, "The Cosmological Constant Problem," *Reviews of Modern Physics* 61(1):1–23 (1989).

Professor Weinberg referred his readers to a non-mathematical article in *Scientific American*.[28] This article said:

> The stupendous failure we have experienced in trying to predict the value of the cosmological constant is far more than a mere embarrassment. . . . Clearly [our assumptions are] spectacularly wrong. There must in fact be a miraculous conspiracy occurring among both the known and the unknown parameters governing particle physics . . . the small value of the cosmological constant is telling us that a remarkably precise and totally unexpected relationship exists among all the parameters of the standard model, the bare cosmological constant and unknown physics. . . . the mysterious relation implied by the vanishingly small value of the cosmological constant indicates that [dramatic and revolutionary new] discoveries . . . remain to be made.

That was a decade and a half ago — what has happened since then? Have the "dramatic and revolutionary new discoveries" been made? Not according to astrophysicist Lawrence Krauss, who worked on the problem a decade later at the European nuclear physics research center in Geneva. In his view the problem got worse rather than better. He quoted a discrepancy of "over 120 orders of magnitude" and says that it "would involve the most extreme fine-tuning problem known in physics, and for this reason many particle physicists would prefer any mechanism that would drive the cosmological constant to be exactly zero today."[29] He then discusses various uncertainties in the measurements and concludes:

> It is getting increasingly difficult to find accord with a flat universe without a cosmological constant. The question then becomes: Which fundamental fine-tuning problem is one more willing to worry about, the flatness problem or the cosmological constant problem? The latter involves fine-tuning of over 120 orders of magnitude . . . while the former involves fine-tuning of perhaps only 60 orders of magnitude.

As time goes by the issue becomes even clearer. The universe is looking flatter, and the energy density due to the cosmological constant is now statistically

28. Larry Abbott, "The Mystery of the Cosmological Constant," *Scientific American*, 258(5):82–88 (May 1988).
29. Lawrence Krauss, "The End of the Age Problem, and the Case for a Cosmological Constant Revisited," *The Astrophysical Journal*, 501:461–466 (1998).

well above zero.[30] The "miraculous conspiracy" is looking ever more like "intelligent design."

In our next chapter we will examine the big-bang model in more detail but, as you can see before we start, the universe is not looking very much like the product of a random "explosion."

30. Adam Burrows, "Supernova Explosions in the Universe," *Nature* 403:727–733 (2000).

CHAPTER 4

THE BIG-BANG MODEL

The big-bang model begins in a singularity — all the matter, energy, time, and space of the universe squashed into a single point of infinite temperature and density. Somewhere between 13 and 17 billion years ago, an unknown event occurred that initiated expansion from the singularity. The expanding universe then near instantaneously inflated by an astronomical amount to iron out "wrinkles" and prevent recollapse. The resulting fireball produced an expanding cloud of mostly hydrogen gas. The gas condensed into stars and galaxies (or perhaps galaxies and then stars). Many generations of stars came and went, each exploding to produce the elements heavier than helium, which were recycled into succeeding generations of stars. About five billion years ago our sun formed by gravitational collapse of a gas and dust cloud. The leftover gas and dust "accreted" by some unknown means into larger and larger "planetesimals." As these planetesimals grew larger, the impacts melted them and eventually they grew large enough to form planets. The earth cooled, the surface hardened, water appeared from somewhere, life formed, and man eventually came to write books on cosmology. That is the story — this chapter examines the various stages in detail, coming to some straightforward yet stunning conclusions about the big bang's much-touted ability to explain the universe.

According to Professor Joseph Silk, head of astrophysics at Oxford University, "virtually all known astronomical phenomena can be understood in the context of big-bang cosmology — if not completely, then at least to a greater degree than in any alternative framework that has yet been proposed."[1] So what do they say happened during the big bang? There are numerous popular books on this subject, but we will take Professor Silk's book as our primary reference, because he is a senior and widely respected cosmologist at the world's oldest and most prestigious university — and because his book is now in its third edition, any problems in the text have had some time to be sorted out.

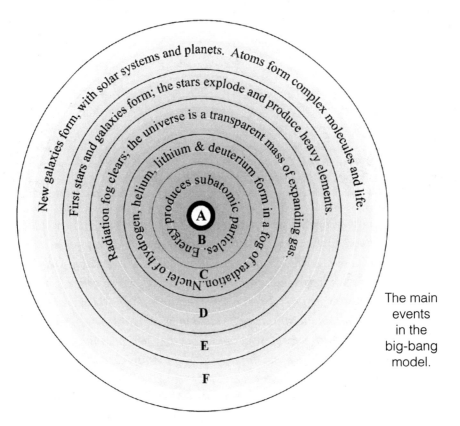

The main events in the big-bang model.

In the above diagram, the letters **A** to **F** refer to the important stages of the big-bang scenario, which are as follows:

Stage A is the unknown region. It contains the singularity where all the matter, energy, space, and time of the universe is contained in an infinitesimal point of infinite temperature and density. The "explosion" from which the

---

1. Joseph Silk, *The Big Bang*, 3rd ed. (New York: Freeman & Co., 2001), p. 102.

big bang got its name is supposed to have happened in this region but no one knows what caused it or how it happened. The time scale is also beyond the reach of any scientific investigation — all descriptions of the big bang begin *after* it allegedly happened. While many cosmologists have tried to avoid the singularity, Professor Silk says "We can say definitely that, subject to certain reasonable assumptions, a past singularity is unavoidable."[2]

Stage B is the period during which physics can begin to describe what is alleged to have happened. Quantum uncertainty shrouds the initial period, but after 10^{-43} seconds (which is called the Planck time) subatomic particles begin to form out of energy. Then at 10^{-36} seconds something very startling happens — the universe suddenly undergoes a near-instantaneous "inflation" by a thousand billion billion billion times. It appears that the big bang was not big enough — another "bang" was needed, which accelerated an unimaginable process into an unimaginably unimaginable process. The purpose of this inflationary episode is to make sure that everything is thoroughly homogenized (because today the CMBR is extraordinarily uniform and it is supposed to be a relic of this period). Once inflation is over and the temperature begins to drop, the more exotic subatomic particles, such as quarks, begin to produce the more familiar ones, such as protons and neutrons.

Stage C is the period during which ordinary atomic matter begins to form. By about one second after the big bang (and its inflationary "bigger bang") stable atomic nuclei develop. These are mainly nuclei of hydrogen (1 proton only), with smaller amounts of helium nuclei (2 protons and 1 or 2 neutrons), and some lithium nuclei (4 protons and 3 neutrons) and deuterium nuclei (1 proton and 1 neutron). At this stage, no complete atoms form because as soon as any electrons link up with these nuclei they are stripped away again in the intense radiation. For the next 100,000 years or so the expansion continues, the temperature drops, and the electrons begin to match up with the protons so that normal atomic structures are then developed.

Stage D is the period when the radiation fog clears — from about 300,000 years onward — and the universe is now a transparent mass of expanding hydrogen gas with lesser amounts of helium and traces of lithium and deuterium. The power of the big bang fades out at this point. Up to now everything has been driven by the transformation of energy into matter caused by the initial "explosion" and inflation of the primordial singularity. The momentum of the expansion will continue, and the faint glow of the intense radiation will remain

---

2. Silk, *The Big Bang*, p. 397

as the cosmic microwave background radiation, but the big bang has now accomplished all that it can do.

Stage E is the period when structure begins to form in the universe — the stars and galaxies. This supposedly commenced about one billion years after the beginning. We can now see why Professor Hawking was unable to explain the origin of the stars and galaxies, because all that the big bang produces is an expanding mass of gas. Something else must have happened during this period to cause the expanding mass of gas to stop expanding and begin collapsing. Of course, once the gas began collapsing, something else again was needed to stop it from disappearing back into a singularity. We will discuss these issues shortly.

Stage F is the period when our solar system, earth, and life were formed — supposedly around five billion years ago. Our earth is not made of gas, it is made primarily of rocks and metal — these were not produced by the big bang and so must have come from elsewhere. Their suggested origin is that the first generations of stars in period E were unstable; they exploded, and produced the metallic elements in their stardust. This stardust was then gathered up into new cycles of star formation and further explosions. The complex molecular structures and information content of living things also had to come from somewhere — they could not have been produced in exploding stars. Their origin will be considered shortly.

So this is the big-bang story, or at least a brief sketch of it. How credible is it? Does it really "agree with all the observational evidence," as Professor Hawking claims? Or has it been made to fit by ignoring the contradictions and inserting ad hoc miracles? Is it internally consistent? We will consider the critical portions of each of the above steps in turn.

Stage A — The Primordial Singularity

We said previously that all thinking has to start somewhere, and thinking about the remote past has to begin with assumptions (beliefs accepted without proof) because no one was there to observe it, and we cannot revisit it in a time machine. The minimum number of assumptions that we must allow is one. So the primordial singularity can be counted as the fundamental assumption of big-bang theory.[3]

---

3. The *existence* of the primordial singularity is not actually the most fundamental assumption in big-bang theory. It is the backward *extrapolation* of the universe's expansion to a singular state that constitutes the fundamental assumption. From this extrapolation, it follows logically from current gravitational theory that there must have been a "beginning" in a singularity.

We pointed out in an earlier section that this primordial singularity is unavoidable. We know from theory that singularities are thermodynamic dead ends. Although known physics permits a universal expansion, any expansion rate — including zero — is allowed. Yet, big-bang supporters must assume that the expansion rate is non-zero. Furthermore, the energy of expansion must match the gravitational energy almost perfectly in order to get a universe like ours. So the first extra ad hoc assumption that is required to sit on top of the fundamental assumption in big-bang theory is that the expansion rate for the primordial singularity is "just right" to produce the universe.

Professor Silk says, "We can visualize the early stages of the big bang as a gigantic explosion,"[4] but not everyone shares this view. Some cosmologists prefer a more orderly explanation. Cosmic expansion at present is (presumed to be) a smooth unfolding of the fabric of spacetime in which matter/energy is "taken along for the ride," so if this is extrapolated backward, then we should get a smooth beginning also. One advantage of the "explosion" view is that it was a one-off event that cannot be observed in the current cosmic expansion so it is beyond the reach of experimental verification.

Recent observations of very distant supernovae and of galaxy cluster X-ray emissions suggest that the cosmic expansion may be speeding up. If this is confirmed, and is indeed caused by some kind of new force, then perhaps this "dark energy," as it is called, may have had a role in the universe escaping the primordial singularity. Prior to this, the expectation of the cosmic expansion was that it should be slowing down due to the braking effect of gravity, so the discovery of this acceleration was a surprise. An accelerating force at work now on the cosmic expansion could perhaps explain the "smooth unfolding" of the universe from its origin. Until we discover more about it, however, the big-bang universe would meanwhile seem to require a one-off "explosion" to get it going.

The primordial singularity worries some cosmologists — they want to stay as far as possible within the realm of physics, but the singularity appears to go "beyond physics." One possible solution can be derived from quantum mechanics. Quantum events usually only occur at the subatomic level. Because

---

4. Silk, *The Big Bang*, p. 96. Quibbles over the use of the word "explosion" can be resolved by recalling the supposed rates of cosmic expansion. The early universe is supposed to have expanded by at least a trillion times in just one second, a rate that is more than a billion times faster than an atomic bomb. And while this Hubble expansion was accomplishing only a tenfold expansion, the supposed inflation expanded it by a further 30 orders of magnitude!

so many of them happen in so many different ways, the effects are generally evened out and we don't usually notice them at larger scales. For example, individual photons of light may behave in a random fashion, but when we turn on the switch in our living room, the light goes on quite predictably (as long as there is a good bulb and no power blackout). The light floods every corner of the room — the individual photons may jump about erratically, but the overall effect is smooth. One of the mysterious implications of quantum theory is that the vacuum is not merely empty space — it is full of "virtual particles" jumping in and out of existence in rapid succession, only appearing for a very brief period of time, in accordance with the "uncertainty principle." It might, for example, contain extremely large amounts of energy in the form of these virtual particles that jump in and out of existence in a perfectly balanced way, giving the impression of nothingness. A clever experiment using two metal plates held very close together is thought to confirm this; it is called the "Casimir effect." So is it possible that the universe just popped into existence out of the vacuum through nothing more than a quantum fluctuation? Some people think so, although they seem to conveniently forget that the laws of quantum physics would have had to already be in existence, so one could not say that the universe created itself "out of nothing." Others have pointed out, however, that the lifetime of quantum events is inversely proportional to the mass of the object and this precludes any such cosmological quantum event. If a universe did pop into existence by quantum fluctuation, nobody would notice — the lifetime of a quantum event the size of our universe would be less than 10^{-103} seconds.[5] Moreover, virtual particles today appear within the vacuum of space. In the primordial singularity there was no space and so no vacuum.

All such speculations about primordial "smooth unfolding" and "quantum jumps" are ultimately unverifiable, however, and the only certainty here is that the big-bang model does indeed begin in a singularity (see "Avoiding the Primordial Singularity" in chapter 3). As Professor Hawking has said, "At the [primordial] singularity, general relativity and all other physical laws would break down: one couldn't predict what will come out of the singularity. . . . This means that one might as well cut the big bang, and any events before it, out of the theory, because they can have no effect on what we observe."[6] Once you accept a singularity, you must let go of your tools (the laws of physics) for

5. Hugh Ross, *The Creator and the Cosmos* (Colorado Springs, CO: NavPress, 2001), p. 170.
6. Stephen Hawking, *A Brief History of Time* (London: Bantam Press, 1988), p. 122.

predicting how a universe might come out of it because those tools no longer work. If the tools don't work, and the "explosion" is hypothetical, then the beginning scenario in big-bang theory is indistinguishable from a miracle.

To help grasp the significance of this crucial point, consider the Friedmann equation, on which all big-bang models are based. A non-mathematical version of the equation can be expressed in words as follows:

$$\begin{array}{ccccc} \text{energy of} & & \text{gravitational} & & \\ \text{expansion} & + & \text{potential energy} & = & \text{a constant} \\ \text{of shell} & & \text{of shell} & & \end{array}$$

Where the "shell" refers to the outer layer of any region of space bounded by a sphere that is expanding along with the universe. What this equation says is that as the shell expands, the energy of expansion increases and the gravitational potential decreases, but the sum remains constant (i.e., total energy is conserved). We can see from this that expansion is *simply assumed*, and not explained, in big-bang theory. The Friedmann equation may describe something of the history of the expansion, but it does not even address the question of its origin. It assumes expansion without explaining how it got started in the beginning.

STAGE B — INFLATION

Inflation is a second miracle, a second necessarily ad hoc faith assumption. The need for inflation is three-fold. First, the early big-bang scenario was in danger of recollapse into a singularity. Because the early stages of the big bang were extremely dense, any deviations from a perfectly smooth expansion would have set up density fluctuations that would likely have caused gravitationally driven recollapse. The postulated inflation scenario conveniently accelerates everything by a thousand billion billion billion times, and in the process irons out all the wrinkles and puts it all beyond fear of recollapse.

Big-bang theorists do not usually describe cosmic inflation as an "explosion" but it is worth taking a moment to compare it with what we usually call an explosion. When the atomic bomb exploded over Hiroshima in World War II, it produced a maximum blast velocity on the ground of 280 meters per second.[7] In one second, therefore, the diameter of the original device (let's suppose it was about 1 meter wide) would have expanded by 560 times (280 meters in either direction) or approximately three orders of magnitude. In

---

7. A-Bomb WWW Museum, Introduction: About the A-Bomb, Figure 2, http://www. csi.ad.jp/ABOMB/data.html version 5.7, July 10, 2000.

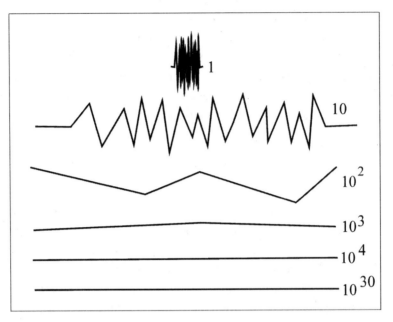

The impact of inflation. Fluctuations at the top of the diagram were extended by the factors indicated. After as little as 10,000-fold inflation the pattern disappears so there can be nothing left after stretching for 30 orders of magnitude.

contrast, cosmic inflation allegedly expanded the universe by about fifty orders of magnitude or 100,000,000,000,000,000,000,000,000,000,000,000,000, 000,000,000,000 times (even though it was still at a minute scale — it started out smaller than the quantum limit of 10^{-35} meters) in a period of less than 10^{-33} of a second.[8] It certainly qualifies as an "explosion."

The second reason for proposing inflation was that magnetic monopoles were supposed to be produced in the early big bang, but have not been found. During the early big bang, when enormous energies were supposedly available, the magnetic force was not yet combined with the electric force, and so just as we now have separate negatively and positively charged particles (electrons and protons, respectively) at that time there would have been separate "north" and "south" magnetic monopoles, but no one has ever found a magnetic monopole. If we take a bar magnet and cut it in half, we don't get a separate north and south pole, we get two magnets each with a north and south pole. The rapid

8. Alan Guth, "Was Cosmic Inflation the 'Bang' of the Big Bang?" *The Beamline* 27:14 (1997), <http://nedwww.ipac.caltech.edu/level5/Guth/Guth_contents.html>.

expansion of inflation is meant to "solve" this problem by "dilution" — i.e., everything is pushed so far apart that, though they may exist, they are now too rare for us to encounter them.

If monopoles are so rare, why is not every other kind of matter equally rare? Inflation has to fudge here and suppose that the more familiar elementary particles were produced *after* the monopoles were dispersed.

The third problem inflation was meant to solve was that the cosmic microwave background radiation (CMBR, which is supposed to be the primary evidence for the big bang) was found to be extraordinarily uniform everywhere one looked. To achieve such uniformity, there must have been some process in the early universe that homogenized the radiation. Inflation comes to the rescue by claiming that the mixing took place when the universe was extremely small (see box "The Horizon Problem," on page 125).

Did inflation do *too* good a job? You see, an amazing thing about the inflationary scenario is its extraordinary precision. One would think that the violence of an explosion upon an explosion would not be able to produce a very precise result. In real life, explosions tend to blow things apart in a very *destructive* manner — that is why we use them in wartime! The universe that emerged from inflation was finely tuned,[9] as we mentioned in the previous chapter, to the extent of perhaps one part in 10^{60} (that's 1 with 60 zeroes following it) and maybe even to one part in 10^{120}. What does this "fine tuning" mean? Here is one of many possible examples. The fundamental forces of physics stabilized at their current values after the end of the inflation era. Now we can see the consequences of this in, among many other things, the remarkable and unique structure of water. The water molecule is made up of two hydrogen atoms and one oxygen atom. The precise arrangement of these atoms depends upon the relative strengths of the strong and weak nuclear forces and the electromagnetic force, plus the quantum rules that govern their interactions. One result is that liquid water consists of varying proportions of four different phases — ice relics, quasi-crystals, fluid, and vacuum.[10] The proportions of these phases depend upon the temperature and pressure, and the behavior of water as a solvent varies correspondingly. Now it turns out that water is in its most versatile configuration at the atmospheric pressure that exists on earth at

---

9. Lawrence M. Krauss, "The End of the Age Problem and the Case for a Cosmological Constant Revisited," *Astrophysical Journal* 501:461 (1998).

10. Karl Trincher, "The Mathematic-Thermodynamic Analysis of the Anomalies of Water and the Temperature Range of Life," *Water Research* 15:433–448 (1981).

sea level, and a temperature of approximately 37°C. Is it a coincidence that the internal temperature of a healthy human being is 37°C and our most agreeable air pressure is at sea level on earth? No, it's "fine tuning."

"Fine tuning" means that the forces that hold the universe together are so delicately balanced that not only do they keep the vast masses and energies of stars and galaxies in harmony, but they also configure the fundamental ingredient of life (water) into its most versatile form to exactly meet the needs of man. By comparison with this impressive precision in the universe, consider now the most precise machine ever built by man — a gravity wave detector that is designed to measure relative motions to an accuracy of 1 part in 10^{23}.[11] No one would ever suggest that such a carefully crafted product of modern scientific and engineering skill was produced by an explosion. Yet big bangers would have us believe that an *explosion upon an explosion* skilfully crafted the whole universe to a standard that is at least 10 trillion trillion trillion (or 10^{37}) times more precise than intelligent human design can achieve!

However, let us not get lost in hyperbole. *Any* explanation of the universe is bound to be extraordinary because it is an extraordinary universe, so we should not get too carried away with how extraordinary the inflation explanation is. We need only note the fact that it *is* an ad hoc assumption.

STAGE C — FROM ENERGY TO MATTER

Once inflation has done its work, the standard model of particle physics takes over. This is the elaborate theory that has emerged from particle accelerators smashing atoms in the laboratory at ever higher and higher energies. The high-energy environment of the early big-bang universe is thought to have been like the high-energy environment inside the particle accelerators, and so the standard model derived from smashing atoms has been applied to the origin of the whole universe. We see no reason to disagree with this approach — a high-energy environment in a laboratory probably *is* theoretically similar to the high-energy environment in the putative early big-bang universe. The energies achieved in the laboratory are still nowhere near those achieved in the early stages of the alleged big bang, but the principle of comparison should be valid.

Einstein's idea that energy and matter are equivalent and interchangeable (remember $E=mc^2$?) is now well established experimentally, and it lies at the heart of what happens in this period. Energy produces matter and the various

---

The Horizon Problem

The problem posed by the homogeneity of the CMBR is sometimes formulated as the "horizon problem." In order for the radiation coming to us from the east, say, to be uniformly the same temperature as that coming to us from the west (and likewise for a north/south comparison) some mixing must have taken place at earlier times to homogenize it all. The radiation coming to us from the east has taken about 15 billion years to get here (or whatever age is assigned to it) and the radiation coming from the west has likewise taken about 15 billion years to get here, therefore the mixing must have taken place more than 30 billion years ago. Of course, the universe is only about 15 billion years old. Thus, the horizon problem.

Inflation theory purports to solve this problem by saying that the mixing took place when the universe was very small and light could have traveled to all parts of it in the time available, but inflation does not solve the problem because the inflation rate allegedly was much faster than the currently measured speed of light, so the early universe did not stay small long enough for light to travel all around it. Only if the speed of light is accelerated to a greater extent than the inflationary expansion rate can it be overcome. This would cause massive distortions to other aspects of physical reality and simply makes the inflation scenario even less believable than it is already. There are other problems also with inflation — two fundamental ones are (a) how to get it started, and (b) how to stop it (see Robert Newton, "Light-travel Time: A Problem for the 'Big Bang,' " *Creation* 25(4):48–49 (2003).

Occam's razor would favor a simpler explanation. One possible simpler explanation is smoothing out of the average temperature of space by thermalization of starlight, as suggested by Eddington in 1926, and as currently favored by Tom Van Flandern, *Dark Matter, Missing Planets and New Comets: Paradoxes Resolved, Origins Illuminated* (Berkeley, CA: North Atlantic Books, 1993), p. 400, 460, 465.

processes depend upon the temperature. The temperature systematically declines as the universe expands and so we end up with ordinary matter like that which we see around us today (well, it only produces hydrogen and a bit of helium, lithium, and deuterium, but it *is* ordinary matter). All sorts of strange things happen along the way and books on cosmology usually go into great detail about them. We will not go into them here except for one principle — that of *quantum pair production.*

This refers to one of the things we noted earlier, namely that when particles of matter are created from energy in the laboratory, they always appear in matter/antimatter pairs. If we get an electron, we also get an anti-electron (called a positron). If we get a proton, we also get an antiproton. If we get a neutrino, we also get an antineutrino, and so on. Just as energy can produce matter by this quantum pair production method, so when the matter and antimatter particles come together again they annihilate one another and revert back to energy.

This has profound and unwelcome implications for big-bang theory, because our universe is made of ordinary matter, not equal amounts of matter and antimatter. The only known way that matter can form from energy is via quantum pair production, and quantum pair production yields equal amounts of matter and antimatter. Since our universe consists only of matter (as far as we can tell — though there are probably small amounts of matter/antimatter pairs associated with localized high-energy events), it is a reasonable conclusion that our universe could not have been produced by quantum pair production.

This is one of those situations where the evidence refutes the paradigm but supporters of the paradigm see it only as an unsolved problem.

Possible solutions to this problem include the suggestion that perhaps the antimatter segregated from the matter and formed separate antimatter galaxies. We have no idea how such segregation might have been achieved, and the concept does not work anyway, for another reason. Some galaxies interact — by colliding, merging, or by the more massive galaxy drawing off matter from the less massive one — and the enormous energy produced by annihilation would be very obvious to astronomers. It is not, so we have no evidence that separate antimatter galaxies exist.

The most popular way of deleting the antimatter is to say that there was a huge bout of annihilation in the early stages of the big bang and the universe we see is simply the residue that was left over. It just happened by chance that a "small" (i.e., universe-sized) imbalance in favor of matter occurred. This is the kind of "cheating with chance" that we mentioned earlier — assigning a positive probability to things that physics does not allow. Indeed, the fact that big-bang enthusiasts can invoke a massive bout of annihilation illustrates how difficult it would have been to separate the matter from the antimatter in the "separate-galaxies" scenario.

On Occam's parsimony scoreboard we must add one more ad hoc assumption to the big bang.

STAGE D — DECOUPLING AND THE CMBR

The cosmic microwave background radiation (CMBR) is widely touted as the definitive proof of the big-bang model, but this is not necessarily so. In 1926, Sir Arthur Eddington argued that because everything is constantly bathed in distant starlight, interstellar space would have a black body temperature of about 3 degrees kelvin (3 K).[12] George Gamow predicted that the afterglow of the big bang would be 5 K, which he revised upward to 50 K in 1961.[13] The CMBR was measured in 1964 by Penzias and Wilson to be 2.7 K. So, is Penzias and Wilson's result a confirmation of the Eddington prediction or the Gamow prediction? We suggest it confirms the Eddington prediction, but big bangers have shouted louder, adjusted their model, and taken it as their own.

The failed predictions didn't stop there. NASA designed a special satellite, called COBE (**CO**smic **B**ackground **E**xplorer), to measure the variations in the CMBR. In the construction phase, they had to predict the size of the variations so that they could make the instruments sensitive enough to measure them. They got it wrong. The actual variations turned out to be below the limit of detection of the instruments — a hugely expensive mistake. A statistical analysis was subsequently carried out on the data and variations *were* found. These were loudly proclaimed to be like "looking at God" — but the authors admitted that they could not point to any spot in the sky and say whether it was hotter or colder than any other. These "variations" were really just noise.

So a new and even more expensive satellite (WMAP) was designed, with 30 times greater sensitivity. This time, they found real variations. These were again widely acclaimed to "prove the big-bang theory," but what really happened was that the model was changed (again) to fit the new data. WMAP actually held some unpleasant surprises. The variations indicated the existence of a cosmic north and south pole, and a cosmic equator.[14] Creationists can explain this in terms of the earth being at or near the center of the universe, but the big-bang model has no credible explanation for it. More precisely, it indicates that earth is located somewhere along a rotational axis, other evidence suggests the center.

The CMBR is supposedly the redshifted light from the time before any galaxies appeared, which means it must be coming to us from the most distant

12. Arthur S. Eddington, *The Internal Constitution of the Stars* (New York: Dover Publications, 1926, republished 1959), p. 371.
13. Tom Van Flandern, "The Top 30 Problems with the Big Bang," *Apeiron*, 9(2):72–90 (2002).
14. D. Whitehouse, "Map Reveals Strange Cosmos," BBC NEWS, March 3, 2003, http://news.bbc.co.uk/go/pr/fr/-/1/hi/sci/tech/2814947.stm.

reaches of space (i.e., beyond the galaxies). There are other explanations for it, some of which you will find in appendix A, where we consider some alternatives to big-bang theory. Halton Arp, for example, believes it is simply the temperature of empty space. Van Flandern has argued that absorption of microwaves in the intergalactic medium, and the lack of any gravitational lensing effects in the CMBR, contradicts the big-bang interpretation.[15]

Given the failed predictions of big-bang theory, the extraordinary pattern in the CMBR, and the existence of alternative explanations for it, we therefore do not feel compelled to believe that the CMBR confirms the big-bang theory.

Stage E — Origin of the Galaxies

The end product of the big bang to this point is not the universe that we know, but simply an expanding mass of gas. The *very* big question then that big bangers face is how to get an expanding mass of gas (that has been homogenized by inflation) to stop expanding and start contracting in localized regions so as to enable stars and galaxies to form. The question following that is: how do you prevent the collapsing gas from disappearing into a singularity again?

Professor Stephen Hawking has not made much progress on this question. In his 1988 best-selling book, he put the origin of the stars and galaxies at the bottom of his unsolved problems list.[16] In his 2001 book he suggested very briefly that they might have formed through the influence of dark matter on a brane world parallel to our own,[17] but parallel brane worlds are imaginary objects (at this stage in history) so this does not qualify as an explanation (remember that an explanation is a description of the unknown in terms of the known). Dark matter should also be treated with some skepticism. It is a term widely used by astronomers to explain motions in the cosmos that they cannot explain with the known laws of physics. In all the known cases where the phenomena have been explained, dark matter has been discarded. Indeed, the appeal to such vague and tentative factors as dark matter, dark energy and brane worlds highlights the lack of any satisfactory explanation within the known world. In his 2002 published lectures on *The Theory of Everything,*[18]

15. Tom Van Flandern, *Dark Matter, Missing Planets & New Comets: Paradoxes Resolved, Origins Illuminated* (Berkeley, CA: North Atlantic Books, 1993), p. 100–107.
16. Stephen Hawking, *A Brief History of Time, from the Big Bang to Black Holes* (London: Bantam Press, 1988), p. 122.
17. Stephen Hawking, *The Universe in a Nutshell* (London: Bantam Press, 2001), p. 188.
18. Stephen W. Hawking, *The Theory of Everything: The Origin and Fate of the Universe* (Beverley Hills, CA: New Millenium Press, 2002), p. 104.

galaxy formation is again on Hawking's list of unsolved problems. However, it is still at the bottom — not at the top, where one would think it belonged. If one cannot explain the origin of a single galaxy, one can scarcely claim to have explained the origin of the universe!

Hawking is not alone in his inability to explain galaxies. A comparison of five different theories of galaxy formation in 1990 led to the conclusion that "we would not give very high odds that any of these theories is a useful approximation of how galaxies were actually formed. [What we need is] a crucial idea that leads us to a new and profitable line of thinking. The great example in cosmology is . . . the discovery of the expanding universe. . . . Another inspiring example, from geology, was the discovery of continental drift and plate tectonics."[19] Since 1990, no such "profitable line of thinking" has emerged — so they are still left with the existing (by implication) *unprofitable* models. The problem was once put this way: "There shouldn't be galaxies out there at all, and even if there are galaxies, they shouldn't be grouped together the way they are. . . . [it] is one of the thorniest problems in cosmology. . . . It's hard to convey the depth of the frustration that this simple fact induces among scientists."[20] The scientists at NASA, the world's leading space exploration agency, have admitted that "We have no direct evidence of how galaxies were formed [or] how galaxies evolved, whether they were formed from aggregations of smaller units or from subdivision of large ones."[21]

It is worthwhile to highlight at this stage the enormous significance of this situation. The definition of our necessary and sufficient universe in our earlier chapter on *Science, World Views and Cosmological Models* consisted of our solar system and our galaxy. We could have expanded our list of course, but in fairness to any explanatory exercise, and in the interests of parsimony, we decided to limit it to just the necessary and sufficient components.

How can we say this simply? Perhaps just this. The universe is, by definition, the planets, stars, and galaxies that surround us. Insofar as big-bang theory does not explain the origin of these objects, then we can say that big-bang theory *does not even address the question* of the origin of the universe. It does not even get to first base. Big-bang theory produces, at best (given the benefit

19. P.J.E. Peebles, and Joseph Silk, "A Cosmic Book of Phenomena," *Nature* 346:233–239 (1990).

20. J. Trefil, *The Dark Side of the Universe* (New York: Macmillan, 1988), p. 3, 55, quoted in Werner Gitt, "What about the 'Big Bang?' " *Creation* 20(3):42–44 (1998).

21. Marcus Chown, "Let There Be Light," *New Scientist* 157(2120):30 (February 7, 1998).

of every doubt), an expanding mass of gas. It does not produce even one solar system, let alone a whole galaxy of billions of solar systems.

Why is it so difficult to produce a galaxy from a big-bang mass of expanding gas? Well, first, as we said earlier, you have to stop the expansion and get localized areas of contraction. Second, once you get contraction started you have to balance the results very carefully or the matter just collapses and disappears into one or more black holes. So is there *any* explanation *at all?* Let's look at what the textbook says.

Gravitational Collapse and Galaxy Formation

Professor Joseph Silk was co-author of the survey of galaxy models just referred to, and, as we said earlier, we are using his textbook as our standard reference.[22] He outlines two different approaches to the problem of galaxy formation — the conservative approach and the revolutionary approach. In the conservative approach we begin with an expanding mass of gas that has been homogenized by inflation, but with tiny ripples of uncertainty flowing on from the quantum fluctuations of the quantum era. Over long periods of time these ripples eventually become amplified and lead to density fluctuations large enough to trigger gravitational collapse on galactic scales. The minute fluctuations in the CMBR that have been observed are said to be these tiny seeds of the later galaxies. In the alternative revolutionary approach we begin with a chaotic early universe in which numerous regions collapsed into black holes, but enough matter was left over in the swirling aftermath to produce the galaxies.

We can see from this how uncertain the whole issue is. The problem is so wide open to speculation that you can start wherever you like, as long as you end up with the universe we see today. In the apparent absence of the primordial black holes, and following his preference for an ordered rather than chaotic approach, Professor Silk prefers the conservative model. He then proceeds to explain how the early fluctuations at the quantum level could have become amplified and turned into self-gravitating galaxy-sized clouds.

It is worth quoting a selection of his actual words:

> Imagine that infinitesimal fluctuations in density were present in the early universe. . . . The expansion of the universe must have exerted a stabilizing influence on such irregularities. The expanding universe has the effect of greatly impeding what otherwise might have been

---

22. Silk, *The Big Bang*.

catastrophic forces. . . . The expansion greatly retarded any amplification of these small fluctuations. Nevertheless, the process of growth of fluctuations went on for a very long time, and the initial degree of inhomogeneity need not have been large for huge fluctuations to develop that could eventually re-collapse. In a region with only a slight excess of matter, compared with its surrounding, the local gravitational field will be increased by a small amount. . . . If density fluctuations with amplitudes between 1 percent and 0.01 percent were present before the decoupling era [Stage D in our earlier summary], the natural accretion from this process of gravitational instability would have ensured eventual collapse — perhaps to form galaxies. . . . We have already seen how the universe inflated from the microscopically small to the macroscopically vast, which accounts for its remarkable isotropy and homogeneity. At the same time tiny density fluctuations were present [due to quantum uncertainty]. . . . [The universe] was not only homogenized and isotropized, yet also permeated by density fluctuations that would be the seeds of the future galaxies.

What is his chain of cause and effect here? Fluctuations in the quantum era lead to density fluctuations in the matter era that are amplified by gravitational attraction until galaxy collapse occurs. At the same time he says that cosmic expansion from the big bang and the subsequent inflation had both a damping and homogenizing effect on any fluctuations. His proposed solution to this paradox is that "the process . . . went on for a very long time." So while the expansion may have "greatly retarded" any amplification of the fluctuations, by continuing the process for a "very long time," we get the amplification we require. This sounds like the shopkeeper who found that his business was losing money, and so decided that if he could only continue trading long enough the accumulated losses would eventually add up to a profit.

In short, Professor Silk has produced amplification by a process of damping going on for a very long time.

One is tempted to ask — why such faulty logic from such an eminent cosmologist on such a vital subject? In the absence of the "new and profitable line of thinking" that he said in 1990 was needed (see footnote 19, this chapter), he went ahead and used one of what he labeled (by implication) "unprofitable" lines of thinking to preserve the illusion that the big bang explains the origin of the universe. This neatly illustrates how paradigms are self-perpetuating — evidence against the paradigm is simply glossed over as a minor problem.

Let's follow his argument, however, and see where it leads us. Let's imagine that the expanding cloud of big-bang gases is indeed permeated with galaxy-sized density fluctuations. Let's further imagine that these density fluctuations eventually defy the dampening effect of cosmic expansion and undergo gravitational collapse into galaxy-sized objects. What would those objects look like? Well, unless something *else* intervenes to stop it, gravity will do what gravity does and will pull it all together again. What happens when you pull together a galaxy-sized cloud of gas? Well, the collapse of just one large star is enough to eventually produce a black hole. There are billions of stars in a typical galaxy, so we can be billions of times more certain that our galaxy-sized cloud of gas would also collapse into a super massive black hole.

Professor Silk describes two possibilities for the "something else" that is needed here. One is *fragmentation*, and the other is *mergers*. There are basically two kinds of galaxies: *spiral* galaxies, like the Milky Way and our sister galaxy Andromeda, and *elliptical* galaxies. (There are also many peculiar types that don't fit either description.) He suggests that in spiral galaxies the gas fragmented — he does not say how, it just did. In elliptical galaxies, two or more protogalactic clouds must have merged. Mergers have indeed been observed, but of course these are mergers of pre-existing galaxies and they do not answer the question of where the galaxies came from to begin with.

So, two more ad hoc events need to go up on our parsimony scoreboard. One is galaxy-sized density fluctuations that can produce gravitational collapse in the expanding gas cloud. The other is "something" that causes fragmentation of the collapsing cloud into suitably sized clumps that will produce stable stars rather than black holes.

Galaxy Distribution and the Cosmological Principle

When we look out at the universe we find much the same picture in every direction — galaxies upon galaxies as far as our telescopes can see. Even when the Hubble Space Telescope was focused for ten whole days (a 153-hour exposure) on an "empty" piece of sky, it turned out to be filled with galaxies, just like everywhere else. This picture poses an interesting question. If the universe is finite in size and we are somewhere nearer to one edge than to another, then we should see fewer galaxies when looking "out" than when looking "in" toward the center, just like we do when looking at stars in the Milky Way. Since we see roughly the same things in all directions, does that mean we are at or near the center? Atheistic cosmologists do not like the idea that we might be at or near the center of the universe because that would suggest that we are in a special or privileged position, perhaps put here on purpose by the Creator. So for them it is convenient when constructing cosmological models to simply *assume* that the universe looks roughly the same from any and every position within it.[23] This assumption is called the "cosmological principle" (or "Copernican principle").

Does that mean the universe is infinite? An infinite universe raises other difficulties. If the universe is infinite then it cannot have begun a finite time ago from a "zero" starting size. To most people, the whole idea of the big bang seems to require that the universe be only a finite size because if it started from "zero" and expanded at a finite rate (the Hubble expansion rate) for a finite time (about 15 billion years) then it must still be of finite size. Even the supposed "inflation" episode was of finite dimensions. However, some cosmologists believe that the universe has always been infinite in extent and began in an infinitely compressed state of infinite extent. As space expanded, the matter density decreased. The universe expands, yet is still infinite in size. Being infinite, the universe appears the same everywhere we look; there is no center or edge.

Another solution to the above problem, which includes the above, one which is incorporated into most big-bang thinking today, was to invoke the concept of four-dimensional "hyperspace." Instead of the universe existing in just three spatial dimensions (length, breadth, and width) they say that our 3-D world exists on the surface of a "four-dimensional hypersphere." Now we can't imagine what a 4-D hypersphere looks like but we can get some idea by comparing a 3-D sphere with its 2-D surface.

Imagine that we lived in a 2-D world on the surface of a 3-D sphere (e.g., a ball, a soap bubble, or a balloon). We would not be able to see anything above or below the 2-D surface, and if the sphere were very large we would think that our 2-D surface was flat in the local vicinity (just like the earth looks "flat" in most terrestrial landscapes). Likewise, if our 3-D world were on the surface of a 4-D hypersphere, we could not see anything in the fourth dimension but it would be there nonetheless. If the hypersphere was large, then it would appear to us to be "flat" in our local vicinity.

Now the clever thing about the surface of a sphere is that it looks the same from any point upon it (i.e., it has no center and no edge), but it is not infinite. So, by analogy, our 3-D universe also has no center or edge. Problem solved?

Well, not quite. The fourth dimension still has to exist somewhere, even if we are not generally aware of it. A mathematical fourth dimension can exist

---

23. This principle is a foundational assumption in the equations that are used to derive the big-bang theory from Einstein's general theory of relativity.

in the head of a mathematician, but a four-dimensional universe has to exist outside of our minds. Where is it then? One possibility is that it is the curved geometry of space that would lead to ultimate collapse in the big crunch. This appears to have been ruled out by observation, however, as the most recent results point to a flat geometry. Another possibility is that it is a matter of scale — it is too small or too large for us to see. This likewise lacks observational support. A diagnostic property of 4-dimensional space is that it causes the intensity of light and the force of gravity to decrease as the inverse *cube* of distance, rather than the inverse *square* of distance, as everyone since Sir Isaac Newton has observed. However, the inverse square law appears to work as far out into space as we can see. The deviation suggested by the MOND theory — which we shall meet shortly — is inverse *linear*, the opposite of the effect needed here. The inverse square law has been verified down to distances of a few millimeters for gravity, and down to atomic scales for light. Clearly, we live in a 3-D space, at least in the region of space we can test. At present, therefore, the 4-D hypersphere is a mathematical abstraction, the reality of which has yet to be demonstrated.

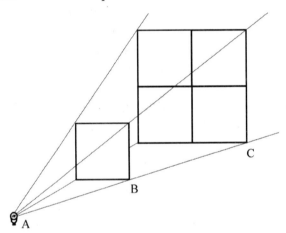

The inverse square law. Frame C is twice as far from light source A as is frame B, so the amount of light striking frame B is spread over an area four times as large in frame C.

Four other lines of evidence are adding strength to the case against the cosmological principle: quantized redshifts, polarization of galactic light and radio waves, anisotropy (which we shall explain shortly) in the CMBR, and the large-scale galaxy map.

Astronomer Geoffrey Burbidge published a paper in 1968 claiming that the redshifts of the then newly discovered quasars showed a regular pattern of clumping around preferred values. The pattern was referred to as being "quantized" — that is, the redshifts were found close to certain discrete values rather than varying continuously. Most people treated it as a curious anomaly, perhaps an artifact of the instrumental or analytical method. However, as time has gone by, and more and more quasars have been studied, the pattern has become clearer and more extensive.[24] Burbidge has suggested that the pattern could be the result of periodic galaxy formation, or perhaps it could correspond to periodic quasar production from active galactic nuclei. This quantization effect was also observed by Tifft in light from galaxies on a much smaller yet very regular scale and with an indisputable level of confidence.

However, creationist physicist Russell Humphreys has pointed out that since we can see these quantized galaxy redshifts in every direction, and at the same discrete intervals, this means that the galaxies must lie on the surfaces of a series of concentric "shells," with each "shell" corresponding to a peak abundance in the redshift distribution. Humphreys further points out that the only way we could see this pattern is if we were at or near the center of it. If we were a long way away from the center then the pattern would be lost. Thus, our galaxy could well be at or near the center of the universe.[25]

The angle between polarization direction of radio waves coming from distant galaxies and the major axis of the source galaxy points to a similar conclusion. In 1997, Borge and Nodland reported that a systematic study of these angles identified what appeared to be cosmic north and south poles. Humphreys interpreted this as evidence that the cosmos is rotating and we are at or near the axis of it.[26]

The anisotropy of the CMBR also points to the same conclusion. The word "anisotropy" means that it is not "isotropic." "Isotropic" means that it looks the same in every direction. Because the CMBR supposedly comes from a period after the big bang when everything was supposed to be isotropic, then it should still be isotropic, but it is not. The Wilkinson Microwave Anisotropy Probe (WMAP) produced detailed maps of the CMBR collected in 2002. While some commentators loudly proclaimed that the results confirmed the big-bang theory,[27] there were other observations that didn't fit. For example,

---

24. G. Burbidge and W.M. Napier, "The Distribution of Redshifts in New Samples of Quasi-stellar Objects," *The Astronomical Journal* 121:21–30 (2001).

25. D. Rusell Humphreys, "Our Galaxy Is the Center of the Universe, 'Quantized' Redshifts Show," *TJ* 16(2):95–104 (2002).

26. D. Russell Humphreys, "New Evidence for a Rotating Cosmos," and "More on the 'Rotating Cosmos,' " in Q & A Section of www.AnswersInGenesis.org, 11/11/02. Some vigorous debate ensued over Borge and Nodland's work, but they remain adamant their analysis was correct and have called for more observational data. See: arXiv:astro-ph/9706126 v2, June 16, 1997; "Nodland and Ralston Reply," *Physical Review Letters* 79(10):1958 (1997).

27. Alan M. MacRobert, "Mapping the Big Bang," http://skyandtelescope.com/news/current/article_877_1.asp, Feb. 11, 2003.

when the data is projected onto a sphere, representing the way it was collected (i.e., from every direction in space) then the components of it called the "octopole and quadrupole components" produce a perfect pattern of cosmic north and south poles and a cosmic equator. Dr. Max Tegmark of the University of Pennsylvania, who processed the image, called the result "bizarre." "It could be telling us something about the shape of space on the largest scales. We did not expect this and we cannot yet explain it," he said.[28] If they could only allow the possibility that we might be at or near the center of the universe,[29] then perhaps they could explain it!

The fourth line of evidence is the recent large-scale map of the galaxies, known as the Sloan Digital Sky Survey (SDSS). It reveals a picture of the universe completely opposed to the cosmological principle.[30] The galaxies appear to be distributed in concentric shells focused on our galaxy, and they are far more dense close in than farther out. A big-bang universe would not produce concentric shells around our location in the sky, and the density of galaxies should increase, not decrease, as you look back in time — because the galaxies were supposedly much closer together in the past.

The Dark Matter Problem

One of the puzzles that face all astronomers today is the "dark matter" or "missing mass" problem. That is, the "missing matter" must be "dark" or non-luminous, which is why we cannot see it against the blackness of space. Or perhaps it could be transparent. So what is it that is missing? If it is not apparent, how do we know it is missing? The problem is not new. There is a long history in astronomy of unexplained celestial motions being attributed to "dark matter" but the problems today are more acute than ever before.

There are four main lines of evidence that lead to the idea that a certain amount of matter is "dark" and/or perhaps "missing" or unaccounted for. First, we can see cold, dark objects, such as dust clouds, against the lighted backgrounds of other galaxies and stars. For all the dark objects that we can see there must be corresponding proportions of other dark objects that we cannot see because they do not happen to be in our line of sight against a lighted background.

28. Max Tegmark, cited in: David Whitehouse, "Map Reveals Strange Cosmos," BBC News http://news.bbc.co.uk/1/hi/sci/tech/2814947.stm, March 3, 2003.

29. Nothing to do with the incorrect notion of the earth being the center of the solar system, of course.

30. John Hartnett, "New Evidence: We Really Are at the Centre of the Universe," *TJ* 18(1):9 (2004).

Furthermore, stellar evolution theory suggests that old stars will die and produce black dwarfs, neutron stars, and black holes, and there are also failed stars called brown dwarfs, that just didn't get to light up; all of these are non-luminous. This latter collection of non-luminous matter is what we might call "true dark matter." It is not invisible in the sense of being transparent, it simply does not emit light. It is therefore not the type of "exotic" dark matter that is mostly sought after, which is *transparent.*

The second kind of evidence comes from spiral galaxies. When we measure the speed of rotation of the gases and stars in the arms in a spiral galaxy, we would expect those speeds to decrease along the length of the arm as one moves away from the center. This is because the bulk of the mass in a spiral galaxy is in the center. The stars nearest the center will be the most strongly influenced by the gravitational force resulting from the central mass, and the outer arms will be least influenced and should not travel as fast as the inner parts. This is not what we observe. The rotation curves for our nearest spiral neighbor, the Andromeda galaxy, show that rotation speeds for the gases and stars in the outer arms are similar to those of the inner parts. Our first thought might be that this suggests that there is a lot of dark matter in the outer part of the galaxy (called the "halo") because a spherical halo of gravitationally interacting matter would maintain constant speed for stars out to the outer edges of the galaxy.

The third line of evidence for "dark matter" is the structure of galaxy clusters and superclusters. Galaxies are supposed to have formed early in cosmic history and are therefore supposedly very ancient. Given the general expansion of the whole cosmos during that time, we would reasonably expect these oldest objects to have been widely dispersed throughout intergalactic space, but surprisingly, most galaxies appear to belong to identifiable clusters and superclusters. The members of the clusters typically move in relation to one another, so why have they remained together for "billions of years"? One answer is that they must have enough gravitational attraction among them to keep them bound together, but when the luminous matter is added up, there is not enough mass to keep the clusters together over such long periods of time.

The fourth line of reasoning is that of the cosmic mass density. You may recall that we said in an earlier section that the "shape" of space is determined by the density of matter within it. For a number of reasons, cosmologists would like the mass density to be in the region of the "critical density" that just avoids the universe collapsing back into a "big crunch." The latest data from very distant supernovae indicate that the mass density is just that and, furthermore, the cosmic expansion appears to be accelerating. For this to be true in the standard big-bang model, the matter density of the universe (both normal and dark components combined) needs to be about seven times what it is measured to be when we only look at luminous matter. So the visible mass in the universe comes nowhere near the expected density.

All four lines of evidence appear independent, therefore they make quite a strong case for the existence of "dark matter," at least some of which might reasonably be described as "missing." How much is missing? Estimates vary, but a common figure is 90 percent. This means that for every star that is seen there are another nine solar masses of "something" somewhere.

The leading candidates are MACHOs and WIMPs. We have met some of the MACHOs already. The name is an acronym for Massive Compact Halo Objects. They are suggested to be objects such as brown and black dwarfs, neutron stars, and black holes (we will learn more about these in the next section). WIMPs stands for Weakly Interacting Massive Particles. These are hypothetical exotic subatomic particles, since nobody has yet discovered them. Since possible MACHO candidates do exist, while WIMPs have yet to make their appearance, the MACHO theory is ahead on points. However, studies of the disk of the Milky Way galaxy show that no dark matter can be found there.[31] So the MACHOs have to take refuge in the galaxy *halo* — a region surrounding the outside of the galaxy — where we can't see them.

Another, quite alarming, possibility has emerged in recent years. Perhaps Newton's inverse square law of gravity is wrong. We know that Newton's law breaks down at velocities approaching the speed of light, and in strong gravity fields, and it gives way to Einstein's theory of relativity, so perhaps it breaks down under other circumstances as well. Perhaps at galactic distances the inverse square law turns into a simple inverse law. Surprisingly, this idea fits the data remarkably well. However, the proposed model is not based on distance *per se* as the key factor, but acceleration. The new theory is called MOND (MOdified Newtonian Dynamics). It proposes that the acceleration due to gravity in the inner reaches of the galaxy is above a threshold value and gravity behaves normally and falls off with distance according to the inverse *square* law. In the outer reaches of the galaxy the acceleration due to gravity is said to drop below the threshold and thus the effect of gravity falls away as an inverse *linear* function of distance. As a

---

31. Michael Oard and Jonathan Sarfati, "No Dark Matter Found in the Milky Way Galaxy" *TJ* 13(1):3–3 (1999).

result, the force of gravity remains unexpectedly strong in the outer arms of the galaxy and thus holds it all together. No one knows why it works (and it appears to work for spiral, elliptical, dwarf, and large galaxies, as well as galaxy clusters and superclusters, and for molecular clouds and globular star clusters) — there is, as yet, no theoretical explanation for either the threshold or the change in gravitational behavior. Indeed there are powerful theoretical reasons for rejecting it.

The inverse square law is fundamental to physics and is an inherent property of our 3-dimensional world. Light intensity propagates according to the inverse square law, and so does the force of gravity, and for very good reasons, which we described in the previous chapter. If gravity fails to obey the inverse square law at galactic distances, then perhaps light does also. This would have an enormous impact on cosmology.

The outcome of the cosmic adventure that will uncover this "dark matter" need not concern us too much in this book, with the exception of one observation. The size of the "dark matter" component is huge. Estimates from galaxy dynamics are usually based on the "mass/luminosity (ML) ratio." Luminosity can be measured directly, but mass has to be inferred from the galaxy motions. If we take the ML ratio for the sun as 1, then the visible regions of the Milky Way have an ML ratio of about 5. That is, only about one-fifth (20 percent) of the matter in our galaxy is luminous. Individual elliptical galaxies have a ratio of about 8, but some rich clusters of galaxies have ML ratios in the region of 200 to 400. This means that there can be up to 400 times as much "dark matter" as visible matter. This factor of 400 translates to 99.8 percent.

This has a profound implication for *any* theory of cosmology. Even if we should come up with a theory that perfectly explained what we do see, we have still not explained the universe — because as much as 99.8 percent of it may still be beyond our perception![32] Humility might one day be added to the list of qualifications for being a cosmologist.

---

32. If the MOND theory does turn out to be correct, then at least some of this problem may go away. When MOND is applied to the rotation speeds of stars in spiral and dwarf galaxies, the ML ratios become more like 0.9 to 2. These are much more realistic figures and indicate that there may be true non-luminous matter in the central galactic bulge or in the spiral arms, but not in some invisible transparent halo. While the MOND hypothesis currently faces strong objections, it would not be the first time in scientific research where an observational result preceded a formal theoretical understanding.

STAGE E — ORIGIN OF STARS

Star formation lies at the heart of cosmology. Stars are the powerhouses for solar systems, and they provide the only source for the heavy elements in the big-bang theory. Without stars there are no galaxies, no planets, and no life. It is also a very exciting field of research to be in because there is a potential for solving the problem of star formation in a way that does not exist in many earthbound sciences. In fields like biology and geology there is an extraordinary complexity, much of which is not understood, that confounds attempts at detailed computer simulation and so simplifying assumptions always have to be used. In star formation, however, the problem can be formulated in terms of the physics of gas particles interacting according to the laws of gravity, electromagnetism, motion, and thermodynamics — all of which are well known and understood. When computers get big enough and fast enough, it is potentially possible to simulate every single event that takes place and thereby reproduce on the computer more or less exactly what takes place in space. At present we still have to make many simplifying assumptions, but computers are getting bigger and faster all the time, and simulations are becoming ever more realistic. It is an exciting time to be an astrophysicist.

Telescopes and space probes are also getting bigger, better, and more far-reaching all the time, and the data they can collect is getting ever more detailed and comprehensive. More information is now available from supposed "star-forming regions" of space than ever before. The problems faced by astrophysicists are still enormous, but there is an excitement growing within the community that will no doubt inspire many generations of researchers yet to come.

The key question from our point of view is this: can stars form by chance and necessity or is intelligent design necessary? No simple answer is available at present. We believe that the weight of the evidence is in favor of intelligent design, but so much is happening so quickly that it is premature to come to firm conclusions.

What Is a Star?

Stars are glowing balls of gas (mostly hydrogen), which are held together by gravity. In the early 20th century, two astronomers, Hertzsprung and Russell, plotted the visible stars on a graph. One axis was luminosity (brightness) and the other was temperature (as determined by the spectrum). They found that the stars fell into three main types. Most stars were on a diagonal that they called "the main sequence," then off to the upper right were exceptionally large but cool stars called "red giants," and off to the lower left were exceptionally small but hot stars called "white dwarfs."

To explain this distribution of star types, astrophysicists have developed a theory of "stellar evolution." The supposed time scales of "stellar evolution" are too long (millions of years) for human observers to verify whether the theory is correct or not, but it does appear to give a reasonable explanation for the observed patterns. According to "stellar evolution" all stars begin via the gravitational collapse of gas clouds. As the gas collapses, its temperature rises. This poses a problem, because as the temperature rises, so will the pressure — and the increased pressure will halt the gravitational collapse. To get over this problem, they propose various mechanisms by which cooling might occur and so the collapse continues. As the temperature continues to rise, the star begins to glow. What happens next depends upon the size of the cloud (or more correctly, the collapsing "core" within the larger cloud).

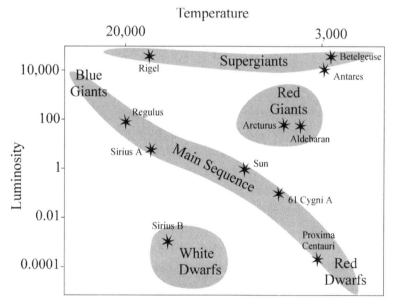

Hertzsprung-Russell star diagram. The shaded areas are where most stars occur; some well-known ones are shown.

If the mass of the gas cloud is less than about one-tenth of a solar mass then it becomes a "brown dwarf." These objects are large enough to produce heat and radiation from the collapsing gas, but are not massive enough to ignite nuclear fusion in the core. After a long period of time, these objects cool down and become cold and dead. They become objects similar to the "gas giant" planet Jupiter.

If the gas cloud is larger, up to about 1.4 solar masses, the collapsing gas becomes so hot that it ignites nuclear fusion in the core — hydrogen is fused to form helium. This allows the star to shine brightly for a very long time (billions of years) as a star on the "main sequence." When it runs out of hydrogen fuel, the core begins to collapse further, and the temperature rises again until the helium begins to fuse into heavier elements. The increased temperature causes the outer layers of gas to swell up and the star turns into a "red giant." When all nuclear fusion ceases, the "red giant" contracts again and becomes a "white dwarf." This extremely dense star remains very bright for a long time and then cools down to become a "black dwarf."

For larger gas clouds up to around 10 solar masses, the "evolution" occurs very much faster because the gravitational field is much stronger and it produces higher temperatures more quickly. It likewise will become a main sequence star, but after only about a million years it will use up its hydrogen and enter the "red giant" phase. When all further nuclear reactions are completed and there is no longer enough heat to hold back the gravity, the star collapses in a gigantic explosion — a supernova. The shock wave from the collapse blows the outer part of the star off into an expanding gas and dust cloud and the remaining core becomes a "neutron star." A neutron star is the densest possible form of ordinary matter. The gravitational field is so strong that it forces the electrons to join up with the protons to produce neutrons. The neutron star is thus almost as dense as an atomic nucleus — a spoonful would weigh about a billion tons. It also has a strong magnetic field and rotates rapidly — like a skater who spins more rapidly with arms and legs drawn in close. Some neutron stars emit beams of radio waves and are called "pulsars" (pulsating stars).

If the mass of the gas cloud is greater than about 10 solar masses, then the resulting star will have a lifetime on the main sequence similar to the previous example. It will likewise enter the "red giant" phase after about a million years, but when the nuclear fuel runs out, a much more catastrophic end occurs. When the core collapses, the gravitational field is now so strong that it even crushes the neutrons that are formed by the collapse of the electrons into the protons. The collapse continues without limit — so far as we know — and the star becomes a "black hole." Yet it is not known how a massive black hole might actually form.[33]

The details of this "stellar evolution" theory will no doubt change as we get to know more about stars, but for the present it represents a reasonable description

33. See A.K. Kembhavi and J.V. Narlikar, *Quasars and Active Galactic Nuclei* (Cambridge, NY: Cambridge University Press, 1999), p. 101, 103; also J.G. Hartnett, "Quantized Quasar Redshifts in a Creational Cosmology," *TJ* 18(2) (2004): p. 105–113.

of what we see in the sky. The Hertzsprung–Russell diagram could well represent stars of differing initial mass, burning nuclear fuel in the main sequence for varying times and then dying off through red giant and/or white dwarf stages.

Star Populations

Creationist attitudes toward the "stellar evolution" theory could probably be summarized somewhat as follows: "Stars have been observed to die on a number of occasions in supernovae explosions, but no one has ever seen a star being born, so we are not necessarily convinced that the star birth scenario is correct. It may perhaps happen in some cases today but we have no reason to believe that it accounted for the first generation of stars." De Young has reported that the white dwarf companion of Sirius was recorded by ancient observers to have changed from what we would call a red giant in about 1,000 years.[34] If this change did occur as suggested, then perhaps the time scale of "stellar evolution" is incorrect. Based solely on present-day observations, however, the major area of dispute between creationists and evolutionists lies in the dynamics of gas clouds. Can a cloud of gas produce a star purely by chance and the laws of physics?

To answer this question we need to distinguish (within the big-bang scenario) between the first generation of stars and present-day stars. The two cases are very different. The first generation of stars only had an expanding cloud of hydrogen and helium gas to form out of, whereas present-day stars — if they are indeed forming today — have their neighborhoods disturbed by whole galaxies of dust, gas, turbulence, ionizing radiation, magnetic fields, and other stars. Astronomers actually distinguish three kinds of stars in this context. "Population I" stars include our sun and are the most common kinds of stars. They are metal-rich, which means they contain a lot of the elements heavier than helium. These elements were supposedly produced in the supernova deaths of previous generations of stars. "Population II" stars are metal-poor and, according to big-bang theory, they must have formed soon after the first generation of stars. "Population III" stars are the first generation stars and contain only hydrogen and helium and a trace of deuterium and lithium — the products of the big bang — and nothing else. No one has ever seen a Population III star. There are a few Population II stars in our galaxy but the majority are Population I.

Gas Cloud Dynamics

So what could cause a star to form out of a cloud of gas? Well, gravity of course — materialists have no other force to call on. Magnetic fields are

---

34. Donald B. DeYoung, "Do Stars Evolve?" *Astronomy and the Bible*, Question No. 55, www.AnswersInGenesis.org/docs/401.asp.

observed in some modern-day gas clouds but they work *against* collapse, so they are of no use in explaining star formation. Turbulence is also observed in modern-day gas clouds, but turbulence also works *against* collapse. So, under what circumstances would a cloud of gas, with the mass of a typical star, undergo the necessary gravitational collapse? As we shall see, gravity is not enough — something else is needed. Without "something else," the outward pressure due to the kinetic energy of the gas molecules in the cloud is so much greater than the inward pressure due to the mutual gravitational attraction of the cloud that the resulting net outward pressure would cause the gas cloud to *disperse* rather than collapse.

To get around the pressure problem, astrophysicists suggest that the gas temperature is very, very low, perhaps in the region of 10 kelvin (that's –263°C), but even that is not enough. Astronomical observations of gas motions in giant molecular clouds — the place where star formation is thought to occur today — indicate that the gas molecules can be moving 10 or 100 times the velocity predicted by the temperature.[35] This "non-thermal" motion is probably caused by turbulence and magnetic fields. In modern galaxies there is a lot of ionizing radiation and this will induce electric currents and magnetic fields within gas clouds. A partially ionized gas cloud would have to exceed about 10,000 solar masses before gravity could begin to cause contraction. The largest stars observed today are far too small to be explained by this mechanism — only about 120 solar masses.

So how do big-bang theorists attempt to solve this problem? The secret ingredient, as in galaxy formation, is "density fluctuations." What is a density fluctuation? It is not turbulence. Turbulent motions stir up the gas and increase its tendency to disperse. To cause star formation, a "density fluctuation" must exert a compressive force upon the gas cloud *as a whole* and squash it into a state whereby gravity has the advantage. The density fluctuation must be just the right size. If it is too small it won't produce a star at all, and if it is too big it will produce a black hole. Where do these density fluctuations come from? The standard answers are supernova explosions, winds and outflows from previously formed stars, and shock waves in the interstellar medium.[36]

---

35. Charles J. Lada, and Frank H. Shu, "The Formation of Sunlike Stars," *Science* 248:564–248 (1990).

36. Derek Ward-Thompson, "Isolated Star Formation: From Cloud Formation to Core Collapse," *Science* 295:76–81 (2002).

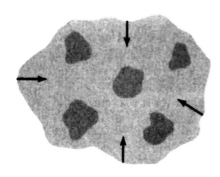

Star formation, according to Professor Silk. A gas cloud collapses (black arrows), and "density fluctuations" (dark areas) cause the cloud to fragment into star-sized objects.

It is instructive to look at Professor Silk's version of these events. The illustration below is taken from his book, *The Big Bang*.[37]

Now, where in this diagram is there evidence of a causal mechanism such as a supernova explosion, a wind, an outflow, or a shock wave? There is none. The causal mechanism is not specified, it is simply assumed. What we are actually looking at is an *implosion*, not an explosion.

Astrophysicists make an important distinction here between the "priming" and the "triggering" of gas cloud collapse. A study of streaming motions along the arms of the spiral galaxy M51 showed that "there is strong evidence that spiral density waves [the force that supposedly created the arms of the spiral galaxy] assemble pre-existing molecular clouds into giant associations and trigger the collapse of suitably primed clouds, leading to the formation of stars."[38] The "strong evidence" was in fact only circumstantial. The authors acknowledged the existence of other evidence "suggesting that density waves do not trigger star formation," and it is entirely possible that the spiral density waves are a consequence, not a cause, of star formation. This study does highlight the distinction between "priming" and "triggering." As the authors explain, "The process that primes clouds so that their collapse can be triggered [by a spiral density wave, for example] has yet to be identified; the global data imply the priming process is not the density wave." What this means is that if a density fluctuation did occur, then it might "trigger" the collapse of an already-primed gas cloud, but it could not "prime" the cloud. That is, "something else" must squash the gas cloud almost to the point of collapse before a density fluctuation could tip it over the edge into actual collapse.

Now if you recall our discussion of the early stages of the big bang, you will remember that cosmic expansion and inflation homogenized all the shock waves and inhomogeneities from the initial explosion, so any subsequent

37. Silk, *The Big Bang*, Figure 10.8, p. 203.
38. S.N. Vogel, S.R. Kulkarni, and N.Z. Scoville, "Star Formation in Giant Molecular Associations Synchronized by a Spiral Density Wave," *Nature* 334:402–405 (1988).

"shock waves in the interstellar medium" must have come from supernovae — the explosion of stars. So even if we solved the "priming" problem, we would be left with a completely circular argument. To form stars, you need density fluctuations, and to produce density fluctuations, you need shock waves — but to produce shock waves, you need stars.

The "supernova solution" to the shock wave theory is also self-defeating for another reason — the nucleosynthesis problem. If you recall, it is alleged that the big bang only produced hydrogen and helium with traces of deuterium (an isotope of hydrogen) and lithium. The rest of the 92 naturally occurring elements have to be synthesized in the interior of stars and in supernova explosions, because the big bang was not energetic enough to do the job. To get enough supernova explosions, they have to postulate "many generations" of early massive stars (of about 100 solar masses each) that die quickly (within about one million years), exploding and producing stardust that gets recycled into new generations of stars, and so on. The problem here is that such massive supernovae do not just produce stardust; they also produce very stable remnants — black holes. In our galaxy, there are about 10^{11} stars and about 3 percent of the galaxy mass is in the form of gas and dust clouds. If the primordial galaxy contained only massive stars of about 100 solar masses each, when they exploded they should have left behind about 10^9 black holes, each containing about 10 solar masses of material — the rest is blown off by the explosion and becomes stardust. If there have been "many generations" of such supernovae that have also left behind equivalent numbers of black holes, then black holes should be about as numerous as stars in our present-day galaxy. This has disastrous consequences for stellar evolution — with so many black holes about, they would get caught up in subsequent cycles of star formation, and gobble up the ingredients so no further stars could form. It also contradicts the observational evidence — we have only about a few dozen candidates for black holes in the Milky Way. There may be supermassive black holes in the cores of some galaxies, but this is no help in solving the problem of star formation, because stars have to form out in the spiral arms to explain what we see. So the "supernova solution" does not work, any way you look at it.

If supernovae really do precipitate gas cloud collapse to form stars, then there should be some observational evidence of it, yet no one has reported such a thing. In a recent survey of supernova data,[39] a variety of cosmological

39. Adam Burrows, "Supernova Explosions in the Universe," *Nature* 403:727–733 (2000).

applications was mentioned, but there was not a single mention of any star formation associated with the shock wave, or with any of the visible remnants of the explosions. About 200 supernova remnants are known from our own galaxy, but not one of them, apparently, has produced any new stars.

What about those Population III stars that formed before there were any other stars to produce shock waves? In a recent paper entitled "The Formation of the First Star in the Universe," the authors appealed to . . . yes, density fluctuations.[40] This illustrates how there is simply no other cause to appeal to. Somehow, the gas has to be squashed to get it to collapse — it won't collapse of its own accord.

"Star Forming" Regions

Modern books on cosmology and astronomy prominently display photographs of "star-forming" regions and confidently proclaim that the stars depicted are in the process of being born. These supposed star-forming regions are gigantic clouds of (usually) glowing dust and gas. Sometimes within the clouds, as revealed by infra-red imagery, are "hot young stars" that are supposedly in the process of formation. It is possible that this may be true, but some cautionary comments are appropriate. First, the fact that the clouds in question are glowing indicates that they are very hot — thousands of degrees. Hot gas clouds are more likely to disperse than collapse. A recent review of the processes of star formation illustrates this point. The author acknowledged that his proposed scenario depended upon molecular clouds remaining intact for long periods of time (i.e., not being dispersed by the energetic activity within them). He wrote as follows: "If molecular clouds are not merely transient structures, then. . . ."[41] Unfortunately, not all authors are as circumspect.

A second reason for caution is that even if the embedded stars are accreting dust and gas from the cloud, it does not prove that we are therefore witnessing star birth. A "cold, old star" embedded in a similar cloud would do exactly the same because the gravitational field of *any* star would cause the infall of surrounding gas and dust. Even the accretion claim is not well established. In 1990, Lada and Shu reported, "We have not yet been able to unambiguously detect the collapse of a molecular cloud core or the infall of circumstellar material onto an

40. Tom Abel, Greg L. Bryan, and Michael L. Norman, "The Formation of the First Star in the Universe," *Science* 295:93–98 (2002).

41. Ralph E. Pudritz, "Clustered Star Formation and the Origin of Stellar Masses," *Science* 295:68–76 (2002).

embryonic star."[42] By 2002, Ward-Thompson was able to say that "spectroscopic evidence of infall has been reported in a number of . . . protostars, although the manner of the collapse cannot be uniquely ascertained from such observations."[43] A great deal more work needs to be done before a convincing case for this kind of "star birth" can be established. Even then, it would not explain the formation of the first stars.

Binaries and Clusters

Stars do not generally exist in isolation. About half the stars in our galaxy are associated with a close companion (and some have more than one) in a binary orbital system. Most stars exist within a distinct cluster. Small "open clusters," such as the beautiful Pleiades group, are not very strongly gravitationally bound, and eventually they will drift apart. Large "globular clusters" can contain a million stars or more, and they are much more tightly bound by their mutual gravitational attraction. According to a recent review, "star clusters form at all epochs of galactic evolution, are associated with galaxies of all Hubble types, and have similar initial mass functions, which suggest a common and robust mechanism of star formation. . . . Star clusters are therefore not exotic novelties in the universe but are the representative products of the process of star formation."[44] So a theory of star formation has to produce not just single stars but large numbers of stars close together. How do they do it?

Surprisingly, the suggested answer is "turbulence." We met turbulence earlier and were told that it increased the likelihood of a gas cloud being *dispersed*. So why is it now being used to cause the gas to collapse? Apparently, there is nothing else to call upon, and one has to use what is available. The proposal is that as a cloud gets closer and closer to the threshold density for collapse, turbulent eddies cause little bumps here and there to cross the threshold and, "Presto!" you have a cluster of stars.[45]

There are at least two weaknesses in this theory. First, it does not explain where the increasing density of the cloud comes from. This is the "priming problem" mentioned earlier and, as we explained on that occasion, we cannot appeal to the magical "density fluctuations" to do the job. Second, if the

---

42. C.J. Lada and F.H. Shu, "The Formation of Sunlike Stars," *Science* 248:564-248 (1990).

43. D. Ward-Thompson, "Isolated Star Formation: From Cloud Formation to Core Collapse, *Science* 295:76-81 (2002).

44. R.E. Pudritz, "Clustered Star Formation and the Origin of Stellar Masses," *Science* 295:68-76 (2002).

45. Ibid.

The globular star cluster Omega Centauri.

turbulence tends to disperse clouds of subcritical density, then it should also tend to disperse a cloud that is near the critical density.

Their globular shape also has intriguing implications. What kind of "density fluctuations" would produce a spherical mass of stars? If the density fluctuations came from an external source, you would expect the stars to form in a ring or arc pattern with its focus on the external source. This is not what we observe — the clusters are spherical with their focus at their *own* center of gravity. The only kind of density fluctuation that could produce a spherical distribution of stars is one that had its origin at the center of the cluster. Could there have been a supernova explosion at the center of every globular cluster? Perhaps, but if so, then we would expect to see similar structure appearing in at least some of the 200 or so supernova remnants that are visible in our galaxy. There are none. Supernova remnants show quite clearly that supernovae blow things *apart*, not together!

Another mystery is the distribution of star sizes (masses) in the cluster. Astronomers have studied large numbers of star clusters and, to their astonishment, they find that the distribution is almost identical in them all.[46] That is, every cluster they look at has approximately the same proportion of small, medium, and large mass stars as all the others. This is most remarkable because star formation is supposed to be the result of random processes in different conditions in different places in the universe. We would therefore expect to find a different mixture of sizes in every cluster. The same mixture of sizes in every cluster points to a common origin for all clusters. Very curious, and perhaps rather alarming for naturalism.

Yet another mystery of the globular cluster is the fragmentation of the parent gas cloud. Why did the cloud break up into star-sized clumps instead of collapsing into a single great blob that would quickly burn and disappear into a black hole? This fragmentation problem is also tied to the size distribution problem. Not only has the cloud fragmented into numerous small pieces — and for no good reason that we know of — but it has produced an identical range of sizes across all clusters. This is beginning to sound rather too precisely engineered! The problem is compounded by the fact that globular clusters supposedly formed at a very early stage from clouds that were relatively unperturbed by nearby galactic activity. Computer simulations under these conditions show that when the cloud is forced to collapse by "density fluctuations" it does not fragment, as they had hoped, it only forms a single massive star.[47]

Summary of Star Formation

So, can chance and necessity explain the origin of stars? A gas cloud of the appropriate size (approximately 0.1 to 100 solar masses) is too small to collapse under its own self-gravity because the pressure is too great. Even at extremely low temperatures, turbulence and magnetic fields maintain a pressure barrier. In all cases, some "other" force is required. The universal solution to this problem is "density fluctuations," but "density fluctuations" are an imaginary solution — no one has ever identified one associated with a star-forming event. Supernovae are supposed to be the primary causes of "density fluctuations," but not one of them has yet been associated with star formation. The commonly cited "star-forming regions" contain hot turbulent gas, which does not provide us with a convincing case for naturalistic star birth. The fragmentation of a parent gas cloud into a dense cluster of star-sized clumps has no satisfactory

46. P. Kroupa, "The Initial Mass Function of Stars: Evidence for Uniformity in Variable Systems," *Science* 295:82–91 (2002).
47. T. Abel, G.L. Bryan, and M.L. Norman, "The Formation of the First Star in the Universe," *Science* 295:93-98 (2002).

explanation. The results appear to be so precisely engineered that it is tempting to conclude that "God did it." However, we will content ourselves by quoting Professor Abraham Loeb of Harvard University's Center for Astrophysics who says, "We don't understand star formation at a fundamental level."[48]

STAGE F — ORIGIN OF PLANETS

The Rocky Planets

Stars are made of gas, primarily, but our planet earth is made of rock, with a central core of molten iron and nickel. How do you get rocks (and metal) from gas? The present explanation is that the heavy elements reached us in the dust from supernova explosions, but how do you produce rock from stardust? Why is it that the earth is hot inside, rather than cold, like stardust? Did it start off hot and cool down, or did it start off cold and heat up?

Many years ago, "hot" theories were in vogue. It was suggested that the planets might have been sucked or blasted off the sun, perhaps by the tidal action of a passing star, or perhaps by an impact between a passing star and a stellar companion of the sun. Neither version of the "hot" theory survived close scrutiny, however. The tidal scenario would have seen any detached material quickly returned to the sun as the visiting star passed, and the impact scenario would have vaporized, rather than fragmented, a companion. Today's favored theory is "cold accretion."

In the "cold accretion" model, the planets and moons form out of the dust and gas left over in the cloud that produced the sun. A number of stars have been observed to be enveloped in dust, and this has been cited in favor of the theory. If such a cloud should begin to rotate, then a "circumstellar disk" will form, and it is supposed that our planets and moons formed within this disk. The disk of rubble that surrounds the planet Saturn is an example of how rotation can form such a disk. Since all the planets in our solar system orbit the sun in a single plane — called the ecliptic — this again is cited as evidence in favor of the theory. But how did they "accrete" from the cloud of dust and gas? Are planets accreting within the disk of Saturn at present? Why are the inner planets made of rock (Mercury, Venus, Earth and Mars) and the outer planets made of gas (Jupiter and Saturn) and ice (Uranus, Neptune and Pluto)?

Two different scenarios are suggested, one for the inner planets and one for the outer planets. Rocky planets are supposed to have formed by the accretion

48. Marcus Chown, "Let There Be Light," *New Scientist* 157(2120):26–30 (February 7, 1998).

of dust granules. These dust granules were supposedly blown into interstellar space from a supernova explosion and are microscopic in size. Somehow these dust granules stuck together to form larger "planetesimals" and these planetesimals continued to grow until self-gravitating bodies were formed. Once gravity began to take over, the speed of the impacts increased to the point where they began to melt the surface of the self-gravitating body. The widespread occurrence of impact craters on solid bodies throughout the solar system is cited as evidence for this theory. When the solar system was cleared of planetesimals, the planets began to settle and cool down. The earth's crust solidified, but the inner core was kept molten by radioactive decay, as it is thought to be today.

The weakness in this scenario is called the "sticking problem." How do you get dust granules to stick together to form solid objects large enough to account for the impact craters that we see, for example, on the face of the moon? Meteorites are often cited as being the material from which the rocky planets were formed, but meteorites are not just aggregations of dust — they are mostly either solid rocks or solid iron. If meteorites were formed from dust granules, they must have undergone either heating and fractionation, in the case of the iron meteorites, or geochemical consolidation, in the case of the stony meteorites. Meteorites actually look more like the fragments of a *broken* planet than the ingredients for *producing* a planet. If you broke the earth into meteorite-sized chunks, you would get iron-rich metallic pieces from the core and stony pieces from the mantle and crust, just like the meteorites we observe.

In an attempt to solve the "sticking problem," a group of German scientists carried out an interesting experiment in the microgravity of the space shuttle.[49] They suspended a dust of powdered glass in a specially designed observation chamber and photographed what happened. The granules did indeed stick together by a force called the Van der Waal's force, and they produced filaments ranging in size up to about 40 granules long. Rather than solving the "sticking problem," this experiment simply illustrated the central issue. Van der Waal's forces are well known in physics and they are very weak. They are produced by the slight imbalances of electric charge that arise in molecular structures. That is why only short filaments were produced in the experiment — the force is not great enough to support longer filaments. Something much stronger is needed to produce planetesimals that can melt

---

49. J. Blum et al., "Growth and Form of Planetary Seedlings: Results from a Microgravity Aggregation Experiment," *Physical Review Letters* 85(12):2426–2429 (2000). Also www.aip.org/physnews/graphics/html/plantesimal.html.

a protoplanet on impact. Filaments held together by Van der Waal's forces would, if they amalgamated with others of like nature, produce "dust bunnies" — balls of fluff. As yet no such objects have been found in the solar system.

There are other objections to the accretion theory as well. The primary evidence for accretion today is the impact craters that litter the solar system. If you look carefully at them you will notice that they are all circular. There are no elliptical craters or elongated furrows such as you might expect to find as a result of varying angles of impact. Indeed, the universal circularity of impact craters caused some early geologists to believe that those on earth were of volcanic origin, and those on the moon were caused by objects falling perpendicularly from the sky.[50] The solution to the problem was uncovered by a young Estonian astronomer, Ernst Opik, in 1916. Meteorites are very hasty objects. They travel at speeds of 50,000 to 150,000 miles per hour. When they hit something, irrespective of the angle at which they hit, their enormous speed causes them to explode with tremendous force — thus producing a round "bomb" crater. Recent photographs of asteroids show that they also have tiny round impact craters. This means that even very small objects, when they collide in space, do so with great violence.[51]

Now when we put this evidence together with the accretion hypothesis, what do we get? Well, we don't get accretion. Planetesimals that collide at around 100,000 miles per hour will not stick together the way that the German glass powder did in the space shuttle. Such objects, when they meet, will either shatter one another or bounce off each other.

It may be argued, not all planetesimals will interact at such high speeds. The objects in the disk of rubble surrounding the planet Saturn, for example, are traveling together and their speed relative to one another is very slight. Are these "planetesimals" in the process of "accreting" today? No, they are not. The pieces of debris are simply bumping into one another, bouncing off one another, or swirling around one another in a kind of "gravity waltz," and gradually being sucked back into the planet.

---

50. James L. Powell, *Mysteries of Terra Firma: The Age and Evolution of the Earth* (New York: The Free Press, 2001), chapter 12.

51. The average speed of asteroids relative to one another is about 18,000 km per hour. This is for objects that are not bound within another object's gravitational sphere of influence. The asteroid Ida was discovered by the *Galileo* space craft to have a moonlet, Dactyl, orbiting it. Co-moving asteroids like this would have much lower relative speeds.

A final problem with this "nebular hypothesis" of the formation of the solar system is momentum. Momentum is the mass of an object multiplied by its velocity. In all physical interactions, momentum has to be conserved. If the solar system began as a swirling cloud of gas and dust with a central collapsing core, the particles that made up the sun would have carried their momentum with them, and because the majority of the mass of the solar system is in the sun, so the majority of momentum would today also be in the sun — that is, the sun should be spinning very rapidly. This is not the case. The sun spins quite slowly, and about 98 percent of the momentum of the solar system is in the planets. Evolutionists cannot explain this contradiction.

The Gas Giants and Ice Planets

What happened to all the gas that must have surrounded the proto-earth? If the earth was made from the same material as the sun, there must have been lots of gas among it. The standard answer is that the solar wind blew it away. Okay, so why then do we have gas giant planets like Jupiter and Saturn? Well, they must have managed to suck up enough gas before the solar wind blew the rest away.

If dust particles have a "sticking problem" in forming rocky planets, then gas molecules most certainly have a very much greater problem in forming gas planets. In fact the "sticking problem" for the gas giants is so great that no one even considers it — gas molecules simply do not "stick" together. What else can they call on? Well, nothing really, so they have to fall back on our old favorite — "density fluctuations."

Computer simulations of gas giant planet formation show that when you have a disk of gas surrounding a star, nothing happens (in the way of planet formation) unless you do something to *make* it happen. This is exactly what we would expect, because the mass of the gas is now very far below the threshold for gravitational collapse. If you have to "squash" a large cloud of gas in order to form a star, as we have discussed, then you will most certainly have to "squash" a small cloud of gas in order to produce a planet. Jupiter is about a thousand times less massive than the sun. If a ball of gas with the mass of the sun is unable to form a star by gravity alone, then it would be much less likely for a similar-sized gas ball with the mass of Jupiter to form a planet by gravity alone.

So what do you have to "do" to make a gas giant? Well, whatever you do has to happen fairly quickly before the solar wind blows the gas away. Moreover, most stars appear to have formed in dense clusters, and the intense combined output of ultraviolet radiation from all these stars can also quickly remove the circumstellar disk. A recent computer simulation began with a very cold disk of molecular hydrogen gas particles at 50 K, or –223 °C. Within just a few hundred (computer simulated) years one or more gas giant protoplanets did form in the outer regions of the disk. So does this demonstrate that gas giant planet formation can occur naturally (as the authors claimed)? Not at all. Why not? Because the simulation *began* with a "gravitationally unstable" disk. That is, the cloud of gas was already dense enough for gravity to begin to work on it. The simulation can only work, in the authors' own words, "if these condensations . . . can contract to planetary densities."[52] This is a circular argument and begs the question of how the disk became so dense to start with. There were other problems as well. The simulation can only work "if the disk remains cold enough for long enough." That is, maintaining the low temperature was also an unrealistic condition.

The ice planets Uranus, Neptune, and Pluto are even harder to explain. The temperatures are so cold out there that everything freezes. Some have claimed that ice crystals can be fluffy and therefore stand a better chance of "sticking" to form a self-gravitating mass. However, there is also very much less material out there and it would take a great deal longer for the protoplanet to move among it and gather it up. It has therefore been suggested that they formed closer in to the sun and were then displaced into their present positions. In so doing, they lose the supposed advantage of the "sticky" ice crystals, so we are back where we started.

Origin of Moons

If planets have a hard time forming out of dust, then moons have even more trouble because they are smaller still and proportionally much less susceptible to the effects of gravity. There are more than 60 known moons in our solar system. The earth's moon is one of the larger ones, with a diameter of 3,476 km. The smallest ones are only around 10 km diameter. According to the planetesimal theory, all these various-sized moons are just representatives of the many different stages of planetesimal development, but as you will recall, the "sticking problem" leaves the planetesimal theory without a credible mechanism, so it is no explanation at all.

Our earth/moon system provides a very useful illustration of the forces that are necessary to produce stars, planets, and moons out of a cloud of gas and dust.

---

52. Lucio Mayer, Thomas Quinn, James Wadsley, and Joachim Stadel, "Formation of Giant Planets by Fragmentation of Protoplanetary Disks," *Science* 298:1756–1759 (2002).

Our moon has no atmosphere. If ever there was a gaseous phase in the moon's history it has long since dispersed because the gravitational field on the moon is not strong enough to hold it. The earth does have an atmosphere however, because its gravity is strong enough to hold onto the gas molecules. The moon is about one quarter the diameter of the earth and about one fiftieth its mass.

Let's think about the gravitational attraction between two molecules of gas. It will be utterly insignificant compared with the kinetic energy of the gas molecule's motion, so if they collide, they will simply bounce off one another. Now let's imagine that we increase the size of one of the particles — let's call it a "protoplanetesimal" — until the gravitational force *is* great enough to hold them together. How big does our "protoplanetesimal" have to be? If we made it the size of the moon this would not be large enough, because the moon's gravity is not strong enough to hold onto gas molecules. We would have to make it about as big as the earth — because the earth's gravity *is* strong enough to hold onto gas molecules. This clearly illustrates how utterly insignificant gravity is within a gas cloud and how huge the "gravitational instability" has to be before it begins to collapse under its own self-gravity. Of course the earth's gravity is only strong enough to *hold* its atmosphere, not enough to squash it into a state of gravitational collapse.

A similar argument can be made for dust grains. The moon's gravity *is* strong enough to hold onto dust grains. Those who have seen the television footage of the *Apollo* moon landings may remember the footprints in the dust that covered the ground. As the astronauts hopped about on the moon's surface they kicked up little puffs of dust that slowly settled back down again. The gravitational attraction between two dust particles in space is negligible. If we then increase the size of one particle until gravity does become significant, how big must it become? Calculations suggest that wind shear would prevent dust accumulation on rocky bodies less than about 500 cubic kilometers in volume. The smallest asteroid that has so far been examined at close range is 433 Eros. With a volume of about 6,000 cubic kilometers, it has boulders, gravel, and finer material that may qualify as "dust" lying on its surface. Once again, you can see from these examples how large a rocky body needs to be before gravity becomes a significant force upon it.[53]

So where did our moon come from? Professor Harold Urey, dubbed the "father of lunar science," was a pioneer in the *Apollo* missions to the moon

---

53. The effects we are talking about here apply to the case where no other large gravitating bodies are present. If another large body is nearby, the smaller body is less able to attract debris from space.

and he looked very carefully into this question. His colleague, and founder of NASA's Goddard Institute for Space Studies, Professor Robert Jastrow, reported that "he [Urey] gave up, saying, 'It is easier to pretend the moon is not in the sky than to explain how it came to be there.' "[54]

In 1986, a review of the subject concluded that "the older hypotheses of lunar origin (fission, capture, and binary accretion) are either physically impossible or extremely improbable."[55] The author concluded that "we will never be able to state with absolute certainty that we know the origin of the moon." His favored suggestion was that perhaps it formed from the impact of a "giant planetesimal" upon the early earth. How big was this "giant planetesimal?" The size of Mars! Subsequent computer simulation studies of various bodies in the solar system have developed this theme. By starting with a large number of Mars- or moon-sized "planetesimals" you can produce all sorts of interesting things. Of course, what these studies are really telling us is that you cannot produce planets and moons by naturalistic means. To produce planets and moons, you have to start with planets and moons!

Origin of Meteorites and Asteroids

More than a hundred tons of meteoritic material enters the earth's atmosphere every day. Most are tiny and are burned up by friction. Of those that survive and reach the ground, about 95 percent of recorded "falls" (those that are seen and then recovered, as opposed to those that are simply "found") are of the "stony" kind — similar in composition to earth rocks. About 4 percent of falls are of the "iron" type — similar in composition to the earth's iron/nickel core. Because they tend to be larger, the "irons" make up about two-thirds of the total mass of recorded falls. About 1 percent of falls are a stony-iron mixture. When the trajectories of falls are traced, the majority indicate an origin within the asteroid belt, a jumble of hundreds of thousands of rocky bodies orbiting the sun between Mars and Jupiter. A small number of "found" meteorites show similarity to moon rocks, and a few others have gaseous inclusions similar in composition to the atmosphere of Mars, so it has been suggested that these might have been blasted off those celestial bodies during the giant impacts that scarred their surfaces. However, the vast majority appear to come from the direction of the asteroid belt and they match the asteroids in composition (as far as we can tell). Some of the small moons throughout the solar system may be captured asteroids as well.

---

54. Robert Jastrow, "Mysteries of the Solar System," *Insight*, p.84–85 (Undated).
55. A.P. Boss, "The Origin of the Moon," *Science* 231:341–345 (1986).

So where did the asteroids come from? Olbers suggested in 1802 that they could be the rubble left over from the disruption of a planet. However, the "cold accretion" theory for the origin of the planets requires that a range of different-sized planetesimals should have formed from the dust cloud in the early solar system, and it is now thought that the asteroids are representative of those planetesimals. Not everyone agrees, however. Asteroids and meteorites are fused solid bodies, but in the "cold accretion" theory there is no heat source to melt the dust particles. The impact-generated heating that is invoked for planets does not work for asteroids because they are not large enough to either attract or absorb sufficient impact energy to cause melting, and heating by radioactive decay doesn't work because the heat is quickly lost through the high surface-area-to-mass ratio. So what are the alternatives? Asteroids and meteorites look very much like the rubble of a disrupted planet. The "stony" types correspond with the outer mantle and crust of an earth-like planet, while the "iron" type exactly parallels the inner core region. Van Flandern has listed a hundred and one reasons for, and two reasons against, the disrupted planet theory as the source of asteroids, meteorites, and perhaps some comets.[56] We think this is much more likely, though we don't accept his model of the origin of the solar system.

Origin of Life

According to Nobel Prize-winning cell biologist Professor Christian De Duve:

> Life is an obligatory manifestation of matter. . . . [Its] spontaneous emergence [was] inevitable under the conditions that existed on the prebiotic earth. [It is] bound to occur similarly wherever and whenever similar conditions obtain. . . . There should be plenty of such sites, perhaps as many as one million per galaxy. . . . The universe is awash with life.[57]

The casual reader would probably not be aware that this statement is not supported by a single experimental result. What Professor De Duve has said here is based entirely upon his ideology. This is what he *believes*, not what he *knows*.

56. Tom Van Flandern, *Dark Matter, Missing Planets and New Comets: Paradoxes Resolved, Origins Illuminated.* (Berkeley, CA: North Atlantic Books, 1993), chapter 11. See also, <www.metaresearch.org>.
57. Christian De Duve, "The Beginnings of Life on Earth," *American Scientist* 83(5) (1995), at http://www.sigmaxi.org/amsci/articles/95articles/cdeduve.html, June 30, 2003.

He is not alone in believing what the evidence so clearly contradicts. When the SETI program — the Search for Extra-Terrestrial Intelligence — had its funding cut by the U.S. Congress, an appeal was launched for home computer users to process the data, and millions of people around the world responded. The rationale for the SETI program is that since life evolved from chemicals here on earth (so they believe), then it must have similarly evolved elsewhere as well. NASA now uses the search for extra-terrestrial life as a primary justification for its space program — its mission statement is "to explore the universe and search for life."

Chemical evolution — the idea that life arose from non-living chemicals in a step-by-step natural progression — is contradicted by the evidence at every step. Others have dealt with these issues in detail[58] so we will give just one example — the problem of hydrolysis.[59]

The NASA space program has identified water as the ingredient to look for in their "search for life." The reasoning is that life evolved on earth in water (so they believe), and water is necessary for all life on earth,[60] therefore planets (or moons) with water are the obvious places to start looking. The recent discovery of water on Mars has greatly fueled their excitement about finding life there as well, but in order to come to these conclusions about life and water, they have to overlook an enormous stumbling block — water actually *prevents* chemical evolution!

The simplest way to explain this amazing statement is to note that virtually all the important chemicals in a living cell are long-chain organic polymers (*poly*=many, *meros*=part). A protein, for example, is a polymer consisting of hundreds or thousands of amino acids. The reaction that joins up amino acids into a chain is called the "condensation reaction," and it looks like the following:

$$\text{Amino acid} + \text{amino acid} \leftrightarrow \text{polymer} + \text{water}$$

The double-headed arrow means that the reaction can go either way. This is the key to understanding what is called the "hydrolysis" problem. The direction that the reaction goes depends upon the concentration of the ingredients.

---

58. Charles B. Thaxton, Walter L. Bradley, and Roger L. Olsen, *The Mystery of Life's Origin* (New York: Philosophical Library, 1984). See also, Q&A at www. answersingenesis.org.

59. Jonathan Sarfati, "Origin of Life: The Polymerization Problem," *TJ* 12(3):281–284 (1998), at: www.answersingenesis.org/Docs/3998.htm, June 30, 2003.

60. Many different kinds of earth life can survive desiccation, but all of them need water to grow and reproduce.

If there is an excess of amino acids, then the reaction will go to the right and produce polymer and water, but if there is an excess of polymer or water then the concentration gradient will push the reaction backward to release the amino acids. It is this "backward" reaction that is called "hydrolysis" (*hydro*=water, *lysis*=to loosen or dissolve). Now chemical evolution scenarios almost invariably involve dilute solutions of amino acids (or other chemicals) in water. That means water is by far the predominant component, in which case the reaction is driven "backward" and any polymer that does form is quickly hydrolyzed and thus destroyed.

Various ways of getting around this problem have been attempted, one of which is to try to mimic what cells do when they produce polymers. Cells use enzymes — clever molecules that can speed up the reaction in the desired direction and overcome hydrolysis, but enzymes are proteins — and to form proteins you need to overcome hydrolysis. So evolutionists have recently turned to mineral surfaces as an enzyme substitute. Huber and Wächterhäuser,[61] for example, used pure solutions of amino acids and tried to get them to join up in the presence of pyrite, an iron sulphide mineral. They managed to get a few to join up in pairs, and a very small proportion to join up in threes, but all of these combinations were rapidly hydrolyzed again. Ferris and colleagues[62] managed to do better. They produced chains of up to 55 amino acids by adhering them to clay mineral surfaces, but this required pure reagents (again) and a series of 50 operator interventions. Pure solutions of amino acids do not occur naturally in the environment, and the 50 operator interventions demonstrate beyond any doubt that the process does not occur spontaneously.

So, the best experimental efforts to prove chemical evolution do just the opposite. They demonstrate beyond doubt that biologically useful molecules do not form spontaneously in water, even in unrealistically pure solutions.

A number of eminent scientists have acknowledged the impossibility of chemical evolution on earth, so they have suggested that it must have come to earth from somewhere else — a view referred to as "panspermia."[63] The recent discovery of microbes in the upper atmosphere has fueled speculation in this

---

61. C. Huber and G. Wächterhäuser, "Peptides by Activation of Amino Acids with CO on (Ni,Fe)S Surfaces: Implications for the Origin of Life," *Science* 281(5377):670–672 (1998).
62. James P. Ferris, Aubrey R. Hill, Rihe Liu, and Leslie E. Orgel, "Synthesis of Long Prebiotic Oligomers on Mineral Surfaces," *Nature* 381:59–61 (1996).
63. See www.panspermia.org.

area.[64] However, even if these were not of terrestrial origin (it is near certain that they are), this would not solve the problem, it would only transfer it to another place. Life that depends upon water (as did the microbes just referred to) cannot evolve in water *anywhere*.

It is therefore no surprise to find a fundamental contradiction lying right at the very heart of the SETI program. SETI pioneer Professor Carl Sagan devised a set of four criteria that they could use to distinguish possible intelligent communications among the constant noise of radio static that comes from all parts of the sky. When those four criteria were applied to the information on the DNA molecule (to see if it comes from an intelligent source), it passed the test.[65] So, the criteria that would alert the SETI astronomers to the presence of "evolved" life in outer space would tell them, if they wanted to know, that life did not evolve — it came from an intelligent Creator.

SUMMARY OF THE BIG-BANG MODEL

The starting assumption of the big-bang model is that all the substance of the universe (in the form of energy) as well as time and space began in a single point of infinite density and temperature. This state of singularity is a thermodynamic dead end, so something else was needed to get it out of the singular state and into a form that could produce the galaxies and stars of the observed universe. This "something else" is called the "big bang," but nobody knows what it was — nothing in the known world of physics could have produced it. Physical descriptions of the big-bang model can only begin *after* the unknown event has already happened.

Even the "big bang" was not enough to explain what we see, so a period of "inflation" that expanded the universe by a very huge factor in a very tiny fraction of a second is proposed. As the inflated fireball expanded, it cooled down, and the energy turned into matter according to the known principles of particle physics. However, this process would have produced equal amounts of matter and antimatter — but our universe consists only of matter, very little antimatter, so this is a major contradiction.

After about 300,000 years, the end product was an expanding cloud of mostly hydrogen gas, accompanied by the cooling glow of radiation from the primordial fireball that we see today as the Cosmic Microwave Background

---

64. All these microbes are earth-type microbes and the finds are quite satisfactorily explained by earth as the source.
65. Walter I. Sivertsen, "SETI and DNA," *Creation Research Society Quarterly* 39(3) (2002). Abstract at: http://www.creationresearch.org/crsq/abstracts/Abstracts39-3.htm.

Radiation (CMBR). There are no galaxies, stars, planets, or people in the big-bang universe, just an expanding cloud of gas. These latter objects are proposed to have formed by "other means" that have nothing to do with the big bang — indeed they have to *counteract* the big bang and *overcome* the cosmic expansion in order to form the stars and galaxies.

There are *no* convincing naturalistic explanations for the origin of the solid objects that we observe in the real universe.

The great achievement of the big-bang theory is that it provides cosmologists with a model to play with, in a subject that previously had no model. Mathematical and computer models are extraordinarily powerful tools to help us with our thinking, but we should never lose sight of the fact that they are models, and not the real thing. No doubt, big-bang theory will go down in history as a stepping stone to our further understanding of the universe, just as many earlier — and now discarded — ideas have also done. Indeed, we can see this happening already. In the May 22, 2004, edition of *New Scientist*, an open letter to the scientific community was published, in which 33 scientists claim that "the big bang today relies on a growing number of hypothetical entities, things that we have never observed — inflation, dark matter, and dark energy are the most prominent examples. Without them, there would be a fatal contradiction between the observations made by astronomers and the predictions of the big bang theory . . . the theory can't survive without these fudge factors." They therefore call for reallocation of funding to test other theories (the letter is reproduced in appendix D). Meanwhile, however, it is alarming (and, we would suggest, ethically and professionally indefensible) that professors at leading universities tell the world that the big-bang model explains the origin of the universe when it most certainly does not.

CHAPTER 5

TIME SCALES

The age of the earth (or the universe) is not a simple concept as you might expect. Nor is time. Both are vitally dependent upon the way you think. They have their objective, measurable aspects, but how you interpret and use those components depends upon your world view. Certain "appearances of age" are a necessary consequence of God creating a functional universe, but events that occur within the cosmos do require scientific explanation. Early attempts by creationists to explain the conflict between the short time scale of the Bible and the vast size of the universe were inadequate. However, relativistic time dilation — a feature of relativity theory — satisfies all the necessary requirements. In fact, when we look at a wide range of time indicators in the universe, the biblical perspective gives a more comprehensive and satisfying explanation than the big-bang model. Once, cosmic time scales were a stumbling block to biblical faith, but now they are a powerful ally.

We saw in the last chapter that the big-bang model does not explain the origin of the universe, nor does it explain the origin of man, the cosmologist. There are many Christians who might agree with us so far but they still embrace the big bang because they cannot believe the biblical time scale. So, in this chapter we will deal with the scientific aspects of cosmic time scales, and in the next chapter we will look at what the text of the Bible says. We will then be in a better position to understand the biblical world view and its cosmological consequences.

WHAT IS "AGE"?

How can we measure the age of the earth? The surprising answer is that we can't directly measure it. Why not? Because the earth does not have a measurable property called "age." Age is a concept that we all understand (or think we do), but it is not a tangible property that can be measured by any measuring device or machine.

We can measure the passing of "time" (but only if the measurement is within human lifetimes), and we have specialized timing devices and international standards to ensure that our timing devices are accurate. But "age" is more than just "time." "Age" is the time that has elapsed *from a given starting point*. This might seem to be a trivial difference, but it is not. The starting point for the earth is perhaps the most crucial issue in all our studies of origin.

Modern-day timing devices were not present when the earth began, so they are useless in measuring the age of the earth. Numerous time-dependent processes go on in and around the earth that can be indirectly correlated with "age," provided we have an agreed starting point. Then we would also need observations and a number of assumptions to establish the correlation. However, there is *no* universally agreed upon starting point.

Any observations on "age" that we might make are limited to the present, and the assumptions that one makes have to be based on what one *believes* happened in the past. So while everyone agrees that the earth has an "age," we cannot directly measure it for two important reasons: (a) because we were not there at its beginning to establish the starting point, and (b) all the time-correlated processes that can be used to estimate the time elapsed since the beginning are crucially dependent upon assumptions.

To illustrate the point in a more concrete way, think about the reasons why we have birth certificates and "use by" dates. Most of us have a birth certificate to mark the beginning of our life on earth (actually the day we left our mother's womb) and we can mark off the number of solar cycles that have passed since then to establish our "age." Without the birth certificate, however, it would be difficult to accurately establish our age. You can easily measure properties like height and weight, but not "age." In a similar fashion, in many countries, manufacturers of perishable food items are obliged by law to print a "use by" date on the package. Why? Because without it there is no easy way to tell how long it has been sitting on the shelf.

Because this is such an important matter, let's look at a quantitative example. Remember in our history chapter, we said that in the third century B.C., a clever Greek called Eratosthenes estimated the circumference of the earth to be about 40,000 km. How could we test the accuracy of this estimate? We could use satellite measuring equipment. When we do, we find a value of 40,074 km. This result confirms the reliability of the earlier measurement — it was within about 0.2 percent of the "true" value — but these modern measurements have increased the accuracy to within about 0.002 percent of the "true" value.[1]

Now let's ask two important questions about this procedure. (1) Does the earth have a property called "circumference"? Yes, it is the maximum perimeter of the earth's surface. The perimeter is slightly different if we measure it around the equator compared with around the poles, but let's not worry about that here. (2) Do we have a standard of length to measure it against? Yes, we have the kilometer, which is 1,000 times the standard meter-length bar housed in Paris.[2]

Let's now do the same exercise for the age of the earth. Professor John Joly, as we will read shortly, used the accumulation of salt in the sea to estimate the maximum age of the earth to be 89 million years. Claire Patterson, however, using isotope ratios in meteorites, came up with an age of 4.55±0.7 billion years. How can we decide who is closer to the "true" value?

There is no standard method for addressing this problem. The reason is that neither sea salt nor isotope ratios are a measure of "age." Sea salt is sea salt, and isotope ratios are isotope ratios. Sea salt only becomes a measure of "age" if a number of unverifiable assumptions are made (we will discuss the assumptions underlying dating methods shortly). Isotope ratios only become a measure of "age" if even more unverifiable assumptions are made. The primary quantities — salt and isotope concentrations — can be accurately measured using standard laboratory techniques. Any disputes over their values can be resolved by calibrating equipment against samples of guaranteed purity and by the use of international interlaboratory comparisons, but the age estimates cannot be subjected to such calibration because they are based on assumptions, and assumptions are

---

1. Measurements of any kind, when repeated, will usually produce slightly different results. This "measurement error" thus prevents us from knowing the exact "true" value, but it does allow us to specify the range of values within which the "true" value lies.

2. This platinum-iridium bar is now only of historical interest. It was superseded in 1960 with the definition of 1,650,763.73 vacuum wavelengths of light resulting from a particular atomic energy level transition of the krypton-86 isotope. Since 1983, the meter has been defined as the distance light travels in $1/2.99792458 \times 10^{-8}$ seconds in a vacuum, where the second is defined by the transition frequency of a certain hyperfine energy level of the ground state of an unperturbed caesium-133 atom.

based on what the practitioners *believe* about what happened in the unobservable past. There are no international standards for testing belief systems.

Let's now ask our two questions. (1) Does the earth have a property called "age?" Yes, but the only way we can access it is by making assumptions about what happened in the unobservable past. (2) Do we have a standard of "age" to measure it by? Well, we have a standard of time. The "second" is the international standard, as determined by a worldwide network of atomic clocks. However, the derivation of time from isotope ratios or sea salt is based on assumptions, and we have no agreed upon starting point.

So, is the question of "age" unresolvable? Evolutionists argue that by using many different isotope methods, a reliable estimate of age can be obtained. However, since all their methods are based on the same (unverifiable) naturalistic assumptions, then the naturalistic assumptions underlying one method will "confirm" the naturalistic assumptions underlying the other methods, by definition, not by objective measurement.

We conclude, therefore, that since we have no objectively definable starting point and no assumption-free method of measuring elapsed time, the age of the earth is not an objective, measurable quantity. It is a matter of opinion that is embedded in a belief system — a world view.

Age and World Views

Evolutionists say that the earth is 4.6 billion years old, so from where did they get this number? They derived it in 1956 from a comparison of isotope ratios in meteorites.[3] What do isotope ratios in meteorites have to do with the age of the earth? Possibly very little — it depends on where you think they came from.

Evolutionists[4] believe that the solar system formed out of leftover dust and gas after the sun formed in a cloud of rubble left over from supernova explosions. They believe that meteorites represent dust-aggregates typical of those "planetesimals" which formed the earth and the other planets. They believe that meteorites have been wandering around in the solar system for the last 4 or 5 billion years, unaffected by the kind of weathering that interferes with earth-bound isotopes. They conclude, therefore, that meteorites contain

---

3. Claire Patterson, "Age of Meteorites and the Earth," *Geochimica et Cosmochimica Acta* 10:230–237 (1956).
4. We use this term here for believers in "cosmic evolution," which includes "progressive creationists." Although these latter eschew biological transformism, they do embrace the big bang and cosmic evolution.

pristine isotope compositions and thus their isotope "clocks" are reliable (we will consider shortly just what makes a "clock" reliable).

The Genesis account, however, suggests that the earth was created separately from other heavenly bodies. While it could have been made from similar materials, there is no reason why we should be bound by this idea. Isaiah 40:26 says, "Lift up your eyes on high and see: who created these? He who brings out their host by number, calling them all by name" and Psalm 147:4 confirms the idea "He determines the number of the stars, he gives to all of them their names." If the heavenly bodies were differentiated by name, then perhaps they were also differentiated in composition. All the known planets in the solar system are different, so perhaps meteorites are too. If, as we suggested in the previous chapter, meteorites are the debris from a disrupted planet, different in composition to the earth, then any "age" derived from meteorite isotope ratios will have little relevance to the "age" of the earth.

As in all other areas of the science of the past, the conclusions you come to about the "age" of the earth depend upon the assumptions that you start with. If you start with long-age evolutionary assumptions, then you will end up with long-age evolutionary conclusions.

What happens if you start with biblical assumptions? You get an age for the earth of about 6,000 years.[5] Is there any physical evidence to support that? Yes, indeed, but before we look at dating methods, we need to understand some underlying principles.

AGE WITHIN THE BIBLICAL WORLD VIEW

There have been numerous attempts at reconciling the billions of years of cosmic evolution with the thousands of years of Genesis creation. Some have simply changed the Bible to fit the evolutionary time scale.[6] Others claim

---

5. While the genealogies in the Bible do not yield an exact date for creation (as some have tried to argue), they do yield an approximate date of around 4000 B.C. Any expansion of the genealogies cannot reasonably be pushed more than a few thousand years beyond that date. For a comprehensive review of the issues surrounding the genealogies, see P. Williams, "Some Remarks Preliminary to a Biblical Chronology," *TJ* 12(1):98–106 (1998).

6. In the next chapter, we will cover theistic evolution, the gap theory and the day-age theory (also called "progressive creation"); there is also the "literary framework" hypothesis, which says that Genesis 1 is not meant to be taken literally. The most vocal of these Bible-changing proponents is progressive creationist Dr. Hugh Ross in his ministry Reasons To Believe <www.reasons.org>; see also Hugh Ross, *Creation and Time* (Colorado Springs, CO: NavPress, 1994).

that the Bible does not speak authoritatively on scientific matters, but Jesus said, "I have spoken to you of earthly things and you do not believe; how then will you believe if I speak of heavenly things?" (John 3:12; NIV). A number of others have attempted to maintain the integrity of the biblical account, but to understand their arguments, we need to clarify just what it is that requires explanation within this slippery concept called "age."

Functional Creation and the Appearance of Age

Imagine that you could visit Adam and Eve in the Garden of Eden in a time machine. Suppose you arrive on day 7. If you didn't know where you were or who these two naked adults were, you might reasonably assume that they were about 20 years old. You would be wrong — they would be only one day old.

This "appearance of age" is not a deception on God's part, it is the logical consequence of creating a functioning universe under man's dominion. A functional human being who is able to reproduce would need to be at least a young, post-puberty teenager. A human being mature enough to exercise dominion over God's creation would need to be at least fully adult. So we infer that a minimum apparent age for Adam and Eve would be in their early twenties.

The "appearance of age" has wide ramifications. Mature trees, for example, have tree rings from their annual growth cycles. Would the trees in the Garden also have had tree rings? If so, they would deceptively suggest annual growth cycles that had never occurred. If they didn't have tree rings would they be "real" trees? Here's another classic one. Would Adam and Eve have bellybuttons like all other human beings? Or would they have none because neither of them was born in the normal way?

We can give three kinds of answers to questions like these. First, we do not know and perhaps we do not need to know (since we are not told). Second, God could have created the original trees *without* tree rings — not all trees have them anyway. Alternatively, God could have created the original trees *with* tree rings — the ring structure has a function and is not just a passive relic of seasons past. Some of the layers provide "plumbing" for liquid transport, some provide active growth regions, some provide protection for the growth regions, and some provide thickened and strengthened areas for maintaining the tensile properties of the trunk. Likewise, God could have created Adam and Eve *without* bellybuttons, since they were not born in the "normal" manner. Alternatively, God could have created them *with* bellybuttons, because the bellybutton is not just the relic of the attachment point of the umbilical cord that provided nutrition from the mother to the child in the womb. In the postnatal child and the adult, it also provides an important structural feature for anchoring the internal organs.

Third, and most importantly, any sense of "deception" here only arises from naturalistic starting assumptions. Tree rings would only deceive us if we based our thinking on naturalistic starting assumptions. If we based our thinking on God's Word, we would know for a certainty that Adam and Eve were only one day old and the trees were of similarly recent vintage.

Following the same line of thinking, some creationists have suggested that a mature cosmos would have light beams from the most distant stars and galaxies arriving on earth on the day they were created (day 4). So even if the most distant galaxies are 15 billion light-years away, Adam and Eve could have seen them (ideally — they did not have modern telescopes, of course) when the stars came out on the evening of day 6.

Let's imagine for a moment what the alternative would have been. If no light beams were part of the original creation, then Adam and Eve would have had to wait for the light to travel to them from the heavenly bodies. So, on the night of day 6 there would have been no stars in the sky at all. Perhaps some of the planets might have been visible, depending on their locations within their orbits. The planets visible with the naked eye (Mercury, Venus, Mars, Jupiter and Saturn) all lie within about 80 light minutes from earth so their light would have arrived on day 4. The nearest star is the Alpha Centauri triplet and it is more than 4 light-years away. So the multitude of stars would not have become visible for many years after the creation, and the full glory of the Milky Way would not have become visible for more than about 30,000 years (i.e., we would still not be able to see it).

This scenario illustrates that the light beams *must* have been part of the original creation because their stated purpose was to be signs in the sky (Gen. 1:14). Signs must be visible, and the distances are vast, therefore created light beams would seem to be essential.

If we apply naturalistic assumptions to a whole universe without created light beams, we must conclude that it is at least 15 billion years old because it would have taken the light that long to traverse a distance of 15 billion light-years. According to God's Word, all that space and all those galaxies were created on day 4. Therefore, God must have created the light beams coming to us from even the most distant galaxies. This would appear to solve the conflict.

There is a snag. We can see events such as supernovae (catastrophic explosions of stars) that have occurred more than 6,000 light-years away. Although

Adam and Eve could see the stars (and nearby galaxies) because the light beams were supernaturally sent to them by the Creator, all the light that has come to earth since that time has (presumably) traveled at normal speed. In July 1054, the Chinese reported seeing, in the region of the Crab constellation, a "guest star" appear suddenly in the sky. It was so bright that for several weeks it was visible in daylight, but then it faded and after a year and a half was no longer visible at all. Today we can see the results of this spectacular catastrophe in the beautiful Crab Nebula, a cloud of expanding gas and dust — the remains of the star that exploded. At the heart of this nebula is the remains of the original star, now a super dense neutron star, spinning at a breathtaking 30 times per second, and sending out pulses of radio signals as it does so. This strange behavior has earned such bodies the name of "pulsars" (pulsating stars).

Now the problem here is that the Crab Nebula is about 6,500 light-years from earth. In A.D. 1054, only about 5,000 years had elapsed since creation, so it should not have been visible. According to the "created light beam" scenario, this supernova should not have become visible until about A.D. 2500 at the earliest, even if it occurred immediately after creation week. This problem is called "the starlight and time problem" and it is the most important scientific issue that any creationist cosmology must address.

A further illustration of the problem occurred in 1987 when astronomers had the rare good fortune of catching a supernova on camera. This one, called "SN1987a" (because it was the first one recorded for 1987) occurred in the nearby galaxy called the Large Magellanic Cloud (LMC). The two Magellanic Cloud galaxies (called Large and Small) are visible at night near the south celestial pole. The LMC is about 12 times and the SMC is about 5 times the apparent diameter of the moon. The LMC is about 170,000 light-years away. According to the "created light beam" scenario, we should not be able to see SN1987a for another 164,000 years!

Could God have created the "appearance" of an explosion in the light beams that He created in transit from the LMC? God can do anything He wants to do, but the great thing about the God of the Bible is that He gives us reason as well as revelation — He is not deceptive or capricious.

In the case of the adulthood of Adam and Eve and the possible presence of tree rings, we can see reasons for the maturity and functionality of the creation, a *side effect* of which is to give the "appearance" of age if viewed from a naturalistic perspective. However, no one has advanced any reasons to explain why God might have created the "appearance of explosions" in light beams that

Problems with the "created light beam" scenario

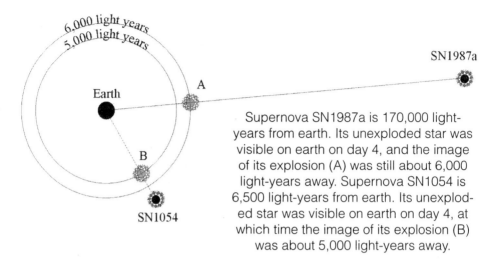

Supernova SN1987a is 170,000 light-years from earth. Its unexploded star was visible on earth on day 4, and the image of its explosion (A) was still about 6,000 light-years away. Supernova SN1054 is 6,500 light-years from earth. Its unexploded star was visible on earth on day 4, at which time the image of its explosion (B) was about 5,000 light-years away.

have no basis in the real history of the stars they represent. Because it involves the creation of a "phony history," it lays God open to a charge of deception in a manner unlike the creation of Adam as a mature adult. A significant challenge for creationist cosmology is therefore to explain events like the supernovae of 1054 and 1987a.

There is another kind of evidence that we also need to consider, which falls somewhere between the bellybutton and the supernova. One example is the fusion power of the sun. The sun emits enormous amounts of energy and, according to the most recent evidence,[7] all of this energy comes from a nuclear fusion reaction in the heart of the sun, but it takes a very long time for a photon of light energy, emitted from the nuclear reaction in the core, to reach the surface. Calculations suggest a time scale of about a million years. The reason for the delay is that the hugely powerful magnetic field and the enormous turbulence created by the nuclear furnace cause the photons to bounce around interminably inside the sun. Now if the sun is only 6,000 years old, it means that the light we receive today never did originate in the heart of the sun's nuclear furnace, but is from the outer parts of the sun's atmosphere[8] where it would have taken less than 6,000 years to escape. Does this imply a deception

7. Robert Newton, " 'Missing' Neutrinos Found! No Longer an 'Age' Indicator," *TJ* 16(3):123–125 (2002).
8. This may have been the result of direct creation by God or due to gravitational compression and heating of the outer atmosphere.

on God's part? Or perhaps a multi-million-year age for the sun?[9] Not if the reason for the creation of the sun was, as stated in Genesis 1, to provide light on earth on the day it was created. Creationist scientist Dr. Jonathan Sarfati writes:

> But this is explained if the main purpose of fusion is *stability* — producing enough energy to balance that lost from the surface. I.e., the sun was created in a *steady state condition*, with the outward pressure generated by fusion matching the inward gravitational pressure, maintaining a constant temperature profile. This means that it could immediately fulfill its function as the 'greater light,' and keep shining at a constant rate. It is no different from believing that God created Adam with oxygen in his bloodstream in his extremities, even though it now takes some time for oxygen to diffuse through the alveoli in the lungs, then be transported by the blood.[10]

Once again, only naturalistic thinking would lead to the idea of deception.

Another example, with much more significance for cosmology, is the relationship between radioactive isotopes and their daughter products. Although we reject the assumptions underlying the general use of long-half-life isotopes to establish a long-age time scale for the earth (see below), we do acknowledge that some explanation is required. The most common isotope of uranium, for example, decays through 16 different unstable daughter isotopes before it reaches a stable lead isotope. All 18 isotopes can be found in rocks. How did they get there? Did God create only the uranium, and then the other elements were produced in the decay process over billions of years (as theistic evolutionists/progressive creationists would claim)? Or did God create all the daughter isotopes in equilibrium with the uranium? There is evidence in the rocks that a great deal of nuclear decay has indeed occurred. For example, when many of the isotopes decay, they produce very destructive, but short range, alpha particles that damage the rock crystals around them. Over time, a spherical "halo" of damage appears, and the radius of the sphere is proportional to the energy of the alpha particles (high-energy

---

9. Rod Bernitt, "Does the New Neutrino Model Ignore Helioseismic Data and Imply a Billion-year Age for the Sun?" *TJ* 17(1):64; Robert Newton replies, *TJ* 17(1):64-65 (2003).

10. Jonathan Sarfati, *Refuting Compromise* (Green Forest, AR: Master Books, 2004), p. 171.

particles produce large spheres). Furthermore, the alpha particles turn into helium atoms and excess helium can often be found in rock crystals. Also, uranium atoms can sometimes spontaneously "fission" — the nucleus breaks into two pieces, called "fission products," which then become isotopes of other elements like caesium and strontium. These nuclear fragments are much larger than alpha particles and they leave "fission tracks" (microscopic holes) in the surrounding rock crystals. Both radioactive decay and isotope fission produce heat, and excess heat can sometimes be found associated with uranium deposits.

All these lines of evidence suggest that considerable decay has occurred, so it is unlikely that all the daughter products were created in equilibrium with the parent isotopes. However, all may not be as it seems. This challenge has been taken up by a group of creationist geologists and physicists, calling themselves the RATE group (**R**adioisotopes and the **A**ge of **T**he **E**arth) and they are researching alternative explanations — one of which is that a time of accelerated nuclear decay occurred in the past, perhaps associated with the creation, the Fall, and/or the Flood.[11] Some intriguing and exciting evidence is emerging suggesting that something like this was indeed the case.

So, in summary to this point, we can say that "appearance of age" is an important and necessary part of God's work of creating a functional universe. However, appeals to this explanation need to uphold God's integrity and not imply deception on His part.

Because of this, we can say that it is probably not necessary for creationist cosmologists to feel obliged to explain the *objects* that we see in the universe. God is clearly a God of diversity — just look at the enormous variety of life on earth — so He could have separately created all the different objects in the universe.[12] However, we most certainly do need to explain the *events* that occur in the cosmos, since it is unlikely that God would deceptively create the appearance of events that never happened.

We will now proceed to look at some of the models that creationists have put forward to explain the time scales and the events of cosmic history.

---

11. Larry Vardiman, Andrew A. Snelling, and Eugene F. Chaffin, editors, *Radioisotopes and the Age of the Earth* (El Cajon, CA: Institute for Creation Research and Creation Research Society, 2000).

12. Isaiah 40:26 is again relevant here: "Lift up your eyes on high and see: who created these? He who brings out their host by number, calling them all by name." If the heavenly bodies were differentiated by name, then perhaps they were also individually created.

Non-relativistic Models

C-decay. In 1986, Norman and Setterfield[13] published an analysis of historical measurements of the speed of light, which showed that a very significant decline had occurred (the theory has been called "*c*-decay" or **cdk**, where *c* is the speed of light). When extrapolated back over the biblical time scale, it produced such an enormous increase in the speed of light that the results appeared to provide an explanation for the appearance of billions of years of time having passed in the cosmos. A lively debate ensued among creationists, and two major flaws in the theory were revealed. First, the result was heavily dependent upon the earliest data, whereas the most reliable measurements were the recent ones, which showed no change at all. And second, a change in the speed of light changes the values of a lot of other physical "constants," so the theory is not viable unless there has been a complicated balance of compensating changes in these other "constants." Recently, a very small change in one of these "constants" was reported, but its magnitude is nowhere near that required by the *c*-decay theory. The observational evidence available to us today would appear to now preclude this model.[14]

Another model in this category is the Harris model.[15] It starts with an infinite speed of light at creation. Then, after the Fall, it changes to the current value as a function of time and linear distance from earth. Like an expanding bubble spreading out through the universe, the speed of light drops from an infinite value to the current value at the surface of the bubble. One problem with this model is that we do not observe the massive blueshifts that would result when the speed of light changed from infinite to finite. In addition, the fine structure of the atomic spectra must change from a stage of no fine structure to their current state of fine structure, as the bubble passes. This should be observable in starlight, but it isn't. There would also be auto-focusing (the bubble acts like a lens) of all starlight onto the earth, which is not observed.

Another version of *c*-decay, by Stuart Burgess,[16] describes a rapid aging process for stars and a faster speed of light. It was all accelerated like fast-forwarding

13. Trevor Norman and Barry Setterfield, *The Atomic Constants, Light and Time* (Menlo Park, CA: SRI International Invited Research Report, 1986).
14. John G. Hartnett, "Is There any Evidence for a Change in *c*? Implications for Creationist Cosmology," *TJ* 16(3):89–94 (2002).
15. D.M. Harris, "A Solution to Seeing Stars," *Creation Research Society Quarterly* 15(2):112–115 (1978).
16. Stuart Burgess, *He Made the Stars Also* (Surrey, UK: Day One Publications, 2001), reviewed in *Creation Research Society Quarterly* 39:39, 2002.

a video tape. After all the light information reached the earth, the rates were reduced to what we now measure. The problem with this model is that the stars would disappear from view as the light slowed down, and then subsequently the light from those stars would take millions or billions of years to get here. Also, such light arriving at the earth would show enormous observable blueshifts,[17] but it doesn't. A more ingenious mechanism is needed to overcome such obvious objections.

At this stage it seems clear that no version of the c-decay theory can explain a young universe. Furthermore, in the process of analyzing this question we have uncovered good reasons to suppose that the constancy of the speed of light is, indeed, an absolute.

The phenomenological model. Newton's time convention[18] model suggests that the language of Genesis 1 is phenomenological (that is, it simply describes appearances). In this scenario, stars and galaxies were made millions and billions of years before day 4, but in such a manner that the light from all stars, no matter how far away, all arrived at the earth on day 4 and would have been seen first at that moment. This provides a reference frame, time-stamping the events from the moment they are seen here on earth. A fundamental problem with this model is that it puts the physical creation of the stars billions of years before creation week — they are only "seen" on day 4 on earth. In contrast, Genesis 1 portrays God as having created by speaking things into existence out of nothing, and they obeyed and came forth. The refrain ". . . and it was so," repeated six times (verses 7, 9, 11, 15, 24, 30), suggests that things happened in the sequence given, as and when God commanded them to happen. Furthermore, in Exodus 20:9–11, the Fourth Commandment reads, "Six days you shall labor, and do all your work . . . for in six days the LORD made heaven and earth, the sea, and all that is in them, and rested the seventh day." This confirms the idea that all the work of creation was accomplished in the six days of creation week. Newton's physical interpretation of his model is also questionable,[19] so we do not consider this a viable explanation of the starlight and time problem.

---

17. If the light speed was much greater in the past, either the frequencies were higher due to higher excitation energies of the sources or the received wavelengths are shortened by the Doppler effect. In either case, referenced against standard sources on earth, such light would appear blueshifted.
18. Robert Newton, "Distant Starlight and Genesis: Conventions of Time Measurement," *TJ* 15(1):80–85 (2001).
19. John G. Hartnett, "Distant Starlight and Genesis: Is 'Observed Time' a Physical Reality?" *TJ* 16(3):65–68 (2002).

Relativistic Time Dilation

The year 1994 will probably go down in history, along with 1961, as a vital landmark in the revival of biblical creationism. In 1961, Drs. John Whitcomb and Henry Morris published *The Genesis Flood*, a reinterpretation of geology in terms of the great flood of Noah. This book launched the modern creationist revival. In 1994, Dr. Russell Humphreys published *Starlight and Time*,[20] an explanation of the biblical time scale in terms of a "white hole cosmology." While Dr. Humphreys admits that it may not be the whole story,[21] his book did bring to the attention of creationists the fact that time is not a constant, and that is enough to break the deadlock.

The principle of relativistic time dilation has been known since the early 1900s with Lorentz and Einstein. However, Dr. Humphreys was the first to apply it to the creationist time scale problem. Einstein's theory has been successfully tested many times on numerous occasions, so we can have reasonable confidence in the underlying theory. There are many potential solutions to Einstein's general field equations and one of those may find an application to the biblical time scale, but that requires further investigation. The currently relevant aspect of relativity theory is that *time slows down* (a) in the presence of strong gravitational fields, and (b) at very high velocity, with respect to another unperturbed frame. We are used to thinking of time as a constant, but according to Einstein both time and space can be stretched and compressed — only the speed of light remains constant.

The relevance to the biblical starlight problem is that variable time allows the possibility that time on earth could have run at a slower rate than time in the outer galaxies. Thus, "billions of years" could have passed in the outer galaxies while only days passed on earth. While other models have tried to achieve this same result by changing the speed of light — and the outcomes have violated other aspects of observed physical reality — the curious thing about variable time is that you wouldn't know it was happening to you (see box on following page, "Changing Time without Noticing").

So when time slows down, it is only relative to some other frame of reference. As far as you are concerned, time is passing at the ordinary rate. And because all physical processes slow down at the same time, nothing seems

---

20. D. Russell Humphreys, *Starlight and Time: Solving the Puzzle of Distant Starlight in a Young Universe* (Green Forest, AR: Master Books, 1994).

21. D. Russell Humphreys, "Seven Years of Starlight and Time," *IMPACT* No. 338 (San Diego, CA: Institute for Creation Research, August 2001).

Changing Time without Noticing

The book *Einstein's Universe* provides a fascinating illustration of what an astronaut might experience near a black hole, depending on the size of the black hole and how close he might be.[22] If he could orbit close enough, he might even get into a time zone where his "clocks" run a thousand times slower. Outside observers would need a week to record his daily 10-minute report,[23] but it would arrive only once every three years. When checking his heart, they would hear it beat once every 20 minutes.

However, and this is the important thing, the astronomer would notice nothing different in his own space ship, but he would see strange things from his friends far from the black hole — everything would appear in superfast-forward. Their daily news bulletin would arrive every 90 seconds, and a U.S. president would be elected five times a week. If he listened to their heartbeats, they would just be a high-pitched hum, but not for long — after a few weeks of the astronaut's time, all his friends would likely be dead. After 10 years of orbiting, when he returned to earth he would find that 10,000 years had passed and his "own" time would be relegated to a few lines in an ancient history book.

Einstein's Universe points out that it would be impossible to orbit a black hole with the mass of a star because of dangerous forces that would rip the craft apart. It indicates that around a very large black hole, these forces would not be a danger.[24] So they should be no problem near a huge galaxy-mass hole, and certainly not near the universe-mass black hole as proposed in the Humphreys' model.

---

22. Nigel Calder, *Einstein's Universe* (London: BBC, 1979), chapter 13 "Methuselah in a Spaceship."
23. The signals would be massively redshifted.
24. Such *tidal forces* are because gravity is stronger on the parts of the body closer to the hole than on the parts away from the hole. The tidal forces near a black hole with a mass of a star are intense enough to stretch a spacecraft and astronaut into tiny pieces. However, while gravitational attraction decreases with the *square* of the distance $(1/r^2)$, the tidal effect decreases with the *cube* of the distance $(1/r^3)$. So the safer black holes to be near are the bigger ones. That is to say that if you have sufficient velocity to prevent you from falling in, across the event horizon, the tidal effects will be much smaller.

amiss. Now one may not understand this rather puzzling phenomenon, but it has been demonstrated experimentally, so it *is* real.

When we apply this principle to clocks on earth and clocks in the outer galaxies it is possible, in principle, for the earth clock to tick at a much slower rate than the outer galaxy clock but physical reality in both places would remain unaffected by it.

Can we see any suggestion of such a "variable time" scenario in the Scriptures? Yes, we can. God makes it clear that He created the whole universe in six days (Gen. 1; Exod. 20:11) but He also "stretched out" the heavens when He created them (Ps. 104:2; Isa. 42:5; 44:24; 45:12; 48:13; 51:13; Jer. 10:12; 51:15; Zech. 12:1). Now we do not know exactly what this means, but a very reasonable inference is that on creation day 4 when He made the heavenly bodies, He "stretched out" the heavens to a vast size in order to make room for all the stars and galaxies. Vast size and a constant speed of light (which, as we concluded from the c-decay debate, is required to maintain a stable universe) necessarily imply the "appearance" of a vast time scale. So the biblical cosmology does indeed imply a "young" earth and an "old" universe — God created a universe that is billions of light-years in size in only one earth day.

It is all a matter of perspective. God, as the Creator of time itself, is above and beyond all time. Time means little to Him, but the time scale He has given us is a six-day creation of the whole universe in earth time,[25] and tucked away within day 4 — an ordinary-length day by earth time — we find the billions of years of cosmic time.

Humphreys' White Hole Cosmology. Humphreys derived his "white hole" cosmology simply by inserting into Einstein's equations the assumptions that the universe has expanded from a previously denser state — which evolutionists accept — and that the universe is bounded[26] in space, with the earth at or near its center — both of which evolutionists reject. As a result, the early universe must have been inside what physicists call a "deep gravitational well." Remember that Einstein said gravity is a "dent" in spacetime caused by the

---

25. Once we realize that time is relative, any discussion of the age of the universe has to ask "by which clock"? The reference frame God has given us in Genesis 1 is clearly from an earth-rotation perspective, i.e., by earth clocks. The creation of the whole universe was thus in six days, about 6,000 years ago in this model. And the whole universe is about 6,000 years old. There is no suggestion of a "billions-of-years ago" date for creation, nor are the stars "older" than the earth (by earth clocks).

26. A bounded universe is necessarily finite. An unbounded one can be finite or infinite. Most big-bang models are finite but unbounded, i.e., have no center and no edge (a balloon surface is a finite two-dimensional space, but it has no center and no edge).

presence of matter. Since the earth would be at the center of all the matter in the universe it would have been at the deepest part of this gravitational well — what we would have called earlier a "black hole." However, there is another possibility — a "white hole." The equations of relativity theory allow the possibility of the opposite of a black hole, a "white hole," in which matter pours out — instead of being sucked in — until the "white hole" evaporates (i.e., it eventually loses all its matter). Dr. Humphreys suggested that this happened in the early universe, and the "event hori-

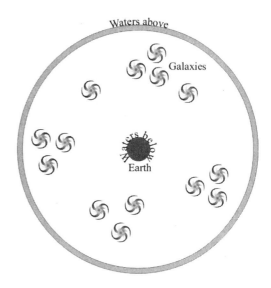

Humphreys' universe. The "waters above" are 20 billion light-years away from earth and its "waters below" at the center of the universe. (Not to scale.)

zon" (the perimeter of the white hole) passed through the earth on creation day 4, so that while billions of years of time were passing in the outer galaxies, only one day was passing on earth.

While Humphreys gives a very detailed creation scenario in his book, we will illustrate here just his model of the "waters" and the "firmament" of Genesis 1. He imagined that, in the beginning, all the matter of the universe was in the form of a sphere of liquid water. The observable mass of the universe would make this sphere about two light-years in diameter. The event horizon would have been much larger, with a diameter of about one billion light-years. He imagined it initially as a "black hole"; the enormous crushing gravitational force at the center of this watery sphere would have caused nuclear fusion in the interior and thus the formation of elements other than hydrogen and oxygen (the constituents of water). When God separated the waters and placed the "firmament" (Hebrew *raquia* = "expanse") between those above and those below, the stretching was associated with a change of the black hole into a white hole. The white hole then spewed out most of the matter within it, thereby evaporating, and causing the event horizon to shrink rapidly, passing through the vicinity of the earth on day 4. Humphreys thus ends up with a universe that looks like that in the illustration above.

The white hole cosmology has sparked a lively debate among Christian physicists. At present, it appears that although the model does account for the passage of billions of years in the outer galaxies while only one day passes on earth, it fails to account for the hundreds of thousands of years that have passed within our own galaxy and those nearby.[27] It predicts large blueshifts in light from nearby galaxies, which are not observed. It therefore needs some modification.

Hartnett's Young Solar System Model. In seeking to address this near-field problem in the white hole cosmology, one of us (J.H.) proposed a "young solar system" model[28] by changing the position of the "waters above." In the Humphreys model, the "waters above" are at the outer limits of the universe,

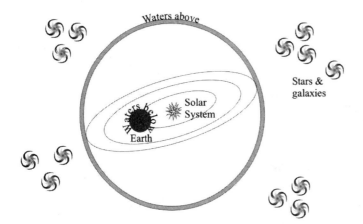

Harnett's universe. The "waters above" are at the perimeter of the solar system, in the form of chunks of ice, and the stars and galaxies lie beyond. (Not to scale.)

far beyond any further interaction in affairs on earth; they appear to be sitting out there doing nothing. However, by putting the "waters above" at the perimeter of the solar system, they continue to have a possible role in affairs on earth. They could, for example, have supplied impacting objects to precipitate the Flood, and they could have supplied comets to the solar system. They could also have provided objects such as the "stars falling from the sky" and the "something like a great mountain, burning with fire was thrown into the sea" of Revelation 8:8, associated with the end-time judgment. Scripturally, this

27. John G. Hartnett, "Look-back Time in Our Galactic Neighbourhood Leads to a New Cosmogony," *TJ* 17(1):73–79 (2003).
28. Ibid.; also John G. Hartnett, "A New Cosmology: Solution to the Starlight Travel Time Problem," *TJ* 17(2):98–102 (2003); and John G. Hartnett, "The Heavens Declare a Different Story," *TJ* 17(2):94–97 (2003).

seems attractive, because the "waters above" are given considerable prominence in the Genesis cosmogony, which suggests they were to have an important role to play.

In this model, maximum time dilation occurred within our solar system, and time passed at the "normal" rate from beyond the solar system to the outer galaxies. This scenario appears to solve the near-field problem, since the time differential is now a function of distance from the solar system.

Let us imagine then that God created the "heavens and the earth" on day 1 with the size of the "heavens" comparable with the current size of our solar system. Then on day 2, God separated the waters and placed the "waters above" near the outer limits of the solar system. Then on day 4, He created the sun, moon, and stars (today we would include here the creation of the other planets and stars of our own galaxy and the other galaxies). He "stretched out the heavens" to make room for them all, and to make the universe vast in size to illustrate His omnipotence and majesty. This process of "stretching out" resulted in a time differential between the solar system and the outer galaxies. On earth, time was passing according to the rotation of the earth, that is, one day per 24 hours, but because the rest of the universe was stretched out from small to vast size in a single earth day, this resulted in physical transformations occurring at rates far exceeding what would be measured by clocks here on earth.

The constraint in this model that forces time dilation to occur is that the heavenly lights were created to be seen on earth, so the light coming from them must have arrived at latest by the evening of day 4. Genesis 1:15 also says, "and it was so," which means that the specified work of creating the heavenly lights took place and was completed at that time (day 4). We would thus conclude that on the night that followed day 4, an astronomer (had there been one) could have looked out and seen the whole universe more or less as we see it today.

Not only would this scenario account for the time differential between the outer galaxies and the earth, it would also avoid the problem that the Humphreys' model stumbles over. We can reasonably infer that the mapping between galaxy time and earth time would be some function of distance, and it may be very steep near our solar system — this is the subject of ongoing research. The result, though, is such that during creation day 4, "billions of years" (corresponding to billions of light-years in distance) of physical transformation would have occurred in the outer galaxies. As we get closer to our galaxy, "billions of years" of aging may still have occurred but the distances only correspond to hundreds of thousands of light-years (the light from their earlier

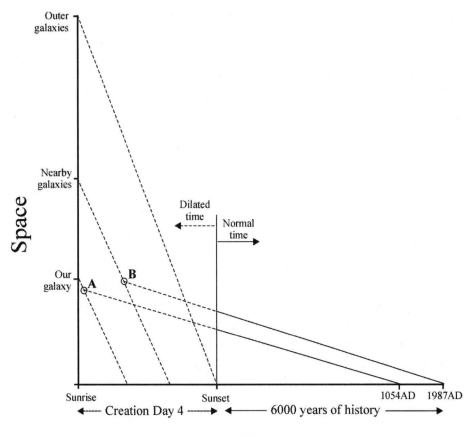

Earth Time

Young solar system time dilation. During creation day 4, light from all parts of the universe reached the earth (dashed lines). During this period, the Crab Nebula exploded in our galaxy and the image traveled to position (A) in the light beam coming to earth, and supernova SN 1987a exploded in the Large Magellanic Cloud galaxy and the image traveled to position (B) in the light beam coming to earth. These images then continued to travel in normal time and arrived on earth in A.D. 1054 and A.D. 1987, respectively.

history may have already passed us by). If we follow Halton Arp's scenario (see appendix A), it would seem that God used a hierarchical process — at a given distance, a cascade of creation events occurred in which galaxies were created from galaxies[29] (but all during day 4, of course). Galaxies at all distances show a roughly similar mix of apparent ages (old and young), which might suggest

---

29. John G. Hartnett, "The Heavens Declare a Different Story!" *TJ* 17 (2):94–97 (2003).

that God created all the parent galaxies at the beginning of day 4, and the younger galaxies were then produced during day 4. During this period, the Crab Nebula supernova would have exploded, as would supernova SN1987a in the nearby Large Magellanic Cloud galaxy. These events were not yet visible on earth during day 4, but the images of those explosions were already on their way to earth and would arrive, in "normal" earth time, in A.D. 1054 and A.D. 1987, respectively. Most of the travel of that light, though, occurred during day 4, which, in the case of SN1987a, would have occupied about 164,000 years of astronomical time, while only one day was passing in our solar system. This would appear to solve the starlight and time problem, at least in principle.

Now the details of this scenario need further study, but it does give us a straightforward, self-consistent model of cosmic origins. Even big-bang cosmologist Professor Stephen Hawking has now added relativistic time dilation to his early big-bang universe — he now says that "time is pear shaped."[30]

Pear-shaped Time. In his 1988 book, Professor Hawking made use of "light cones" to illustrate his big-bang theory.[31] A "light cone" is the region of spacetime within your field of view as you look out into the universe (and thus back in time) that is allowed by the finite speed of light. In other words, the regions outside your light cone are those places beyond which light has not yet had time to travel to you. He illustrated his light cones as having straight sides, as follows:

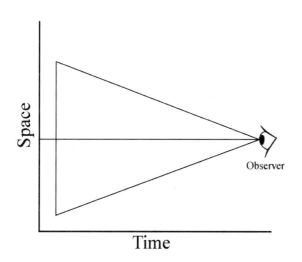

A linear-time light cone. As an observer looks out into the universe, he looks back in time, and surveys an ever-increasing volume of space. The slope of the oblique lines is the speed of light.

30. Stephen W. Hawking, *The Universe in a Nutshell* (London: Bantam Press, 2001), p. 40.
31. Stephen W. Hawking, *A Brief History of Time* (London: Bantam Press, 1988), p. 25–29.

However, in his 2001 book he changed this picture and said that time is "pear-shaped." His illustration of the "pear-shaped light cone" looked somewhat like the following:

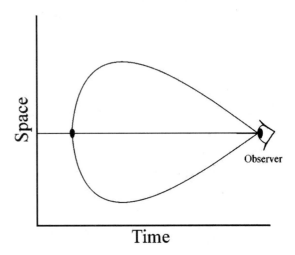

Pear shaped light cone. As an observer looks out into the universe, his field of view converges to zero at the point of the big-bang singularity. The huge gravitational field in the early universe causes time to go slowly on the horizontal line, compared with that in the outer regions.

This illustrates the exact principle we are proposing here. A clock moving on the horizontal center line just after the beginning would indicate the passing of less time than a clock that followed the "pear-shaped" outline. Hawking's diagram suggests a fairly extended time period for the non-linear region near the singularity, but when we realize that the big-bang and its inflationary successor both occurred in less than one second, we see that the time dilation zone could well fall within a single creation day. Because Hawking does not believe we are at the center of the universe (or even that there *is* a center) he did not pursue the full implications of "pear-shaped" time, but creationists do believe that we may be at, or near, the center of the universe (i.e., on the horizontal center line), so it is extremely interesting to us.

In summary, relativistic time dilation now provides creationists with a credible explanation of cosmic time scales, even though the details remain to be sorted out. An illustration of where we are up to could be drawn from the history of flight. The Wright brothers, Wilbur and Orville, were the first human beings to fly. It took them many years of trial and error, accidents and injuries, to achieve this seemingly impossible feat. Why did they persist in the face of such failure and its accompanying opposition and ridicule? Their first inspiration came from kites.[32] Kites can fly, so perhaps people can too. Then followed a detailed study of birds. Birds can fly, so perhaps people can too. We, likewise, from the experiments that demonstrate relativistic time dilation, know that it is possible to have varying time scales within the cosmos. That, at present, is all the encouragement we need to inspire us to continue our pursuit of a full-blown God-honoring cosmology.

Time Indicators in the Cosmos

We now come to the matter of the methods of "age" determination, for both the earth and the universe beyond. There are numerous processes in the cosmos that give some measure of the passage of time, but to understand their relevance we once again need to consider some of the underlying principles.

The Clock Problem

Let's imagine that in our space exploration program we came across a curious new planet, landed upon it, and proceeded to explore and study it. One worker digs up a cache of clocks — thousands of them, all ticking away merrily. Let's ignore, for the moment, the question of who put them there, and just focus on the time that they tell. Clocks tell time, don't they? Here we have lots of clocks, all telling us the time. What time would they tell? Which, if any, is telling the "right" time? How would we know the "right" time even if we did come across it?

These are not simple questions. If the universe is infinite in time and space, then there is *no* time that is the "right" time. If the universe did have a beginning, then perhaps the "right" time might be that which has elapsed since the "beginning," but who knows when the "beginning" began?

Our usual concept of "clocks" and "time" is very much more local. Earth clocks are aligned to the earth's movement on its axis (day) and around the sun (year), but our "new" planet might have rotation periods very different from earth.

How do we decide, on earth, which among our many clocks are telling the "right" time? Those that are set according to our *standard* are considered to tell the "right" time. What is our standard? Nowadays we have two standards. The traditional one — the rotation of the earth — continues as a standard because it is what we all experience every day. The actual definition of time units (the second) is now made in terms of atomic clocks (a large number of them,

---

32. Ann Lamont, "The Wright Brothers: Pioneers in the Skies," *Creation* 13(4):24–27 (1991).

many of which are housed at the U.S. Naval Observatory in Washington). The atomic clocks are periodically adjusted to match the earth's rotation; one leap second is added about every 500 days.[33] The earth is divided into 24 time zones, based on longitude, with zero at Greenwich in England, and our local clocks are set according to this system. What makes our local time the "right" time? Nothing at all. It is purely a convenient (but arbitrary) standard in what would otherwise be a continuum of "time."

The point of this little illustration is to show that we can have any number of "clocks" ticking away and telling "time," but unless we have some standard reference point it will be impossible to tell the "right" time.

Actually, *three* standard reference conditions must be fulfilled for any clock to tell the "right" time. If these conditions are not met, then we cannot be sure the clock is telling the right time. First, you need a known **starting point**. In isotope dating,[34] for example, you need to know how much isotope was present in the beginning. Since this is never known, isotope dating can never be the "absolute" dating method it is often claimed to be. Second, you need a reliable process of "**ticking**" that will measure the passing of time accurately. This is why isotope dating is so popular, because it provides an (apparently) accurate "ticking" process to mark the passing of time. However, the RATE project is producing some interesting evidence to show that accelerated nuclear decay occurred in the past. We can see from the example of the cache of clocks on our newly discovered planet that ticking alone tells us nothing about the "right" time. Third, you need to know that **nothing has interfered** with the clock since the last time it was "set" against the standard (which is the known starting conditions and the reliable "ticking" process). This again is a fundamental weakness in isotope dating — the rocks with the isotopes in them are supposed to have been sitting around for billions of years without any interference, yet interference is an ever-present and unknowable possibility. Isotope dating experts are aware of this and they readily invoke interference to explain

---

33. This adjustment is purely a result of the definition of the second; it does not imply a rapid slowing of the earth compared with the atomic clocks. The earth is slowing down through tidal friction with the moon, but the rate is insignificant at about 1.4 milliseconds per day per century.

34. Isotope dating is based on radioactive elements (such as uranium, thorium, unstable isotopes of potassium, carbon, and many more) that decay over time. By measuring the amount of the parent isotope and its daughter product, and taking into account the known rate of decay, a "time interval" can be calculated. What these "time intervals" really mean, however, is very much disputed.

anomalous results — but nobody ever knows, of course, if the "interference" actually occurred or not!

The Age of the Earth

The history of attempts to measure the age of the earth neatly illustrates these problems that we have just outlined.

Sediment clock. Until about 200 years ago, Christians generally accepted the biblical time scale for the age of the earth. Bibles of the time frequently carried Bishop Ussher's chronology, with Genesis 1 beginning in the year 4004 B.C. The first inkling of millions of years of earth history came from British geologists. They discovered that sedimentary rocks frequently showed multitudes of layers. Since such rocks often also showed evidence of having been laid down by water, they reasoned that perhaps the layers reflected flood events and sea level variations. If vast numbers of layers could be observed in the great depths (thousands of meters) of sedimentary rocks that appeared on every continent, and if significant periods had intervened between the depositions, then years beyond number were cast in stone beneath our feet. The earth must be very ancient indeed. By the mid-19th century, geologist Charles Lyell was claiming an earth history covering measureless time.

Heat clock. Lyell's measureless geological time was challenged and soundly contradicted by Lord Kelvin's meticulous physics calculations based on the second law of thermodynamics. According to the second law, if the earth was once a molten mass (i.e., the hottest such a solid body could be — perhaps because it was flung off from the whirling young sun), then it could not be infinitely old or it would have cooled down to be an entirely solid body. Volcanoes, and temperature measurements made in deep mine shafts, showed that the interior of the earth was very hot. By using such measurements, and a mathematical model of heat flow from the earth's surface, Kelvin calculated that the earth could not be more than 100 million years old. Further refinements of his calculations brought the maximum age down to only 24 million years.[35]

Salt clock. Professor John Joly, head of the Geology and Mineralogy School at Trinity College in Dublin, looked to the sea to try to mediate in the conflict between Lord Kelvin's physics and the geological ages. He calculated that all the sodium in the sea (in the form of common salt, sodium chloride)

---

35. James L. Powell, *The Mysteries of Terra Firma: The Age and Evolution of the Earth* (New York: Free Press, 2001), p. 23.

could be accounted for in 99 million years. Salt is carried into the sea by the world's rivers, but when the water evaporates from the ocean, it leaves the salt behind. Therefore, if we assume that the starting condition is zero salt, that the annual input is what we observe today, and that there has been no loss or gain in the accumulating salt, then the salt clock should be a fairly reliable chronometer and give us an approximate age for the earth. When he corrected for the presence of some original sodium, he came to an age of 89 million years.[36]

Isotope clock. The "end" of the age problem — for evolutionists — came with the discovery of radioactivity in 1896 by Henri Becquerel. Although it was not well understood to begin with, radioactivity was quickly perceived to be a source of energy, and if the earth's rocks contained their own heat source then Lord Kelvin's calculations must be wrong. In 1913, Arthur Holmes published the first book on the age of the earth using radioactivity (see isotope dating diagram below), and while much still remained to be clarified, he claimed that the most ancient rocks must be at least 1.6 billion years old, so the earth must be older than that. In 1956, Claire Patterson used isotope ratios

ISOTOPE DATING

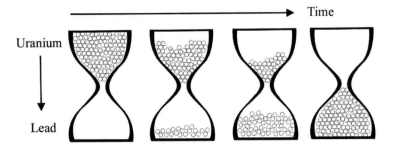

Isotope dating of rocks is based on the assumption of regular decay of a radioactive isotope such as uranium, into its daughter product, which in this case is lead. By measuring the amount of uranium and the amount of lead, and also by assuming some initial conditions and no loss or gain from outside over time, an "age" for the rock can be calculated. However, the assumptions can never be proved true, so the "age" can never be known for certain.

---

36. Ibid., p.25–26. Powell tries to explain away this embarrassingly "young" age by claiming that sodium does not remain dissolved in seawater but is removed by sea spray and by sedimentation. When all such processes are included, however, we still get a similarly "young" age — as explained later in this chapter.

in meteorites to obtain a figure of 4.55±0.07 billion years,[37] and the age of the earth has not changed since then.

Creationist Views of Earth Age Indicators

So what are creationists to make of these results? Are they irrefutable, as many evolutionists proclaim? Definitely not. While this is not the place for a detailed critique of isotope dating,[38] we can outline three of the major problems.

First, all isotope dates are interpreted within the framework of stratigraphy — the fossil record in the geological column (i.e., the layers of rock, the fossils within them, and the order in which the layers occur). If an isotope date conflicts with this framework, it is discarded or reinterpreted. This demonstrates three important points: (a) those who use isotope dating methods know how fallible they are and discard them or reinterpret them without hesitation; (b) isotope dating is therefore not the "absolute" dating method it is often claimed to be, because you never know (independently of other alleged "age" indicators) when it is giving the "right" date; and (c) most important of all is that if the dates assigned to the stratigraphic record (well before the discovery of radioactivity, and based on the assumption of slow, uniform processes for sedimentation) are wrong, then the isotope "dates" are also wrong. Creationists have pointed out that the sedimentary rocks show abundant evidence of *rapid* deposition, and say that the great flood of Noah, and its aftermath, was the source of most of that rapid deposition. Therefore, if the rocks were laid down rapidly, then the isotope ratios are not an accurate measure of time at all — they are simply reflecting an inextricable tangle of radioactive decay and geochemistry.[39]

---

37. Claire Patterson, "Age of Meteorites and the Earth," *Geochimica et Cosmochimica Acta* 10:230–237 (1956). The calculated age was first announced in 1953.

38. Comprehensive critiques are given in John Woodmorappe, *The Mythology of Modern Dating Methods* (El Cajon, CA: Institute for Creation Research, 1999), and Donald DeYoung, "Radioisotope Dating Review," in Larry Vardiman, Andrew A. Snelling, and Eugene F. Chaffin, editors, *Radioisotopes and the Age of the Earth* (El Cajon, CA: Institute for Creation Research and Creation Reseach Society, 2000), chapter 2.

39. For a comprehensive review of geochemical processes that affect isotope ratios, see Andrew A. Snelling "Geochemical Processes in the Mantle and Crust," in Larry Vardiman, Andrew A. Snelling, and Eugene F. Chaffin, editors, *Radioisotopes and the Age of the Earth* (El Cajon, CA: Institute for Creation Research and Creation Research Society, 2000), chapter 5.

Second, as pointed out earlier, isotope dating methods cannot fulfill the requirements of a good chronometer. Although the isotope "clocks" tick away at a (usually) predictable rate,[40] the original isotope composition is never known,[41] and the extent of interference can never be ascertained.[42] Only a time machine could verify the assumptions underlying isotope dating, and no one has a time machine so no one really knows. That is why evolutionists discard isotope dates so readily, because they know how fallible they are. A classic example is quoted by creationist Dr. John Morris.[43] Carbon dating is the most accurate of all isotope dating methods because it deals with short periods of historically verifiable time (i.e., a time scale of only thousands of years[44]). However, when he asked a famous archaeologist if he had sent timber samples, from a recently discovered site, for carbon-14 dating, he replied that he would never believe anything that came from a carbon-14 laboratory. He was obliged to carbon-date artifacts to keep the grant money coming in and so he always did so. If the date agreed with what he "knew" it should be historically, he would publish the result, but if not the data would simply be ignored.

A very important example of this kind of evolutionary "selection" of dates is illustrated in G. Brent Dalrymple's "authoritative" book, *The Age of the Earth*.[45] Dalrymple was, at the time of writing, one of the world's leading geochronologists. Now in the "real" isotope dating literature (i.e., the few rare

---

40. This is not always the case, and creationists have suggested (and put forward evidence for the proposition) that a period of accelerated decay occurred in the early universe. See D. Russell Humphreys, "Accelerated Nuclear Decay: A Viable Hypothesis?" in Larry Vardiman, Andrew A. Snelling, and Eugene F. Chaffin, editors, *Radioisotopes and the Age of the Earth* (El Cajon, CA: Institute for Creation Research and Creation Reseach Society, 2000), chapter 7.

41. Isochron methods are promoted as solving the initial conditions requirement, but the method can produce different results in the same rock samples. Mixing of parent materials can produce false isochrons and this may be a better explanation than "age" interpretations. See Andrew A. Snelling, footnote 39, this chapter.

42. Whenever an isotope "date" conflicts with stratigraphy, the practitioner will unhesitatingly look for other explanations in processes of interference. Thus, interference is routinely used as a tool for making the dates "fit" the evolutionary preconceptions.

43. John D. Morris, *The Young Earth* (Green Forest, AR: Master Books, 1994), p. 65. Morris is the president of the Institute for Creation Research.

44. Calibrated and carefully carried out carbon-14 dating may well be valid over the biblical time scale, but we do not accept the assumptions required to extrapolate the results, as evolutionists do, back to 50,000 years or more.

45. G. Brent Dalrymple, *The Age of the Earth*, (Stanford, CA: Stanford University Press, 1991).

papers that publish all their data[46]), the results tend to be very messy and it is not uncommon that large proportions of the data are unusable. However, in Dalrymple's book, he presents page after page of immaculate data, all pointing to the unerring conclusion that the earth, the moon, and meteorites are 4.5–4.6 billion years old. There is no sign of the "messy," "contradictory," "real" data. Everything he presents is squeaky clean and unequivocal. Anyone who is familiar with the real world of isotope dating cannot help but conclude that Dalrymple selected the data he wanted and discarded the rest — which is after all the standard practice in isotope dating.

Third, when isotope dating methods are applied to rock formations of "known" age, they can give wildly erroneous results. We will give just three examples. (1) Basalt rocks from lava flows over the top rim of the Grand Canyon were clearly laid down *after* the basalt rocks buried in among the sediments at the bottom of the canyon. There is about a mile of sedimentary layers separating the top and bottom, and evolutionists interpret this interval as representing about a billion years of geological activity. However, isotope dating suggests just the opposite. Using four different isotope methods, the rocks at the top turned out to be about 300 million years *older* than rocks at the bottom.[47] If we did not know that the rocks at the top must be younger, the isotope dates would have given us the wrong answer. (2) Lava deposits in New Zealand that were laid down in a volcanic eruption in 1954 yielded isotope dates of up to 3.5 million years.[48] If we had not seen the eruptions take place and did not know that the rocks were only half a century old, isotope dating would have given us the wrong answer. (3) Carbon dating of fossilized wood in coal at the Crinum coal mine in Queensland yielded a carbon-14 date of 37,500 years. However, the deposits the coal came from are supposedly about 30 to 47.5 million years old according to stratigraphy and other isotope methods.[49] Which isotope result is correct? Or are both wrong? If isotope dating methods can give the wrong answer on rocks from a known sequence, on rocks of observed age, or can differ by as much as a thousand-fold in the same formation, why should we trust them when used on rocks where we don't have such standards to judge them by?

---

46. See, for example, Alexander R. Williams, "Long-age Isotope Dating Short on Credibility," *TJ* 6(1):2–5 (1992).
47. Steven A. Austin, editor, *Grand Canyon: Monument to Catastrophe* (Santee, CA: Institute for Creation Research, 1994), p.120–131.
48. Andrew A. Snelling, "Radioactive 'Dating' Failure," *Creation* 22(1):18–21 (1999).
49. Andrew A. Snelling, "Conflicting 'Ages' of Tertiary Basalt and Contained Fossilised Wood, Crinum, Central Queensland, Australia," *TJ* 14(2):99–122 (2000).

Accelerated Nuclear Decay

While creationists have numerous and good reasons to reject or reinterpret the "dates" produced by conventional isotope dating methods, the isotopes themselves are associated with features that do need explanation in the short time scale of the biblical world view.

When unstable isotopes decay they can produce a number of different tangible effects, which include: (1) daughter products, (2) visible tracks and halos in surrounding rocks, (3) helium gas, and (4) heat. It can be shown in many rock types that all four products are present in amounts that indicate millions of years of decay at present decay rates. It seems unreasonable to propose that they were created in place, since many of these rocks show evidence of having been reprocessed since creation. Therefore, the RATE group is examining the idea that one or more periods of accelerated decay occurred in the past, either during creation, the Fall, and/or the Flood. This, at present, is an ad hoc assumption, but the evidence for it is mounting.

In 2000, Dr. Russell Humphreys said, "Accelerated nuclear decay is a good answer to the problem . . . the data require it, Scripture suggests it, theory allows it, and observations can test it."[50]

Two years later, after completing some crucial experimental work, Dr. Humphreys was able to say, "1.5 billion years" worth of nuclear decay took place in one or more short episodes between 4,000 and 14,000 years ago" in a suite of rock crystals they had studied.[51] The estimated age of the zircons, based on their helium retention, is not 1.5 billion years (the supposed "geological age" of the Precambrian granite from which they were taken) but 6,000 ± 2,000 years.[52]

50. D. Russell Humphreys, "Accelerated Nuclear Decay: A Viable Hypothesis?" in Larry Vardiman, Andrew A. Snelling, and Eugene F. Chaffin, editors, *Radioisotopes and the Age of the Earth* (El Cajon, CA: Institute for Creation Research and Creation Reseach Society, 2000), chapter 7.

51. D.Russell Humphreys, "Nuclear Decay: Evidence for a Young World," *Impact* No.352 (Santee, CA: Institute for Creation Research, 2002), available at www.icr.org.

52. D. Russell Humphreys, Steven A. Austin, John R. Baumgardner, and Andrew A. Snelling, *Precambrian Zircons Yield a Helium Diffusion Age of 6,000 Years*, American Geophysical Union Fall Conference, San Francisco, December, 2003, Abstract # V32C-1047, http://www.icr.org/research/misc/aguconference.html.

It is premature to draw conclusions about this work in detail at present but it is certainly showing excellent promise. Furthermore, it may turn out not to be an ad hoc assumption at all, but rather a logical consequence of creation. Dr. Humphreys explains as follows.

God upholds the universe by His word of power (Heb. 1:3), and one way He holds it together is by the four forces of physics — gravity, electromagnetism, strong and weak nuclear forces. So when God intervenes to judge the world (e.g., during the Fall, and/or the Flood), one way for Him to change the world is to change the forces that hold it together. If He changed gravity or electromagnetism, the earth and its life-forms would all be destroyed — because the earth and life crucially depend upon molecules that are held together by electromagnetism and gravity. If God changed the nuclear forces just a small amount, nuclear decay rates could increase quite dramatically and produce heat to precipitate the deformation of the earth's crust during the Flood, for example, without interrupting the molecular structures that life depends on. Humphreys argues that this may be the mechanism God has already placed within the elements to make them melt in the coming Judgment (2 Pet. 3:12). We await their further research findings with keen interest.

Evidence for a young earth. Finally we come to the evidence for a young earth. There are numerous examples, but we will give just some parallel arguments for the long-age methods already mentioned.

The layers in sedimentary rock were first used to establish the idea of millions of years. However, it is now known that layers can be produced spontaneously whenever you have fluid flowing and carrying a mixture of particle sizes.[53] In fact, many evolutionary geologists now acknowledge that rapid deposition characterizes much of the sedimentary rock record, but they still cling to the idea of millions of years by inserting long periods of time *between* the different rock formations. Morris has argued, however, that the evidence for long gaps in the record is imaginary.[54] He cites evidence such as: (a) Frequent

53. Guy Berthault, "Experiments in Stratification," *IMPACT* No.328 (El Cajon, CA: Institute for Creation Research, 2000).
54. John D. Morris, *The Young Earth* (Green Forest, AR: Master Books, 1994), chapter 8.

preservation of surface features such as ripple marks, rain drops, and animal tracks, which means that the layer below was soft when the impressions were made, and it was rapidly covered by the layer above in order to be preserved. If long periods of weathering and erosion had intervened, then these ephemeral marks would have been quickly obliterated; (b) Lack of sufficient bioturbation. Animals and plants quickly colonize fresh surfaces, particularly those in watery environments, and their burrowing activities can quickly mix up the layering patterns;[55] (c) Lack of soil. Soil can form fairly quickly (tens to hundreds of years) on exposed surfaces, so if many long periods of time (millions of years) intervened between sedimentation events, then fossil soils would be common, but they are not; (d) Undisturbed bedding planes. Frequently, totally different rock types are found lying directly on top of one another with no intervening activity, such as erosion, evident; (e) Polystrate fossils. Sometimes tree trunks protrude up through many different layers of rock. Obviously all the layers were laid down before the tree trunks had time to rot away; (f) Coal is said to form slowly in swamp forests, yet it frequently is found lying between layers which show no sign of root penetration. Recent evidence shows that rapid formation from water-transported vegetation is the best explanation for the origin of coal; (g) Deformation of multiple sedimentary layers often shows no sign of (even microscopic) cracking, which means all the layers were deposited and deformed while still wet and pliable; (h) Multilevel petrified forests were once claimed to be clear evidence of continuing forest growth over many successive deposition events, but recent evidence reveals that catastrophic deposition of the whole formation is a better explanation (tree-ring evidence indicates that the trees at all levels were growing at the same time).

While all these lines of evidence point to rapid deposition of the whole geological column, the sediment clock does not identify how long ago this occurred. A rough estimate can be gained, however, from the current rate of sediment deposition in the oceans. All the sediment at the bottom of the world's oceans can be accounted for using the current rate of input from rivers in only about 15 million years.[56] The Genesis flood would have deposited much of that

---

55. Burrowing animals buried quickly during a flood catastrophe could initiate a brief frenzy of burrowing activity, which is observed. The minimal degree of such bioturbation, even its frequent absence, between many layers belies the notion of millions of years of time.

56. Morris, *The Young Earth*, p. 90. Note that even allowing for plate tectonic activity (subduction) to "get rid of" the excess sediment does not come anywhere near compensating for this.

anyway, so the age of the oceans must be much less than that. The sediment clock, when rightly interpreted, thus destroys the foundation of the long-age evolutionary methods.

The heat clock appears to be on the verge of a revolution in creationist thinking. Lord Kelvin compared his heat flow measurements with the evolutionary assumption of a molten primordial earth, which then cooled down. However, deep drilling into the earth's crust has shown that temperature varies with *rock type*, not depth. Different rock types contain different amounts of heat. When heat flow in surface rocks is compared with their radioactivity content, there is a strong correlation — the more radioactivity, the more heat is produced, but when there is little or no radioactivity, significant heat flow still occurs. This means that present-day radioactivity is an important heat source, but it is not the only one. Baumgardner has suggested that enormously accelerated radioactive decay may have occurred on creation days 1–3, together with massive (supernatural) redistribution of materials and heat within the earth. The heat distribution we observe today, he suggests, is the aftermath of a more modest period of accelerated decay that God used as the triggering mechanism for the Genesis flood. This model is testable, and the RATE group is actively investigating it.[57]

An issue related to the heat clock is that the molten core of the earth is supposed to constitute a "dynamo" to fuel the earth's magnetic field. If the earth really were 4.6 billion years old, its magnetic field should have died away long ago. Since it is still there, evolutionists have had to invent the "dynamo" idea to support it, but rather than behaving like a field that is continuously maintained by a dynamo effect of the earth's constant rotation around its molten core, the field is *rapidly decaying* and thereby behaving much more like a freely decaying primordial (i.e., created) field.[58] With a half-life of 1,465 years (i.e., it loses half its energy every 1,465 years), it points to an age consistent with the biblical time scale, even (actually, especially) taking the many reversals into account.[59]

57. John R. Baumgardner, "Distribution of Radioactive Isotopes in the Earth," in Larry Vardiman, Andrew A. Snelling, and Eugene F. Chaffin, editors, *Radioisotopes and the Age of the Earth* (El Cajon, CA: Institute for Creation Research and Creation Reseach Society, 2000), chapter 3, citing p. 80–91.

58. Russell Humphreys, "The Earth's Magnetic Field Is Young," IMPACT No. 242 (El Cajon, CA: Institute for Creation Reseach, August 1993).

59. D. Russell Humphreys "The Earth's Magnetic Field is Still Losing Energy," *Creation Research Society Quarterly* 39(1):1–11 (2002).

The salt clock, when all the sources of input (gains) and output (losses) are accounted for, yields a maximum age for the oceans of 68 million years according to evolutionists,[60] and 62 million years according to creationists.[61] Remember this is an upper limit, not the actual age. The oldest salt lakes on earth, in Australia, yield a maximum age for their origin of just a few thousand years.[62]

The isotope clocks yield some remarkable examples that support a young age. Carbon-14 in the atmosphere, for example, has not yet reached equilibrium with its rate of formation in the upper atmosphere,[63] which points to an age for the atmosphere of much less than 30,000 years.[64] When carbon dating experts went looking for "ancient" fossil carbon with no carbon-14 in it, they could not find any. All "ancient" fossil carbons (coal, graphite, seashells, etc.) were found to contain small amounts of carbon-14. This isotope is only produced in the upper atmosphere, and it decays away with a half-life of 5,730 years (after 10 half-lives, or 57,300 years, 99.9 percent disappears). After some 50,000 to 100,000 years or so, there should be no detectable carbon-14 remaining. So instead of these fossils being hundreds of millions of years old, as evolutionists claim, the evidence is consistent with the fossil record being laid down recently during the great flood of Noah and its aftermath, when there was much less carbon-14 in the atmosphere.[65] The RATE group also analyzed carbon-14 in diamonds from Precambrian basement rocks.[66] The presence of

60. James L. Powell, *The Mysteries of Terra Firma: The Age and Evolution of the Earth* (New York: Free Press, 2001), p. 26.
61. Steven A. Austin and D. Russell Humphreys, "The Sea's Missing Salt: A Dilemma for Evolutionists," *Proceedings of the Second International Conference on Creationism*, Pittsburgh, 1990, vol. 2, p. 17–33.
62. Alexander R. Williams, "World's Oldest Salt Lakes Only a Few Thousand Years Old," *Creation* 17(2):52 (1995).
63. Carbon-14 is produced in the upper atmosphere when cosmic rays impact upon nitrogen atoms.
64. Morris, *The Young Earth*, p. 64–67.
65. John R. Baumgardner, D. Russell Humphreys, Andrew A. Snelling, and Steven A. Austin, "Measurable ^{14}C in Fossilized Organic Materials: Confirming the Young Earth Creation-Flood Model," *Proceedings of the Fifth International Conference on Creationism*, Pittsburgh, August 4–8, 2003. See also, <www.icr.org/research/icc03/pdf/RATE_ICC_Baumgardner.pdf>.
66. John R. Baumgardner, D. Russell Humphreys, Andrew A. Snelling, and Steven A. Austin, *The Enigma of the Ubiquity of C in Organic Samples Older Than 100 ka*, Poster presentation at American Geophysical Union Fall Conference, San Francisco, December 2003; pdf version at: <http://www.icr.org/research/misc/aguconference.html>.

measurable carbon-14 indicates that it is primordial (it could not have been incorporated via the usual biological mechanism), which indicates that the earth itself is only thousands, not billions of years old.

Isotopes of uranium and thorium emit alpha particles when they decay, and these alpha particles turn into helium atoms. Helium is an unreactive gas that diffuses readily through rocks, yet it can exist in anomalously high concentrations in apparently "old" zircon crystals. For example, in zircon crystals dated by the lead isotope method at 1.5 billion years old, the helium concentrations were far too high for such an old age, and were much better explained by a young-earth model with an early burst of accelerated decay.[67] Fossil radioactive halos in rocks and coal indicate that millions of years of evolutionary time can be reduced to a matter of months and less.[68]

All these ages are maxima and so are consistent with the possibility that the earth really is as "young" as the Bible indicates — about 6,000 years. They all severely contradict the 4.6 billion year evolutionary "standard," as can be seen in the scale diagram below:

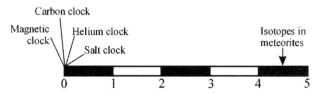

Estimates of earth age, in billions of years.

Age as myth. The invariance of the "standard" age of the earth, at 4.55±0.07 (variously quoted as 4.5 or 4.6) billion years, points to its status as a myth. The estimated age of the universe, as based on the Hubble constant,

67. D. Russell Humphreys, "Accelerated Nuclear Decay: A Viable Hypothesis?" In Larry Vardiman, Andrew A. Snelling, and Eugene F. Chaffin, editors, *Radioisotopes and the Age of the Earth* (El Cajon, CA: Institute for Creation Research and Creation Reseach Society, 2000), chapter 7, p. 344–350; D. Russell Humphreys, " Nuclear Decay: Evidence for a Young World," IMPACT No. 352 (El Cajon, CA: Institute for Creation Research, October 2002).

68. Robert V. Gentry, *Creation's Tiny Mystery* (Knoxville, TN: Earth Science Associates, 1986). See also Andrew A. Snelling, John R. Baumgardner, and Larry Vardiman, *Abundant Po radiohalos in Phanerozoic Granites and Timescale Implications for Their Formation*, Poster presentation at American Geophysical Union Fall Conference, San Francisco, December 2003; pdf version at: <http://www.icr.org/research/misc/aguconference.html>.

for example, has varied from 2 to 25 billion years since Hubble first did the calculation in 1929, and different methods continue to yield different results, which are freely published. However, the age of the earth has remained fixed and unvarying over the 50 years since it was first derived in this fashion. No one ever questions it and no one ever revises it. If someone finds rocks that are "older" than this "known age," the results are simply discarded.[69] If it were a real number, then it would be subject to revision, at least fine tuning, as new information and new methods become known. The fact that it never varies strongly suggests that it is a mythical number that people embrace by faith, not by reliable calculation.

The Age of the Solar System

The Bible indicates that the earth is young, and (indirectly) that the universe is "old," but what about the solar system? The young solar system model (YSS), as the name indicates, proposes that the solar system is young, and three important lines of evidence support this contention.

Comets. Comets are solid bodies a few kilometers in diameter, with the composition of a "dirty snowball" or iceberg, consisting of water, methane and ammonia ices together with dust. They orbit the sun in an elliptical pattern and every time they come near the sun, some of the ice is evaporated and blown away by the solar wind — thus creating the characteristic "tail" that always points away from the sun. Because of the evaporation problem, comets cannot survive too many close encounters with the sun and so have maximum lifetimes in the range of 10,000 to 100,000 years. Evolutionists therefore require a mechanism to replenish the supply of comets. They propose that a reservoir of long-period comets exists in the "Oort cloud," way out beyond the orbit of Pluto, and a reservoir of short-period comets exists in the "Kuiper belt," just outside the orbit of Pluto. The Oort cloud has never been observed, and the objects so far located in the Kuiper belt are too big to explain the observed comets.[70] The observations at this stage do not preclude the YSS "waters above" ice belt, but they would appear to rule out the vast reservoirs needed to explain the billions of years of evolutionary time. There is some observational evidence to support the hypothesis that the earth is being constantly bombarded by

---

69. Alexander R. Williams, "Flaws in Dating the Earth as Ancient," *Creation* 18(1):14 (1996).
70. Robert Newton, "The Short-period Comets 'Problem' (for Evolutionists): Have Recent 'Kuiper Belt' Discoveries Solved the Evolutionary/Long-age Dilemma?" *TJ* 16(2):15–17 (2002).

cometesimals — small icy bodies from as little as grain-size to as big as houses.[71] This also points to a young age. If the solar system were billions of years old, the sun and major planets would have sucked up all this material before now.

Planetary rings. While the beautiful rings around Saturn have been known for centuries, one great surprise of the space exploration program was the discovery that *all* the outer planets have rings. These rings consist of dust and rock debris. All the primordial dust from the early solar system has been blown away by the solar wind, according to evolutionary theory, so a more local source must have produced them. The most likely source is the gravitational disruption of moons or other bodies that wandered too close to the planet. They could also have been created by God as ephemeral signs of a young solar system. Whatever their source, however, they cannot last for billions of years, and thus could not be billions of years old.[72] Long before such a time period can elapse, gravity will do what gravity does and suck them back into the planets. While these ephemeral rings do not prove that the solar system is young, they do add to the list of objects and events that are consistent with a young age.

Planetary magnetic fields. The earth's magnetic field is supposed to be maintained by a "dynamo" in its interior, fueled by the rotation of the planet around a molten core. One of many problems with this theory is that the strength of the field is decaying at a rapid rate, while the mechanism (the rotation and the molten core) remains constant. A better explanation, as mentioned earlier, is that the magnetic field was created in place and is now freely decaying. Using this theory, Humphreys predicted the magnetic fields of all the planets, and the results upon subsequent measurement matched far better than the dynamo models.[73] Freely decaying magnetic fields in all the planets thus point to a young solar system.

The Age of the Universe

The simplest way to calculate the age of the universe, within the big-bang world view, is to wind its expansion back to zero. This is called the "Hubble

---

71. Louis A. Frank and John B. Sigwarth, of the University of Iowa, have maintained since 1986 that satellite images of the upper atmosphere show the daily "small comet" bombardment, constantly adding water vapor to the atmosphere. Other workers, however, have argued against this interpretation, saying it is simply noise in the images. See "Other Views of the Small Comets Debate" on the NASA Marshall Space Flight Center website, <http://science.nasa.gov/default.htm>.

72. Andrew A. Snelling, "Saturn's Rings: Short-Lived and Young," *TJ* 11(1):1 (1997).

73. D. Russell Humphreys, "Beyond Neptune: Voyager II Supports Creation," IMPACT No. 203 (El Cajon, CA: Institute for Creation Research, May 1990).

age" because it is the inverse of the Hubble expansion constant. The best current estimate is 15 billion years, with an uncertainty of about ±2 billion years. Astronomers also calculate the ages of star clusters by the patterns they make on the Hertzsprung-Russell diagram, using their theory of stellar evolution. These give ages of 12–15 billion years. They also use their theory of nucleogenesis and galaxy evolution to arrive at an age range of 10–15 billion years.

While we do not accept all the assumptions that underlie these figures, there is no doubt that distance alone, plus a constant speed of light, yields a light-transit time far in excess of the biblical time scale, so we do accept the idea of an "old" cosmos within its own frame of reference, but the entire universe is young in earth-clock terms.

However, there are some profound anomalies within the big-bang time scale, which turn out to be better explained by relativistic time-dilation cosmologies (e.g., our YSS model, Humphreys' white hole cosmology).

Galaxies are largely found in clusters — and clusters of clusters, called "superclusters." Some clusters contain as many as a thousand galaxies. Space is supposed to have expanded enormously since the galaxies were first formed, yet these galaxies are still grouped together. The only "glue" available to bind them together is gravity. Yet when the speeds and masses within individual galaxies are calculated, it frequently turns out that they are moving much too fast to be held together by gravity. That is, if such movements were continued for the supposed multiple billions of years that the clusters have existed, the clusters would have ceased to exist long ago. The calculated break-up time for a typical cluster is a billion years or so, far less than their presumed age.

Time dilation models *can* explain the galaxy cluster problem, as the following sequence shows: (a) God created the galaxies in clusters; (b) the light beams arriving on earth on creation day 4 would have been the first light beams to be emitted from the newly created galaxies; (c) we, today, are therefore viewing those galaxies only 6,000 years after they were created, which is very short on the galaxy "evolution" time scale, so we are seeing the galaxy clusters still in roughly the same positions as when they were created.

Let's put it another way to make sure the point is not missed. The light from those distant galaxies took billions of years of galaxy time to reach earth, but the light that arrived here on creation day 4 (of earth-time, having traveled for billions of years in galaxy-time) was the first light emitted from the newly created galaxies. So Adam and Eve would have viewed them (had they been able to see them through a modern telescope) in their created positions. We today are seeing them 6,000 years after their creation as measured by earth clocks (even though the light took billions of years as measured by galaxy clocks to get here).

Further research is needed to develop a plausible mapping of the events of creation day 4 into the time scale of the cosmos. If it turns out that the light which arrived on earth at the end of the time dilation period was not the first light emitted from the galaxy clusters (it depends on when during day 4 the bodies were created), our argument is still valid because the extra cosmic time will only be a fraction of the supposed age of the universe. There is some evidence that we are currently still seeing the day 4 creation process,[74] so the time scale of those creation events is likely to be very short compared to the supposed age of the universe.

Also, evolutionary cosmologists suppose that all the galaxies were formed early in the universe's history and hence, for example, that spiral galaxies should have wound around their centers hundreds of times by now, but only about two or three turns are ever observed.[75] This indicates a very short time in comparison to the age of the universe and a real problem for the big bangers to explain. In time-dilation models such as the YSS, we can apply the same explanation as for galaxy clusters — we are viewing the spiral galaxies only a relatively short time after their creation (even though it has taken a lot longer in cosmic time for the light to get here).

Another problem with the big-bang time scale is that the farther we look out into space, the earlier in time we are supposed to be seeing. When telescopes get big enough they should be able to see into the era before the stars formed. That is, they will eventually see the era when, according to the big-bang model, the universe was only radiation and plasma (charged particles) but no stars and galaxies. Surprisingly, however, when the Hubble Space Telescope was trained for a very long time onto an "empty" region of space, it turned out to be filled with galaxies, and a large fraction of those galaxies looked pretty much like those in our local vicinity. Moreover, using infra-red imagery from ground-based telescopes (infra-red can see things that are not visible in ordinary light), galaxies were seen that the Hubble Space Telescope could barely detect. Once again, these galaxies looked much like those nearby.[76] This should

74. John G. Hartnett, "The Heavens Declare a Different Story," *TJ* 17(2):94–97 (2003).

75. This description assumes that the spiral galaxies commenced as simple bars; they may have been created as spirals. Even then, though, the point remains valid, namely that if the spiral galaxies were as old as claimed, they should have been completely "wound up" long ago.

76. Andy McIntosh and Carl Wieland, " 'Early' Galaxies Don't Fit!" *Creation* 25(3):28–30 (2003).

not be so if the big-bang theory is correct. The most distant galaxies should be the most "primitive" and "least evolved," while the nearby ones should be the most advanced. Yet they all look much the same (actually the galaxies are very different individually, but taken as a whole they cover a similar range of the different types).

As more data comes in, the evidence becomes ever more broadly based — we now have "mature" galaxies at the earliest observable times, quasars and super-massive black holes appearing too early, and elements appearing before they are supposed to have had time to form. In the same way as before, time dilation models, including our "young solar system" one, can also explain these results. God created all the galaxies in a functional (i.e., mature) state and the light we receive from the most distant galaxies is the light that first left them just after they were created, or very close to that time. We are therefore now seeing them only 6,000 years after they first appeared. So they look pretty much the same as those nearby, which we are also viewing 6,000 years after they were created.[77]

Closer to home in our own galaxy, supernova remnants provide a time scale that defies explanation in the big-bang time frame. When a star explodes as a supernova, its remnants are scattered into space in all directions. Many of these remnants provide spectacular viewing for astronomers. Models of the physical processes involved suggest that three separate stages occur. The first stage, up to the point where a blast wave forms, emits lots of energy and endures for about 300 years. The second stage strongly emits radio waves and lasts about 120,000 years. The third stage emits little energy and lasts for 1 to 6 million years, after which it becomes no longer visible. Since it is believed that supernovae occur in our galaxy about once every 25 years on average, there should be thousands of second- and third-stage remnants if the galaxy is really billions of years old. However, only about 200 stage two remnants have been found, with no stage three remnants found at all.[78] Since the Milky Way galaxy is also a spiral galaxy, the combined testimony of its evident spirals (not wound up yet) and its missing supernova remnants powerfully supports our young-earth scenario.

---

77. Once again, depending on when during day 4 these particular ones were created, the most astronomical time that they would have "aged" in appearance would be a few million years, a minuscule period on the time scale of galactic "evolution."

78. Jonathan Sarfati, *Refuting Compromise: A Biblical and Scientific Refutation of "Progressive Creationism" (Billions of Years) as Popularized by Astronomer Hugh Ross* (Green Forest, AR: Master Books, 2004), p. 346–350.

SUMMARY OF TIME SCALES

The universe appears to be vast beyond our ability to even imagine it. We infer that the Creator made it so in order to display His majesty, omnipotence, and transcendence. Vast space would seem to demand vast time for the light to reach earth, if we accept (which we appear compelled to do) that the speed of light has remained constant. However, it is now well established that *time* is not a constant, and variable time allows for the possibility of six earth days of creation, in which vast amounts of time pass in the outer reaches of the universe while only one creation day passes on earth. We thus come to a model of the universe in which the earth (and, we suggest, the solar system) is young, but the rest of the universe is as "old" as the light-travel time suggests that it is — but only within its own reference frame. By the reference frame given in Genesis, *the entire universe is young — thousands of years old, not billions.* This model explains a wide range of age-related phenomena (that cover a wide range of time scales) better than does the big-bang model. Time dilation models need further investigation and elaboration, but they would appear to vindicate the stand of those who take God at His word and worship Him as the six-day Creator.

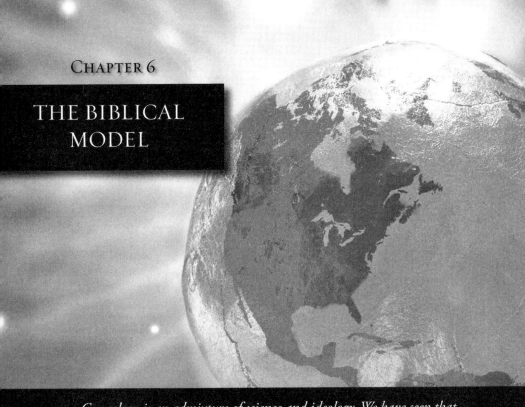

CHAPTER 6

THE BIBLICAL MODEL

Cosmology is an admixture of science and ideology. We have seen that the big-bang ideology does not provide an adequate explanatory framework for the origin of the universe nor for all of its time scales. We are therefore free to explore other ideologies. Free to rethink what the universe is — to see God's will behind it all; to read the Bible with fresh eyes and open ears, looking anew at Jesus' and Moses' attitudes toward Genesis; to consider the interplay between the method and timing of creation, and to see it as an outsider might, who only had the Bible as his guide. The main components of our biblical model are summarized in a table presented at the end.

WHAT IS THE UNIVERSE?

Our modern concept of the word "universe" has developed during a period when scientific thinking has increasingly diverged from biblical thinking. As a result, everyone today, including most Christians, has a concept of the universe that is very different to the biblical concept. Today the word "universe" means "the world as revealed to us by modern physics (e.g., through astronomy and space exploration)." It consists of energy, matter, space, and billions of years of time, and within this "natural universe," the laws of physics determine every interaction. When scientists build models of the universe it is gravity (and, to a lesser extent, the other forces of physics) that determines its fate. Christians generally adopt this description unquestioningly, and add God and the spiritual realms to it in some adjoining and/or underlying, unseen sphere.

This "natural universe" is very different to the biblical concept. The "universe" of the Bible is not just the physical world, and it is more than a physical-plus-spiritual world. It is a very special manifestation of a much greater reality — the will and character of God. God brought the universe into existence by His will, through His Word, and He upholds it even now by His will, through His word. He periodically judges it by His will, through His Word, and He will do so a final time soon, after which, by the same will and through the same Word, He will bring it to total destruction and re-creation. In the biblical world view, it is God's will (through the agency of God's Word), not gravity or any other force, that determines the nature and fate of the universe.

Physical confirmation of this world view, if we should need confirmation, is to be found in the DNA molecule. The Bible was inspired by God but written by man, and so it can be subjected to critical analysis by man — it passes the test very well, as we shall shortly see. However, the information on the DNA molecule was not written by man. Though it can in principle be read and understood by man, just like any written book, it cannot be explained by man. All our studies of information show that it cannot come into existence spontaneously, nor can any law of physics produce it,[1] but there it is. Where did it come from? No materialist can explain it. So, we find that even the materialist's universe consists not just of energy, matter, space, time and the laws of physics, it also contains *information*. Once one admits that the information on the DNA molecule is the product of intelligent design, then the evidence of design in the rest of the universe — as summarized in the anthropic principle — becomes immediately understandable as the manifestation of the same creative will.

We believe that Christians need to change their attitude toward the universe, and to help them do so, we propose a new description — the "thelein universe." The word "thelein" (pronounced "THELLain") is the New Testament Greek word frequently used for God's will.[2] The "thelein universe" is the universe in which God's will is the dominant force. As we pursue our study of

---

1. Werner Gitt, *In The Beginning Was Information* (Bielefeld, Germany: Christliche Literatur-Verbreitung, 1997).

2. "Thelein . . . denote[s] the will that commands, e.g., God's rule and purpose in creation and history." Geoffrey W. Bromily, *Theological Dictionary of the New Testament* (Grand Rapids, MI: Eerdmans, 1985), p. 319.

the thelein universe, we will discover that the key to understanding it is God's written Word. God's written Word is the key to understanding God's will, and God's will is the key to understanding the universe.

The Seven Cs of Thelein History

The Bible is the history book of the universe. As a framework for what lies ahead, the biblical world view can be conveniently summarized by "the seven Cs of thelein history," as follows:

- Creation — in the beginning God created the heavens and the earth by speaking them into existence, and He holds them in existence by His same word of power.

- Corruption — Adam and Eve disobeyed God and brought upon themselves, their offspring, and the whole universe, the Curse of decay, suffering and death.

- Catastrophe — mankind continued their rebellion against God and He brought upon them the world-destroying flood of Noah.

- Confusion — mankind continued their disobedience and refused to disperse after the Flood, so God confused their languages at the Tower of Babel and forced them to disperse, with a side effect being the formation of the "races" or different people-groups that we see today.

- Christ — the Creator was revealed to us in Jesus of Nazareth, the "seed" of Eve, through Abraham and David.

- Cross — Christ died for us, taking the penalty for our sins in himself upon the cross, so that in Him we might become the righteousness of God. In His resurrection, we see both a validation of the biblical world view and a preview of the new creation.

- Consummation — when Christ returns, this world will be destroyed and a new world will be created, where righteousness dwells, and believers shall reign with Christ forever.

Not all Christians would agree with this summary of cosmic history. We therefore need to explain how we arrived at it.

Principles of Biblical Interpretation

Theologians and Bible commentators differ in their interpretations of the Bible — especially in the foundational passages in Genesis 1–11. As we present our case, therefore, it is important that we clearly state our methods and principles of interpretation. There are three fundamental principles that we shall use:

First, is the question of **authority**. We take the authority of the Bible as supreme, since it is the Word of God: "All Scripture is God-breathed and is useful for teaching, rebuking, correcting, and training in righteousness, so that the man of God may be thoroughly equipped for every good work" (2 Tim. 3:16–17; NIV). Some people divide their thinking into non-overlapping areas of science and theology. Thus, science, they say, tells us things like the age of the earth, but the Bible tells us things like God's purpose in creation. We reject this position because Jesus said, "I have spoken to you of earthly things and you do not believe; how then will you believe if I speak of heavenly things?" (John 3:12;NIV). If we cannot trust what the Bible says about earthly things, how can we trust what it says about heavenly things? We believe that every-thing relates to everything else and there is no science/theology divide. Conse-quently, we believe that our personal integrity and spiritual stability requires an undivided mind (James 1:8). All Christian compromise positions on Genesis (gap theory, day-age theory, framework hypothesis, progressive creation, theis-tic evolution, and NOMA doctrine) arise from this mental division.

People accept the billions-of-years dating methods thinking that it is "sci-ence" and then they change the Bible to fit the long-age framework. As our previous chapter shows, all long-age dating methods are *interpretations* based on assumptions, and they yield different results if different assumptions are used. The Bible is not a scientific textbook, nor was it meant to be, but it does give us a framework for thinking about the world and interpreting scientific evidence. In particular, it tells us that man's thinking has become corrupted by lies (1 John 5:19; John 8:44) and the truth is in Christ, the Creator, alone (John 1:1–3, 14:6). If the Bible is authoritative only in part of our thinking, then the other part may not be under the lordship of Christ and may thus be subject to error.[3] Like Paul, "We demolish arguments and every pretension that sets itself up against the knowledge of God, and we take captive every thought to make it obedient to Christ" (2 Cor. 10:5). We urge others to "see to it that no one takes you captive through hollow and deceptive philosophy, which depends on human tradition and the basic principles of this world rather than on Christ" (Col. 2:8;NIV). To do this, like the Bereans, we check everything against the Scriptures (Acts 17:11).

---

3. We do not claim infallibility, of course, only that thinking which is not under the authority of the Bible is exposed to deception.

Second, we shall endeavor to **interpret the Bible within the culture of the major characters that it deals with**. The meaning of language is crucially dependent upon the culture of the people who use it, so the understanding of language needs to go hand in hand with the understanding of culture. The two persons whom we will focus on are Moses — the most important person in the Old Testament — and Jesus — the most important person in the New Testament. We will endeavor to read Genesis as Moses and Jesus would have read it. If we interpret Genesis within the culture of the modern world, we would most likely read into it some things that were not intended by the original authors, and we might miss some things that they had intended. Language is not entirely culture-bound, however, as there are many things common to all cultures (walking and talking, for example) and these can be translated across cultures without significant error. There are other things, like world views, idioms, historical references, and word usage, that are culture-bound and need to be taken into account in order to achieve correct translation of the author's intended meaning. Aside from this, however, we believe that the Scriptures were intended to be just as understandable to Moses and Jesus as they are to us. That is, they did not require modern science to tell them what the Scriptures mean. They could derive the intended meaning from the Scriptures for themselves, within their own culture.

Third, we will use **principles of interpretation that are given in the Bible itself**. These include things like:

- Reading the books of the Bible in the order they were given. Moses' readers did not have the New Testament to help them interpret Genesis, so to understand Genesis we need to read it in its own right, in the context of Moses' other writings. Jesus said that Moses' writings were authoritative in their own right (Luke 16:19–31) so we should not underrate or misrepresent their unique, stand-alone value. Having read Moses' books in their own right we can then refer to the other parts of Scripture to see what further light is shed upon them.

- Using Scripture to interpret Scripture — it was all inspired by the one Spirit so there will be an internal consistency within it (2 Tim. 3:16–17; 2 Pet. 1:19–21; John 14:26; 16:14; 1 Cor. 2:12).

- Important matters in Scripture required the testimony of two or three witnesses (Matt. 18:16; 2 Cor. 13:1; 1 Tim. 5:19; Heb. 10:28), so we will not use single "proof texts" but rather gather together a range of teachings on the subject in hand.

- We will avoid arguments based solely upon the meaning of individual words (1 Tim. 6:4; 2 Tim. 2:14). Individual words may have a range of possible meanings but the author always defines the intended meaning by the context in which the words are used. So we will read our meanings not from individual words (like "day," for example) but from the context of sentences, paragraphs, chapters, and books, within the whole framework of God's plan of redemption.

Jesus' View of Genesis

Jesus made it exceedingly clear that He viewed the whole of the Old Testament as authoritative. He staked the credibility of his own ministry upon the credibility of Moses' writings, saying, "If you believed Moses, you would believe me, for he wrote of me. But if you do not believe his writings, how will you believe my words?" (John 5:46–47). In John 10:35, He said, "Scripture cannot be broken." In the Sermon on the Mount, He said, "Do not think that I have come to abolish the Law or the Prophets. I have not come to abolish them but to fulfil them. I tell you the truth, until heaven and earth disappear, not the smallest letter, not the least stroke of a pen will by any means disappear from the Law until everything is accomplished" (Matt. 5:17–18;NIV). Jesus clearly expected the Old Testament Scriptures to be fulfilled to the letter. So much so that after the Resurrection, on the road to Emmaus, He rebuked His two companions for not sharing this attitude, saying, "How foolish you are, and how slow of heart to believe *all* that the prophets have spoken" (Luke 24:25;NIV, emphasis added). A little later he said to all of His disciples: "This is what I told you while I was still with you: *Everything* must be fulfilled that is written about me in the Law of Moses, the Prophets and the Psalms" (Luke 24:44;NIV, emphasis added). Now the Jewish Bible is divided into three parts: the first part consists of the five books of Moses, the second part consists of the books of the prophets, and the third part contains the poetic and wisdom books which begin with the Book of Psalms. So Jesus was here saying that *everything* in the *whole* of Scripture that was written about Him *"must be fulfilled."*

In regard to Genesis, Jesus quoted directly from it or alluded to it 25 times in the Gospels. On every occasion, His attitude was that the material, as written, was historical, authoritative, and definitive. For example, in Mark 10:2–8 and Matthew 19:3–8, the Pharisees came to Jesus to test Him and asked why Moses had allowed divorce. Jesus answered by quoting from both Genesis 1 and Genesis 2. He said, "For your hardness of heart [Moses] wrote you this commandment. But from the beginning of creation, 'God made them male and female.' [Gen. 1:27] 'For this reason a man shall leave his father and mother and be joined to his wife, and the two shall become one flesh.' [Gen. 2:24] So they are no longer two but one flesh."

These quotations also make clear Jesus' view on the time scale of creation. According to Jesus, the events He referred to in Genesis took place at "the beginning of creation." Now if God had used evolution (or even creation in "batches" as progressive creationists argue) over billions of years as His method of "creation," then it would have been highly inappropriate to describe this time as being "the beginning of creation" — it should more appropriately have been described as "the end of creation," because man appeared last on the geological time scale. From the perspective of a six-day creation a few thousand years ago, however, the difference between man appearing on day 6 and "the beginning" being on day 1 is so trivial that Jesus quite appropriately referred to these events as happening in "the beginning."

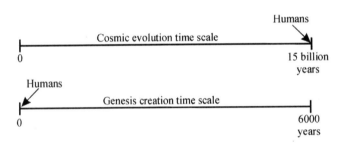

On the time scale of cosmic evolution, humans appeared at the "end," but on the Genesis time scale, humans appeared at the "beginning," as Jesus said in Matthew 19:4.

Jesus also made it clear from His references to Genesis that He considered the subsequent history of the world to have been entirely embraced within the Old Testament record. In Luke 11:47–51 and Matthew 23:34–36, He said that "the blood of all the prophets, shed from the foundation of the world, [will] be required of this generation, from the blood of Abel to the blood of Zechariah, who perished between the altar and the sanctuary." According to Jesus, "all the righteous blood shed on earth" was included in the list that began with Abel, and the list began at "the foundation of the world." Once again, He equates the origin of man (a few thousand years prior to when He was speaking) with the origin of the creation, a view that doesn't make sense if billions of years of evolutionary (or any other) history had intervened. In Mark 13:19, Jesus also equates the period of human suffering (tribulation) with the time since "the beginning of creation."

It is also clear from the rest of the New Testament that Jesus' followers were convinced by, accepted, and adopted, His attitude toward the Scriptures, starting with Genesis, including its time scale. Henry Morris[4] has listed 200 direct quotations from, or allusions to, Genesis in the New Testament, more than half of which were taken from the foundational chapters 1–11, and 63 of these (one-third) refer to the creation and Fall narratives in chapters 1–3. The general attitude in these quotations is that the material is historical, definitive, and authoritative. Adam and Eve are referred to as real people who lived in a real garden, who behaved as Genesis says they behaved and suffered the consequences that Genesis says they suffered.

According to Paul, sin entered the world by one man and death was the consequence of that sin, and thereby death spread to all men because all men have sinned (Rom. 5:12; 1 Cor. 15:21–22). Moreover, the whole creation is suffering under the curse of man's sin, as Genesis says, and the redemption of mankind will also mean the liberation of the whole creation from the Curse (Rom. 8:18–23). Paul's cosmic time scale also has man at "the beginning" — men have seen the Creator's eternal power and divine nature "ever since the creation of the world . . . so they are without excuse" (Rom. 1:20). According to Peter, the world was destroyed in a real flood and only eight people survived on the ark (1 Pet. 3:18–20; 2 Pet. 3:3–13). This event constitutes a type of the judgment to come (2 Pet. 3:5–7). Moreover, in 2 Peter 3:4, he equates early human history with "the beginning of the creation."

The list of the great heroes of faith given in Hebrews 11 begins with Abel (Cain is also mentioned), Enoch, and Noah. They are treated as being as real as Gideon, Samson, David, Samuel, and Abraham, who is, of course, the greatest of the patriarchs, being mentioned or alluded to no less than 58 times in the New Testament.

Now it is true that some passages in the New Testament do treat the material in Genesis allegorically. For example, Galatians 4:24 treats the story of Hagar and Sarah as an allegory, but the context clearly shows that Paul is *using* the story as an allegory, not that he believed the original story was itself allegorical. He goes on to say, "Now Hagar is Mount Sinai in Arabia; she corresponds to the present Jerusalem." He compares a real woman with a real mountain and a real city — the characters and places are simply *used* by Paul as an allegorical teaching aid.

---

4. Henry M. Morris, *The Genesis Record* (Grand Rapids, MI: Baker Book House, 1976), appendix 4.

Why the Intensity?

The very intensity of Jesus' commitment to the Scriptures — which He clearly communicated to, and duplicated in, His followers — should prompt us to ask why? Why was Jesus *so committed* to the Scriptures?

We will deal with this question in more detail in appendix B on theological issues, but for the moment, the short answer is that the *honor* of God is inextricably tied up with the fulfillment of His Word. God is "a man of his word" and it is a matter of honor that He keeps His word. In Psalm 138:2, the Psalmist says of God, "You have exalted above all things your *name* and your *word*" (NIV).[5] In Isaiah 55:10–11, God says, "For as the rain and the snow come down from heaven, and return not thither but water the earth, making it bring forth and sprout, giving seed to the sower and bread to the eater, so shall my *word* be that goes forth from my mouth; it shall not return to me empty, but it shall accomplish that which I purpose, and prosper in the thing for which I sent it." In Isaiah 44–48 God repeatedly says things like, "I am God, and there is no other; I am God, and there is none like me, declaring the end from the beginning and from ancient times things not yet done, saying, 'My counsel shall stand, and I will accomplish all my purpose . . . I have spoken, and I will bring it to pass; I have purposed, and I will do it.' " (Isa. 46:9–11). In Revelation 10:6–7 these words are dramatically fulfilled when the mighty angel who stands on land and sea announces, "There will be no more delay! . . . the mystery of God will be accomplished, just as he announced to his servants the prophets." God will do what He said He will do. His honor and glory depend upon it. That is why Jesus was so committed to the Scriptures.

Jesus' commitment was not restricted to the Old Testament. He made it clear that an essential condition of Christian discipleship was not just to believe the (Old Testament) Scriptures, but to believe what *He* said, "If any man would come after me, let him deny himself and take up his cross daily and follow me. For whoever would save his life will lose it; and whoever loses his life for my sake, he will save it. For what does it profit a man if he gains the whole world and loses his soul? For whoever is ashamed of me *and of my words,* of him will the Son of man be ashamed when he comes in his glory and the glory of the Father and of the holy angels" (Luke 9:23–25, emphasis added). If we belong to Jesus, clearly we must honor what He says. Is this just because Jesus is the boss and we must do what He says? Certainly not. The words of Jesus are

---

5. The KJV translates this as "thou hast magnified thy word above all thy name" but the word order and the larger context favors the NIV, quoted here.

far more than just authoritative, wise, and good advice; they are words of life (John 6:68; Matt. 4:4) that uphold the universe (Heb. 1:3) and stand forever — "Heaven and earth will pass away, but my words will not pass away" (Matt. 24:35; Mark 13:31; Luke 21:33).

MOSES' VIEW OF GENESIS

The traditional Jewish view is that Moses wrote the first five books of the Bible, which together are called the Pentateuch (from the Greek, meaning "five scrolls") sometime between 1500 and 1400 B.C. Higher critics have pulled the Pentateuch to pieces and would have us believe that it was the work of four separate authors/editors (called J, E, D and P) and that it was not written down until hundreds of years after the time of Moses. They also claim that the task was not completed until after the return from the Babylonian exile in the 6th and 5th centuries B.C.

A fundamental answer to this challenge is that the Pentateuch itself establishes a tradition of written history/Scripture from the very earliest times. Genesis 5:1 says, "This is the book of the generations of Adam" — Adam wrote down his family history. God commanded Moses to write down what He said in a book (Exod. 24:4), which Moses read to the people (Exod. 24:7). God then made repeated references to what had been written in the book (seven times in Deuteronomy) and Moses commanded that the book should be kept alongside the ark of the covenant because, "I know how rebellious and stubborn you are; behold, while I am yet alive with you, today you have been rebellious against the LORD; how much more after my death!" (Deut. 31:27).

Many other lines of evidence now contradict the views of the higher critics, of which the following four are examples. (1) Recent linguistic and historical research has shown that the two separate manuscript traditions — the Masoretic text and the Samaritan Pentateuch — point to the existence of a unified original source *prior to* the Babylonian exile. (2) The favorite starting point for higher critics is to point out that there are two separate and quite different creation accounts in Genesis 1 and Genesis 2, therefore we must conclude that there were at least two different authors. We certainly agree, but one only needs to examine the context to see who those authors were. Genesis 1 is written from God's perspective (and no one else was around for the first five days anyway),[6] while Genesis 2 is written from man's perspective — obviously

---

6. What we are suggesting is that God was the author of the narrative, not necessarily the one who wrote it down.

Adam, since he is the person in the story! (3) Analysis of Genesis shows it has a structure consistent with it being compiled from archival material by a single editor/compiler. (4) The higher critics based their theory on evolution and considered the earliest stories to have come from "primitive" oral traditions. Archaeological finds are continually revealing sophisticated technology, including writing, at earlier and earlier times. We therefore see no good reason to doubt the traditional view, especially in the light of Jesus' *total and unreserved commitment* to it.

There are certainly editorial additions to the writings of Moses. He could not have written the story of his own death, for example (in Deut. 34), but we need only look as far as Joshua, his successor, to locate that source. Also, Moses did not live through the events of Genesis, and he could well have used family histories handed down from the earlier patriarchs. Indeed, when we look at the structure of Genesis we find that it consists of a compilation of family histories, each being named for a particular person and identified by the Hebrew word *toledoth* ("these are the generations of . . ."). Henry Morris identified nine separate compilations: heavens and earth (probably God's revelation to Adam, since Adam did not appear until day 6), 1:1–2:4; Adam, 2:4b–5:1; Noah 5:1b–6:9; the sons of Noah, 6:9b–10:1; Shem, 10:1b–11:10; Terah, 11:10b–11:27; Isaac 11:27b–25:19; Jacob, 25:19b–37:2; and the sons of Jacob, 37:b–Exodus 1:1.[7]

There are some obvious later insertions in Genesis. For example, in Genesis 14:14 Abram is said to have pursued Lot's captors as far as Dan, but the name "Dan" was not given until after the Danite tribe captured the city at the time of Joshua (Josh. 19:47), but such amendments could have been inserted by later copyists to make the place name more recognizable. On return from the exile, for example, Ezra, the learned priest and teacher, was charged with the duty of teaching the Law to the Israelites (Ezra 7). This involved translating the Hebrew into Aramaic, the language of the returning exiles. Just as Bible translators today use modern language and idioms to reach modern audiences, we can reasonably suppose that Ezra used similar methods to make the text understandable to his audience. Jewish tradition identifies Ezra as having consolidated the whole collection of Jewish sacred books, but this in no way casts doubt upon their origin or original authorship.

Despite the length of the history recorded in Genesis, we do not need to imagine a cumbersome and error-prone process of transmission in "primitive" societies over thousands of years. As we have already noted, Genesis 5:1

---

7. Morris, *The Genesis Record*, p. 26–30.

indicates that Adam wrote down his family history, and there are centuries of overlap in the lives of the patriarchs during which transmission could have taken place.[8] Noah's father, Lamech, and his grandfather, Methuselah, lived for many years during the latter part of Adam's lifetime, so Noah could have had living witness testimony to accompany the written records that he no doubt took with him on the ark. Noah's son Shem would have still been alive in Abraham's time, so it is not unreasonable to believe that Abraham himself could have had living witness testimony of the great events of the Flood. So, in fact, the whole sweep of history from Adam to Abraham could have been communicated by as few as four people: Adam, Lamech, Shem, and Abraham. Of course, the person who transmits a family history need not be the author of it. We ourselves pass on to our children segments of our family histories that have been written by others.[9]

So how did Moses view Genesis? The central event of the Pentateuch is the appearance of Yahweh at Mount Sinai. To make that event understandable, Moses needed to write the history of Yahweh's dealings with His people, so they could properly understand who it was that had appeared to them. Genesis provides that historical background. It describes (a) who Yahweh is and (b) what His relationship is with the Israelites.

Who Is Yahweh?

The first thing that Genesis tells us about Yahweh is that He is the Creator of the universe (Gen. 1:1). The word used in this verse is not "Yahweh" (or "Jehovah," the translation used in the KJV) but "Elohim" which is simply the common noun in Hebrew for "God." Interestingly, it is in the plural form, which suggests that the Trinitarian concept of God can be seen here, right from the beginning. This is further confirmed in verse 26 (and 3:22) when God says "Let *us* make man in our image, after *our* likeness." However, the main thrust of Genesis 1:1 is that the person(s) identified as "Elohim" is (are) defined as being the Creator of the universe.

Then in 2:4 we are introduced to Yahweh. It says, "In the day that the LORD God made the earth and the heavens." The words "LORD God" are the English translation of the Hebrew "Yahweh Elohim." In Exodus 3:14 we are told that "Yahweh" is the personal name of the God of Israel. It means "I am" and signifies that He is "the eternally self-existing one." In Jewish tradition, the

---

8. Russell Grigg, "Meeting the Ancestors," *Creation* 25(2):13–15 (2003).

9. Obviously, in the case of the Bible, the inspiration of the Holy Spirit ensured that the transmission and compilation of these histories was originally free of error.

word "Yahweh" is not spoken or translated as such, but is replaced with the Hebrew word "Adonai," which simply means "lord." They were afraid that the sacred name might be taken in vain, thus breaking the third commandment (Exod. 20:7). In English translations it is usually written in small capitals as "LORD" to indicate that the original word was "Yahweh," to distinguish it from places where the word "Adonai" simply means "lord" or "Lord" in the more general sense.

So Genesis tells us that Yahweh, the God of Israel, is the Creator of the universe. This simple statement is so familiar to Christians that we easily overlook the enormous significance that it had for someone living in the time of Moses. To understand this cultural context, we need to look at what we might call the "spiritual geography" of the Bible.

Genesis tells us that God created mankind to have dominion over the creation (Gen. 1:26–28). However, when Adam and Eve chose to believe (and obey) what Satan said rather than what God said (Gen. 3:1–7), they ceded their dominion to Satan (Rom. 6:16). Therefore, Jesus called Satan "the ruler of this world" (John 12:31, 14:30, 16:11). John said that the whole world (except for those in Christ) is under the power of the evil one (1 John 5:19). So, all nations are ruled by Satan and his demons — the "principalities and powers, the world rulers of this present darkness, and the spiritual hosts of wickedness in the heavenly places" that Paul spoke about (Eph. 3:10, 6:12; Col. 1:16, 2:15). The chief characteristic of their rule is deception — Jesus said that Satan is a liar and the father of lies (John 8:44).

Accordingly, the gods of the nations in the time of ancient Israel were demon gods. The Bible describes them in terms such as "Ashtoreth the vile goddess of the Sidonians, for Chemosh the vile god of Moab, and . . . Molech, the detestable god of the people of Ammon" (2 Kings 23:13;NIV). In a world of nations committed to demon gods, it was a matter of the most extraordinary significance that the people of Israel should have been chosen by the Creator of the universe to be His special people. In Deuteronomy 7:6 we read, "For you are a people holy to the LORD your God; the LORD your God has chosen you to be a people for his own possession, out of all the peoples that are on the face of the earth." If Yahweh had *not* chosen them, then they would have shared the fate of the other nations — slaves to the rule of demon gods.

Who Are the Israelites?

The Israelites were a light in a dark world. Not because they were in any way superior to any other peoples, but simply because God chose them to be the bearers of His plan of salvation. In the nation of Israel we do not see a race of super humans leading the world out of darkness and into the light. What we do see is the Creator God being totally committed to those He loves.

The name "Israel" was given by God to the patriarch Jacob. Jacob was the grandson of Abraham and he became the father of the 12 tribes of Israel. God changed his name following a personal encounter when Jacob "wrestled with God" and would not let him go until God blessed him (Gen. 32:24–30). The intended meaning of the new name "Israel" is given as "for you have struggled with God and with men and have prevailed" (Gen. 32:28; NKJV).

The Israelites were also called "Hebrews" (Exod. 1:15–19) and they spoke the Hebrew language. This name is derived from their ancestor Eber, the great-great-grandson of Noah, who outlived all his descendants down to the time of Abraham. In addition, they (along with Arabs) are sometimes called "Semites," a name derived from their ancestor Shem, one of the three sons of Noah.

In later times, King Solomon's sin of idolatry caused the kingdom of Israel to be divided in two. The northern kingdom (called "Israel") was eventually destroyed, and the southern kingdom (called "Judah") was sent into exile. On return from exile, people from all 12 tribes became known as "Jews" (after Judah), and so it continued into New Testament times and down to our own day.

So why did God choose the Israelites? To answer this question we need to go back to the beginning.

The Garden of Eden, the Fall, and God's Great Plan of Redemption

God created man to be like himself (Gen. 1:26–27). We can reasonably infer that this meant God desired fellowship with man, in a similar way that Adam found fellowship with Eve (he did not find it among the animals, only with another like himself — Gen. 2:18–23). This is confirmed by the Great Commandment, to love God with all our heart, soul, mind, and strength (Mark 12:28–30). We can also reasonably infer that God wanted this relationship to endure, and thus man would live forever like God does — there would be no death. Biology affirms the idea that we could (theoretically) live forever; our cells have the ability to repair and replace themselves. The only reason we die of old age (even if we had perfect nutrition and were able to avoid all injury and disease) is that there appears to be a genetic program that limits the number of times our cells can divide to replace those that are damaged or worn — presumably a result of the Curse (which we will discuss shortly). Genesis also implies that our physical immortality depended upon continuing access to the tree of life (Gen. 3:22–24). The tree of life will also reappear in the new creation (Rev. 22:1–2), where we will remain alive for eternity.

God gave Adam and Eve everything they needed — food, companionship, and fruitful labor in their care of the Garden. They had no immediate need for clothing or shelter as the environment was perfect and their moral character unspoiled. God gave them just *one* rule — they were not to eat the fruit of the tree of the knowledge of good and evil.

Why did God do that? We suggest that the forbidding of the fruit was a token of dominion. If Adam and Eve had kept the one rule, they would have lived in obedient submission as creatures in a right relationship with their Creator. In breaking the rule, however, they chose to reject God's dominion so they could decide "good" and "evil" for themselves and become "gods" by their own authority (Gen. 3:5, 22).

The penalty for Adam and Eve's disobedience was immediate death. ". . . in the day that you eat of it you shall die" (Gen. 2:17). However, Adam lived for hundreds of years after the Fall and died when he was 930 (Gen. 5:5). Some Bible commentators therefore interpret this to mean that the "death" referred to was spiritual death (spiritual separation from God). This may be so, but in fact on that day they did begin to die physically, as well. The Hebrew is literally translated, "Dying, you shall die."

There seems to be something much more fundamental here that comes right from the heart of God. Throughout the Bible we see God being merciful to sinners and giving them time to repent. On rare occasions, sin was judged with immediate death. For example, in Leviticus 10:1–2, two of Aaron's sons offered "strange fire" to Yahweh that he had not authorized, "and fire came forth from the presence of the LORD and devoured them." Ananias and Sapphira fell down dead at the words of the apostle Peter as a result of their deception in Acts 5:1–11. In the vast majority of cases, however (considering that *everyone* who has ever lived is a sinner), God is merciful toward sinners and gives them time to repent. Paul urged his readers not to take God's kindness, forbearance, and patience for granted, as it was intended to lead them to repentance (Rom. 2:4). Peter went even further and said, "The Lord is not slow about his promise as some count slowness, but is forbearing toward you, not wishing that *any* should perish, but that *all* should reach repentance" (2 Pet. 3:9, emphasis added). In Revelation 6:10, the martyrs cry out to God asking how long until the Judgment comes, and they are told to rest a little longer, until the number of their fellow servants and their brethren should be complete, who were to be killed as they themselves had been. Then in Revelation

10:6, the mighty angel standing on land and sea announces the dreaded words "There will be no more delay" (NIV). Judgment will be delayed no longer.

So, following this line of argument, we suggest that one reason why Adam and Eve did not die physically on the day that they sinned is that God began His plan of redemption by *delaying the judgment to give them time to repent.*[10]

The next thing that God did was to allow Adam and Eve to experience *some* of the consequences of their actions — not enough to kill them, but just enough to give them *reason* to repent. This is called "the Curse," and is outlined in Genesis 3:14–19. If God had not done this, and had allowed them to continue their idyllic life in the Garden, they would have continued in their rebellion, thinking that sin was of no consequence. The Curse made sure that the time during which God was waiting for them to repent would be filled with reminders of their fallen condition.

Some may think that the Curse is not a very "nice" idea, but those who understand the horror of sin and its inevitable consequences — eternal separation from God, who cannot look upon sin due to His holy nature — are not so inclined. One Psalmist who obviously understood this declared: "Before I was afflicted I went astray; but now I keep thy word. Thou art good and doest good; teach me thy statutes. . . . It is good for me that I was afflicted, that I might learn thy statutes" (Ps. 119:67–71). So, we suggest that in delaying the judgment, God gave them *time* to repent, and in imposing the Curse, he gave them *reason* to repent.

We are not told the exact mechanism of the Curse, but we can infer the essential elements of it. Hebrews 1:3 says that Jesus *upholds* the universe with His Word of power. We can imagine that in the original perfect creation, part of its perfection lay in its perfect design and construction, but an important part of its ongoing perfection must have been the perfect *upholding* provided by the powerful Word of God. A post-Fall example would be the experience of Shadrach, Meshach, and Abednego in the fiery furnace (Dan. 3). Because God was with them, they came through the fire without even the smell of burning upon them — not a single hair was singed! In a perfectly upheld universe, there would likewise be no injury, accidents, sickness, or mutations.

---

10. This line of argument is derived from the general principles outlined here, not from the specific case of Adam and Eve; we are not given enough detail in their case to know how much time was involved.

In the resurrection of Jesus we see the perfect upholding in His glorified body. He had paid the penalty for sin, so He was no longer subject to the Curse, and the bones and sinews, heart, blood, flesh, and skin were restored, renewed, and glorified[11] into the state that He enjoyed before the incarnation (John 17:5 — except now, of course, he had a glorified material body as well). We suggest that by withdrawing just a small amount of His upholding power, God has given mankind a small taste of what life without Him is like — injury, accidents, illness, and mutations.[12] Indeed, it is quite possible that in order for man to die, God *had* to withdraw some of His upholding power. So the Curse may in fact be a necessary consequence of the death penalty. Life without God altogether would be absolute hell, but life under the Curse works well most of the time, yet it is seasoned with just enough suffering to remind us of our fallen condition and our continuing need to repent and depend upon God.

Some people may be shocked by the idea that God causes suffering. How can this be when the major part of Jesus' ministry was devoted to the alleviation of suffering? This apparent paradox is easily resolved. While God may be the immediate cause (that is, He has arranged things so that we *will* suffer) He is not the ultimate cause. The ultimate cause of our suffering is sin — our own sin, and the sin of others. The reason that God causes us to suffer is that He loves us and wants to restore us to himself eternally. God is not at all reticent about claiming responsibility for our suffering, so neither should we be reticent about attributing it to Him. When He pronounced the Curse in Genesis 3:15–16, He said, "I will" twice, thus taking full responsibility for their resulting suffering. Job suffered greatly at the hands of the devil, yet he never attributed any of it to the devil, he attributed all of it to God — and God commended him for it (Job 42:7–8). In Exodus 4:11, God says, "Who makes [man] deaf or mute? Who gives him sight or makes him blind? Is it not I the Lord?" (NIV). Exodus 15:26; 21:13, and Isaiah 45:7 reaffirm this theme, and in Leviticus 26, Deuteronomy 28, and Amos 4:6–11 God links His imposition of suffering with His larger purpose of man's repentance. Earthly suffering, in its extremes,[13] can

---

11. Jesus' resurrected body still retained the scars of his crucifixion; Revelation 5:6 also describes Christ as bearing the marks of having been slain. In recalling His suffering on our behalf, we suggest these marks are a part of His eternal glory.

12. The immediate effects of the Curse suggest that some active redesign of the biological world took place as well; the serpent would now crawl upon its belly, thorns and thistles appeared in the plant kingdom, the earth was to become less productive, and childbirth would involve more pain (Gen. 3:14–19).

13. See, for example, Ken Ham and Carl Wieland, *Walking Through Shadows* (Green Forest, AR: Master Books, 2002).

be horrific, beyond all imagining, yet the conclusion we come to here is that God would rather us suffer terrible things for a short time in His comforting presence (i.e., by faith), than to suffer eternally, separated from Him.

The next thing that God did, in His great plan of redemption, was to exile Adam and Eve from the Garden so that they would not eat from the tree of life and their bodies continue to live forever while their souls remained in alienation (Gen. 3:22–24). The result of this exile was that without the divine nourishment of the tree of life, their bodies began to deteriorate and eventually die. This, again, may not appear to be a very "nice" solution to the problem, but it highlights how horrendous sin is, and how awful its consequences. Death was designed by a loving Creator to bring sin and its appalling consequences to an end.[14]

The final thing that God did, which lies right at the very heart of His plan of redemption, was *to provide a substitute to die in our place* (Isa. 53:4–6; 2 Cor. 5:21). We see the beginnings of this in the Garden. God covered Adam and Eve's nakedness (a sight now corrupted by their guilt, and therefore a symbol of guilt) with "garments of skin" which *God himself made* (Gen. 3:21). The "skin" referred to is animal skin, so at least one animal must have been slain to provide the covering. God did not need to kill an animal to clothe them — He could have woven linen garments using fiber from the flax plant. Why did God kill an animal? Surely it was to illustrate, in the most graphic manner possible, the horrific consequences of sin. It was a visual aid to show Adam and Eve that the consequence of sin is death. This theme is richly developed in Exodus where *daily* animal sacrifice at the tabernacle was instituted as the formal acknowledgment that forgiveness of sin was an essential prerequisite for Israel's enjoyment of their intimate personal relationship with God (Exod. 29:38–46).

While animal sacrifice could provide a "covering" for man's sin (as the skin clothing did), it could never *take away* the sin (Heb. 10:4). It was only meant to be a *reminder* of the terrible consequences of sin, and to be a *symbol* of the amazing love and compassion of their Savior (Heb. 10:1). The real sacrifice was to be God himself. "God so loved the world that he gave his only Son that whoever believes in him should not perish but have eternal life" (John 3:16). "God made him who had no sin to be sin for us, so that in him we might become the righteousness of God" (2 Cor. 5:21;NIV). "Without the shedding of

---

14. Death is referred to as "the last enemy" in 1 Corinthians 15:26, but in this context it is a metaphor for sin and its consequences; death is the final obstacle — overcome by Christ — to the liberation of humanity from the Curse of sin.

blood there is no forgiveness" (Heb. 9:22). But Christ did not enter the Most Holy Place by the blood of animals — He entered by His own blood, shed on our behalf (Heb. 9:12). The innocent one died in the place of the guilty.

Now these things are very familiar to Christians. Too familiar perhaps. Let's imagine an entirely different salvation scenario. Let's imagine that Jesus arrived on earth in a spaceship (or perhaps a time machine) and died on a cross for the sins of the world. What would have been the outcome? Well, no one would have had a clue what He was doing. No one could possibly have ever understood the significance of it.

This illustrates the crucial importance of culture. To make sure that we understood what He was doing, God created a *context* within which Christ could carry out His work of atonement. God created a language, a people, a culture, a history, a sacrificial system, and a written scriptural tradition, so that we could understand who He was, where He came from, what He did, why He did it, and how we can benefit from it.

To accomplish all this, God chose a man, Abraham, sent him to the land He had chosen, and made him the father of a nation with all the characteristics listed above. The key promise to Abraham is Genesis 12:1–3: God would (a) bless him, (b) make him a blessing to others, and (c) through him all people on earth would be blessed. When Jesus came, born of Mary, as a descendant of Abraham, He grew up as a Jew, in the context of the law of Moses and their divine national history. When He then went on to fulfill God's promise to Abraham, through fulfilling the requirements of the law of Moses (Matt. 5:17; Rom. 10:1–4; Gal. 3:21–29), we today can read about it and understand who He was, where He came from, what He did, why He did it, and how we can benefit from it.

That is a further reason why the Scriptures were *so important* to Jesus, because they explained who He was and what He was doing. A critic of Christianity once said that we don't really know what Jesus believed because He never wrote anything down, but we can see from the line of reasoning presented here that we know *exactly* what Jesus believed — He did not need to write it down because it was already written down in the Jewish Scriptures.

Now we are not suggesting that Moses understood all of this. However, by setting it in this context we can see *how essential all the pieces are to the puzzle*, especially the foundational pieces in Genesis. Genesis is the foundational history for the person and work of Christ. It is not meant to be poetry or wisdom or prophecy. It *contains* poetry (a handful of lines only), wisdom, and prophecy, but it is fundamentally a historical account of who Yahweh is and who the Hebrew people are. Moses would have understood the importance of this history for understanding his part in God's plan — the giving of the Law at Mount Sinai. That, in turn, provides the foundation for everything else in the Bible. When Jesus said in John 5:46, *"If you believed Moses, you would believe me, for he wrote of me"* it was not just a throw-away line — He was there claiming to *be* the God whom Moses wrote about, and He was affirming that *the writings of Moses, beginning with Genesis, formed the foundation for His incarnation and atonement.*

THE SIX DAYS OF GENESIS CREATION

While "cosmology" means the study of the universe in general, the word "cosmogony" is the technical term for the study of the origin of the universe. Because it is such an important issue, Genesis gives us a detailed statement of the biblical cosmogony, and because it forms the foundation for everything else, it comes before everything else, *at the beginning.*

"In the beginning God created the heavens and the earth" (Gen. 1:1). This majestic statement performs two functions in the narrative. First, it provides a summary statement of all God's work of creation. The "heavens and the earth" in this sense refers to the whole universe. Who created the universe? God created it. When did He create it? In the beginning. Before that, there was no time, no space, no matter. God created the universe *ex nihilo* (from nothing), by simply calling it into existence (Heb. 11:3; Ps. 33:6, 9).

Some scholars have argued that this verse is a subordinate clause to verses 2 and 3, where the first act of creation is "let there be light." According to this reading, the unformed earth already existed when God began the work described here, and thus there is room for an ancient cosmos, and/or events such as the fall of Satan and the geological ages. Grammatically, however, the evidence favors the idea of an absolute beginning of all things. Other words could have been chosen to create a subordinate clause, but the word for "beginning" used here is related to the word for "end," and thus the two ideas stand in counterpoint.[15] This conclusion is confirmed by the Fourth Commandment in Exodus 20:8–11 where the Israelites were commanded to do *all* their work in six days, because in six days God "made heaven and earth, the sea, and *all* that is in them." The New Testament adds no less than 24 references to "the beginning" or "the foundation of the world," where the

---

15. John H. Sailhamer, "Genesis," in Frank E. Gaebelein, editor, *The Expositors Bible Commentary*, Vol.2 (Grand Rapids, MI: Zondervan, 1990), p. 21.

context implies the originating events within the biblical world view (e.g., Mark 10:6; Rom. 1:20; etc.). All things in heaven and on earth were created in Christ (Col. 1:16; John 1:3), and since He calls into existence things that do not exist (Rom. 4:17) there is clearly no room for anything other than what He called into existence. Scientific evidence supports the idea of an absolute beginning also, because time, space, and matter form a continuum — when space and substance come into existence, so does time (see box below).

The second function of this statement within the narrative is to specify the

---

The One-Particle Universe

Imagine a universe consisting of an unbounded space in which there is just one object, say, a spherical particle. How big is this particle? Well, we cannot measure its size because we have no standard of length, width, or height to compare it with. What is the particle's mass? Again, we don't know because we have no standard of mass to compare it with. Is the particle moving? Well, we cannot tell, because there is no other object to compare movement with. Is it rotating? No, we cannot tell that either, and for the same reasons. Can we measure time in a one-particle universe? Not as long as our particle endures (which could be "forever," but who knows?).

Let us now add another particle, and see what happens. Presto! We have a measure of length — the distance between the two objects. We can now measure the length, width, and height of both particles (and of the space they occupy) in terms of the distance between the two. Mass? Yes, we can have the particles collide; the one with the larger mass will be least deflected by the impact. Motion? Yes, a sequence of measurements of the distance between the particles will reveal whether they are moving farther apart or closer together. Rotation? Yes, any spin will now become obvious in terms of the relative location of the other particle. Time? Yes, any movement of the particles, relative to one another, will provide a measure of the passing of time.

This imaginary universe is overly simplistic, of course (it assumes an observer able to manipulate particles and make measurements) but it does illustrate the physical integrity of Genesis 1:1. Space, time, and mass are inextricably related, and none can exist without the other. The Bible thus correctly portrays God as bringing them all into existence at the same time, "in the beginning."

initial acts of creation. We know that verse 1 does not stand alone but is linked to verse 2 via a *waw* disjunctive in the Hebrew. This indicates a parenthetic statement describing the earth when it was created — formless and empty; it does *not* indicate a later judgment where it *became* this way. Then the rest of Genesis 1 is a series of linked statements starting with a *waw* consecutive, typical of a historical narrative sequence of events. It is not a series of poetic reflections, since poetry in Hebrew has quite a different structure. God's first act of creation was to create the earth and the heavens (i.e., the space beyond the earth). The next part describes the state of the earth at that point in the sequence.

We can also infer here that since the heavenly bodies (sun, moon, stars — and today we would add the galaxies) were not created until day 4, the "heavens" were created empty to begin with. Having a universe of empty space — that is subsequently filled — is an important foundational concept in a cosmological model. It differs from the big-bang model, in which time and space begin from an infinitesimal point and expand conjointly — it does not expand "into" anything because space itself is created only as the cosmos expands. If space beyond earth was indeed created empty, then it could have a definable temperature, that which we now measure as the Cosmic Microwave Background Radiation (CMBR).[16]

In the "gap theory," which attempts to fit the geological ages into Genesis, verse 1 is said to refer to an initial creation that was corrupted and destroyed by Satan's rebellion and then verse 2 refers to a second work of creation. The geological column, in this view, resulted from the destruction of the first creation. There are numerous objections to this view, both theological and scientific.[17]

"The earth was without form and void" (Gen. 1:2). The "and" at the beginning of this verse is deleted in some translations. This is unfortunate because it loses the power of the narrative sequence. Verse 1 tells us that God created the earth and verse 2 tells us that its condition was "without form and void." Gap theorists suggest that the earth *became* formless and void as a result of Satan's rebellion, but the grammar and context favor "was." "Without form and void"

---

16. Sir Arthur Eddington, in the final chapter, "Diffuse Matter in Space," in his book *The Internal Constitution of the Stars* (New York: Dover Publications, 1926), p.371, estimated the temperature of interstellar space to be about 3 K. The measured value today is 2.7 K.

17. Henry M. Morris, *The Genesis Record* (Grand Rapids, MI: Baker Book House, 1976), p.46–48; Don Batten et al., *The Answers Book* (Green Forest, AR: Master Books, 1999), chapter 3.

simply means it was not yet in its finished state. God still had a lot more work to do to make the earth a special place for life and to populate it with countless amazing life forms, including man. The results of our space exploration have shown just how true this statement is — the rest of the universe, as far as we know, is lethal to life. Only the earth is suitable for human habitation, because God went to a lot of trouble to make it so; and the original result, as we will see shortly, was perfect in every way.

". . . and darkness was upon the face of the deep; and the Spirit of God was moving over the face of the waters" (Gen. 1:2). The primordial surface of the earth was liquid water. The earth did not begin as a high-temperature stellar offshoot, nor was it (wholly, at least) molten magma. There was no light on the earth, but God's Spirit was at work there. The presence of God's Spirit upon the earth provides us with the proper reference frame for understanding the time scale of creation. Time in Genesis, as we pointed out in the previous chapter, is earth time.

"And God said, 'Let there be light'; and there was light. And God saw that the light was good; and God separated the light from the darkness. God called the light Day, and the darkness he called Night. And there was evening and there was morning, one day" (Gen. 1:3–5). Here we have the introduction of the contentious word "day." Some commentators suggest that it can mean an indefinite period of time (as in Gen. 2:4 or 2 Pet. 3:8) and so they begin to insert here the billions of years of cosmic and geological time.[18] My dictionary gives 27 different usages for the word "day" in English. How do we know which one the author intends? The intention of the author is always revealed by the *context* in which a word is used. Among these many applications of the word "day" in English, the basic meanings all fall under three headings: (a) sunrise to sunset (the daylight hours), (b) sunset to sunset (one rotation of the earth on its axis), or (c) an indefinite period of time. The Hebrew word for day, *yom*, covers the same range of meanings. The context in Genesis 1:3–5 specifies (a) as the intended meaning of the first occurrence, and it specifies (b) as the intended meaning for the second occurrence, and the context identifies (c) as the intended meaning in Genesis 2:4. If you were to translate this passage into any language anywhere on earth, the speakers of that language would unerringly understand "evening and morning, one day" to mean an ordinary 24-hour cycle of light and darkness. No one would ever have any reason to believe otherwise, given the text as it stands.[19] The only reason that people today want to insert billions

18. Hugh Ross, *Creation and Time* (Colorado Springs, CO: NavPress, 1994), Ch. 5.

of years into this narrative is because they erroneously think that the scientific evidence demands it. This error was exposed in our previous chapter and it no longer need be a stumbling block.

Given that Moses is the editor of this narrative, it is significant that this context in Genesis 1 is internally consistent with the Fourth Commandment in Exodus 20:11, where the Israelites were told to keep the Sabbath as a memorial to the fact that God created the universe in six days and rested on the seventh day. Not only does this internal consistency affirm the idea of six-day creation, but it reveals the absurdity of the alternative — it would be absurd to interpret the Fourth Commandment to mean that the Israelites should work for six billion years and then rest for one billion years. Furthermore, God wrote down the Ten Commandments with His own finger in stone — a "set in stone" guarantee of its crucial importance (Exod. 31:18). Added to that, God summarized the whole of the Mount Sinai revelation by commanding the Israelites to keep the Sabbath cycle as a *perpetual* memorial to the fact that He created the universe in six days (Exod. 31:12–17). To make sure this eyewitness account would be treated with the reverence it deserves, Exodus 32:16 says, "The tablets were the work of God; the writing was the writing of God." The fact of six-day creation is therefore clearly established beyond any reasonable doubt. The question of *why* six-day creation is so important, both scientifically and theologically, will be dealt with shortly.

Some have argued that it is impossible to have an ordinary-length day on earth before the sun was created on day 4, yet this is not so. All that we need is (a) a source of light, and (b) rotation of the earth, both of which are clearly contained within the Genesis account. When God created light, He separated it from darkness. If He did this near the earth, then there would have been a gradient, or other kind of disjunction, between the two, in our region of space. If then the earth began to rotate, the alternation from light to dark would produce the "evening and morning, one day," as reported. Now the rate of rotation of the earth needs to stay within a very narrow band of values so we cannot invoke

---

19. Ibid., p. 48. Ross has argued that the unusual syntax of the sentences enumerating the specific creation days suggests that something other than ordinary-length days are in mind. This is not so, however. The sequence is "one day . . . second day . . . third day . . . fourth day . . . fifth day . . . the sixth day . . . the seventh day." Thus, the first occurrence defines what a day is (a light/dark cycle marked by evening and morning); then follows a sequence of similar days, with the last two highlighted as special — man was created on the sixth, and God rested on the seventh. See Jonathan Sarfati, "The Numbering Pattern of Genesis: Does It Mean the Days Are Non-literal?" *TJ* 17(2):60–61 (2003).

a very long day — that is, a very slow earth rotation. If the rotation is too slow, the temperature gradients on earth become too extreme, and the oceanic and atmospheric currents and tides, so vital to life, are disrupted. On the other hand, if the rotation is too fast, cyclonic winds would disrupt everything on the surface. So, it is logical that the initial rotation of the earth was approximately the same as we observe today, and the Genesis sequence makes perfect sense.

What was the source of light before the sun? In the new creation, there will be no sun or moon for God himself will provide the light (Rev. 22:5), so He could have done the same in the primordial creation as well. There is no real reason to invoke anything more than what the text says — God created light, separated it from darkness, the earth rotated, and it produced a day/night cycle. The light need not have had any source other than the command of God, and it could have continued until day 4 when the sun took over as the ongoing source. Furthermore, a good theological reason for placing the creation of the sun after the creation of light, is to make the point that the sun is a created object and should not be worshiped, as the Egyptians and many other ancient peoples did.

"And God said, 'Let there be a firmament in the midst of the waters, and let it separate the waters from the waters.' And God made the firmament and separated the waters which were under the firmament from the waters which were above the firmament. And it was so. And God called the firmament Heaven. And there was evening and there was morning, a second day" (Gen. 1:6–8). The "firmament" is called "heaven." This is the place "across" which the birds fly, and "in" which is the abode of the sun, moon, and stars.[20] It appears to refer to space beyond (and perhaps including at least a portion of) earth's atmosphere. The waters above it are variously thought to be a vapor canopy around the outer atmosphere,[21] a collection of ice-bodies in the outer reaches of the solar system,[22] or a watery region beyond the farthest reaches of the galaxies.[23] It is also possible that, since the earth was made out of water (2 Pet. 3:5), the rest of the solid objects in the universe were also made from water. In this view, water is the primary

---

20. It has been suggested that the stars could have been created beyond the firmament and the "waters above." See John G. Hartnett, "Look-back Time in Our Galactic Neighbourhood Leads to a New Cosmogony," *TJ* 17(1):73–79 (2003).

21. Don Batten et al., *The Answers Book, Updated & Expanded* (Green Forest, AR: Master Books, 1999), p. 161–163.

22. See Hartnett, footnote 20, this chapter.

23. D. Russell Humphreys, *Starlight and Time* (Green Forest, AR: Master Books, 1994), p. 76–78.

substance of creation out of which all the other elements are formed. Russell Humphreys used this model very successfully to predict the magnetic fields of the planets in our solar system.[24] Psalm 148:4 implies that at least some of the waters above the firmament are still there, so perhaps all of these interpretations are possible.

"And God said, 'Let the waters under the heavens be gathered together into one place, and let the dry land appear.' And it was so. God called the dry land Earth, and the waters that were gathered together he called Seas. And God saw that it was good. And God said, 'Let the earth put forth vegetation, plants yielding seed, and fruit trees bearing fruit in which is their seed, each according to its kind, upon the earth.' And it was so. The earth brought forth vegetation, plants yielding seed according to their own kinds, and trees bearing fruit in which is their seed, each according to its kind. And God saw that it was good. And there was evening and there was morning, a third day" (Gen. 1:9–13). The gathering of the waters "into one place," and then the dry land appearing, suggests that there was originally one land mass, and one ocean. The hydrological impact of the receding waters would have been enormous, and would have produced considerable depths of sediment. These sediments would have no fossils in them, since life had not yet appeared. Affirming this, we find that the deepest sedimentary rocks in the geological column are indeed devoid of fossils. The land/water division is also confirmed by geology, which reveals an original single landmass, which subsequently split up into the present-day continents.

Creation geologists[25] have shown that catastrophic crustal plate movements may have been associated with Noah's flood and these can explain continental break-up on a short time scale. Some have suggested that the sequence of events in Genesis 1 parallels the sequence of evolution, but the record clearly contradicts this. Evolution says the sun came before the earth, and aquatic life came before any terrestrial life, but Genesis 1 puts earth before sun, and terrestrial plant life before aquatic life (which appears only on day 5). Why this sequence? One obvious reason is that God was making the earth habitable for man. As every home gardener knows, terrestrial vegetation is the key to agreeable living spaces. Our joy in gardens is no cosmic

24. D. Russell Humphreys, "The Creation of Planetary Magnetic Fields," *Creation Research Society Quarterly* 21(3) (1984).

25. Batten et al., *The Answers Book*, chapter 11; Steven A. Austin et al., "Catastrophic Plate Tectonics: A Global Flood Model of Earth History," *Proc. Third Int. Conf. on Creationism*, Pittsburgh, PA, 1994, p. 609–621.

coincidence — God created the plant kingdom to furnish and supply our terrestrial home.

"And God said, 'Let there be lights in the firmament of the heavens to separate the day from the night; and let them be for signs and for seasons and for days and years, and let them be lights in the firmament of the heavens to give light upon the earth.' And it was so. And God made the two great lights, the greater light to rule the day, and the lesser light to rule the night; he made the stars also. And God set them in the firmament of the heavens to give light upon the earth, to rule over the day and over the night, and to separate the light from the darkness. And God saw that it was good. And there was evening and there was morning, a fourth day" (Gen. 1:14–19). The rest of the universe was made on day 4. In an attempt to reconcile the apparent age of the universe (currently about 13 billion years) with this verse, some commentators have suggested that the remote stars and galaxies existed before day 4 but simply became apparent to observers on earth on day 4. The reason for this is given as a clearing of the previously vaporous and dusty atmosphere so that the heavenly bodies could be seen clearly for the first time.[26] The straightforward meaning of the text, however, is that God made things in the sequence given, and on day 4 He made the heavenly bodies, both near and far. Their stated purpose includes "to separate the day from the night . . . for signs . . . for seasons . . . for days and years." This reaffirms the earlier definition of the meaning of "day" as the period that alternates with the night, to give a diurnal cycle in the context of "days, seasons, and years" — this context cannot possibly be twisted to mean billions of years.

We will not consider in detail what happened next. On day 5, God created the sea creatures and the winged creatures, and on day 6, He created the land animals and man. Then on day 7, He rested. We infer that His special creative forces were withdrawn from this point on, but the conservative physical forces (gravity, electromagnetism, strong and weak nuclear forces) that we see today continue to hold the universe together.[27]

However, two cosmically important points are set forth in this latter part

---

26. Job 38:9 is used to justify this position in G. Gray, *The Age of the Universe: What are the Biblical Limits?* (Washougal, WA: Morningstar Publications, 2000). Gray concludes that the Sabbath was not a commemoration of creation, but simply of God "working on" the biosphere. We believe it is overwhelmingly clear that the Sabbath commemorates creation.

27. In stating this, we are not implying that these laws operate independently of God's sustaining power.

of the creation narrative. First, the appearance of man only two days after the stars and galaxies highlights the impact of Jesus' statement, quoted earlier, which implies that human history is coincident with cosmic history. When we add up the ages of the ancestors of Jesus, as recorded in Luke 3:23–38, we get an approximate date for creation of around 4000 B.C.[28] Second, God was very pleased with what He had created. Seven times it is recorded that He looked at what He had made and said that it was "good" (Gen. 1 in verses 4, 10, 12, 18, 21, 25, 31), and on the seventh time, he added that "everything" was "very good" (v. 31). We interpret this to mean that the whole creation was perfect and without defect in every part. We suggest that its perfection lay in three things: (a) divine design, (b) divine construction, and (c) divine upholding (Heb. 1:3; Col. 1:17). This latter condition allowed the universe to function and maintain itself perfectly. This is a very important part of the biblical world view. A creation that is perfect and endures forever must include an "upholding" force — which we have traditionally called "providence" — to counteract the effect of the second law of thermodynamics. According to this latter law, stars, for example, cannot shine forever because they will consume their nuclear fuel and eventually die. Without this upholding, animals and man would be likely to suffer from accident, injury — perhaps even leading to death.

This is the thought behind the devil's temptation of Jesus to throw himself off the pinnacle of the temple (Matt. 4:5–7; Luke 4:9–12). Jesus was tempted to use His supernatural "upholding" power to protect himself, but He chose not to do so — and He suffered as a result. So in our "thelein universe" we see that the dominant force — God's will — is primarily carried out by the power we call providence.[29] While the withdrawing of some of this providential upholding has contributed to the Curse, as we outlined earlier, God's will is still the dominant force in the universe because Romans 8:28 says that God is working all things (even our suffering) together for good for those who love Him and are called according to His purpose.

---

28. For a comprehensive review of the issues surrounding the genealogies, see P. Williams, "Some Remarks Preliminary to a Biblical Chronology," *TJ* 12(1):98–106 (1998).

29. It may not be obvious to a physicist doing an experiment on gravity that God's will is the dominant force in the universe, but that is because he is not aware that it is God's will that holds him and his experiment in existence. Romans 8:28 assures believers that God's will is still the dominant force in the universe.

God's Method and Timing of Creation

The method and timing of God's work of creation are inextricably connected and cannot be separated without doing violence to both. God spoke the universe into existence out of nothing, as indicated by the repeated phrasing: "And God said, 'Let there be . . . and there was.' " This is also explicitly affirmed in Hebrews 11:3 and 2 Peter 3:5, and is implicit within the creation statements in John 1:1–4 and Hebrews 1:1–3. Psalm 33:6–9 sums it up as follows: "By the word of the LORD the heavens were made, and all their host by the breath of his mouth. . . . For he spoke, and [the earth] came to be; he commanded, and it stood forth."

It is worth pausing at this point, to reflect upon God's absolute dependence upon His word in His work of creation. When we think of "making things," we think in terms of manually constructing and assembling parts, but God is a spirit being and has no "hands" as we do[30] — He does not need them because His method of manipulating His world is *entirely* through His verbal commands. God creates and sustains via His Word, as we have already seen. He commands His angels to work on His behalf (the word means "messenger," e.g., Exod. 23:20; Luke 4:10) and He elicits faith in His chosen ones via His Word (John 10:27; Rom. 10:17). This demonstrates very clearly why Jesus was *so* committed to the Scriptures as God's Word, and why faith in God's Word is the central dynamic of Christianity.

God did not make the universe out of some pre-existing matter. This is crucially important, because pre-existing (and therefore eternal) matter would contradict Yahweh's claim to be the unique "eternally self-existent One" as indicated by the meaning of His name, "I am," and the exclusive claims He made about himself (e.g., Isa. 42:8; 45:5, 6, 14, 18, 21, 22; 46:9). Many non-biblical creation accounts begin with pre-existing matter. For example, the Babylonian creation account in the *Enuma Elish* features Marduk creating the universe out of the slain body of Tiamat. In contrast, the Bible says that God not only spoke it into existence, but He currently holds it in existence by the same word of power (Heb. 1:3) and by the same word will bring it to judgment and re-creation (2 Pet. 3:7ff).

God's *method* of creation is also intimately involved with its *time scale*. We dealt with the scientific aspects of the time scale in the last chapter, but the logical implications of the time scale are crucial to the theology.

---

30. Jesus, God the Son incarnate as man, does have hands, but they are a derivative part of His eternal being.

Let's consider an example of the principle that is at stake here. Remember when Jesus raised Lazarus from the dead. They rolled the stone away and Jesus called, "Lazarus, come out," and he came out. Let's imagine what would have happened if Lazarus hadn't come out until the following day. Everyone would have gone home. Lazarus would have been wandering around in a daze, still wrapped in grave clothes. He wouldn't have known what had happened to him. In fact, if anyone had found him wandering about they might not even believe that he *was* Lazarus.

What would have happened if Lazarus hadn't come out until, say, five years later? Could anyone credibly have said that Jesus had raised him from the dead? Of course not! They would have had to look for some other explanation.

Now some Bible commentators would have us believe that when God created the universe by commanding things to happen, some of those things didn't happen for billions of years. Does this sound like "God spoke, and it came to be; he commanded, and it stood forth"? Not at all! If the events did not happen when God commanded them to happen, then we cannot say that "God did it." The events would have been subject to time, chance, and the laws of nature over billions of years and any number of alternative "natural" causes could be invoked to explain them.

If, and only if, the events happened within a short period of God having commanded them to happen, can we reasonably attribute the cause to God's supernatural work of creation. Billions of years of delay destroy all vestiges of a miraculous cause.

Thus, to be internally consistent, if God created the universe by calling it into existence out of nothing, then the universe must have been created during a short interval of time. The inflationary version of big-bang theory inadvertently supports this notion. According to inflation, the scale of the universe was established in less than one second. It seems that if you are going to make a universe, you have to do it very quickly!

There's more. The irreducible complexity of much of the creation demands a cause that could have assembled all the required parts over a short period of time. "Irreducible complexity" is such an important concept that we will take a few moments to explain it.

Irreducible Complexity

A simple example is a bicycle. Two bicycles are shown in the diagram below, one a penny-farthing from the 19th century, and the other a more recent version with chain and sprocket drive. Each is an irreducibly complex design. On the penny-farthing, the essential parts are the two wheels, the frame, the handlebars, the seat, and the pedals — which, in this case, are directly connected to the axle of the front wheel. Irreducibly complex systems, such as these bicycles — and virtually all man-made machinery and the molecular machinery in living cells — have four important characteristics, each of which can be seen in the bicycle designs:

- The parts are *specifically structured* to do a particular job. For example, the wheels are round so they will roll along with ease, and the frame is made to join the wheels and support the rider.

- The parts are *functionally integrated* in a way that allows each of them to contribute their function to the whole system. For example, the wheels are connected to the frame via a lubricated axle mount at their center.

- The whole unit is *precisely regulated* to do the job at hand. For example, the size of the wheel and the length of the pedal arms has to be within narrow limits for a given rider to be able to ride the bicycle (length of legs, power of legs), and a braking system is required to stop, thus avoiding accidents and injury.

- The system does not work if any part is missing (perhaps the seat may be optional in this case — but every other part is certainly essential).

Note the crucial link between irreducible complexity and the time scale. All the components need to be structured, integrated, and regulated *on a short time scale* for the system to work. If the components were to be left lying around for millions of years, they would become degraded and/or dispersed and no longer able to function.

Now there is irreducibly complex design in our solar system. Many examples could be given but we will note just one.

Humans, and most other forms of life (except some microbes) need oxygen to burn the carbon compounds in their food to release the energy on which their molecular machinery runs. The process is called "respiration." Once the oxygen is used up in this way, it becomes bound to carbon atoms (as carbon dioxide) and is no longer available for respiration. Unless the oxygen is regenerated, most life on earth would quickly die out. God's solution to this problem is green plants — the familiar trees, shrubs, and herbs on the land masses, and the vast numbers of macroscopic and microscopic algae in the oceans. Green plants have the remarkable system of "photosynthesis" which turns carbon dioxide back into oxygen and carbon-based food, using the energy of sunlight.

Now without going into the details here, we can say that the necessary components of this system include, among many other things, (a) the astonishing molecular machinery of photosynthesis in the green plants (which has never yet been duplicated in the laboratory), (b) sunlight of tolerable intensity, (c) liquid water, (d) an average temperature range in the region of 5–35°C, (e) a hydrological cycle to provide water for the land vegetation, and (f) an atmosphere containing about 20 percent oxygen. No other known planet has these properties. If we were much closer to the sun the water would evaporate, and if we were much farther away it would freeze. If the earth did not turn on its axis, the light side would become unbearably hot and the dark side would freeze up. As it is, the combination of the 23° tilt of the earth's axis, plus the rotation on its axis, plus the annual orbiting around the sun, spreads the incoming sunlight over most of the surface in a way that provides the right temperature balance to sustain the hydrological cycle and allow life to flourish. All the other necessary factors likewise need to exist within a fairly narrow range of their actual values.

The earth, as you can see, is part of an irreducibly complex system. If any of these components were not present, the system would not work. The implication, therefore, is that it must have been created and assembled, more or less in its present form, during a short period of time. Just the kind of thing you would expect if "God commanded, and it stood forth."

There is more still. *Why* did God choose to create the universe in six days rather than six seconds, or perhaps instantaneously? The reason is given in the Ten Commandments (Exod. 20:8–11; 31:12–18). God wanted His people to regularly commemorate His work of creation. He knew how fickle we are, and how prone to forget Him, so He gave us a time scale that would be a convenient reminder. A six-day work week, with one day of rest, gives a perfect rhythm to our lives. If God had created the universe in six seconds we could not regularly commemorate the fact. By the time we had even said the words once it would be time to say them again. Notice the implications for the "billions of years" argument. If God had created the universe over billions of years, no humans would have yet had a chance to commemorate the event even once.

All these different lines of evidence indicate a very complex interplay between the *method* and *timing* of God's work of creation. Evolution over billions of years destroys these logical connections, yet the Bible gives a story that is perfectly consistent.

The Nature of Truth

The Bible presents a view of "truth" quite different to the common perception of it. According to Jesus, "truth" is a person, and He himself is that person (John 14:6). When we understand the nature of the thelein universe we begin to understand something of what Jesus meant when He said "I am the truth." If the universe was created and is currently upheld by the Word of God, and its ultimate fate will be guided and determined by that same Word, then that Word is the fundamental "truth" about the universe. There is *ultimately* no other guiding principle, no other authority, no other source of power or influence or inspiration. The Creator is the beginning and the end, the Alpha and the Omega (Rev. 1:8; 21:6; 22:13). John's Gospel begins: "In the beginning was the Word, and the Word was with God, and the Word was God . . . all things were made through him" (John 1:1–3). This gives us insight into both the nature of God and the nature of the universe. God's Word is so much an integral part of His person that He *is* His Word. The universe is a created expression of that Word — originally, at present (even in its fallen state), and in its future consummation.

Seekers after "truth" should therefore not expect to find it anywhere other than in the person of the Creator.

THE SUPER-ALIEN GALAXY COLLECTOR

The Bible is not a textbook on cosmology, so it would be inappropriate to compare it in a one-to-one fashion with a book on big-bang theory. Yet the Bible does contain a cosmology that goes beyond the creation accounts (the cosmogony). To see it in its own context, let us examine the question of what we would *expect* the universe to look like, if all the information that we had was that which is in the Bible. Because we are so evolutionized in our thinking and so familiar with Bible stories, we need some means of "cleaning the slate" so we can see more objectively what the Bible says.

Imagine, for the moment, that you are a "super-alien galaxy collector" able to visit our universe, though from another dimension entirely. In your annual galaxy collector's catalog you see our Milky Way galaxy offered for sale at a bargain price. You write in for a prospectus and you are sent a copy of the Bible. You read the Bible and then decide to visit the Milky Way, with a view to buying it. Your only knowledge of the Milky Way is what you read in the Bible — so what would you *expect* to see when you got here?

[This imaginary scenario is meant to be read in the context that "the galaxy is the necessary and sufficient universe," as outlined in our chapter on *Science, World Views and Cosmological Models*. We could have put it in terms of a "universe collector" wanting to buy "our universe" but by restricting it to "the galaxy" we have retained an imaginable spatial context. Although aliens do not exist in our universe, we have allowed an imaginary alien to arrive from another dimension.]

The following lists a few of the things that we might expect, simply from reading the Bible alone.

A man-centered universe. The Bible presents a world view in which the whole creation is centered on earth and humankind. Until God made the earth habitable, and populated it with life, the universe was void of life. Evolutionists laugh at this as a ridiculously anthropocentric point of view, yet that is what we see. So far, no life has been found beyond the earth and its immediate surroundings. Furthermore, the anisotropy in the CMBR and the quantization of galactic redshifts (as described in our chapter on the big-bang model) points to the earth being at or near the center of the universe. Moreover, the structure of the laws of physics seem to be finely tuned to support life, which of course means life on earth. In contrast, evolutionists believe that because life arose spontaneously on earth, so it should have also formed spontaneously elsewhere. The evidence so far supports the Bible.[31]

The earth being a safe haven for life at a prime location in the galaxy. It is easy for us to take for granted the privilege in which we live here on earth. Genesis tells us that God went to special lengths to make the earth

---

31. Even if life (in some microscopic form) is eventually found on Mars, this will not be proof that it arose there independently of earth. Most likely it would be due to contamination from earth. Microbes live in the upper atmosphere of earth and could easily be blasted off into space. Also, Mars has already had visits by spacecraft from earth.

habitable, and then to populate it with a great variety of creatures to provide sustenance and companionship for man. Everywhere else in the universe except earth, as far as we know, is lethal to life. On earth, the sun warms us and provides the source of all our food, and of all of our fossil, hydroelectric, wind, and wave power. Yet venture beyond the earth's protective "force shields" (the atmosphere, the ozone layer, and the magnetic field) and your life is immediately in grave danger. In 1972, in between the *Apollo 16* and *17* moon landings, a solar storm occurred that would likely have killed any astronauts out in space, had they been there. Visit any of the other planets and it gets worse.

Mercury is totally covered with impact craters, it is continually blasted by the solar wind (a stream of charged particles accelerated into space by the sun's magnetic field), its daytime temperature is a life-destroying 350°C (660°F), and its night-time temperature plunges to a killer -170°C (-310°F).

Venus is completely enveloped in clouds of toxic gases, and the resulting greenhouse effect causes surface temperatures to reach an incredible 480°C (900°F) — hot enough to melt metals such as lead, tin, and zinc.

Mars is a barren wasteland with a suffocating atmosphere of carbon dioxide, and the moon is likewise barren but with no atmosphere at all.

Jupiter is called a "gas giant" planet because it is virtually *all* "atmosphere," the outer parts of which are continually ripped by unbelievably violent winds, and storms that rage for hundreds of years.

Beautiful Saturn, another "gas giant," is as intensely violent as Jupiter. The *Voyager* spacecraft measured wind gusts near its equator of 1,700 kilometers per hour. Beyond Saturn, we have the ice planets where the temperatures drop below that of liquid nitrogen — so cold that virtually nothing happens there. No other planet is like earth.

Our solar system is also a very civilized one. Numerous other solar systems have now been found, and the majority have very massive planets quite close to their parent stars.[32] If that were the case in our solar system, the earth would be thrown about by the gravitational impact so much we would likely be destroyed. We are also in a very placid part of the galaxy. The center of the Milky Way is thought to host a humungous black hole that is swirling its near neighbors into violent, spiraling death throes before they are swallowed up. We also have an ideal view of the galaxy. Our solar system is about halfway out

---

32. Rod Bernitt, "Extrasolar Planets Suggest Our Solar System Is Unique and Young," *TJ* 17(1):11–13 (2003).

along one of the spiral arms, but we are not in the ubiquitous dust clouds that inhabit spiral arms, we are out to the side far enough to get a perfectly clear view of the magnificent display of the hundred billion other stars in the galaxy. Furthermore, being in a spiral galaxy gives us these special opportunities that do not exist at all in the other major kind of galaxy — ellipticals. Elliptical galaxies have all their stars close together, rather than spread out as in spiral galaxies. The resulting radiation environment in most of the galaxy would be so intense that it is likely we could not survive.

The earth is indeed a unique safe haven for life, and it is in a prime location to gain a glorious view of the rest of the galaxy.

Evidence of eternal power. Paul says in Romans 1:20 that God's "eternal power" is clearly revealed in His works of creation. Psalm 19:1 says, "The heavens declare the glory of God" (NIV). Part of God's glory is His "power," according to Revelation 4:11, so these verses agree — God's omnipotence is on display in His creation.

Since today we know far more about the universe than the Psalmist did, we need to consider this question from two different points of view — that of the Psalmist, and the modern-day astronomer.

What would the Psalmist have seen in the heavens? The list would include the sun, the moon, the fixed stars, and the "wandering" stars (planets). It would also include ephemeral things like comets and meteorites. So how might the "eternal power" of God have been revealed in these heavenly bodies? The Psalmist mentions two things — the light (day) and the heat of the sun.

Light and heat are so much a part of our daily lives that we need to step back from our technology in order to see them as the Psalmist did. When the sun went down, the blackness of ancient night could be awesome. There was no electricity and no streetlights. When the moon was up, the ancients could see fairly well at night. Even by starlight it is possible to discern shadows and shapes, but by far their most important source of light in the darkness was fire. Candles, oil lamps, firebrands, campfires, and hot coals were as essential to them as electricity, gas, and matches are to us today.

Now a very obvious and pesky thing about fire, for a person living in ancient times, is that it consumes its source. This would have been a daily problem in the semi-arid lands of the Middle East, where firewood was scarce, and where olive oil was an expensive and seasonal commodity. It would have been even more evident to nomads who had to carry their fuel supplies with them. Yet the sun came and went every day, and had been doing so for thousands of years, without ever (apparently) consuming its source. This would certainly have seemed, to our ancient brethren, a sure sign of the Creator's "eternal power."

The same line of reasoning could have formed the background to their understanding of the moon and the stars. These lights would appear night after night, yet never consume their source. Yes, the moon waxed and waned, but it always returned to its full glory so it did not diminish, as a campfire would, through the watches of the night. When God called Moses from the burning bush, Moses knew it was a miracle because the bush was not consumed (Exod. 3:2–6), and so it would have been for their understanding of the heavenly bodies.

There would have been other "heavenly," but more local, signs of power evident to ancient man as well. Lightning and thunder, for example, and the floods that could accompany them. The Great flood of Noah became proverbial as a sign of God's awesome power (e.g., Ps. 29).

What of modern man? Does our discovery that the sun indeed consumes its source of fuel reduce God's glory to simple physics? Anyone who has witnessed an unmoderated nuclear chain reaction (atomic bomb explosion) up close will quickly affirm that it magnifies the concept beyond the wildest dreams of the ancient Semite. The sun shines because it continually feeds upon itself in nuclear reactions so violent that its heart blazes at a staggering 15 million degrees Celsius, and as a result of its enormous power output, billions of tons of its outer layers can be blasted off into space at millions of kilometers per hour, in dozens of eruptions every day. So huge is the energy output of the sun that if the Creator had not protected us in various ways we would have been wiped out by it long ago. The sun's power is not just a local phenomenon; it reaches out with its solar wind to a massive 22 billion kilometers into space — about four times the distance to Pluto, the outermost planet.

Such power is certainly impressive, but is it the "eternal power" of the Creator? Or just the inherent power of matter? In chapter 4 on the big-bang model we said that the origin of primordial stars is inexplicable in naturalistic terms, so we conclude that the Creator has indeed placed these enormous energies within matter, and He has also created the stars, which put that energy on display for us to see. Since God is jealous of His glory, we could perhaps go further, and suggest that it is likely that no naturalistic explanation for star formation will ever be found.

Modern astronomers see far more than the antics of our sun, which is a quite modest and average kind of star. Other stars out there beggar the imagination with their periodic and/or ongoing displays of "eternal power." One indication of their potential magnitude is shown below.

In January 2002, a previously unknown star, now called V838 Monocerotis, erupted and briefly became the brightest star in the galaxy.[33] Baffling astronomers, it did not self-destruct, as supernovae do, and after a few months quieted down again, in the process leaving behind a spectacular light show in the surrounding dust clouds. While the mechanism of this event remains a mystery, the scale is certainly not. In the image below, our *entire solar system* would occupy only about one tenth of the smallest pixel in the picture!

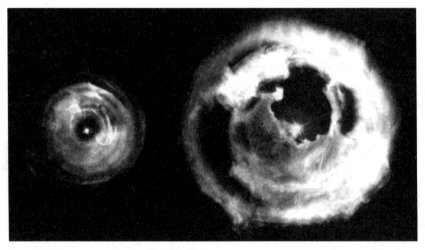

V838 Monocerotis on April 30 (left) and October 28, 2002 (right). Our solar system, by comparison, would be smaller than the smallest pixel in this image.

If the sun provides abundant evidence of the Creator's "eternal power," then events such as this, elsewhere in the universe, show even more.

Evidence of divine design. Paul says further in Romans 1:20 that God's "deity" or "divine nature" is also clearly revealed in His works of creation. Psalm 19:1 says that "the firmament proclaims his handiwork." Psalm 136:5 says, "to him who by understanding made the heavens." The early chapters of Proverbs are an ode to wisdom and in Proverbs 3:19 it says, "The LORD by wisdom founded the earth; by understanding he established the heavens." In Proverbs 8:22–27 it is said of wisdom, "The LORD created me at the beginning

33. Howard E. Bond et al., "An Energetic Stellar Outburst Accompanied by Circumstellar Light Echoes," *Nature* 422:405–408 (2003).

of his work, the first of his acts of old. Ages ago I was set up, at the first, before the beginning of the earth. . . . When he established the heavens, I was there, when he drew a circle on the face of the deep." The companions of wisdom are prudence, knowledge, and discretion (Prov. 8:12). All these references assert that God's personal characteristics of intelligence, wisdom, and skill are on display in His work of creation.

The sun shows forth astonishing power, but does it also show intelligence, wisdom, and skill? Or just brute force? Let's try to look at the heavens through the eyes of the Psalmist.

Psalm 19:4–6 says, "In [the heavens] he has set a tent for the sun, which comes forth like a bridegroom leaving his chamber, and like a strong man runs its course with joy. Its rising is from the end of the heavens, and its circuit to the end of them; and there is nothing hid from its heat."

A "tent" for the sun. A dwelling place. The wind can be violent and unpredictable; the rain can deluge the land and destroy it; the thunder can shake the foundation of all man's achievements; and the lightning can destroy in one stroke the work of a lifetime, but the sun remains constant, predictable, calm, and "civilized." We tend to think of a tent as being a primitive device, but in the semi-arid grazing lands of nomads, it was in some places the *only* sign of civilization. Thus, the Creator's provision of a dwelling place for the sun, a home base from which it can conduct its daily activities, is a sure sign of civilized intelligence.

The sun "comes forth like a bridegroom leaving his chamber." The bridegroom leaves his wedding chamber after consummating his vows with his beloved. He is radiant, satisfied, fulfilled. He does not need to go wildly wandering like the wind or the storm, he is now settled and can come and go with confidence. The sun likewise is settled and assured in its "coming forth."

The sun also "like a strong man runs its course with joy." The Hebrew word for "strong man" refers to a champion or hero. The radiance of the bridegroom is accompanied by the strength of the champion. There is no sign of the sun faltering in its course — it takes exactly the same path every day without wavering. Only a strong athlete can run his course with such precision. Moreover, there is no sign of sluggishness nor lethargy, the champion accomplishes it all with constancy and joy.

The daily circuit of the sun goes from "end to end" of the heavens. The lightning might strike here or there on the earth, but the sun goes from "end to end." The wind may blow this way or that but the sun goes the whole way on the same course every day. Such precision, persistence, regularity, radiance, and strength all speak loudly of intelligent design. Yet the sun does move, imperceptibly each day, but perceptibly over the course of the year — but even this variation is so precise that it coincides exactly with the seasonal patterns of life on earth. So, the daily regularity is precise, and its seasonal wandering is precise — sure signs of intelligence in a world of capricious change.

And "nothing is hid from its heat." In our air-conditioned offices and our heated cars and homes we lose touch with the heat of the sun. In summer, everything is radiant in its heat, and in winter, everything laments its remoteness. In the natural world, nothing is hid from its heat; heat which brings life, and the absence of which can mean death. Here we have a sign of grace. Jesus used this very thing to define grace in Matthew 5:45: "Your Father in heaven . . . makes his sun rise on the evil and on the good, and sends rain on the just and on the unjust." Not only could the Psalmist see the intelligence, wisdom, and skill of the Creator in the heavens, but also His love and provision for His creatures.

What about the modern astronomer? Where is the Creator's divine nature on display through the telescope?

As we pointed out in an earlier chapter, the evidence of design (in the fine-tuning of the universe) has become so abundant in recent years that cosmologists have invented the anthropic principle to try to explain it away. The anthropic principle says that if the universe *didn't* appear to be designed for life, then we would not be here to observe the fact. They then try to imagine that there are countless other possible universes and we just happen, by chance, to be in one of those where the conditions are right for life. As we said earlier, we know of only *one* universe. Chance cannot accomplish what the laws of nature forbid. Evidence of design is evidence of design.

There is an abundant literature on the anthropic principle, but we will consider here just one example — the marvel of water — to illustrate the issues involved.

Water is so common on earth that we take it for granted, yet it is unique in all the world of chemistry and physics. Water is made of the very common elements hydrogen and oxygen, and its physico-chemical properties should resemble a number of similar related compounds — but they don't. Its strange properties are called "anomalies." For example, all liquids show an inverse relationship between density and temperature — except water. Below 4°C, water reverses this relationship. As a result, ice is less dense than water, and it floats. If it did not do so, then ice would sink, and lakes and oceans would freeze up in winter and not thaw. As it is, in winter, lakes can freeze over and life can go on, protected under the floating ice. Among the several other anomalies of water, there is the one we mentioned earlier — its fascinating internal structure.

Water is the major component of all living cells. No life form is known that is not made up mostly of water.[34] Molecular biologists generally explain life processes in terms of the carbon-based molecules such as DNA and proteins, but much of the intriguing function of these organic molecules is made possible only by the unique structure of water. Liquid water consists of four different components: ice relicts, quasi-crystals, fluid, and vacuum. All the surprising anomalies of water can be explained by the differing proportions of these components at different temperatures and pressures.[35] The two most important components are the quasi-crystals and the fluid, and it turns out that some organic molecules preferentially dissolve in one of these phases, while other kinds of molecules prefer the other phase. The amazing thing is that the point at which these two phases are equally present, so that the water displays its maximum possible structural diversity, is approximately 37°C, the internal temperature of the healthy human body!

The crucial aspect of design here is not so much the fascinating relationship between the structure of water and the physiology of the human body. It is the fact that the forces that hold the water molecules in their various delicate configurations, and the forces which hold the whole biosphere system in place here on earth also hold the planets, stars, and galaxies together and guide them in their courses. If you varied these forces just a small amount either way, the whole structure of life, the earth and the universe would become unrecognizable.

As physicist Professor Paul Davies says, "The impression of design is overwhelming."[36]

Cryptic clues. Some have suggested that the Bible contains cryptic clues that reveal its supernatural authorship — things that could not have been understood by the original author or audience, and can only be seen via modern technology. These include the following:

- *The paths of the sea* (Ps. 8:8). God has given man dominion over all creatures, including "whatever passes along *the paths of the sea."* This could

34. A number of different life forms can survive drying out, but they all need water to grow and reproduce.
35. Karl Trincher, "The Mathematic-thermodynamic Analysis of the Anomalies of Water and the Temperature Range of Life," *Water Research* 15:433–448 (1981).
36. Quoted in Hugh Ross, *The Creator and the Cosmos* (Colorado Springs, CO: NavPress, 2001), p. 157.

be a metaphor of the fact that sea creatures make migratory journeys and thus follow "pathways" of who-knows-what making. Or it could refer to the amazing network of globe-circling sea currents that migratory sea creatures use, and which have long been known — but only in part — to mariners. American naval officer and oceanographer Matthew Maury pieced them together in the 19th century, based on his belief in the Bible, [37] and the driving force — the thermohalocline fronts — was only discovered in the 20th century. These truly are worldwide "paths" in the sea that allow travelers (both marine and maritime) to journey much more quickly than elsewhere.

- *People flying like clouds and birds.* In Isaiah 60, God speaks of a time when the people of Zion shall return to a glorified city, the majesty of which will attract people from all nations. It then describes the coming of large numbers of people, by land, sea, and air — so it seems. A multitude of camels shall come by land, bearing people and treasures (v. 6) together with flocks of sheep (v. 7); then "Who are these that fly like a cloud, and like doves to their windows?" (v. 8); then "the ships of Tarshish . . . bring your sons from far, their silver and gold with them" (v. 9). If verse 8 had not been framed as a question, we could reasonably infer that it was simply a poetic image, but the question reveals that the prophet was puzzled. He "sees" something that he cannot interpret. The context is the gathering of people and he can understand them coming by land on camels, with their flocks, and by sea in their ships. Perhaps his puzzlement results from the fact that he is "seeing" them also come on airplanes and (understandably) does not comprehend what he sees.

- *The earth as a sphere.* Proverbs 8:27 says that the Creator "drew a circle on the face of the deep," and Isaiah 40:22 says that God "sits above the circle [*kug* = sphere or circle] of the earth." In our introductory chapter on the history of cosmology we showed that ancient peoples figured out the shape of the earth, but the final proof has come only with imagery from space. The fact that it is here written in the Bible is confirmation that the author(s) had real knowledge of the real world, beyond that of many other "primitive" peoples.

---

37. Anon., "Matthew Maury's Search for the Secrets of the Seas," *Creation* 11(3):30 (June–August 1989); <http://www.answersingenesis.org/home/area/magazines/docs/v11n3_maury.asp>.

- *The fountains of the deep.* At the beginning of the great Flood catastrophe in Noah's time, the "fountains of the great deep burst forth, and the windows of the heavens were opened" (Gen. 7:11). At the end of the inundation phase, "the fountains of the deep and the windows of the heavens were closed" (Gen. 8:2). Present-day deep-sea exploration has revealed the most remarkable, and unexpected, fountains of super-heated water feeding into the deepest ocean trenches. These seem to be in mind in Job 38:16, where God questions, "Have you entered into the springs of the sea, or walked in the recesses of the deep?" Huge reserves of water still exist within the earth's mantle,[38] perhaps ten or more times the amount of water in all the present oceans, so it is not hard to imagine that even more existed there in previous eras, to provide an adequate source for the great Flood.

- *The earth suspended in space.* Job 26:7 says that God "stretches out the north over the void, and hangs the earth upon nothing." This accurate picture of the earth in space could not have been known to earth-bound observers in ancient times. It also provides a remarkable contrast to other ancient world views which picture the earth being supported in various physical ways (e.g., on the back of a turtle, an elephant, a fish, a bull, or a god-man).

- *The number of stars.* Until the invention of the telescope, the number of stars was counted by numerous early astronomers to be less than ten thousand. However, several references in the Bible indicate that the stars were countless (Gen. 15:5), just as the sand on the seashore (Gen. 22:17; Jer. 33:22). Even today we cannot count the stars — there are too many. A reasonable estimate might be ten million billion billion (10^{25}).[39]

- *Cosmic expansion.* There are numerous references to God having "stretched out" the heavens, both during creation (Ps. 104:2; Isa. 42:5; 44:24; 45:12; 48:13; 51:13; 51:16; Jer. 10:12; 51:15; Zech. 12:1) and perhaps ongoing as well (Isa. 40:22). Humphreys[40] interpreted these to mean the Hubble expansion of the cosmos, which was only discovered in the 20th century and could not have been understood by any previous generation.

---

38. Alexander R. Williams, "Drowned from Below," *Creation* 22(3):52–53 (2000).

39. Werner Gitt, *Stars and Their Purpose* (Bielefeld, Germany: Christliche Literatur-Verbreitung, 1996), p. 19.

40. D. Russell Humphreys, *Starlight and Time* (Green Forest, AR: Master Books, 1994), p. 66–68.

Evidence of corruption. When you look at the Bible as a whole, it presents a picture of a universe in pain. It starts off with "all things bright and beautiful," and it ends up in a transformed and glorified state of deathless perfection, but in-between it presents a tragic saga of sin, suffering, and death. According to Romans 8:22, the *whole* creation is groaning under the curse of man's sin and God's judgment. Evidence of such corruption of the created order is all about us on earth, but where do we see the signs of it in the heavenly creations?

Corruption and design go together, because it was a designed universe that was corrupted. Indeed, we would not know what corruption was unless we had at least some aspects of a functional universe to compare it with. When a car breaks down, for example, we know something is wrong because there are numerous other cars about us that are functional and being driven around. However, if we were born in a junk yard and all we had ever known was broken-down cars, then perhaps we might expect that to be the norm. Likewise, when we look at the heavens, we know what a functional star and solar system looks like because we have one right here that works very well (most of the time).

So what would a broken-down — or breaking down, or at least somewhat imperfect — star and solar system and galaxy look like? Once again, we will examine this question from the point of view of an ancient observer and a modern astronomer.

To get some idea of what the ancient observer might have seen, let's look at some Bible verses that speak of unusual events that can, or will, happen in the heavenly realm. Matthew 24:29 lists three kinds of celestial phenomena that are also referred to in several other places: "Immediately after the tribulation of those days [1] *the sun will be darkened, and the moon will not give its light,* and [2] *the stars will fall from heaven,* and [3] *the powers of the heavens will be shaken*" (emphasis added). Isaiah 34:4 adds to this list, "All the host of heaven shall rot away, and [4] *the skies roll up like a scroll*" (emphasis added). Isaiah 51:6 confirms these ideas with "the heavens will vanish like smoke, the earth will wear out like a garment."

All these references are prophetic, and seem to refer to events in the future. However, it is reasonable to assume that God chose images which mankind could understand because they had already experienced something of a similar nature. We will therefore examine these four phenomena to see if they might be signs of corruption and judgment in the celestial realm (i.e., beyond the earth's atmosphere) that could have been evident to readers of the ancient Scriptures.

- **Sun, moon, and stars darkened.** It is unlikely that the darkening of the sun, moon, and stars at any time in history has been a sign of corruption in the celestial realms. Such darkening is most likely to have resulted from an eclipse, or from atmospheric smoke and dust obscuring and distorting our *view* of the heavens. The continued functioning of the earth as a haven for life — which we know is God's will because the purpose of the Curse was not to destroy us but to give us time and reason to repent — is crucially dependent upon the stability of the sun and nearby stars. If the sun's energy output were to permanently reduce to the level observed in an eclipse, for example, or if a nearby star were to explode, it would destroy all life on earth. A special sign of the moon turning to "blood" is associated with the end times (Joel 2:31; Acts 2:20; Rev. 6:12). This can happen when an eclipse of the moon occurs near sunset, and the refraction of sunlight through the earth's dusty atmosphere turns the moon to a coppery or blood red color. This could provide a fairly precise astronomical indicator of the end times, but it is not a sign of celestial corruption.

- **Stars falling from heaven.** We noted earlier that the regular motion and stable light output of heavenly bodies was a sure sign of the Creator's eternal power and divine nature. When stars "fall from heaven," and perhaps burn more brightly for a short time and then die, as meteors do, this would certainly be a sign that something is very wrong in the celestial realm. Meteor falls are evident every night to a patient observer, but just one or two now and then against a background of thousands would be a sign of corruption in the face of otherwise stable design. A meteor shower, however, could be a portent of real disaster — so many "falling stars" might temporarily obscure the background of stable stars and the large numbers could give the impression that "the sky is falling in." The prophetic value of this image is likely to have been that the "end times" are to be a world-shattering event.

To the modern astronomer, "falling stars" are purely local phenomena in the earth's atmosphere, and do not refer to actual star "death." Star death in a supernova would be rarely observed on earth and it would not cause the star to "fall" from the sky, only brighten for a while and then fade. The Chinese referred to the Crab nebula supernova of A.D. 1054 as a "visitor" — it came for a while, and then went away (without appearing to "fall"). "Falling stars" are meteors, objects entering the earth's atmosphere and burning up because of their enormous speed. Meteors can be tiny grains of debris left behind by comets, and large amounts of such debris can lead to meteor showers. Most meteorites are larger objects, and have trajectories that suggest they come from the asteroid belt, a collection of thousands of rocky bodies orbiting the sun between Mars and Jupiter. A meteorite is a meteor that has fallen to earth. The range of compositions of meteorites also matches the range of compositions of asteroids, so it is not unreasonable to conclude that meteorites originated as asteroids. Evolutionists say they represent the "planetesimals" that the earth was formed out of but they look more like the remains of a broken planet. If the earth were to be broken into meteorite-sized pieces, the majority would be stony (from the outer mantle and crust region) and some would be iron-rich (from the inner iron/nickel core region), just as we observe among meteorites and asteroids. If "falling stars" are indeed a result of the break-up of a planet, then they are a dramatic sign of corruption in the celestial realm.

Throughout our solar system, there is also widespread evidence of impact craters. The whole surface of the moon, for example, is pock-marked with craters. The same is true for all other rocky bodies in the solar system that do not have erosional processes to remove the scars. Most impact craters on earth have been eroded by wind and water and ground movements. Impact scars could well be a sign of corruption and could have been produced at the Fall and/or during the Flood.

If a nearby planet was destroyed, as the asteroid belt almost certainly witnesses, then a rain of meteorites could have ensued and produced all these impact craters. Hartnett[41] has suggested that ice comets from the "waters above the firmament" might have been a contributory factor to cratering, and also as a water source and as a tectonic trigger for the devastating earth movements that would have accompanied the Flood. Cratering appears to be an important part of the creation/corruption/catastrophe cosmology and should be actively researched.[42]

- **Powers of heaven shaken.** It is unlikely that the shaking of the powers of heaven could have indicated corruption in the heavenly realm.

41. John G. Hartnett, "Look-back Time in our Galactic Neighborhood Leads to a New Cosmogony," *TJ* 17(1):73–79 (2003).
42. The various creationist views on cratering can be found in Carl R. Froede Jr, "Extraterrestrial Bombardment of the Inner Solar System: A Review With Questions and Comments Based on New Information," *Creation Research Society Quarterly* 38(4):209–212 (2002); see also Danny Faulkner, "A Biblically-based Cratering Theory," *TJ* 13(1):100–104 (1999).

Shaking means a rapid back-and-forth movement. On earth, cataclysmic shaking occurs during an earthquake. No such phenomenon in the galactic realm is visible as such from earth. It is most likely that this image refers to the visual effects of an earthquake, causing our *view* of the galaxy to "shake."

- **Skies roll up like a scroll.** Since there are numerous references to the heavens being "stretched out" (Ps. 104:2; Isa. 40:22; 42:5; 44:24; 45:12; 48:13; 51:13; 51:16; Jer. 10:12; 51:15; Zech. 12:1) in the context of creation, it is likely, as Humphreys has claimed,[43] that cosmic expansion was an important component of creation week, and perhaps it is ongoing. If indeed the stretching out is a creation event, then it is likely that when the "skies roll up like a scroll" (Isa. 34:4) this will be a terminal cosmic event. The universe that we know will cease to exist and God will create a new heaven and a new earth. If the original "stretching" was primordial and the future event is terminal, then such things are unlikely to have been witnessed on earth before, and therefore cannot be listed as signs of corruption due to the Curse.

- **Supernovae and cosmic dust.** If we follow the line of reasoning that the glory of God which was evident in the heavens to ancient observers was (a) the constancy of the celestial lights (they did not consume their sources) and (b) their predictable movements (thus showing order and intelligent design), then it follows that the death of stars in supernova explosions and the spread of the resultant stardust would be signs of corruption caused by sin and the Curse.

  Modern astronomers are very familiar with supernovae and cosmic dust because they provide some of the most spectacular of all celestial viewing. That, in itself, may contradict this line of argument. Just as the clouds in our terrestrial skies can show forth the glory and majesty of God in the most spectacular ways during sunrises and sunsets, so also the glory and majesty of God can be seen in the cosmic light shows, in which stardust plays a crucial role. Jesus used the earthly glory of clouds as an image of the heavenly glory of His second coming (Matt. 24:30; 26:64; Rev. 1:7). It is possible that this indicates a reversal of the natural order (i.e., God glorifies what we disdain) but it would seem more natural if the logic were as follows: (a) earthly clouds show forth created

---

43. D. Russell Humphreys, *Starlight and Time* (Green Forest, AR: Master Books, 1994), p. 66.

glory, therefore (b) they provide a suitable setting for the glory to come. If cosmic dust clouds show forth created glory, then we should look elsewhere for signs that show the modern astronomer that the galaxy has been corrupted by man's sin and God's curse.

In summary, the evidence of corruption available to ancient observers in the heavenly realms beyond earth's atmosphere would primarily have been "stars falling from the sky." We can understand this today as the destruction of a planet, the remains of which orbit the sun as the asteroid belt, fragments of which continue to rain down on earth as meteorites. Perhaps ice comets may be included as well. Impact craters throughout the solar system are consistent with this view. Further afield, supernova explosions and the resulting stardust (or at least some of it) could be signs of corruption evident to modern astronomers.

So, would our "super-alien galaxy collector" recognize the Milky Way when he got here? Would he consider the author of the Bible to be a trustworthy reporter? We believe so. Given the purpose and time for which it was given, the Bible presents a remarkably accurate and internally consistent picture of both the inner workings of the human heart,[44] and the outer world inhabited by the human body.

SUMMARY OF THE BIBLICAL MODEL

When we read the Bible in the way that Jesus and Moses would have read it, we find no sign whatever of God having created by means of evolution or over billions of years. The God of the Bible created the universe in six ordinary-length days, just a few thousand years ago. His method of creation and its timing are diametrically opposed to the evolutionary view: "He spoke, and it came to be; he commanded, and it stood forth" (Ps. 33:9). If we intrude billions of years into this process we destroy the many logical connections between the cause and the effect. These logical connections are extremely important because not only did God create the universe by calling it into existence, but He upholds it in existence by that very same Word, and has reserved it for future judgment by that same Word.

The miraculous works of Jesus, the Creator incarnate, powerfully corroborate the method and timing of creation, as described here. He spoke and people were healed and raised from the dead; water was turned into wine; a

---

44. This term is, of course, used here not to refer to the muscular pump that drives the circulation, but to the inner core of our being — volitional, emotional, and spiritual.

storm was calmed; one meal was multiplied to thousands; and the divine up-holding was brilliantly displayed in the marvel of His bodily resurrection.

Scientifically, the evidence also supports the biblical account. Creation needed to be rapid because irreducibly complex systems need to be assembled within a short time frame in order to achieve functionality and to avoid the ravages of time in the degradation and dispersal of their components.

Theologically, six days is an ideal choice of timing because it gives us, as God intended, an opportunity to commemorate and celebrate His work of creation, and it provides a convenient rhythm to our social and personal lives with six days work and one day of rest. Recent creation is also a theologically necessary ingredient because the purpose and fate of the universe is focused on humankind — if the universe had existed for billions of years and man ap-peared only at the last moment, then our presence could have had no signifi-cant impact on its history. The New Testament viewpoint, however, is that the *whole* creation is groaning under the curse of man's sin, and its liberation will come only with the redemption of mankind — it is God's will, not gravity, that decides the future. Just as the future of the universe is tied up with the fate of mankind, so it is consistent to read that Jesus believed the whole of cosmic history is embraced within the history of mankind — creation occurred only a few thousand years ago.

If we read the Bible without evolutionary preconceptions, we see that the description it presents of the universe (from an earthly perspective) is consis-tent with what humans, both ancient and modern, have observed. Life exists only on earth; God's eternal power and divine nature are clearly revealed in what He has made; and the corruption of man's sin and God's curse can be seen both on earth and in the heavens. What we read in God's Word, we can see in God's world.

Yet, since the invention of modern telescopes, it appears that the universe does have a "billions of years" time scale — it is out there, implied by the vast-ness of space and the constancy of the speed of light. Relativistic time dilation can reconcile the billions of years of cosmic history with the thousands of years of earth history, but we should be careful not to lose the biblical perspective. God's time for us is earth time, and within that time frame there are no billions of years, either past or future. God created the universe for us, and in Christ has restored our dominion over it. We shall rule with Him over the world to come — which the Bible says is coming "soon" in earth time, not billions of years hence.

A BIBLICAL MODEL OF THELEIN HISTORY

CREATION Day 1	God created the heavens as empty space, which was of indeterminate size. The earth as a body of matter, either all water or at least covered in water, was created from nothing within this space. This was also the point where He created time in which physical processes could occur. He created light and separated it from darkness, suggesting that a gradient existed in the vicinity of earth. The earth began to rotate and there was evening and morning, one day. It is important for us to identify this separation event. Is the remnant of this light with us today as the Cosmic Microwave Background Radiation (CMBR)? Or is the CMBR simply the temperature of the created empty space resulting from the radiant energy (light) of His presence in the unformed universe?
CREATION Day 2	God separated the "waters above" from the "waters below" the firmament. The former, we suggest, may be a halo of icy material surrounding the outer regions of the solar system. Perhaps it also includes the icy material that is now found in the planets beyond Neptune, that is, Pluto and other bodies. The "waters below" formed the oceans. The "firmament" is the space that includes the earth's atmosphere and the solar system, the region that now contains the sun, moon, and planets.
CREATION Day 3	God separated the land from the water on the earth and produced land vegetation. There was probably one land mass and one ocean, and the first layers of sediment — that later hardened into rocks without fossils in them — were formed as the water ran off the land.

CREATION Day 4	God created the sun, moon, stars, and galaxies, and stretched out the heavens in the process to make room for them all. This stretching out resulted in an enormous amount of time dilation; billions of years of physical transformation occurred in the galactic realms while only one ordinary-length day passed on earth and in the solar system.
CREATION Days 5 and 6	On day 5 God created the sea creatures and flying creatures, and on day 6 He created the land animals and man.
CREATION Day 7	God rested from His work of creation.[45] The special creative forces were withdrawn and the conservative forces that we know today continued to hold the universe together. A special providential upholding continued, however, to maintain the universe in perfect working condition, preventing accidents, injuries, decay, and death.
CORRUPTION	When Adam and Eve disobeyed God, they brought the Curse of decay, suffering, and death upon themselves and the whole creation. The Curse was effected in large part by God withdrawing just a small amount of His providential "upholding" power. This gives man a small taste of what life without Him is like, and therefore a reason to repent. The evidence of the Curse is all around us on earth, but in the heavens, the primary evidence of it is meteorites — "stars falling from the sky." This

45. Some have suggested that the lack of a closing "evening and morning" formula for the seventh day implies that it is still ongoing — and therefore can be interpreted as a long period of time. However, the Sabbath law contradicts this view — the Israelites were to work for six days and rest for one day, just as God did. It is more reasonable to focus on what the author put *in* Genesis 1, rather than what is left *out*; and what is put *in* is a clear description of a six-day creation.

	was probably the result of a planet being destroyed between Mars and Jupiter, the remnants of which today are called the asteroid belt, the apparent source of the meteorites.
CATASTROPHE	Although the Flood was primarily an earthly event (it was the major source of the sedimentary rocks with their fossils), it may well have had a celestial trigger. There are two periods of cratering evident upon the moon,[46] so the second round could have occurred during the Flood. We suggest that a narrow band of ice bodies from the "waters above" were sent in toward the earth to trigger the opening of the "fountains of the great deep," and precipitate the catastrophic crustal plate movements. Froede[47] has pointed out that celestial bodies which caused cratering on the biblical time scale should have visible remnants in the solar system today. Meteorites and asteroids would be the remnants of the cratering objects of the first bombardment (the planet break-up perhaps occurring at the time of the Curse), and comets would be the remnants of the second bombardment (from ice chunks at the time of the Flood). A period of accelerated nuclear decay (as mentioned in chapter 5 on time scales) may also have occurred at this time to facilitate the earth movements.
CONFUSION	This appears to have been an earth-only event, but one of its cosmic implications is that it highlights the miraculous nature of human

46. Danny Faulkner, "A Biblically-based Cratering Theory," *TJ* 13(1):100–104 (1999).
47. Carl R. Froede Jr., "Extraterrestrial Bombardment of the Inner Solar System: A Review With Questions and Comments Based On New Information," *Creation Research Society Quarterly* 38(4):209–212 (2002).

	language, thereby refuting any possible evolutionary origin.[48] Man, the cosmologist, is a unique creation and we would not expect to find alien counterparts elsewhere in the universe, as the SETI program continually confirms.
CHRIST	The Incarnation is both the centerpiece and the proof of the biblical cosmology. Earth is not simply an insignificant "pale blue dot," lost in the vastness of a purposeless universe. Earth is the focus of the Creator's attention, and the very place where He chose to be with His beloved people. Nowhere else in the whole creation has ever been so blessed!
CROSS	The Curse affected the whole creation, so the Cross, in redeeming man, redeemed the whole creation, with the full outworking yet to come. The price has been paid! The Resurrection proves beyond doubt that Christ is who He said He was and that the Bible is accurate as He said it was.
CONSUMMATION	The Final Judgment is yet to come. Some prophetic Bible passages refer to celestial phenomena, including "stars falling from the sky." One of these is described as "something like a great mountain, burning with fire, was thrown into the sea" and another as "a great star fell from heaven, blazing like a torch" (Rev. 8:8–10). These could well be asteroids or ice chunks (comets) from the "waters above," reserved by God for this final judgment. Those in Christ will have nothing to fear from such phenomena, however, for their

48 Alexander R. Williams, "Apes, Words and People," *Creation* 25(3):50–53 (2003).

redemption will be near at hand. We do not have to wait billions of years for a big chill, or a big crunch, or a big rip. We have a new creation on the way, and it will be much, much sooner than that!

God has declared the end from the beginning (Isa. 46:9–10) and His people will be His witnesses at the Judgment to testify that this is so (Isa. 43:9–12). Christ is the Alpha and the Omega, the Beginning and the End (Rev. 22:13).

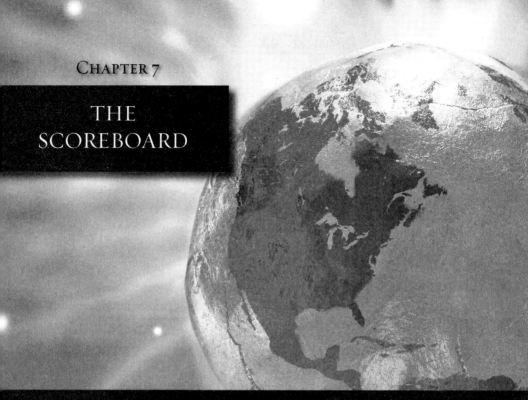

CHAPTER 7

THE SCOREBOARD

The time has now come to "add up the scores" as it were. You may recall from our earlier discussion that all theories of the past have to involve assumptions because we cannot revisit the past to directly test our theories. We now need to look at each model, the assumptions underlying them, and the secondary assumptions made within each model, to see which is more directly consistent with the evidence. Some assumptions can be ruled out on the basis of contradictory evidence, but among those that remain, we can use "Occam's Razor" — the theory requiring the least number of ad hoc assumptions (i.e., assumptions just invented for that particular purpose and not derived from the general principles of the theory) is to be preferred. So which model fits the data best? The big-bang model? Or the biblical model?

Because the big-bang theory and the Bible are different kinds of explanations, different kinds of assessments are required. Big-bang theory can appeal to any and every possible physical cause, so it needs to be assessed against those causes. The Bible appeals to supernatural causes, which cannot be scrutinized, but the consequences of God's stated actions can be.[1] So, the procedure

---

1. This is why compromise positions on Genesis (gap theory, day-age, progressive creation, theistic evolution, etc.) produce a scientifically worthless world view. When the Genesis account is compromised with naturalistic theories, its evidence becomes debased as a source of testable predictions.

we will follow is to assess the big-bang theory against its own claims, and see how it matches the observations, and likewise to assess the Bible against its own claims and see how they match the evidence. Then we will assess both explanations across any common criteria. Before we do this comparison, we need to briefly return to our study of logic — the logic of causality.

Causality

A fundamental issue in any theory of origins is causality. We spoke earlier of "necessary" and "sufficient" causes in scientific explanations, and we now need to highlight the idea of a "competent" cause. A competent cause is a cause that *can* do what it is said to have done. Because it happened in the past, we cannot know for sure if it *did* do what it is claimed to have done, but if it is a competent cause for the nominated effect then we can reasonably infer that it *might* have done so. For example, an ant cannot push a bulldozer so it is not a competent cause in explaining the movement of a bulldozer. However, a bulldozer can push an ant. Therefore, a bulldozer is a competent cause as a possible explanation for the movement of an ant.

When we apply this thinking to the universe, we can ask, "Can cause X produce a universe?" Or in other words, "Is cause X a competent cause as a possible explanation for the origin of the universe?" So, let's examine the basic causes which each model appeals to and see which, if any, is a competent cause.

The basic features of the big-bang model are that it begins with a singularity, which "exploded," and it then produced the universe that we observe, via chance and the laws of physics. We can formulate three questions here about competent causes. First, "Can a singularity with the mass of the whole universe exist?" Second, "Can such a singularity explode?" Third, "Can the explosion of such a singularity produce a universe?" The answer to the first question is probably "yes" — there appears to be no limit to the mass of possible singularities. The equations of general relativity do allow for an expanding singularity; however, as mentioned earlier, these equations do not apply at the exact moment of the singularity due to the extremely small scales involved. So the second question cannot be answered with certainty since the physics at singularity scales is not known.

Let's concede for argument's sake, however, that our science is inadequate when it comes to primordial singularities. So what happens if we proceed? Can the explosion of a singularity produce a universe? It can (theoretically, at least) produce an expanding cloud of gas. An expanding cloud of gas is not the galaxy/star/planet/life/man universe that we defined as our "necessary and sufficient" universe.

We must conclude, therefore, that the big-bang theory is not based on a competent cause, even allowing for a crucial amount of ignorance regarding primordial singularities.

What about the biblical model? Does it fare any better? The starting point is God, the eternally existing One (His personal name is Yahweh — meaning "I am"). The causal argument is "In the beginning God created the heaven and the earth." Our three parallel questions will therefore be: "Does God exist?" "Can God create?" and "Can God create the universe that we observe?"

Our answer to the first question is that any system of thought has to start somewhere and we choose to start with God. We cannot prove the existence of God, nor do we try. Those who come to God "must believe that he exists and that he rewards those who earnestly seek him" (Heb. 11:6). The answer to the second question is yes, God (if we mean by that the God of the Bible) can create — it is the primary characteristic by which He distinguishes himself from false gods (Isa. 40–46; Jer. 10:11–12). Furthermore, God incarnate — Jesus of Nazareth — displayed His creative power in many and varied miracles. The answer to the third question is that the universe described in the Bible as having been made by God corresponds in many important ways with the universe we observe, even to the extent of making known beforehand (by thousands of years) things that have been discovered only in recent times. We conclude, therefore, that the Bible does present us with a competent cause for the origin of the universe.

INDIVIDUAL AND COMMON SCORES

The detailed comparison tables are given in appendix C, *The Scoreboard Tables*.

There are 19 items on the list for the big-bang theory. The first one is acceptable on purely philosophical grounds (any theory has to start somewhere), one (the CMBR) may have some explanatory power, although there are other possible explanations, and the remaining 17 are either ad hoc or are directly contradicted by the evidence. The best possible score for the big-bang theory is therefore 2 out of 19, or 11 percent.

There are 13 items in the list for the biblical model. None are inconsistent with the evidence. The time scale for supernova events is explained in principle by relativistic time dilation, but their relation to the Fall still needs to be explained. We have therefore given a score of 12 out of 13, or 92 percent.

On the common scoreboard, where both models address the same phenomena, 20 items are listed. All 20 are consistent with the biblical model, but only 4 are consistent with the big-bang model.

So what does it all mean? We think it is very clear. The Bible presents us with a better explanation of the universe than the big-bang theory. When assessed against its own criteria, the biblical cosmology was consistent with the evidence in 92 percent of cases. On the other hand, the big-bang theory is woefully inadequate — when assessed against its own criteria, only 11 percent of the items were consistent with the evidence, and on the criteria common to both, the biblical model is ahead by a margin of 20 to 4.[2]

Are we presenting a fair assessment of big-bang cosmology? Or are we simply coming to a conclusion that was predetermined by our starting assumptions? When evolutionary cosmologists of the stature of Cambridge University's Professor Stephen Hawking acknowledge that the origin of the stars and galaxies (i.e., our necessary and sufficient universe) remains an unanswered question within the big-bang paradigm, we believe we can rest our case; big-bang theory is indeed inadequate. This conclusion is further confirmed by the widespread disaffection among the cosmological community concerning the fundamental weaknesses in the theory itself (appendix D).

On the other hand, are we presenting an unwarranted positive view of the biblical model? Are there any potentially insurmountable problems facing the Genesis cosmogony that we have overlooked? Prior to Humphreys' pioneering work in relativistic time dilation, many would have said that the time scale was an insurmountable problem. We believe this is no longer the case; on the contrary, over a wide range of time indicators in the cosmos, the biblical model is now well ahead of the big-bang model.

It is common among evolutionists to say, when challenged over the inadequacy of their theory, that it is "the best scientific theory that we have." By this they mean that since nothing better is available, then this one is good enough. This is a fallacious argument. If it were true, we could apply the same logic to turn a bicycle into a time machine. We could say that a bicycle is "the best time machine we have" and is therefore "good enough" to do the job, because no one else has a better time machine. This is ludicrous. The lack of a better alternative does nothing to improve the adequacy of the bicycle. Likewise, the lack of a better alternative does nothing to improve the adequacy of big-bang theory.

---

2. We do not claim any particular significance for the absolute values of the numbers presented in this comparison, only that the outcome favors the Bible. Other authors might take a different approach to the criteria we have used and this may improve the apparent performance of the big-bang model, but we do not believe that different authors could come to a different conclusion to the overall comparison.

In fact, the big-bang theory is not the "best we have." The Genesis cosmogony is far superior, both philosophically and scientifically. At this point, evolutionists might counter-argue that creation is not scientific, it is religious, and has no place in science, but we have pointed out that all theories of the past have to be based on assumptions, because no one can revisit the past to test their theories. Assumptions are always made within a *belief* system (a world view). So the big-bang theory is just as much based on faith as is the biblical model, and is therefore no more scientific nor less religious. Both models therefore have equivalent philosophical foundations, and in the above comparison, the biblical model "wins" by a large margin.

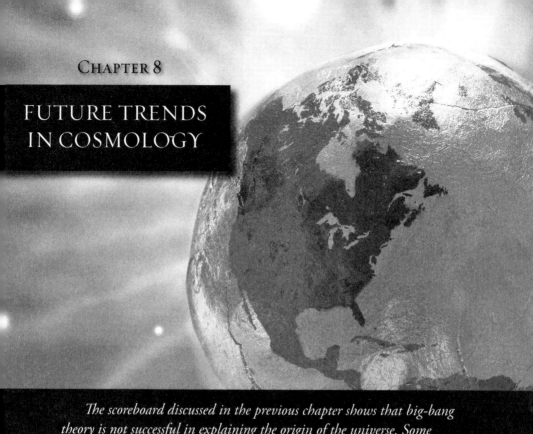

CHAPTER 8

FUTURE TRENDS IN COSMOLOGY

*The scoreboard discussed in the previous chapter shows that big-bang theory is not successful in explaining the origin of the universe. Some naturalistic materialists refuse to give up their belief, however, and point to the enormous progress made by science, saying that future discoveries will surely vindicate their point of view. This is a logically invalid position to take, however, because it bases a present-day conclusion on what we don't yet know of the future. What we **do** know at present is that naturalistic materialism has no answer to the question of origins. Nevertheless, it is worth tracing out the present trends in cosmology to see where they may be pointing.*

To refresh our memory, let's recall the major tasks of cosmogony — they are to explain the origin of the universe, galaxies, stars, planets, life, and cosmologists.

Origin of the universe. The first law of thermodynamics says that matter/energy cannot be created or destroyed. Naturalistic materialists cannot explain the origin of matter/energy, just as creationists cannot explain the existence of God, except to say that it (or, in the latter case, God) has always existed. We cannot foresee any future change in this position.

Early history of the universe. At present, there is enormous interest in precision measurements of the Cosmic Microwave Background Radiation (CMBR) and its implications for big-bang theory. However, as can be seen in our appendix A on *Some Other Cosmological Models*, all this speculation is conditional upon the assumption that the CMBR is the leftover radiation from the decoupling phase in the big-bang scenario. If this is not the case, as a number of eminent scientists have suggested, then it will be much ado about nothing (or rather, about something else).

New physics. Will new discoveries in physics lead to better explanations of origin? We do not believe so. The current forces of physics are conservative, not creative — God's creative forces ceased their general operation when He rested on creation day 7. We expect that new discoveries will bring new understanding of how the universe is held together and how it works, but not where it came from. Advances in gravity research, for example, may reveal its quantum structure and its wave behavior, but this will merely deepen our understanding of gravity — it is unlikely to allow gravity to do things that it previously could not do. If string theory or M-theory can be validated experimentally, it will reveal the universe to be even more complicated than it appears at present, and so will add to the burden of explanation, not reduce it.

Origin of galaxies. Peebles and Silk's pessimistic survey of models of galactic origins in 1990 has not been advanced in any significant way in the intervening years. As more information comes in, to shed further light on galaxy structure and diversity, we expect that the task will become harder rather than easier.

Origin of stars. Models of stellar origin continue to begin with gravitationally unstable gas and dust clouds, but with no credible explanation for the "priming" mechanism. The more we get to know about our own star, the sun, the more surprises we discover. We expect this trend to continue for other stars as well. We suggest that the stars will appear more and more diverse as time goes by, and our solar system will progressively stand out as being more and more special.

Origin of planets. The search for extrasolar planets is throwing up lots of new information about planets, but the trend is one of revealing new problems rather than solving old ones. We expect this trend to continue.

Origin of life. Molecular biologists recently succeeded in fabricating viruses from pre-existing components (DNA and protein) so the technology for eventually fabricating a living cell appears to be advancing. However, the technology is so specialized that it clearly illustrates how life requires intelligent design and manufacture. NASA's search for extra-terrestrial life is, we predict, heading for a disappointment. We expect Mars to be as barren as the moon. If some microbial life is found on Mars, we predict it will be of the familiar earth-kind and will have come originally from earth, either via man-made spacecraft or ejecta from celestial impacts on earth.

Origin of man. Man, the cosmologist, is absolutely unique in all the known universe, despite widespread claims that we are just mammals, like the apes and the dolphins. Human language and capacity for true abstract thought and creativity sets us apart in a quantitative and measurable way that is beyond refutation.[1] We do not expect to find any creatures like ourselves "out there" (except for the angels in the spiritual realms).

Space travel. Some people are arguing that man's journey of discovery to Mars and beyond is as necessary and inevitable as Columbus's journey of discovery to the New World, but the comparison is false and misleading. The New World of the Americas was a vast, fertile, well-watered land, rich in natural and human resources, which repaid many times over the investment in the original journey of discovery. In stark contrast, human space travel is enormously expensive and it has so far yielded no material gains that could realistically fund continued expenditure into the future. Virtually all the technological benefits of the space program have been gained by research and development carried out here on the earth. Unless space travel can generate money to support itself (such as tourism to the moon) it seems likely that the future of space research will be by small intelligent machines. Human space travel to Mars appears to be technically feasible, but a somewhat bleak prospect. Nowhere else in our solar system is benign enough to welcome visitors. Human travel to other star systems is certainly not feasible with present-day technology, so an entirely new kind of technology would be required to search beyond our solar system. Man's future presently appears tied to the earth. There are no obvious escape routes.

Time travel. The only way (other than waiting for the return of Christ) to gain observational evidence of what happened "in the beginning" is to revisit it in a time machine. No one that we are aware of is making any substantial progress on this subject. As we pointed out earlier, the absence of time tourists would appear to preclude any future invention of such a time machine. It does

---

1. Alexander R. Williams, "Apes, Words, and People," *Creation* 25(3):50–53 (2003); Brad Harrub, Bert Thompson, and Dave Miller, "The Origin of Language and Communication," *TJ* 17(3):93–101 (2003).

not preclude the development of a time machine that can return an observer to the time that machine was switched on, but such a machine would not be able to revisit "the beginning."

UFOs. Despite the continuing lack of any reproducible evidence, a worldwide culture of "alien visitation" has persisted for the last half century. People report UFO sightings and abductions, sometimes with deep conviction as to the causes and the consequences. One observation that we believe is crucial to interpreting these reports is that all of them seem to be limited to the human sphere of activity — the SETI project has not found anything to confirm the idea of alien intelligence beyond earth. We therefore conclude that their cause is also limited to the human sphere of activity. We suggest that a combination of hoax, misinterpretation, coincidence, delusion, and demonic deception[2] can variously explain these things. While it is possible that Satan may raise up opposition to God through the cults of "alien visitations," we do not expect them to have any significant consequences for the scientific study of cosmology.

New cosmological theories. There are many possible theories of cosmological origins. Is it likely that a new one may explain it all better than the current front runner — the Bible? There are basically only two kinds of objects under consideration in cosmology — the *matter* of its substance and the *mind* that contemplates it. Two components only allow for three different possible combinations of kinds of origin scenarios: (1) mind produced matter (the Bible says God spoke the universe into existence); (2) matter produced mind (by self-organization of galaxies, stars, planets, life, and eventually people, over millions of years); or (3) matter and mind are both primordial (creative spirits formed primordial matter into the objects we see today, or their original precursors). At present, the first kind is the leading contender and none but biblical creationists are actively pursuing it. Self-organizing scenarios of the second kind appear to be defeated at the present time, although no doubt new variations will come and go. Combined scenarios of the third kind are held among a number of traditional societies and are also promoted by UFO "alien

---

2. Paul warned that "The coming of the lawless one will be in accordance with the work of Satan displayed in all kinds of *counterfeit miracles, signs, and wonders*, and in every sort of evil that deceives those who are perishing. They perish because they refused to love the truth and so be saved. For this reason God sends them *a powerful delusion* so that they will believe the lie" (2 Thess. 2:9–11). Revelation 12 indicates that Satan has been thrown out of heaven and down to earth, which would be consistent with him being limited to the sphere of human activity. See Gary Bates, *Alien Intrusion* (Green Forest, AR: Master Books, Inc., 2005).

visitors," but no significant contributions to scientific understanding are yet forthcoming in these areas. We do not foresee any imminent change to this current situation.

SUMMARY OF FUTURE TRENDS

While enormous strides of progress in astronomy, astrophysics, and particle physics no doubt lie ahead, we do not expect any such discoveries to overturn the general conclusions that we have reached in this study. The current trend of circular reasoning (new discoveries interpreted within the prevailing paradigm so as to appear to bolster it, especially through the popular media) may of course continue to foster the hopes of secularists from time to time, but naturalistic materialism has no satisfactory explanation for cosmic origins. Famous astronomer the late Sir Fred Hoyle considered that big-bang theory was "dull-as-ditchwater expansion which degrades itself adiabatically [i.e., without gain or loss of heat] until it is incapable of doing anything at all. The notion that galaxies form, to be followed by an active astronomical history, is an illusion. Nothing forms; the thing is dead as a doornail."[3] The Bible presents a far more self-consistent explanation: In the beginning *God* created the heavens and the earth.

---

3. Fred Hoyle, "The Big Bang in Astronomy," *New Scientist* 92:523 (November 19, 1981).

THE CHOICE

We hope that you agree with us by now that no one can interpret the universe without making some preliminary assumptions about it. We pointed out in the chapter on *Science, World Views, and Cosmological Models* that we all have a choice when it comes to these starting assumptions. We face at least three options for our choice, and it is now appropriate to review those options in the light of the evidence that we have considered.

(a) We can choose to **decide for ourselves** what happened "in the beginning." Many people do this but it is not an option that we can recommend, for the following reasons: (1) we were not there so we have no direct knowledge of what happened; (2) we do not have all the relevant information on the subject, and much of the "information" that we do have is biased (and thus inadequate) *interpretation* of the evidence; (3) our imagination, knowledge, and wisdom are all limited by our own personal character and experience. This option can do little more than build us a "castle in the air."

(b) We can choose to follow the method of **scientific naturalism**. This entails beginning with observable things such as matter and energy and seeking explanations within the laws of physics. The most widely accepted naturalistic theory of cosmic origins is the big-bang theory, but, as we have seen, it does not explain the origin of galaxies, stars, planets, or people. As a theory of origin, and therefore as a basis for a "scientific" world view, big-bang theory is a dramatic under-achiever. Anyone who is tempted to put their trust in it is putting their life in the hands of a demonstrably inadequate theory.

(c) We can choose to follow the advice of **someone else** who knows more about the subject than either we, or the scientific natural-ists, know. Out of all the great figures in human history, only one has risen from the dead to validate His claim to authority on cosmic issues — Jesus of Nazareth. He pointed to the writings of Moses (and thus the Genesis creation account) as the basis for His own life and minis-try, and He commended it to His followers.

We, the authors, have chosen to follow Jesus because His miracles and His resurrection demonstrated His surpassing power and authority over both the physical and spiritual worlds, and His self-giving love is an example that we desire to follow. He claimed to be God incarnate and proved it by rising from the dead. As a result of following Jesus, we have found that His life and His words, and the Scriptures that He based His life and words upon, are consis-tent within themselves, are consistent with the physical world that we have studied, and are consistent with the personal experience that we have of Him. We have taken Him at his word, and accepted His offer of forgiveness for the sins that separated us from Him; we have received the gift of His Spirit and we now rejoice in His presence. We have found, in Jesus, peace and fellow-ship with God in the present world, and a sure hope for the world to come. We have a cosmology that is internally consistent — the God who created and who sustains the universe has come to us as Savior and friend. We *know* whom we have believed and are persuaded that He is the personal truth that underlies the universe that we live in.

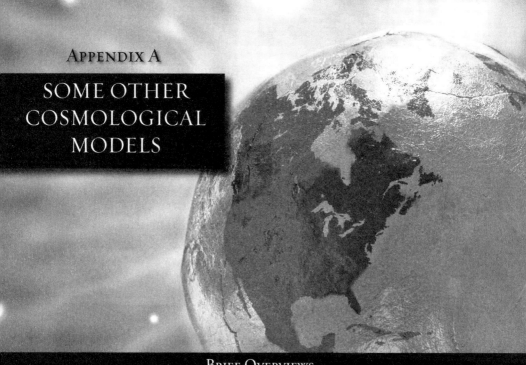

Appendix A

SOME OTHER COSMOLOGICAL MODELS

Brief Overviews

B ig-bang theory doesn't work. Are there any other more plausible models? Well, there are quite a few alternative viewpoints, and in this appendix we will briefly outline four other cosmological models that contribute new insights not present in big-bang theory. Some of the discussion is quite technical, so for those who might get lost in the details we will list here some of the interesting features of each model:

- **The Arpian Universe** — Astronomer Halton Arp has produced convincing (to several significant others as well as himself) evidence that quasars are not vastly distant objects, but they are new "infant" galaxies being ejected from the hearts of mature "parent" galaxies. Their high redshifts (the reason that others think they are very distant objects) result from the fact that the matter in the quasars is newly created, initially with zero mass; as they accumulate mass with time, their initially high redshift declines in inverse proportion to their accumulating mass. According to Arp, quasar redshift is a measure of age, not recession velocity. As a result, Arp's universe consists of the (relatively nearby) Fornax and Virgo superclusters of galaxies, surrounded by vast reaches of empty space. The CMBR is simply the temperature of this empty space.

- **Quasi-Steady State Universe** — Astronomers Hoyle, Burbidge, and Narlikar believe Halton Arp's work to be the correct interpretation of quasars and their redshifts, but they have developed an infinite, cyclic universe that undergoes compression and expansion phases (but not total collapse such as in the "big crunch"). In their universe, we are about 11 billion years into the current expansion cycle, and we can see back to objects that were created as much as 18 billion years ago, but the universe is actually infinite in extent. New matter is continually being created in the hearts of existing galaxies (via Arp's mechanism) and the redshift correlation is the result of us observing objects at different times after their matter was created.

- **Carmeli's Cosmological General Relativity** — Theoretical physicist Moshe Carmeli has rewritten relativity theory in terms of velocity (redshift) rather than time, so his universe is made up of *spacevelocity*, an analogue to Einstein's *spacetime*. It is an intriguing idea and produces a cosmology that is based on what astronomers actually observe (redshift and luminosity) rather than what they infer (time). It makes predictions that are testable — in 1996 it predicted that the universal expansion would be accelerating, which was confirmed in 1998, and tests of other predictions may become available soon.

- **Van Flandern's Meta Model** — Astronomer Tom Van Flandern has created a cosmological model from the ground up, simply using interacting particles. His meta-gravity is not an attractive force, but a repulsive force — the apparent attraction results from nearby objects shielding one another from constant buffeting in a universal sea of gravity particles. For such a simple model, the meta model provides some very interesting and elegant explanations of cosmological phenomena. Meta-gravity has a limited range of about the size of a typical spiral galaxy core, so each galaxy is a world of its own and there is no universal expansion or contraction. The galactic redshift correlation with distance is not a result of cosmic expansion, but the cumulative effect of interference between gravity particles and light waves. Because of gravity's shielding effects, maximum shielding is reached in supernova remnants, which do not suffer infinite collapse into black holes — rather, they produce quasars.

We can see here the truth of Professor Silk's earlier quote, that there are numerous different possible models of the early universe — the only constraint is that they produce the world that we observe today. All these models contribute something to cosmology, but none of them provides a complete picture, so none of them constitutes a reliable foundation for one's eternal destiny.

The Arpian Universe

When Halton Arp was in seventh grade at school, he discovered that the solution to a problem in his textbook, as given in the back of the book, was wrong. This revelation — that the received wisdom of the day can be wrong — started Arp on a path of independent thinking that has caused him the deepest grief, perhaps of all contemporary scientists of his high caliber. His skepticism toward mainstream thinking and his persistence in pursuing an alternative view of the universe have led him through unfair dismissal, ostracism, rejection, ridicule, denial of funding, and a long sequence of disappointments in his fellow man and in the ideals of science.

The seat of Arp's trouble lies in the decades of astronomical observations that have proven to him, over and over again, that the highest redshifts among celestial objects are not due to expansion of the universe, as the Hubble orthodoxy tells us. How does he know? Because over and over again he has discovered that quasars, the most highly redshifted objects in the universe, are often associated in tangible ways with galaxies that are (relatively) close by. If the quasars are close by, then their redshifts cannot be mostly the result of cosmic expansion over vast distances.

To see the significance of Arp's findings, we need to understand the visible universe as seen through the eyes of a big-bang theorist. It looks approximately like this:

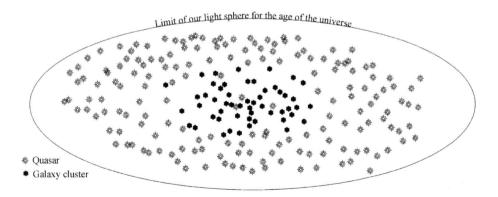

The distribution of quasars and galaxies in the big-bang universe.
Note that the outer regions contain mostly quasars.

According to the Hubble law, redshift is proportional to distance (that is, recession speed times the supposed age of the universe). It does seem to work for the brightest galaxies in any cluster, but the big bangers have applied this to quasars as well. Quasars are generally the highest redshifted objects in the universe, so therefore they must be the farthest away. Therefore, the big-bang universe consists of galaxies and galaxy clusters (and superclusters) in the inner regions, and mostly quasars in the outer regions (a few faint, very distant galaxies have been observed).

Now one of the embarrassing things about this picture is that big bangers do not really know what quasars are.[1] In volume terms, therefore, most of the visible universe is inhabited by inexplicable objects. How can a respectable astrophysicist be expected to explain a universe that is filled with inexplicable objects? Arp's answer is that they shouldn't be expected to. He believes that he knows what quasars are, *and* where they came from.

Quasars

The name "quasar" is derived from "**QUA**si-Stell**AR** radio source," sometimes also called a "quasi-stellar object" or QSO. This means that they *look* like stars, but there is something different about them. They don't look like galaxies — and the importance of this point will become clear shortly. Until 1963, these objects were universally considered to be ordinary stars. However, in that year their "something different" was uncovered — they have extraordinarily high redshifts. Under the Hubble law, a high redshift means that they are traveling away from us at enormous speeds (some of them supposedly at up to 90 percent of the speed of light!). If they are traveling at enormous speeds — very much faster than any known galaxy — then they must be a long way away from us, since they have been traveling fast for a very long time.

If they are a long way away from us then they must also be massively luminous — far beyond any star in our own galaxy (or most of the known galaxies). According to the inverse square law, an object that looks like it is a star in our own galaxy but is actually 100,000 times farther away must therefore be 10,000,000,000 times more luminous than such a star. Since the stars in our galaxy only range up to about 100,000 times the luminosity of our sun, these quasars pose a considerable challenge. Their estimated energy output can supposedly be hundreds of times that of a *whole galaxy*. All of this in a "star-like" object!

---

1. Tom Van Flandern, "Quasars: Near or Far?" (lists 21 properties of quasars that are not well explained by big-bang theory) <http://www.metaresearch.org/cosmology/QuasarsNearVersusFar.asp>.

The contemporary big-bang view is that quasars are the active nuclei of remote galaxies that are fueled by massive black holes surrounded by an accretion disk, but this is little more than guesswork.[2] Very few observable galaxies (where we *can* see the stars) have quasar-like properties. Quasars are star-like, not galaxy-like. The luminosity of some quasars also varies over periods as short as one day. The time scale of such a light-emission-varying process must be comparable to the light-travel time across the object. So if the period of light variation is one day, that would limit the size of the object to one light-day in diameter, tens of millions of times smaller than the diameter of a typical galaxy. If the process causing the variation is rotation, it means the object's rotation period is also of the order of one day. Galaxy-sized objects normally take millions of years to complete a full rotation, so it seems most unlikely that an object that rotates once per day is a galaxy. Galaxies also usually have visible evidence of stars — that is, a fuzziness around the edges. Surprisingly, some quasars do have "fuzz" as well, but according to the big-bang interpretation they should be too far away for stars to be seen at all.

Arp has no such problems. He has discovered a repeating pattern of paired quasars either side of large active galaxies that are relatively nearby. The low probability of such associations occurring by chance, together with frequent evidence of luminous matter (which is often found to be emitting X-rays) connecting the quasars with the galaxies, forms a solid case as far as he is concerned. If quasars are at the same distance as their associated galaxies, then their high redshift is not the result of recession due to cosmic expansion.

Arp's interpretation of these observations has not been accepted by the astronomical community — they say the alignments are the result of chance — and his work has been repeatedly rejected from publication. He has refused to be quiet, however, and has published the essence of his work in three books, *Quasars, Redshifts and Controversies* in 1987,[3] *Seeing Red: Redshifts, Cosmology and Academic Science* in 1998,[4] and *Catalogue of Discordant Redshift Associations* in 2002.[5]

---

2. They say that matter falling into the black hole causes enormous amounts of energy to be emitted, such that it can be seen over distance scales of the order of the size of the visible universe.

3. Halton Arp, *Quasars, Redshifts and Controversies* (Berkeley CA: Interstellar Media, 1987).

4. Halton Arp, *Seeing Red: Redshifts, Cosmology and Academic Science* (Montreal: Apeiron, 1998).

5. Halton Arp, *Catalogue of Discordant Redshift Associations* (Montreal: Apeiron, 2003).

So what are the quasars doing next to the galaxies? Why are they in pairs? Arp believes that the quasars were produced from the nuclei of their parent galaxies, which usually show evidence of being active and disrupted, and that they are themselves balls of "new matter" that will eventually turn into new galaxies. Quasars, according to Arp, are embryonic galaxies.

Why are their redshifts so different from that of their parent galaxy? Because the "new" matter emits light at longer wavelengths, giving the impression of a Doppler-type shift. Arp believes that the new matter emerges from its parent galaxy with zero inertial mass, and that the mass of these new particles then proceeds to accumulate with time. Light is produced from matter when electrons fall between energy levels within atoms. The wavelength of light coming from a "new" low-mass hydrogen atom will appear to be highly redshifted compared with light from "normal" hydrogen from a laboratory source. The emitted light will become more "normal" with time as the "new" hydrogen gathers mass and becomes more like ordinary hydrogen. Redshift, according to this theory, is a measure of *youth*, not of recession velocity.

How does the "new" matter gather mass? This is where most physicists part company with Arp. Yet history may well be on Arp's side, because he bases his explanation on a venerable concept — Mach's principle. Ernst Mach was an Austrian physicist in the latter part of the 19th century whose work formed an important impetus and base for Einstein's general theory of relativity. Mach's explanation for where the inertial mass of an object (its resistance to acceleration) comes from was that it is the result of the gravitational attraction of every other particle in the universe. Most of modern physics, based on general relativity, ignores Mach's principle and settles for an approximation based on "local" events and objects. That is, when a gravitational computation is carried out, it takes into account only those particles within a particular radius of the object in question, and it ignores everything in the universe beyond that "local" radius.[6] Modern physics is therefore "local" physics, according to Mach's principle.

Arp takes Mach's principle seriously (as do a number of other contemporary astrophysicists) and says that "new" matter with zero mass will accumulate mass as the "light sphere" around its position expands throughout the universe. According to relativity, gravitational fields travel at the speed of light,

---

6. One of the principles of General Relativity, Local Position Invariance, means that any local experiment only need be concerned with the local space curvature, which is the combined result of all matter acting to curve the space.

so the new matter will accumulate inertial mass (and gravitational mass) at the same rate that light travels through the universe. A resulting prediction of Arp's model is that quantum pair creation (e.g., electron-positron pairs) in the laboratory should show they have zero inertial mass initially and they should accumulate it over time. The effect *has not been observed,* so it remains to be seen how significant this might be. On the surface, it is a very big problem for Arp, and he does not answer the objection very well in his book.[7]

The quasar "galaxy babies" do not continue indefinitely on their journey away from the parent. As their mass grows, they are gravitationally attracted back toward their parent, and as they age and become recognizable galaxies, they form clusters of galaxies around the parent galaxy. In time they, too, produce quasar pairs, which in turn become new galaxies. As a result, Arp's model produces galaxy clusters, something that the homogenized, hyperinflated, hot big-bang model cannot do.

The process results in multiple births of galaxies in hierarchical structures, spatially and temporally; something like a fireworks display where

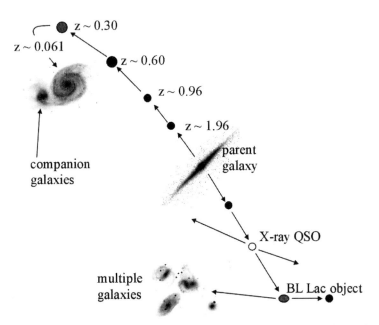

This schematic diagram of the changes occurring in the ejected quasars as they turn into normal galaxies is from Arp's *Seeing Red*.[8]

---

7. Arp, *Seeing Red: Redshifts, Cosmology and Academic Science*, p. 234.
8. Ibid., figure 9.3, p. 239.

many explosions eject small glowing centers that then explode to liberate more glowing centers.[9] On top of this, due to the forces of gravity, these galaxies of stars form whirlpools in space, some in spirals, some highly distorted and peculiar. The galaxies then form into clusters and these clusters into superclusters. The superclusters viewed from earth appear to form into gigantic spiral structures.

Note in the figure below that in the Fornax supercluster of galaxies, there is a general S-shaped or spiral pattern visible. The bottom part of the S is not all visible.

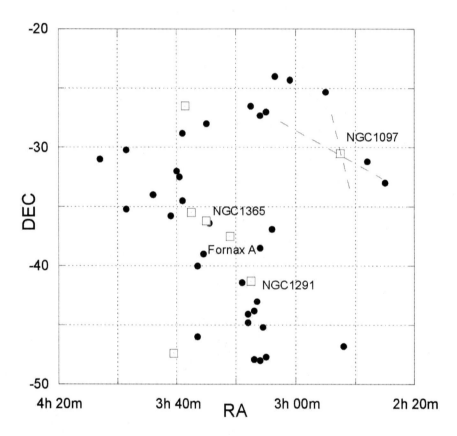

Schematic diagram of the Fornax supercluster, showing spiral structure (from Arp, *Seeing Red*).[10] Galaxy magnitudes : • ≤ 17.0, □ < 10.9.

---

9. The actual process of creation in this model could be the direct creative work of God, which we are seeing just 6,000 years after it occurred on creation day 4. However, Arp assigns to it a "natural" process, since he believes in the quasi-steady state model of Hoyle, Burbidge, and Narlikar (see next section).

10. Arp, *Seeing Red: Redshifts, Cosmology and Academic Science*, figure 6.12, p. 152.

It is like a signature that is repeated throughout the cosmos — structure within structure and new galaxies born from the dense hearts of active existing galaxies. Arp describes what he sees as the evolution or aging of the ejected quasars into new galaxies. The elliptical galaxies were the original (created) galaxies. They tend to be very large and often are associated with groups of spirals, like M31 (the most massive in our local group) and M81 in the next major group.

Arp mentions in particular two major superclusters, Virgo and Fornax, one in the northern sky and the other in the southern sky. He says of these, "I am tempted to say that if there is a Creator (and if so I would not presume to attribute anthropomorphic properties to it [shows his bias]) we might expect to hear: "Look, you dummies, I showed you the Virgo cluster and you did not believe it so I will show you another one just like it and if you still don't believe it — well, let's just forget the whole thing." It is amazing how he comes so close to the biblical view; the observations are pointing him to the obvious conclusion, but he turns away!

Arp's universe therefore consists of two relatively local superclusters of galaxies — Virgo and Fornax — surrounded by empty space stretching out to about 15 billion light-years distance. Beyond that, he says the universe is unknown, and at present is unknowable because we cannot see it yet, for light has not had enough time to travel that far. Arp's universe is non-expanding, unbounded, and ageless. Time is local to each galaxy. Newly formed galaxies have clocks that run slow compared with older galaxies. The cosmic microwave background radiation is simply the temperature of the "empty" space beyond our galactic neighborhood.

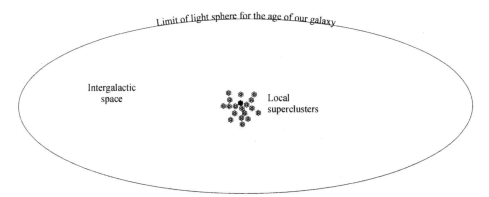

The Arpian universe. Most of the known galaxies are in our local Virgo and Fornax superclusters because they were all produced locally. We cannot know what else lies beyond our light spere.

Anyone who is interested in the details of Arp's universe, and the observational data that he has based it on, should consult his books. The interesting points for our purpose are as follows:

- The same astronomical observations are available to Arp as to mainstream astronomers, but Arp has been able to interpret the observations in a totally different way and yet remain within the laws of physics. There may well be other, yet again totally different, ways of interpreting the same observations that we have not yet discovered.

- Arp has taken up a dormant principle of science (Mach's principle) and made ingenious use of it. Perhaps there are other such things under our noses that we are not seeing either.

- Arp has proposed a mechanism for producing "self-gravitating" gas clouds — something that is essential to all cosmology but is severely lacking in big-bang theory. Arp's "new matter" with zero mass is in a compact quasar form, and as mass grows within a cloud of new matter, densities increase and (perhaps plausibly) produce self-gravitating bodies. A process of fragmentation is still required — to turn a quasar into a galaxy of stars — but at least Arp has suggested a way to get over the self-gravitation hurdle.

- Big-bang theorists have consistently chosen to focus on observations that support their theory and have sidelined, minimized, or rejected observations that contradict it. There is thus a bias in the information that they present to the world.

- Arp has highlighted the fact that big-bang theorists have allowed their theory to determine the validity of his observations, rather than using the observations to shape the theory. In the ideal world, observations and theories need to progress together. When a person walks, they put one foot forward and then the other. Likewise, in science, as new observations are made, an advance in theory is required in order to maintain progress, but if one foot is allowed to remain in front all the time, no progress is made. Likewise, when big bangers allow the theory to take precedence over the observations they stall the progress of science.

- Astronomy is now dominated by very large and expensive equipment that no individual can afford to buy. Allocation committees decide who gets to observe what, and Arp has been frequently denied observation time on his anti–big-bang projects. You obviously don't have to be a six-day creationist to suffer at the hands of those who "know better." Not surprisingly, Arp is one of the signatories to the dissenting open letter to the scientific community reproduced in appendix D.

- NASA has a stranglehold on space technology and it has to justify huge budgets every year to the U.S. Congress. Its use and promotion of space technology is therefore heavily influenced by motives other than pure science. This is not meant to be a criticism of NASA *per se*, it is just the financial reality in the world of "big science," and seekers after truth should be aware of such influences.

Arp's work provides us with abundant evidence for the main theme of this book — that current cosmology is crucially dependent upon current starting assumptions, and its progress is dominated, not by what is "out there" in the universe, but by what is "in here" in people's heads — the ruling big-bang paradigm.

The Quasi-Steady State Model

Arp's work has played an important role in the revitalization of the steady state theory (SS). The original SS model, introduced by Bondi, Gold, and Hoyle in 1948, was based upon what is called the "perfect cosmological principle." This says that the universe looks the same in every direction (it is isotropic), it looks the same from every location (it is homogenous) and it looks the same from every epoch in time. Because the universe is also expanding, some kind of continuous creation of matter is necessary, so that the SS model can maintain a constant matter density. This creation was originally said to take place in otherwise empty space. The required rate of creation was too low to be detected by any of our modern instruments, so it could not be refuted by experimental observation. For a while, many cosmologists preferred this theory because it avoided the rather embarrassing singularity at the beginning of the big-bang theory. However, when the cosmic microwave background radiation (CMBR) was discovered in 1964, this was interpreted as favoring the big-bang theory, and the steady state theory was generally thought to have been refuted.

Hoyle did not give up on it, however. In 1982, Wright[11] suggested that metallic (or carbon) "whiskers" might be the cause of large infrared emissions from interstellar gas clouds and Hoyle recognized that here was the kind of

---

11. E. L. Wright, "Thermalization of Starlight by Elongated Grains: Can the Microwave Background Have Been Produced by Stars?" *Astrophysical Journal* 255:401 (1982).

thermalizing mechanism that his earlier model lacked — and which could now explain the CMBR, but it was 20 years too late to impress the big-bang advocates. It further turned out that McKellar[12] had already determined in 1941 that thermal excitation of rotational states of cyanide molecules (CN, quite common in interstellar gas clouds) indicated that 2.3 K microwave radiation was being produced. Had this been realized earlier, the big-bang model might never have taken center stage at all.

In the new quasi-steady state (QSS) model of Hoyle, Burbidge, and Narlikar,[13] radiation produced by stars is scattered by interstellar clouds of carbon whiskers to produce the CMBR. The new matter is now said to be created within the "nearly black holes" that inhabit the cores of active and disturbed galaxies. The light elements are created and ejected from galactic centers, in line with Arp's observations as described earlier.

Hoyle et al. also postulate the existence of a new heavy particle, a Planck particle (mass about 10^{-5} gram), which is the result of gravitational energy and is able to "tear open" the structure of spacetime, from which process the creation events emerge. These events result in showers of particles with masses of this order, which eventually decay into quarks, which in turn combine to eventually form hydrogen and helium. In both big-bang and QSS models, the creation of matter must occur. The difference is whether the products expand as a universal sea (big bang) or in separated fireballs (QSS). The big bang allows only for a balanced particle–antiparticle creation process but the QSS theory requires fireballs of (matter not antimatter) particles only. The results of their QSS calculations correspond rather well with the observed abundances of hydrogen and helium in the cosmos.

The steady-staters point to three major themes that support the QSS model over the big bang:

- Not all redshifts are the result of the general expansion of the universe (as Arp has shown).

- There is much evidence that galaxies, quasi-stellar objects (quasars), etc. are generated and ejected from galactic nuclei (as Arp has shown), and not from initial density fluctuations in the universe shortly after the big bang.

---

12. A. McKellar, *Pub. Dom. Astrophys. Observatory*, Victoria, B.C. 7, No. 15, p. 251 (1941).

13. Fred Hoyle, Geoffrey Burbidge, and J.V. Narlikar, *A Different Approach to Cosmology: From a Static Universe through the Big Bang Towards Reality* (Cambridge, UK: Cambridge University Press, 2000).

- The observed rapid release of large amounts of energy from galactic nuclei could conceivably come from creation processes that are occurring in the present-day universe.

Redshift and Quasars

Hubble showed a good correlation between redshift and apparent magnitude (which he attributed to cosmic expansion) for normal galaxies, but for quasars there is no such correlation. Compare the figures below. The first shows a classic Hubble diagram plot for galaxies, and the second shows a similar kind of plot for 7,000 quasars. The galaxies show a clear and strong correlation between redshift and apparent magnitude (and thus distance), but the quasar data show no such correlation.

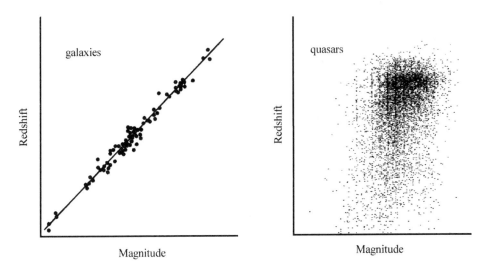

Galaxies show a strong correlation between apparent magnitude and redshift (left, redrawn from Alan Sandage, *Astrophysical Journal* 178:1 (1972)). In contrast, quasars show no such correlation (right, redrawn from A. Hewitt and G.A. Burbidge, "Revised and Updated Catalog of Quasi-stellar Objects," *Astrophysical Journal Supplement* 87:451–459 (1993)).

Among the group of 7,000 quasars, it was found that their apparent magnitudes were better explained as a loss of energy correlated with the redshift itself, rather than with distance. What this suggests is that the observed redshift (z_o) consists of a Hubble-type cosmological expansion component (z_c), plus a component intrinsic to the quasar (z_i). They suggest that it is the intrinsic component that causes the large scatter in the apparent magnitude/redshift plot.

The evidence for this interpretation began to accumulate as far back as 1967 and 1968 when Arp[14] first started to identify radio sources near interacting galaxies. His observations suggested that there was a physical association between some of them. However, the redshifts of the galaxies were usually small, whereas the redshifts of the radio-sources, usually associated with quasars, were very large. Arp argued, on statistical grounds, that the systems must be physically linked and that the redshifts of the quasars cannot therefore be of cosmological origin, but must have an intrinsic origin. Because his work was heavily criticized, he searched for radio-quiet quasars near bright spiral galaxies with small redshifts. He found many candidates, which turned out to be high-redshift quasars. Burbidge and others were able to develop the relationship between the observed redshift of the galaxy (z_G) and the angular separation (Θ) of its associated quasar. The results, taken from 392 pairs, indicate that $\Theta \cdot z_G =$ constant. This shows without doubt that the vast majority of pairs are physically associated — therefore the observed redshifts of the quasars must have a strong intrinsic component.

Hoyle et al. therefore believe that quasars have their own intrinsic redshifts, and, like Arp, they believe that they are ejected from active galactic centers. The strong rejection that greets this view in the wider astronomical community is well illustrated by the following example, cited in their book. They discovered four quasar images with $z = 1.69$, symmetrically placed around (and within 0.3 seconds of arc of) the center of a galaxy with $z = 0.039$. Arp and Crane, using Hubble Space Telescope (HST) images, suggested in 1992 that this was a galaxy ejecting four quasars with non-cosmological (i.e., intrinsic) redshifts. The paper was turned down by all leading astronomical journals on the grounds that, as a number of referees put it, "It must be a gravitational lens." Finally, it was published in a general physics journal.[15]

The QSS and the Big Bang

The QSS model describes an oscillating universe with episodes of intense creation when the size of the universe approaches its minimum. It is a long-age evolutionary model, like the standard big-bang model, but with cycles of the order of 100 billion years from one minimum to the next. The "big crunch"

14. Halton Arp, "Lines of Galaxies from Radio Sources," *Proceedings of the Astronomical Society of the Pacific* 80:129 (1968); Halton Arp, "Peculiar Galaxies and Radio Sources," *Astrophysical Journal* 148:321 (1967).

15. Halton C. Arp and P. Crane, "Testing the Gravitational Lens Hypothesis in G2237+0305," *Physics Letters A* 168 (1):6–12 (1992).

does not occur, only an increase in the density of galaxies. The model has the bulk of optical radiation being thermalized in the contracting phase through the agency of carbon whiskers that absorb it and re-emit in the microwave region. The whiskers are not uniformly distributed, but are lumpy on the scale of galaxy clusters. According to these authors, this is consistent with the COBE (COsmic Background Explorer) satellite results on an angular scale as measured across the sky where one beam width contains a rich galaxy cluster and the other not. As a result, fluctuations in the measured temperature of the CMBR of the order of 30 μK are expected, in agreement with the COBE data.

The QSS model predicts that galaxies observed at the last maximum in the oscillation will be faint because of distance, but comparatively blue with a small redshift of about z = 0.2. The authors claim that this has actually been observed and small redshifts have been measured. In the QSS model, the time period between maxima and minima is about H_0^{-1}, the reciprocal of the Hubble constant. According to the model, because of our position in the current expansion phase, one would not expect to see redshifts much greater than 5. For larger distances, one would be observing a region in the previous contraction phase of the universe.

In fact, looking back toward the last maximum would yield blueshifts of the order z = –0.5. However, a typical galaxy of absolute magnitude –21 would be unobservable at an apparent magnitude of about +28.5 (allowing for about 6 magnitudes of absorption due to carbon whiskers occurring near the last oscillatory minimum). They predict that the best chance of seeing galaxies from the previous cycle would be from stars that are just a little beyond the last minimum which haven't had their light shifted too far into the blue to be affected by carbon whiskers. They maintain that there should be a profusion of galaxies at about +27.5 magnitude with very red stars due to their low mass and some reddening due to overall expansion. They argue that the larger modern telescopes are already seeing into the last oscillatory minimum of the QSS.

The QSS model predicts a period back to the last oscillatory minimum of 11 billion years, hence also the age of Population I stars. They explain the apparent anomaly in the standard big bang cosmology of the Population II stars being older, because they were born in a period before this, as far back as 18 billion years ago, but the Hubble law doesn't work past this oscillatory minimum and therefore the apparent contradiction. The standard big-bang model predicts a maximum age of 0.667 H_0^{-1}, which is little different from 0.652 H_0^{-1} for the QSS model, the time back to the last minimum. They make the point that although the technology exists, very few galaxies with redshifts z > 5 are ever observed. Also, there is a sharp decline in observed quasars past z ≈ 2.5. The QSS authors believe the facts are better explained by their cosmology with its intrinsic redshift components.

The big bangers have had to revise their star/galaxy formation period down from z = 100 to z ≤5,[16] brought about by observational necessity from deep field observations with the HST. Moreover, the proposed United States $1 billion SKA (square kilometer array radio telescope) has as one of its objectives to examine the epoch of peak galaxy and star formation, which they now claim occurred in the region of z = 1 to 3.[17] Of course, the big-bang model requires that the entire visible universe came from a minute fraction of the post-inflation universe no more than a few centimeters in size. Dirac once said, "That which is not observable does not exist," but these days what is said is, "I know my theory is right. Therefore anything required to make it work must also be right whether observable or not."

Hoyle et al. distance themselves from anyone believing in the Bible. Their new QSS model presents a cosmological model very different from the standard big-bang model, but it contains just the same philosophy of atheistic naturalism. Their aim is to explain the origin of the universe without acknowledging the existence or the work of the supernatural Creator God.

They rather rely on what they call "common sense." This "common sense" is the belief that energy appears in the universe in compensating positive and negative forms (this avoids violating the first law of thermodynamics, which says that energy cannot be created or destroyed). Negative energy fields are inherently explosive and, concentrated locally, they offer the advantage of explaining the quasars, radio galaxies, and active galactic nuclei. When distributed uniformly, negative energy fields exert a negative pressure that manifests in the overall expansion of the universe. Note that this negative energy is that which maintains the conservation of energy when, according to the model, normal matter is created near compact near-black holes. Their model does offer an explanation for the intrinsic redshift observed in quasars and the like, by attributing it to the different times the matter was created as compared with the time of observation, much the same as Arp's idea.

16. Hoyle, Burbidge, and Narlikar, *A Different Approach to Cosmology: From a Static Universe through the Big Bang Towards Reality*, p. 267–269.

17. H. Sim, *The Square Kilometre Array* promotional pamphlet (Australia: CSIRO, July 2000).

Carmeli's Cosmological General Relativity

In the years pre-dating Einstein's relativity theory, it was assumed that space and time were independent and that there existed a frame of reference, fixed in space, in which time had the universal property such that it would be the same for all observers independent of their motion. Lorentz and Einstein broke that connection. In Einstein's special theory, the universal constant became the speed of light (in a vacuum). Time and space became entwined as *spacetime* and it would warp according to the motion of the observer. No one observer's determination of when and where an event occurred was any longer absolute. Another observer moving with a different relative velocity would determine the sequence of events differently. This seemed crazy at the time, but it has been borne out with many experiments over many decades since then.

A theoretical physicist, Moshe Carmeli, has extended this concept to the cosmos. Though he was in his early sixties, he developed a new description of the universe around the kitchen table in his home in Beersheba, Israel. Being from the old school, he did most of his calculations on paper. He had spent most of his early years working on Einstein's special and general theories and has published a number of detailed books on relativity. This gave him excellent training for developing his new theory.

Carmeli observed that there are really only two things that astronomers actually measure: distance and velocity. In fact, they are both derived in turn from other measurements, like the apparent magnitudes and redshifts of sources. On the largest scales of the universe, he saw that astronomers really could only take still pictures of the galaxies as they are seen in the sky. From these pictures, the redshifts are derived and then, using the Hubble law, distances are determined. From this, he developed a new idea: cosmological special relativity (CSR).[18]

In this view, the parameters to be observed were the relative distances and velocities of the galaxies in the universe. He then theorized that any physical description must relate these quantities in the same way as Einstein did in special relativity. The substance of his universe therefore is called *spacevelocity* instead of *spacetime*. In Carmeli's case, the Hubble-Carmeli time constant, τ, which is the inverse of the Hubble constant in the limit of zero gravity, is the universal constant for all observers in any epoch. As observers, we look back into space and see light from ever more distant objects. We are essentially looking back to an earlier cosmic time (t). On earth we are at cosmic time $t = 0$. In Carmeli's CSR,

---

18. Moshe Carmeli, *Cosmological Special Relativity* (Singapore: World Scientific, 2002).

cosmic time, by analogy, takes the role of velocity in special relativity. So instead of the famous Lorentz factor $(1 - (\frac{v}{c})^2)^{1/2}$, involving the relative velocity of the observer as a fraction of the speed of light (v/c), in the Carmeli theory the new factor $(1 - (\frac{t}{\tau})^2)^{1/2}$ involves cosmic time as a fraction of the Hubble-Carmeli time (t/τ). From this, Carmeli's theory predicts unusual effects in the cosmos, like length contraction and velocity dilation for large-scale structures in the universe.

Carmeli then extended his theory to describe what he understood astronomers were observing. By including matter into his theory, he developed his "cosmological general relativity" (CGR). He chose his energy-momentum tensor with the Hubble-Carmeli time constant playing an analogous role to the speed of light. This means that when the average mass-energy density of the universe equals a critical value, space is totally unstressed or relaxed. From these basic assumptions and solving Einstein's field equations for the motion of the galaxies in the Hubble distribution, which he assumes to be true, he generates his own cosmology. He assumed a spherically symmetric matter distribution around the observer. Therefore, his model assumes isotropy, but not necessarily homogeneity as is necessarily assumed by the big bang. This cosmology has challenged the standard big-bang model and is not (yet) taken very seriously by that community.

The CGR model is elegant in that it is simple. His model describes the motion of galaxies in the expanding *observable* universe. Carmeli says that he is not very much interested in what happened in the unobservable past. Only the Hubble constant, the locally measured average mass density of the universe and the familiar well-known constants are needed in his model. From this, in 1996, Carmeli predicted the accelerating universe,[19] which was only observationally verified in 1998.[20] His model indicated the universe to be spatially flat, due to an appreciable amount of dark energy. His model also predicted the amount of dark energy, about 70 percent, which is the amount currently held to be the case by the big bangers. He does not specifically incorporate a cosmological constant (Λ) as do the big bangers. However, by comparison with standard big-bang Friedmann-Lemaître (F-L) cosmology, a cosmological constant can be determined from his model. It turns out to be non-zero and positive, about $\Lambda \sim 10^{-35}$ s^{-2}.

Carmeli's model does not require the strange negative pressure to force the galaxies apart, as invoked in the standard big bang. The standard big-bang model needs a form of dark energy, which can be interpreted to be a sort of

19. Moshe Carmeli, *Communications in Theoretical Physics*, 5:159 (1996).
20. S. Perlmutter et al., "Measurements of Ω and Λ from 42 High-redshift Supernovae," *Astrophysical Journal*, 517:565–586 (1999), http://www.lbl.gov/supernova/1988.

"pushing gravity" instead of the familiar pulling type. This is described by the cosmological constant Λ, but in the F-L models the pressure exerted on space is negative, consistent with the "pulling" effect of Λ. By contrast, in Carmeli's model there is a pressure exerted on space due to the dark (or vacuum) energy component but it is the normal positive type. No exotic parameters are needed, though he does assume a certain amount of dark matter, about 30 percent,[21] and dark energy as mentioned above. His model describes three phases of the universal expansion, initially decelerating, then passing through a constant phase (where the pressure is zero) to an accelerating phase. The CMBR temperature is seen to vary in accordance with observation and is described by his Lorentz-like factor (mentioned above) involving the cosmic time.

The tri-phase expansion of his model should be testable. Supernova SN 1997ff, with a redshift a little less than 2, should be near the limit where astronomers could see into the decelerating phase. Uncertainty in the visual magnitude of that very distant source puts it at the edge of, but within, the uncertainty of what his model would predict.

Though Carmeli's model is a challenge to the big bang, it really is a description of the structure of the visible universe, taking into account what we can, rather than cannot, observe. Its strength lies in its simplicity. It may offer solutions to some puzzling questions that astronomers and physicists have yet to solve. For instance, it offers a solution to the dynamics of galaxies in the universe without requiring the assumption of dark matter.[22]

VAN FLANDERN'S META MODEL

Astronomer Tom Van Flandern began his cosmology from the bottom up, rather than the more conventional top-down approach.[23] In the top-down approach, one begins with the observable universe, and works down to a model that will explain it. In the bottom-up approach, one begins with the simplest possible model — in this case a "one-particle universe" — and then adds further

---

21. This has since been shown to be unnecessary. Only normal matter need to be assumed for his theory to work. See John Hartnett, "Carmeli's Accelerating Universe Is Spatially Flat without Dark Matter," *International Journal of Theoretical Physics,* vol. 44, no. 3 (April 2005): p. 495–502; also at http://arxiv.org/abs/gr-qc/0407083.

22. John Hartnett, "The Carmeli Metric Correctly Describes Spiral Galaxy Rotation Curves," *International Journal of Theoretical Physics,* vol. 44, no. 3 (March 2005): p. 359–372; also at http://arxiv.org/abs/gr-qc/0407082.

23. Tom Van Flandern, *Dark Matter, Missing Planets & New Comets: Paradoxes Resolved, Origins Illuminated* (Berkeley, CA: North Atlantic Books, 1993); see also www.metaresearch.org.

details until the model begins to behave like the real world. Van Flandern appears to have achieved remarkable success — if not yet the acclaim of the establishment. We will not attempt a detailed description of the meta model here, but just give a few examples.

The simplest interaction in a universe of particles is a collision between two particles. The meta model describes gravity as being the result of the collision between very tiny gravity particles — which he calls "C-gravitons" — and matter particles. Meta-gravity is thus a repulsive force, not an attractive force as Newton assumed. Its "apparent" attraction results from shielding within the "sea" of gravitons that pervades the meta-universe. Ordinary matter is mostly composed of empty space, and C-gravitons are extremely tiny so they penetrate matter very deeply before they strike anything. So, when two bodies such as the earth and its moon are close together, they mutually shield one another in the region directly in between them. As a result, the decreased bombardment of C-gravitons on the near side of each body sets up a net attraction between them.

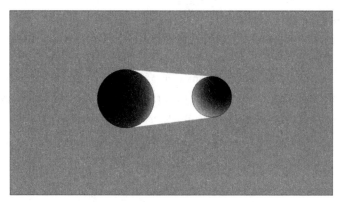

Meta model gravity. The sea of gravitons surrounds the two solid bodies and they shield one another on their near sides. The imbalance of graviton collisions thus draws the two bodies together with an apparent "attractive" force.

Now the interesting thing about this version of gravity is that it explains the "missing mass" needed in the big-bang universe. You may recall that one example of the need for "missing mass" was the rotation speeds of stars in the outer parts of spiral galaxies. Big bangers must postulate a great deal of invisible mass to account for the motion, which of course is not observable and probably does not exist. The MOND theory suggests that gravity behaves in an inverse linear way in the outer parts of galaxies rather than the usual inverse square behavior that we measure in our physics laboratories on earth. This radical behavior is rather ad hoc in conventional physics, but it turns out to be a natural result of the meta model. Because C-gravitons are tiny solid particles, they occasionally collide with one another. When they do, they reduce the gravitational force, and thus we find that gravity has a limited range, which corresponds to the average distance that C-gravitons travel before they collide. Van Flandern suggests that the range of C-gravitons is about 2 kiloparsecs (roughly the radius of a typical spiral galaxy core). This means that the core of the spiral galaxy is held together by the gravity of the mass within it, but in the outer regions, the sea of gravitons behaves like a "perfect gas" — particles[24] freely moving around — and rotation velocities remain constant at all distances from the center, as observed.

Another interesting result of the meta model's view of gravity is that it denies the possibility of singularities and thus black holes. Because meta gravity is the result of shielding, supernovae will produce matter densities great enough to produce total shielding. As a result, there is not the infinite collapse into singularity that results in Newtonian and Einsteinian gravity. In the meta model, quasars are the end-products of supernovae, and they are nearby objects, not out at the edges of the observable universe as the Hubble redshift interpretation would suggest.

What causes the Hubble redshifts? The gravitons that pervade all space are small enough not to scatter light waves but are large enough to cause them to lose energy as they propagate through it, so their wavelengths become longer the farther they travel. Light from the most distant galaxies thus has the greatest redshift, as Hubble observed. So, the universe is not expanding in the meta model, but static. Why does the static universe not collapse in on itself? Because meta gravity has a limited range which is less than the typical size of a galaxy, so each galaxy is a little island unto itself, not significantly affecting other parts of the universe.

Apparently, Van Flandern is not the first to propose this view of gravity. It was raised 300 years ago by Le Sage, it was promoted at one time by Lord Kelvin, and it has since become known as Le Sage's theory of gravity. In a recent book on the subject,[25] Van Flandern is joined by numerous other astrophysicists (including a foreword by Halton Arp) in developing the theory. According

---

24. These suffer inelastic collisions with the ingredient particles of matter. The unbalanced force due to the inelastic collisions supplies the needed force of gravity.

25. Matthew Edwards, editor, *Pushing Gravity: New Perspectives on Le Sage's Theory of Gravitation* (Montreal, Quebec: C. Roy Keys Inc., 2002). See review at: <http://www.metaresearch.org/publications/books/PushingG.asp>.

to Van Flandern, "Le Sagian gravity produces all the features of Newtonian and Einstein gravitation, and several more features presently unrecognized by physics as well." We look forward to further developments with eager anticipation.

Summary of Other Cosmological Models

Big-bang theory is based on three main ideas: (1) Einstein's theory of gravity (general relativity), (2) galactic redshifts, interpreted to mean that the universe is expanding (Hubble's law), and (3) the observation (given Hubble's interpretation of the redshifts) that the universe from earth looks much the same in every direction (on a large enough scale). This is in turn interpreted via the assumption of the cosmological principle to mean that this is true for every other location in the universe as well. The primary evidence in support of big-bang theory is the CMBR, interpreted to be the afterglow of the primordial fireball.

The differing models presented here show that it is possible to explain all these features of the universe in entirely different ways. The universe could be expanding or static. Gravity could be attractive or repulsive. Quasars and their high redshifts could be nearby or far away. The CMBR could be interpreted as the redshifting of radiation due to the expansion of the universe or due to the temperature of space resulting from the thermalization of starlight — nothing to do with expansion. The universe might consist mostly of "dark matter" and "dark energy," or it could just consist of what we see around us; it could be everywhere like we see it, or what we see could be surrounded by vast reaches of "empty" space. These possibilities vary over colossal scales, and demonstrate that our ignorance far outweighs our knowledge.

Big-bang theory does not explain the origin of the universe, and none of these alternative models do either. All of them, in some way or other, fall short. Our journey into understanding the universe has hardly yet begun. Cosmology is an exciting field that has an enormous future, but our present-day naturalistic models are certainly not a reliable foundation for one's eternal destiny.

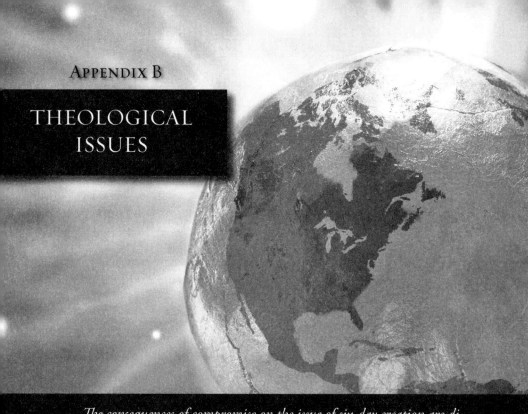

Appendix B

THEOLOGICAL ISSUES

The consequences of compromise on the issue of six-day creation are disastrous: doctrinal collapse, destroying the gospel, falling into the sin of unbelief, dishonoring God, flirting with idolatry, insulting God by retreating into deism, and undermining the authority of the written Word of God, to name just some. Claims by some compromising Christians that they uphold "biblical inerrancy" are contradicted by their violation of the purpose of the Scripture. The widespread deception that characterizes teaching on origins has its source in man's corrupt heart, the devil's schemes, and the judgment of God; many Christians underestimate the importance of the latter. Rightly understood, cosmic history — what we have called thelein history, the history of God's will — is a stronghold for Christian faith.

The Consequences of Compromise

Compromise positions — such as gap theory, progressive creation, theistic evolution, and the framework hypothesis — all try to avoid facing the straightforward meaning of Genesis 1, that God created the universe in six ordinary-length days, a few thousand years ago. They all embrace the old-earth world view of modern science, and the theological consequences are disastrous.

Doctrinal Collapse

Many modern Christians live inconsistently with their faith; they accept evolution over billions of years, but do not follow through on the consequences of that belief system. For those who want to live consistently, however, once they stop believing in the first chapter of the Bible, they enter a path that, consistently and logically, eventually leads to not believing the rest of it.[1]

Typical of many possible examples is Reverend Adam Ford,[2] an astronomer/priest who was, at the time of writing, priest to the queen of England at the Chapel Royal in London. He says, "The insights of science, particularly astronomy, require that the Christian today develop a new creation story, a fresh understanding of the nature of God, and a new concept of the inspiration of scripture. . . . The stories in the opening chapters of the Bible are not history, nor science. The Book of Genesis and the account of God creating in six days is a myth" (p. 44–45). "Gone is the idea of an original perfection, an ideal world spoilt by man's sin in the Garden of Eden" (p. 75). "The laws of nature working on the materials created in stars with the opportunities offered by chance, given time, generate the human soul" (p. 57). "Mankind is just one of the accidental products of an aimless process . . . a by-product of an unfolding purposeless accident" (p. 77). "The return of Christ and the end of the world is not just around the corner as traditionally expected by Christians. Two possibilities face the universe — a Big Crunch or slow decay. In perhaps 100 billion years the universe may collapse back on itself, or it may go on expanding forever, slowly using up all its available energy, until it is spread out into the desolate silence of an exhausted void" (p. 54).

Theologically, the "exhausted void" seems to have already descended upon the former Episcopalian (Anglican) bishop of Newark, New Jersey, John Shelby Spong. Citing the work of Copernicus, Galileo, Newton, Darwin, and Freud as his justification, he has called for a "New Reformation" of the Christian Church, and has posted 12 theses on the Internet for debate.[3] These include:

---

1. Some people are able to mentally compartmentalize enough to be able to live with all manner of logical inconsistencies. However, history has repeatedly shown that the faith-destructive consequences of such inconsistencies relentlessly surface in not only the majority of individuals, but given time, will *invariably* do so in entire institutions, denominations, and cultures.
2. Adam Ford, *Universe: God, Man and Science* (London: Hodder & Stoughton, 1986).
3. John S. Spong, "A Call for a New Reformation," http://www.dioceseofnewark.org/jsspong/reform.html.

- theism is dead;

- the incarnation is nonsense;

- Christology is bankrupt;

- the perfect original creation is mythical nonsense;

- the virgin birth is impossible;

- the miracles cannot be believed;

- the sacrificial death of Jesus is primitive barbarism;

- the Resurrection was not physical;

- the ascension of Jesus does not make sense in the space age;

- there is no revelation valid for all time;

- prayer can have no impact on history;

- there will be no rewards and punishments beyond this life.

As you can see, compromise on the creation issue is not just a matter of revising the first few pages of the Bible — it completely changes the whole fabric of the Christian faith.

Destroying the Gospel

The saddest legacy of old-earth theology is its impact upon Christ's precious work of salvation. We dealt with this in the biblical model chapter, but here we will highlight the importance of a correct understanding of the fossil record.

The Genesis world view is that the original creation contained no suffering and no death. Suffering and death entered the world only through man's sin and God's judgment upon it. Now the fossil record is a record of suffering and death, and so our interpretation of the fossil record is crucial to our theology of redemption.

The Genesis chronology would suggest that most of the fossils were laid down during the great flood of Noah and its aftermath. They stand as a visual reminder that the consequence of sin is suffering and death, but if the fossil record was laid down *before* the Fall, as virtually all compromise positions hold,[4]

---

4. A recent effort to solve this problem in an old-earth context is: Gorman Gray, *The Age of the Universe: What are the Biblical Limits?* (Washougal, WA: Morningstar Publications, 2000). In this view, the six days of Genesis 1 do not report the creation *ex nihilo* of the whole universe, but merely the days during which God "worked on" the already-existing biosphere. The error of this view will become evident in the section below on "Undermining the authority of the written word of God."

then death is a natural part of life and it was in the world (along with cancer and other kinds of suffering) for millions of years before man appeared on the scene. Death, therefore, has no relationship to man's sin. Indeed, in theistic evolutionary views, death is not just a natural part of life, it is an *essential* part of life because death is fundamental to the Darwinian mechanism of natural selection — the "unfit" die, but the "fit" survive long enough to reproduce.

If death is a natural part of life, then it cannot be the special penalty for sin. If death is not the penalty for sin, then the death of Christ, as payment of the penalty for sin, is an empty myth. The logic of the Atonement is shattered to its foundation.

As a consequence of this, theistic evolutionists therefore have to deny the "penal substitution" theory of the Atonement (i.e., the idea that Christ paid the penalty for our sins by dying in our place). They have to invent some other meaning to replace it. Astronomer/priest Reverend Adam Ford, as quoted above, now puts his faith in man, science, and evolution.

Progressive creationist Dr. Hugh Ross believes in penal substitution, but in his attempt to salvage it he has to deny the perfect upholding of God in the pre-Fall creation. He has to suppose that the death penalty for man's sin was only spiritual death for man, not physical death for man and all other *nephesh* creatures.[5] A creation that is not upheld perfectly, as Dr. Ross proposes, would indeed be subject to accident, injury, illness, and death, but that does not sound like the "*good . . . good . . . good . . . good . . . good . . . good . . . very good*" vision of the original creation that Genesis 1 presents us with. In His curse upon Adam, God very clearly specifies physical death: "In the sweat of your face you shall eat bread till you return to the ground, for out of it you were taken; you are dust, and to dust you shall return" (Gen. 3:19). Dr. Ross is clearly wrong.

Reverend Ford denies the Atonement entirely, Bishop Spong calls it "barbaric," and Dr. Ross destroys its foundation.

Sin

In his classic book *The Genesis Record*, Henry Morris pointed out that in technical writing it is crucial that important words and concepts be defined when they are first used, otherwise the reader may not understand, or may

---

5. The Bible identifies three basic kinds of life — vegetation and non-air-breathing animals; *nephesh* creatures that breathe air and so include the mammals and man; and man, a *nephesh* creature, but also made in the image of God.

misunderstand, the author's intended meaning. Since many important words are used for the first time in the Bible in Genesis, we can therefore expect that God will have defined his intended meanings in the context of those first-use passages. The most famous illustration of this principle is Morris's exposition of the word "love," which is well worth reading.[6]

So numerous are the important words and concepts introduced in Genesis that Christians who compromise on the creation issue are likely to find their understanding to be faulty in other areas as well. One of the most important of these is "sin."

The word "sin" first occurs in Genesis 4:7 in the story of Cain and Abel, but of course the *concept* first occurs in the Garden of Eden. What was Adam and Eve's sin? Some say "rebellion," and this is true — they acted against God's direct instruction to Adam. *Why* did they rebel? When you look at what God said ("[if you eat] you will die" — Gen. 2:17) and what the devil said ("You will not die" — Gen. 3:4) and whose advice Adam and Eve followed (the devil's), then we can say that they rebelled against God because they did not believe what He said. So, Genesis is here defining the concept of "sin" as being fundamentally the result of not believing what God says. This idea is affirmed by Jesus in John 16:9 (and its corollary in John 6:28–29) and by Paul in Romans 14:23: "Whatever does not proceed from faith is sin." Abraham is presented in the New Testament as the paragon of righteousness, and the defining passage is Genesis 15:6 — Abraham *believed* God and God reckoned it to him as righteousness (Rom. 4:3, 20–24; Gal. 3:6; James 2:23). The righteous live by faith (Hab. 2:4; Gal. 3:11; Heb. 10:38) and the corollary of this is that the unrighteous die by unbelief.

So, a fundamental consequence of compromise is that you condemn yourself by your own words. You worship God as Creator (as all Christians do) but you do not *believe* what He says on the subject of creation.

The extraordinary absurdity of this position can best be illuminated by some ordinary examples. In our personal and working lives, if we have a problem, we usually ask an expert for help. If we are sick, we consult a doctor; if our plumbing fails, we consult a registered plumber; if an electrical device fails, we consult a licensed electrician; if our car needs servicing, then we consult a mechanic — and perhaps look for his certificate of accreditation to assure ourselves that he is a reputable tradesperson.

---

6. Henry M. Morris, *The Genesis Record* (Grand Rapids, MI: Baker Book House, 1976), p. 374–376.

Now no human beings witnessed God's work of creation. Not even Adam and Eve — they were the last in line during creation week, so they did not witness any of the creative events that occurred before them. No human being can revisit creation week in a time machine to check out what God did. Therefore, the only eyewitness is God himself. If we do not accept God's eyewitness account, then we have *no accurate information at all* on the subject. In fact, we do not even have enough information to confidently *reject* what God says about it, because all human theories are based on unverifiable assumptions. The big-bang theory, as we have shown, does not explain the origin of the universe, so there is no reason to trust it.

Those who reject six-day Genesis creation are therefore under a cloud not only of sin, but of foolishness. They reject the word of the only eyewitness, and substitute for it the demonstrably fallible theories of men who were not there, who don't know everything, who don't have all the relevant facts on the matter, and whose theories fail to explain even the present world, let alone the past world.

Dishonoring God

When Christians compromise on the creation issue to suit their scientist contemporaries, they overlook the impact on the most important player — God himself.

In Ezekiel 36:25–29, God presents a marvelous promise of salvation: "I will sprinkle clean water upon you, and you shall be clean from all your uncleanness, and from all your idols I will cleanse you. A new heart I will give you, and a new spirit I will put within you; and I will take out of your flesh the heart of stone and give you a heart of flesh. And I will put my spirit within you, and cause you to walk in my statutes and be careful to observe my ordinances . . . and you shall be my people, and I will be your God. And I will deliver you from all your uncleanness." What a wonderful promise — God will take away our sin, give us a new heart and a new spirit, and give us the grace to obey Him and to love Him. Then God cautions them: "It is not for your sake that I will act, says the Lord GOD; let that be known to you" (v. 32). God is going to redeem His people, but He is not doing it for their sake. How is that possible? The answer is in verse 22: "Therefore say to the house of Israel, Thus says the Lord GOD: It is not for your sake, O house of Israel, that I am about to act, but for the sake of my holy name, which you have profaned."

God is redeeming His people in order to restore the honor and glory that is due to Him, and which we have defiled through our sin. The "big picture" of Christianity is that when we sin we do far more than just condemn ourselves to death. When we sin, we dishonor God, and not only do we dishonor God, but we defile His creation. When we sin, not only do we go down, but we bring God's name down with us, and we bring God's creation down with us as well.

The good news, however, is that when God redeems us, He not only redeems us but He also redeems His own honor and glory and He redeems the whole creation along with us (Rom. 8:18–21; Rev. 21:1–5)!

So when the Reverend Adam Ford and Bishop Spong change the creation story into cosmic evolution, they are not simply updating the Bible, and thereby removing sin and redemption from the heart of the gospel — they are defiling the honor and glory of God!

Honor. In our society today we have lost sight of the meaning of honor, which is no longer a central value in our culture. To properly understand God's honor, we need to go back to those cultures in which honor was a central value. We will give just two of many possible examples from the Old Testament.

The first is when David, the young shepherd boy, heard the insults that the Philistine giant Goliath was hurling at the Israelite army. His response was this: "What will be done for the man who kills this Philistine and takes away the reproach from Israel?" (1 Sam. 17:26). When David went out to face Goliath on the battlefield, he said, "You come against me with sword and spear and javelin but I come against you in the name of Yahweh Sabaoth, the God of the armies of Israel that you have dared to insult" (1 Sam. 17:45; JB). David was a man of honor who understood the honor of God and he defended God's honor — with his life.

The second example is one of the most tragic among many tragic stories in the Book of Judges, this one about Jephthah. Jephthah faced the Ammonites in battle and he made a foolish vow to God, saying, "If you give the Ammonites into my hands, whatever comes out of the door of my house to meet me when I return in triumph will be the LORD's, and I will sacrifice it as a burnt offering" (Judg. 11:30–31;NIV). When Jephthah subsequently defeated the Ammonites and returned home in triumph, who should come out the door of his house to greet him but his daughter. She was his only child. Now Jephthah was a fool, but he was also a man of honor and knew that his word could not be broken. His daughter also was a woman of honor and she knew that her father's word could not be broken. Do you know what she said when he told her what he had done? She said, " 'Father, you have given your word to the Lord. Do to me just as you have promised. . . . But grant me this one request. . . . Give me two months to roam the hills and weep with my friends because

I will never marry.' 'You may go,' he said" (Judg. 11:36–38;NIV After the two months, she returned to her father and he did to her as he had vowed to God.[7]

These events are shocking beyond belief to us, and they are even more shocking when we see that Jephthah is listed among the heroes of faith in the New Testament. In Hebrews 11 we read about all the great heroes of faith in the Old Testament, and there along with Noah and Abraham and Moses and David is immortalized the name of Jephthah. How can this possibly be? Jephthah is certainly not a hero because he killed his own daughter. Jephthah is, we infer, a hero of faith because he kept his word at great personal cost to himself and his family. In a culture of honor, among people who understand these things, honor is more important than life itself.

Now in a society where honor is a central value, it is perceived to reside primarily in certain objects and persons.[8] For example, the honor of a tribe or clan resides primarily in the head of that tribe or clan. The honor of a family resides primarily in the head of that family. The honor of a married woman resides primarily in her ability to produce a son and thereby establish an inheritance for herself in her husband's clan. The honor of a young woman resides primarily in her virginity. The honor of a young man resides in a lifestyle that reflects well upon his family and, if possible, enhances their standing in the community — the Fifth Commandment says, "Honor your father and mother . . . that it may be well with you and that you may live long on the earth" (Eph. 6:2–3).

When it comes down to the personal level, the honor of a person resides most especially in their name and in their word. David said to Goliath, "I come against you in the name of the LORD Almighty, the God of the armies of Israel, whom you have defied" (1 Sam. 17:45;NIV). David was defending

---

7. Some have suggested that Jephthah did not kill his daughter, but rather gave her into service at the tent of meeting, but the Hebrew and Greek (Septuagint) texts of Judges 11:31 clearly specify a "burnt offering" and they are translated as such by all major English versions. Some translations insert "[instead of] a burnt offering," or "[or] a burnt offering." The reason given is that the Mosaic law prohibited human sacrifice. However, Jephthah was the son of a prostitute, he was outcast at an early age, lived among pagans, and was thrust into leadership with no preparation, so it is not unlikely that he would have fallen back onto pagan practice in an hour of need. He tore his robes in grief, she grieved for two months prior to the event, and the Israelite women lamented her fate for four days every year — hardly the response expected if she was simply one of many women who were privileged to serve at the tent of meeting.

8. Bruce J. Malina, *The New Testament World: Insights from cultural anthropology* (London: SCM Press, 1981), chapter 2.

the honor of God and that honor resided in the name of God. When Jephthah killed his only child he did so because he had given his word to God.

At the personal level then, honor resides in one's name and in one's word. Your honor resides in your good reputation (i.e., your name) and in whether your word can be trusted. So it is with God. God's honor resides in His name, and in His word. He is a person of good reputation (among those who know and love Him) and He keeps His word. In Psalm 138:2 the Psalmist says of God "You have exalted above all things your name and your word."[9]

If we understand this principle, then we can also begin to understand Jesus' statement in John 10:35, "Scripture cannot be broken." Why not? Because Scripture is the Word of God and the Word of God cannot be broken. If the word of Jephthah could not be broken, how much more can the Word of God not be broken?

That is also why Jesus expected the Old Testament Scriptures to be fulfilled to the letter, because the honor of God resides in the fulfillment of His Word. That is why Jesus made it a condition of Christian discipleship that we not be ashamed of His words (Luke 9:26), because His honor is likewise at stake!

When Christians disbelieve God's Word on a subject so close to His heart as creation, not only do they condemn themselves, they dishonor God.

Glory. It is not only God's honor that resides in His Word — His glory does, too. Jesus said in John 15:7–8 "If you abide in me, and my words abide in you, ask whatever you will, and it shall be done for you. By this my Father is glorified, that you bear much fruit, and so prove to be my disciples." When the word of God is believed and obeyed, God is glorified. In Isaiah 55:11, God says, "My word . . . that goes forth from my mouth . . . shall not return to me empty . . . it shall accomplish that which I purpose, and prosper in the thing for which I sent it." When God fulfils His Word, His honor is vindicated and His name is glorified!

In Revelation 4–5 we are given a picture of what is going on in heaven. The heavenly host worship and praise God for three things — first, for His eternal being; second, for His work of creation; and third, for the Lamb's work of redemption.

The four living creatures surrounding the throne sing without ceasing: "Holy, holy, holy, is the Lord God Almighty, who was and is and is to come!"

---

9. RSV, NIV; the KJV translates this as "thou hast magnified thy word above all thy name." The Hebrew word order is "[you have magnified] [above all] [your name] [your word]" so in context, the modern translation is preferable.

(Rev. 4:8). This is the eternal being of God, the great "I am." God is eternally self-existent and He is worshiped unceasingly for this great fact.

Then the 24 elders who reign with God respond in a similar mode of worship: "Worthy art thou, our Lord and God, to receive glory and honor and power, for thou didst create all things, and by thy will they existed and were created" (Rev. 4:11). God's work of creation shows forth His honor and *glory* and power.

The hosts of heaven are here telling the whole universe that the holiness of God lies in His eternal being, and the honor and glory of God lies in His work of creation.

How then do you think God feels when compromising Christians say that God is not the six-day Creator that He claims to be? Will those compromising Christians be willing to stand up in heaven and tell the worshiping hosts that God did not create the universe in six days? Are they willing to tell God himself?

Idolatry

Idolatry is the worship of man-made gods. Idols are not just objects of wood, metal, or stone — they can be made of ideas. In Ezekiel 14:3, God says, *"These men have taken their idols into their hearts."* If Christians worship the "billion-year evolver" or the "billion-year progressive Creator" rather than the six-day Creator, then they worship an idol, a man-made god.

The contemporary answer to such a challenge has been that science reveals the truth about the world, and we must face the truth wherever science leads us. However, as we have shown in this book, science has only a very limited ability to uncover the events of the past, so it is not an infallible guide to the truth.

On Judgment Day, the honor and glory of God will be on center stage. Since the honor of God resides in His name, one of His many glorious names that will be on display there will be six-day Creator. Since the honor of God also resides in His Word we will find that the Word made flesh, Jesus Christ, will also be on center stage. Jesus said, "Whoever is ashamed of me and of my words, of him will the Son of man be ashamed when he comes in his glory and the glory of the Father and of the holy angels" (Luke 9:26). Let us be careful then, lest we be led astray to worship idols.

Retreat into Deism

Progressive creationists hold to the idea of "biblical inerrancy," and so they have to insert the billions of years of modern cosmology into the six days of creation. As a result, God's creative acts are spread out over long periods of time, corresponding to the big-bang time scale of cosmic history and the uniformitarian time scale of earth history. One tragic consequence of this is that, as we pointed out in the chapter on the biblical model, the connection between the cause (God commanding things to happen) and the effect (the creation coming into being) is destroyed by the intervening billions of years.[10]

This is not just a disruption of biblical logic; it is an insult of the first magnitude. Those who insist that billions of years intervened between God's command and the creation's response, necessarily portray God as being remote from His creation. He spoke, and it was millions or billions of years before the things happened. This is a retreat into a form of *deism* — the idea that God created the universe and then left it to run by itself.

Deism is probably one of the greatest insults that one could make against the God of the Bible. The God of Genesis 1 was present with His creation, His Spirit moving over the face of the waters. The God of Eden was present, walking and talking with Adam and Eve in the cool of the day. The God of Moses was present with His people — by day in the desert in a pillar of cloud, and by night in a pillar of fire, and later above the mercy seat in the tabernacle. The God of the New Testament is with us even more intimately. One of Jesus' names is Emmanuel, meaning "God with us" (Matt. 1:23). In John 14:23, Jesus said, "If a man loves me, he will keep my word, and my Father will love him, and we will come to him and make our home with him." This dramatic presence of God with His people was spectacularly demonstrated on the Day of Pentecost (Acts 2:1–4). Jesus said of this time "In that day you will know that I am in my Father, and you in me, and I in you" (John 14:20). In his high priestly prayer for all believers (John 17:21), He asked the Father "that they may all be one; even as thou, Father, art in me, and I in thee, that they also may be in us."

How would a God, so extraordinarily intimate with His creation, feel if told that He commanded, and billions of years later something happened? The God of the Bible upholds His creation by His word of power (Heb. 1:3), so He is closer to us than our very breath. He knows when a hair falls from our head (Matt. 10:30; Luke 12:7), not only because He is omniscient, but also because He is paying attention — He is that intimate with us and that committed

---

10. Another consequence is, of course, that it puts death and suffering before sin. This has enormous logical ramifications for the gospel, but also for the nature of a Creator who would call millions of years of bloodshed and suffering "all very good."

to our welfare. We may be slow to obedience, but that is not because God is remote from us, and we should never even suggest that He is.

Undermining the Authority of the Written Word of God

Because Christ has fulfilled the law for us, Christians have generally lost sight of the extraordinary life-and-death significance of the Sabbath for the ancient Israelites. The first recorded victim was a man who did nothing more than gather firewood on the Sabbath, and he was stoned to death for it (Num. 15:32–36). The Sabbath was clearly identified by God to be a commemoration of His work of creation, as spelled out in the Fourth Commandment in Exodus 20:8–11. It also appears in God's summary statement to Moses in Exodus 31:12–18. After God gave all the law to Moses, He summarized his intentions in His final words, as follows:

> And the LORD said to Moses, "Say to the people of Israel, 'You shall keep my sabbaths, for this is a sign between me and you throughout your generations, that you may know that I, the LORD, sanctify you. You shall keep the sabbath, because it is holy for you; every one who profanes it shall be put to death. . . . Six days shall work be done, but the seventh day is a sabbath of solemn rest, holy to the LORD. . . . It is a sign for ever between me and the people of Israel that in six days the LORD made heaven and earth, and on the seventh day he rested, and was refreshed.' "

Out of all the things that God had said to Moses on Mount Sinai (in the preceding 12 chapters), He chose the Sabbath to be His summary sign. It was to be "a sign forever" for the Israelites that He "made heaven and earth" in six days. As if to make the point indelibly clear, the very next verse says, "And he gave to Moses, when he had made an end of speaking with him upon Mount Sinai, the two tables of the testimony, tables of stone, *written with the finger of God.*" In case we should miss the point, Exodus 32:16 tells us, "The tables were the work of God, and the writing was the writing of God."

So when compromising Christians teach that God did not create the universe in six ordinary-length days they are not only undermining the authority of the words that God inspired men to write (e.g., Genesis 1), but the words that *God himself personally wrote down in stone.*

BIBLICAL INERRANCY

Many Christians who compromise on six-day creation claim to believe in "biblical inerrancy," so this raises the question of just what that term means. Annotated versions of the Bible show on virtually every page at least one, and sometimes several, alternate readings that arise from variations among ancient texts, but "inerrancy," of course, relates to the original writings, not to the current copies of copies of copies . . . that we have today. Yet for all the copying, if you follow through those footnotes and marginal readings, you will find that not a single basic doctrine of Christianity is in any way compromised by textual variations. The text is remarkably consistent. If the *copies* have been preserved so well, it is therefore not hard to believe that the Holy Spirit also preserved the integrity of the *originals.*

Why has God given us an "inerrant" Scripture? The idea may seem rather arbitrary in light of the fact that every other document of human history is "errant" to a greater or lesser degree. The answer lies, as we pointed out earlier, in God being a "man of His word." His honor lies in the fact that His Word can be trusted. Consequently, He has given us an accurate written record of His revelations and prophecies so that we can understand what is going on. It makes sense that He providentially protected its accuracy in order to preserve its message.

The key issue is not even so much the accuracy of the text of the Bible, it is the *purpose* for which it was given. In the Sermon on the Mount, Jesus said: "Think not that I have come to abolish the law and the prophets; I have come not to abolish them but to *fulfil* them. For truly, I say to you, till heaven and earth pass away, not an iota, not a dot, will pass from the law until all is *accomplished*" (Matt. 5:17–18, emphasis added). This suggests that the authority of the Scriptures lies not just in its textual accuracy, but in the message it contains — the plan that is to be "fulfilled" and "accomplished."

We would therefore say that the correct approach to six-day creation is not so much a question of, "What is the meaning of the word 'day' in Genesis 1?" but rather, "What was God's purpose in giving us the creation account in Genesis 1?" One important purpose, which was later fulfilled, is stated clearly in the Fourth Commandment — that God's people should regularly commemorate and celebrate His work of creation.[11]

If the time scale of creation had not been important, then God could have placed a statement like John 1:1–3 in the beginning of Genesis. John 1:1–3 gives a perfectly adequate statement of creation, without any reference to the time scale.[12] The inclusion of a very clear time scale in Genesis 1 shows that

---

11. A primary, transcendent purpose of six-day creation is also that it displays God's omnipotence — He can do all that in just a short time!

12. There are also about a dozen different Hebrew words that God could have used to indicate long periods of time, had He desired to do so.

God had a purpose and that purpose was fulfilled (at least in part) in the Israelite observance of the Sabbath cycle. Now within this "plan-fulfillment" theme, the meaning of the word "day" is, of course, important. You can now see that it does not stand alone, but is part of the much larger *purpose* of God — in giving the Scriptures so that they might be *fulfilled*. There is absolutely no room here, whatever the word "day" might mean, for billions of years, because the *purpose* was that man should be able to commemorate and celebrate God's work of creation. That limits possible meanings to the time scale of a human lifetime, and the most reasonable meaning is, of course, six ordinary-length days.

It also happens to be the overwhelmingly obvious meaning of the Hebrew word for "day" (*yom*) in this context of Genesis. If not for the perceived need to compromise with "billions-of-years" beliefs, reinterpreting the word "day" in Genesis would be as inconceivable as suggesting that Jesus lay in the tomb for three vast periods of time.

This clearly shows that anyone claiming to retain "biblical inerrancy" must not just keep the words intact, but also keep the *purpose* intact as well.

The Source of Deception

Many suppose science to be our touchstone of truth in the modern world. How is it then that on the crucial question of origins we see such a vast sweep of deception ruling the world? Why is it that our most learned professors are so far off the track? The Bible identifies three causes — God, the devil, and man. We shall consider these in reverse order.

Man is born sinful (Ps. 51:5), and outside of Christ his heart is incurably corrupt (Jer. 17:9) so it is not surprising that deception characterizes his works. We are not suggesting that evolutionists are deliberate liars; merely that corruption is in our nature and therefore easily contaminates our world view.

The devil is a liar and the father of lies (John 8:44); he rules the world as usurper (John 12:31; 14:30; 16:11; 1 John 5:19), so again it is not surprising to see his lies gaining the upper hand.

If it were only man and the devil behind the deception, then we could fight on, as lights in the darkness, confident of ultimate — if not immediate — victory. The Bible tells us that there is a third force at work here — God himself.

In 2 Thessalonians 2:9–11, Paul says:

> The coming of the lawless one by the activity of Satan will be with all power and with pretended signs and wonders, and with all wicked

deception for those who are to perish, because they refused to love the truth and so be saved. Therefore *God sends upon them a strong delusion, to make them believe what is false*, so that all may be condemned who did not believe the truth but had pleasure in unrighteousness (emphasis added).

What is the biggest lie that rules our world today? No doubt there are numerous candidates. If the Bible says that the primary truth about God is that He is Creator, and the world says that the universe made itself and no Creator is necessary, then surely this must be the biggest lie there could ever be. So if God is sending a strong delusion upon the world to make people believe what is false, how should faithful Christians respond?

Are we opposing God when we oppose evolution? Certainly not. Paul described his ministry in the following way: "We destroy arguments and every proud obstacle to the knowledge of God, and take every thought captive to obey Christ" (2 Cor. 10:5). So, then, should we.

Are we thereby fighting against God, as sender of the delusion? The answer, of course, is that we are not fighting against God. God is at work in the world continually (John 5:17), and when we fight for the truth of the gospel we are joining battle with Him. Likewise, even though God is the ultimate source of the Curse, whenever we fight, however locally and temporarily, against any of the consequences of the Curse, we can never be fighting God. Thus, making peace, healing disease, and so on is "blessed" and follows Christ's example.

What then is the purpose of this "strong delusion?" It is, we believe, yet another evidence of God's judgment upon sin. Just as the fossils in the rocks remind us of judgments past, so the great lie of evolution is a sign of judgment present. Both point clearly to the final Judgment to come. We are being warned — again.

THELEIN HISTORY — A STRONGHOLD OF FAITH

God saves us because He chooses to do so; He then works in our hearts by His Spirit to bring us to a knowledge of, and belief in, His truth (2 Thess. 2:13). Thus, as Paul says, it is by grace that we are saved, through faith (Eph. 2:8–9). Once we have begun this journey of faith, however, we need nurture and protection, otherwise we may fail to mature and bear fruit (Matt. 13:1–23). Thelein history provides us with nurture for our faith and protection for our journey.

Before we go on, let us reflect upon the opposite — compromise. Our two examples given earlier, Reverend Adam Ford and Bishop Spong, have both lost their way. They still call themselves Christians, but their "Christian faith" bears little resemblance to that outlined in Scripture. They have substituted man's opinions for God's Word.

How then can we feed our spirits upon thelein history and walk safely under its protection? Let's revisit each of the seven Cs in turn, in the light of what we have learned.

- **Creation** — This is *the* foundational doctrine of Christianity. Jesus affirmed it, and demonstrated His creative power over both the spiritual and physical worlds. It is God's will (thelein) that brought the universe into existence, that holds the universe together, and that guides it to its eternal destiny.

- **Corruption** — It was not just Adam and Eve who sinned, but we also. The inherent corruption of the human heart, made manifest in our own personal sin, is the only ground upon which we can approach our Maker — "Have mercy upon me, a sinner" (Luke 18:13;NIV). We live daily with the consequences of sin in the form of all-pervading suffering and death. We, too, although eternally safe in Christ, will suffer from the multiple effects of the Curse, and the tragic consequences of our own and others' sin — but God is disciplining those He loves and He will meet us in our suffering (Heb. 12). Jesus' ministry of healing assures us that God desires to alleviate our suffering, and Romans 8:28 tells us that even under the Curse, God is working all things together for the (eternal) good of those who love Him and are called according to His purpose.

- **Catastrophe** — Mankind's continued rebellion led to God's judgment in the world-destroying flood of Noah, and this constitutes a warning of the Judgment to come (Matt. 24:33; Luke 17:26; 2 Pet. 2:5). The Flood and its aftermath produced the fossil record — a constant reminder that the consequence of sin is suffering and death.

- **Confusion** — Mankind's continued disobedience led to further judgment. Repeated judgments throughout the Bible should give fair warning that our turn may soon come, also. The different language families in the world today, created originally at Babel, stand as a monument to creation — there is no evolutionary explanation — and the miracle of Pentecost reunited mankind by bridging the language gaps (Acts 2:1–11).

- **Christ** — the Creator was revealed to us in Jesus of Nazareth. None of the other great religious leaders dealt with sin, none of them did miracles as Jesus did, and none of them rose from the dead in fulfillment of their own predictions. There is simply no one else like Him.

- **Cross** — Christ died for us, taking the penalty for our sins in himself upon the cross, so that in Him we might become the righteousness of God. In His resurrection, we see the proof of His Genesis world view, and a preview of the world to come.

- **Consummation** — Christ is the beginning and the end. When Christ returns, this world will be destroyed and a new world will be created, where righteousness dwells. We shall reign with Him forever. Come, Lord Jesus. Amen.

God will accomplish all His purpose and fulfill the word that He has sent forth (Isa. 55:10–11).

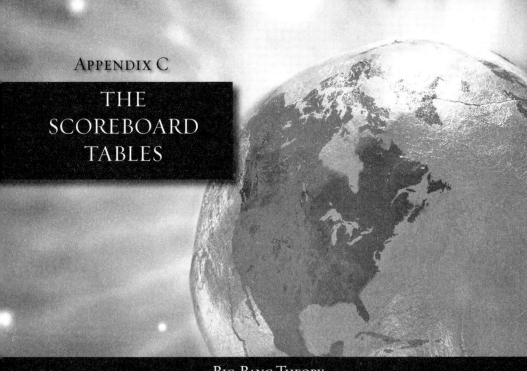

THE SCOREBOARD TABLES

BIG-BANG THEORY

The following table identifies stages in big-bang theory that can be matched against the evidence, and the adequacy of the explanation assessed.

ITEM	EXPLANATION	ADEQUACY
Universe	Initial singularity (obtained by extrapolating cosmic expansion back to its beginning).	Acceptable, since at least one starting assumption is needed in any model of origins.
	The singularity "exploded" at just the right rate into the presently observed expansion mode, and the expansion of space carried the energy along with it out of the singularity.	Ad hoc.

	The "explosion" exploded further in an instantaneous and exceedingly vast inflationary event.	Ad hoc.
	Energy converted into matter via quantum pair production, eventually producing hydrogen, helium, deuterium, and lithium.	Contradicted by lack of evidence of the predicted 50% antimatter.
	The decoupling of matter and energy left behind the CMBR.	This is supposedly the great achievement of big-bang theory, but George Gamow predicted a CMBR temperature of 50 K in 1961 while the value was measured in 1964 at 2.7 K. Eddington predicted in 1926 (on non–big-bang grounds) that the temperature of space would be around 3 K.
	The big-bang model is based on the cosmological principle, which says that the universe looks the same from any point within it, and therefore exists on the surface of a 4-dimensional hypersphere.	The cosmological principle is contradicted or weakened by lack of evidence for a 4-D hypersphere (latest indications are that the universe is comprised of flat Euclidean space), quantization of galactic redshifts, patterns in the polarization of radio waves from galaxies, the anisotropy of the CMBR, and the pattern in large-scale galaxy survey.

Galaxy	The uniformly expanding cloud of gas stopped expanding locally and collapsed due to "density fluctuations."	Ad hoc.
	The collapsing "density fluctuations" did not uniformly collapse but "fragmented" into hundreds of billions of stars.	Ad hoc.
Stars	Population III stars formed by unknown means.	Ad hoc.
	Population III stars were very large and they soon exploded and produced the heavier elements.	These explosions should have produced about as many black holes as stars but this is not observed.
	Population II and I stars formed by "density fluctuations" caused by supernovae.	Evidence is lacking in supernova studies.
	Most stars formed in groups or clusters.	Computer models do not produce globular clusters.
Solar system	Originated in a swirling dust cloud with a collapsing core that formed the sun; planets formed out of leftover dust and gas.	Collapsing core would have concentrated the majority of momentum in the sun but this is not the case — 98% of momentum is in the planets.
Planets	Stardust "aggregated" into small planetesimals.	"Sticking" mechanism unknown.

	Dust aggregates fused into solid planetesimals.	There is no heat source in the cold dust cloud left over from the formation of the sun. Observed "planetesimals" are fused solid meteorites and asteroids, not the experimentally produced and theoretically expected "dust bunnies."
	Planetesimals "aggregated" into self-gravitating bodies.	Gravity cannot overcome wind shear until kilometer-sized objects are formed.
Moon	Same sequence as planet formation.	Same objections as for planet formation.
Life	Chemicals assembled themselves into living cells.	Contradicted by vast amounts of chemical evidence, both theoretical and experimental.
Man	Evolved from lower forms of life by mutation and natural selection.	Natural selection can only select from organisms/genes that already exist. Neither mutation nor natural selection produces new genetic information, so they cannot lead to totally new kinds of organisms. They actually both lose information, and so point to creation.

There are 19 items in this list. The first one is acceptable on purely philosophical grounds (any theory has to start somewhere), one (the CMBR) may have some explanatory power, although there are other possible explanations, and the remaining 17 are either ad hoc or are directly contradicted by the evidence. The best possible score is therefore 2 out of 19, or 11 percent.

THE BIBLICAL MODEL

The following table identifies stages in the biblical model that can be matched against the evidence, and the adequacy of the explanation assessed.

ITEM	EXPLANATION	ADEQUACY
Time scales		
Light travel from distant galaxies	To display His majesty, God created a vast universe that takes light many billions of years to traverse; to display His omnipotence He created it all in six days. The resolution to this apparent paradox is suggested to be the principle of relativistic time dilation.	The principle has been demonstrated experimentally, but not at the magnitude required; we suggest that creation week involved magnitudes not seen since that time.
Hubble expansion of space	God created a functional universe of large size, and "stretched" it out, as several Scriptures describe.	Described in Scripture.
Galaxy evolution	Galaxy clusters should not exist in the big-bang scenario, but we can explain them on the grounds that God created them in clusters and we are seeing them only 6,000 years after their creation in earth time or hundreds of millions of years in cosmic time — a very short time in universal history.	A reasonable deduction from Scripture.

Stellar evolution	God created many different kinds of stars; the fact that we can arrange them in a Hertzsprung-Russell diagram may simply illustrate their diversity and does not require them to have evolved. Stars could move along the H-R diagram following their creation at differing original masses.	Variety noted in Scripture.
Nuclear decay	Accelerated nuclear decay is possible by God changing the nuclear forces — without destroying the molecular structures necessary for life.	A reasonable inference from Scripture, with some important experimental/ observational confirmation.
Geological column	The geological time scale was constructed on the assumption of slow deposition, but the evidence indicates rapid deposition — and the Flood and its aftermath can explain this.	Follows from Scripture.
Archaeology	The Bible gives a short chronology of human civilization, but the opposing archaeological time scale is heavily dependent upon carbon dating.[1] The evidence for a stronger magnetic field in the past, together with substantial burial of carbon biomass in the Flood, can explain small concentrations of carbon-14 in human artifacts and bones as reflecting environmental conditions and not great age.	Deduction from the evidence and Scripture.

---

1. It is also dependent on Egyptian chronology (which in turn has some reliance on carbon-14). Even a number of secular authorities are beginning to suggest that Egyptian dating is in need of drastic revision downward.

Human "evolution"	A crucial difference between man and the apes is language. Man is supposed to have diverged from the apes about 5 million years ago, yet all human languages can be traced (on the evolutionary time scale) to a rapid originating event between 6,000 and 25,000 years ago.[2] This time scale is dominated by carbon-14 dates, which, when corrected for magnetic field and Flood effects, can be telescoped down to the Tower of Babel incident about 4,000 years ago.	Deduction from the evidence and Scripture.
Intelligent life only on earth	Evolutionists mostly believe the universe is "awash" with life, but the Bible presents man as being very special — the intimate companion of God, higher even than the angels (in his final state). We would not expect to find intelligent life elsewhere in the universe, and that is what we observe.	Scripture and evidence agree.
Earth at the center of the universe	According to the Bible, the earth is the center of God's attention, but it may also be at the physical center of the universe. Isotropy — the fact that the universe looks the same in every direction (in CMBR, galaxy distributions, galaxy redshifts) — can reasonably be explained by the earth being at the center. Quantization of galaxy redshifts suggests that we are at or near the center of a series of concentric shells on which the galaxies are located. The anisotropy (variations) in the CMBR produce a startling pattern of celestial north and south poles, together with a celestial equator — all pointing to us being at or near the center. Large-scale galaxy survey reveals a pattern consistent with us being at the center.	A reasonable deduction from Scripture.

2. Alexander R. Williams, "Apes, Words and People," *Creation* 25(3):50–53 (2003).

Evidence of design	The abundant evidence of design caused evolutionists to invent the anthropic principle to explain it away. However, their "multiple universes" scenario is pure speculation — there is only one universe that we know of.	Taught in Scripture, confirmed by symbolic language in the DNA molecule. Irreducible complexity is evident in the structure of the earth's biosphere within the solar system.
Evidence of corruption	The Curse is obvious everywhere on earth, in the suffering and death of the myriad forms of life. Our major evidence of corruption in the celestial realm is "falling stars," the remnants of an exploded planet, the remains of which are the asteroids and meteors.	Convincing evidence. The relation of star "death" (supernovae) to the Fall needs to be clarified, as our YSS model puts these events before the Fall.
Evidence of grace	The Curse causes suffering but does not destroy grace, since its purpose (we suggest) was to provide man with a reason to repent. The earth continues to be a safe haven for life in an otherwise lethal universe — the "falling stars" do not wipe out life, they just give a warning.	Scripture continually interweaves the themes of love and discipline.

There are 13 items in this list. None are inconsistent with the evidence. The time scale for supernova events is adequately explained by relativistic time dilation, but their relation to the Fall still needs to be explained. We will, therefore, give a score of 12 out of 13, or 92 percent.

THE COMMON SCOREBOARD

We will now present a summary of the common areas where predictions and/or explanations can be derived from both the big-bang and the biblical models, and add up the scores:

ITEM	BIG BANG	BIBLE	Evidence Favors:	
			BB	Bible
Causality	No competent cause, even allowing for uncertainty about the physics of the primordial singularity.	God is competent to create a universe. Jesus Christ, the Creator incarnate, demonstrated His creative power in miracles and Resurrection.	☒	☑
Singularity	The mechanism that caused space to begin expanding from the primordial singularity, and carrying all the energy of the universe along with it, is unknown.	Creating a small-scale universe and then "stretching it out" and filling it with the stars and galaxies would avoid collapse into a singularity.	☒	☑
Entropy	Second law of thermodynamics points to low primordial entropy, but the big bang is a high-entropy event.	God created a highly structured, low-entropy universe in the beginning.	☒	☑

Cosmic Microwave Background Radiation	Light from the "decoupling era" has been redshifted into the microwave spectrum.	The temperature of empty space; may be redshifted light from creation day 1.	☑	☑
Cosmic Geometry	Cosmological principle says the universe looks the same from every position within it, and we exist on the surface of a 4-D hypersphere, but there is no evidence for the latter.	Earth is the center of God's attention and possibly therefore at or near the center of the universe. Several lines of evidence support this view.	☒	☑
Nucleosynthesis				
Light elements	Only normal matter hydrogen produced in the big bang, via quantum pair production, then helium, lithium, and deuterium produced by fusion; contradicted by absence of anti-matter.	Primordial creation of all elements (atmosphere, water, earth) by day 3.	☒	☑
Heavy elements	Produced in numerous cycles of star formation; models suggest that earliest stars were very massive, but these would have produced large numbers of black holes, which have not been observed.	As above.	☒	☑

Time scales				
Cosmic expansion	Hubble relation indicates billions of years; but Arpian objects (see appendix A) contradict the redshift/distance correlation.	Bible says God "stretched out" the heavens; outward motion of galaxies consistent with need to prevent gravitational collapse.	☑	☑
Light-travel time	Furthest galaxies billions of light-years away, therefore it took billions of years to get here.	Relativistic time dilation can explain a vast universe which was all created 6,000 years ago in earth time.	☑	☑
Galaxy clusters	Clusters should have drifted apart if really billions of years old.	We are seeing clusters only 6,000 years after creation; they are at most only hundreds of millions of years old in astronomical time, a short period on the universal time scale.	☒	☑
Spiral galaxies	Spirals should have performed about two or three hundred rotations by now if billions of years old, and thus be completely "wound up," i.e., no longer spirals.	Only enough astronomical time available for a few rotations at most.	☒	☑

Planetary magnetic fields	Require some means of sustaining in face of rapid decay. "Dynamo" theory not applicable to all planets and not proven for earth.	Rapid decline consistent with free decay of created fields; this and the discovery of extremely rapid reversals in basalts supports young solar system.	☒	☑
Comets	Oort cloud not observed.	Rapid decay of comets supports young solar system.	☒	☑
Sea salt	Contradicts billions of years.	Low value supports young earth.	☒	☑
Sea floor sediment	Should be much deeper, even given tectonic plate movements.	Shallow depths support young earth.	☒	☑
Stratigraphy	Slow deposition of whole geological column needed but contradicted by widespread evidence of rapid deposition and carbon-14 profile.	Rapid deposition consistent with world-destroying flood of Noah and its aftermath. This also explains the carbon-14 profile.	☒	☑
Isotopes	Long-age isotopes support billions of years; but contradictions exist in a number of other areas.	Carbon-14, helium, radiohalos support young earth; accelerated decay and selective reporting can account for "long age" data.	☑	☑

Momentum in the solar system	Nebular hypothesis leads to majority of (angular) momentum in sun; contradicted by 98% of this momentum being in the planets.	Planets and sun created separately, each with their own angular momentum.	☒	☑
Evidence of design	Not expected. Explained away via anthropic principle, but the multiple universe interpretation is purely hypothetical.	Primary prediction of model; originally perfect design marred by the Curse, as observed.	☒	☑
Life in the universe	Universe "awash with life"[3] but none found.	Man is alone in the physical universe, as observed.	☒	☑
Totals			4	20

---

3. Some people might insist that life is not a prediction of big-bang theory, but our definition of the "necessary and sufficient universe" included man. Any theory of cosmology must explain the cosmologist.

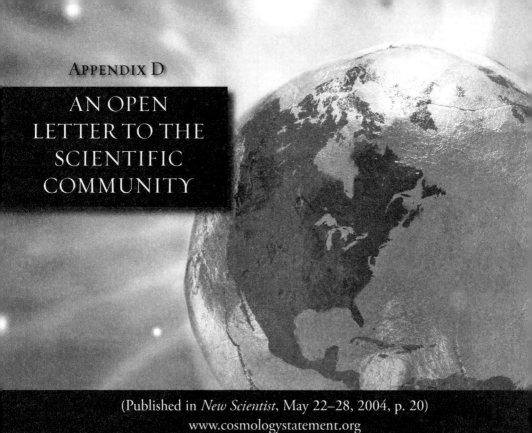

Appendix D

AN OPEN LETTER TO THE SCIENTIFIC COMMUNITY

(Published in *New Scientist*, May 22–28, 2004, p. 20)
www.cosmologystatement.org

The big bang today relies on a growing number of hypothetical entities, things that we have never observed — inflation, dark matter, and dark energy are the most prominent examples. Without them, there would be a fatal contradiction between the observations made by astronomers and the predictions of the big-bang theory. In no other field of physics would this continual recourse to new hypothetical objects be accepted as a way of bridging the gap between theory and observation. It would, at the least, raise serious questions about the validity of the underlying theory.

But the big-bang theory can't survive without these fudge factors. Without the hypothetical inflation field, the big bang does not predict the smooth, isotropic cosmic background radiation that is observed, because there would be no way for parts of the universe that are now more than a few degrees away in the sky to come to the same temperature and thus emit the same amount of microwave radiation.

Without some kind of dark matter, unlike any that we have observed on earth despite 20 years of experiments, big-bang theory makes contradictory predictions for the density of matter in the universe. Inflation requires a density

20 times larger than that implied by big-bang nucleosynthesis, the theory's explanation of the origin of the light elements. And without dark energy, the theory predicts that the universe is only about 8 billion years old, which is billions of years younger than the age of many stars in our galaxy.

What is more, the big-bang theory can boast of no quantitative predictions that have subsequently been validated by observation. The successes claimed by the theory's supporters consist of its ability to retrospectively fit observations with a steadily increasing array of adjustable parameters, just as the old earth-centered cosmology of Ptolemy needed layer upon layer of epicycles.

Yet the big bang is not the only framework available for understanding the history of the universe. Plasma cosmology and the steady-state model both hypothesize an evolving universe without beginning or end. These and other alternative approaches can also explain the basic phenomena of the cosmos, including the abundances of light elements, the generation of large-scale structure, the cosmic background radiation, and how the redshift of faraway galaxies increases with distance. They have even predicted new phenomena that were subsequently observed, something the big bang has failed to do.

Supporters of the big-bang theory may retort that these theories do not explain every cosmological observation. But that is scarcely surprising, as their development has been severely hampered by a complete lack of funding. Indeed, such questions and alternatives cannot even now be freely discussed and examined. An open exchange of ideas is lacking in most mainstream conferences. Whereas Richard Feynman could say that "science is the culture of doubt," in cosmology today doubt and dissent are not tolerated, and young scientists learn to remain silent if they have something negative to say about the standard big-bang model. Those who doubt the big bang fear that saying so will cost them their funding.

Even observations are now interpreted through this biased filter, judged right or wrong depending on whether or not they support the big bang. So discordant data on redshifts, lithium and helium abundances, and galaxy distribution, among other topics, are ignored or ridiculed. This reflects a growing dogmatic mindset that is alien to the spirit of free scientific inquiry.

Today, virtually all financial and experimental resources in cosmology are devoted to big-bang studies. Funding comes from only a few sources, and all the peer-review committees that control them are dominated by supporters of the big bang. As a result, the dominance of the big bang within the field has become self-sustaining, irrespective of the scientific validity of the theory.

Giving support only to projects within the big-bang framework undermines a fundamental element of the scientific method — the constant testing of theory against observation. Such a restriction makes unbiased discussion and research impossible. To redress this, we urge those agencies that fund work in cosmology to set aside a significant fraction of their funding for investigations into alternative theories and observational contradictions of the big bang. To avoid bias, the peer review committee that allocates such funds could be composed of astronomers and physicists from outside the field of cosmology.

Allocating funding to investigations into the big bang's validity, and its alternatives, would allow the scientific process to determine our most accurate model of the history of the universe.

Signed: (Institutions are listed for identification only)

Halton Arp, Max-Planck-Institute Fur Astrophysik (Germany)
Andre Koch Torres Assis, State University of Campinas (Brazil)
Yuri Baryshev, Astronomical Institute, St. Petersburg State
    University (Russia)
Ari Brynjolfsson, Applied Radiation Industries (USA)
Hermann Bondi, Churchill College, University of Cambridge (UK)
Timothy Eastman, Plasmas International (USA)
Chuck Gallo, Superconix, Inc.(USA)
Thomas Gold, Cornell University (emeritus) (USA)
Amitabha Ghosh, Indian Institute of Technology, Kanpur (India)
Walter J. Heikkila, University of Texas at Dallas (USA)
Michael Ibison, Institute for Advanced Studies at Austin (USA)
Thomas Jarboe, University of Washington (USA)
Jerry W. Jensen, ATK Propulsion (USA)
Menas Kafatos, George Mason University (USA)
Eric J. Lerner, Lawrenceville Plasma Physics (USA)
Paul Marmet, Herzberg Institute of Astrophysics (retired) (Canada)
Paola Marziani, Istituto Nazionale di Astrofisica, Osservatorio
    Astronomico di Padova (Italy)
Gregory Meholic, The Aerospace Corporation (USA)
Jacques Moret-Bailly, Université Dijon (retired) (France)
Jayant Narlikar, IUCAA(emeritus) and College de France (India, France)
Marcos Cesar Danhoni Neves, State University of Maringá (Brazil)
Charles D. Orth, Lawrence Livermore National Laboratory (USA)

R. David Pace, Lyon College (USA)

Georges Paturel, Observatoire de Lyon (France)

Jean-Claude Pecker, College de France (France)

Anthony L. Peratt, Los Alamos National Laboratory (USA)

Bill Peter, BAE Systems Advanced Technologies (USA)

David Roscoe, Sheffield University (UK)

Malabika Roy, George Mason University (USA)

Sisir Roy, George Mason University (USA)

Konrad Rudnicki, Jagiellonian University (Poland)

Domingos S.L. Soares, Federal University of Minas Gerais (Brazil)

John L. West, Jet Propulsion Laboratory, California Institute of
     Technology (USA)

James F. Woodward, California State University, Fullerton (USA)

Index

Abraham, 207, 212, 216, 218, 223, 299, 302

accelerated nuclear decay, 173, 186, 190, 192, 197, 256

Adam and Eve, 15, 63–64, 168–170, 200, 207, 212, 217, 219–220, 222, 255, 299–300, 305, 310

Adonai, 217

age and world views, 166

age as myth, 197

age of the earth, 31, 163–167, 173, 187–190, 192, 195, 197–198, 208

age of the solar system, 198–199

age of the universe, 50, 178, 197, 199, 201, 231, 276, 297

age, definition of, 164

algebra, 36

Alpha and Omega, 63, 237, 258

alpha particles, 172–173, 197

American Civil War, 67

amino acids, 159–160

Andromeda, 41–42, 132, 137

animal sacrifice, 15, 222

anisotropy in the CMBR, 134–135, 238, 314, 319

annihilation, 126

ant, 260

anthropic principle, 72, 74, 206, 244

anti-matter, 14, 88, 126, 161

anti-matter galaxies, 126

anti-neutrino, 88, 126

anti-proton, 47, 88, 126

Apollo moon landings, 156–157, 239

appearance of age, 168, 170, 173

appearance of explosions, 170

Aristarchus, 28, 35

Aristotle, 23, 28

Arp, Halton, 128, 182, 273–284, 286, 288, 293, 329

Arpian universe, 273, 275, 281

assumptions, 19, 14–16, 55–56, 58–61, 64–65, 68, 72, 88, 102, 111, 113, 117–118, 140, 164–167, 169, 172, 178, 188, 190, 200, 208, 259, 262–263, 271, 283, 290, 300

assumptions in big-bang theory, 48–49, 117–121

assumptions in dating methods, 186, 189–192

asteroid 433 Eros, 156

asteroid belt, 157, 250, 252, 256

asteroids, 95, 153, 157–158, 250, 256–257

astronaut, 156, 177, 239

astronomical unit, 39

atheism, 14, 27, 53, 57, 62, 71, 74, 75, 77, 107, 132, 288

atheistic materialist world view, 75

atmosphere, 78, 90, 103, 156–157, 160, 171, 196, 199, 229, 231, 236, 238–239, 248–249, 252, 254

atmosphere, as protective shield, 239

atomic bomb, 45, 47, 119, 121, 241

atomic clocks, 166, 185–186

atonement, 15–16, 298, 223–224

authority of the Bible, 208, 237, 272

avoiding the primordial singularity, 100, 120

Babel, Tower of, 207, 310, 319

Baumgardner, John R., 192, 195–197

Becquerel, 188

bedding planes, 194

bellybuttons, 168

biblical concept of the universe, 206, 238, 262, 269

biblical cosmogony, 32, 181, 224, 262–263

biblical inerrancy, 295, 304, 306, 308

biblical interpretation, principles of, 207

biblical time scale, 16, 163, 174, 176, 187, 190, 195, 200, 256

biblical world view, 16, 20, 25, 63, 164, 167, 192, 206–207, 225, 232

big-bang model, 13–14, 49, 53–54, 62, 70, 73, 100, 114–116, 120, 127, 137, 161–163, 201, 203, 226, 238, 241, 259–262, 279, 284, 290–291, 328

big-bang theory, 13–14, 16, 47, 50, 53, 55, 58–59, 66, 69, 72, 79, 87–88, 99–100, 102, 106, 110, 118–119, 121, 126–129, 133, 135, 140, 143, 162, 183, 202, 234, 237, 259–263, 265–266, 269, 271–272, 273, 276, 282–283, 294, 300, 313, 325, 327–328

big-bang universe, 13–14, 53, 88, 100–103, 119, 124, 136, 162, 183, 275–276, 292

big chill, 87, 107–110, 258

big crunch, 87, 107–110, 134, 137, 258, 274, 286, 296

big rip, 108, 258

binary accretion, theory of moon's origin, 157

bioturbation, 194

birth certificates, 164

Bishop Ussher's chronology, 187

black dwarf, 138, 142

black hole, 20, 78, 87, 96–97, 99, 101–102, 107, 130, 132, 138, 142, 144, 150, 177, 179, 202, 239, 277, 284

black hole, mini, 99

blueshifts, 174–175, 180, 287

Bohr, Niels, 45

Bondi, Gold, and Hoyle, 73, 283

Borge and Nodland, 135

bouncing universe, 62, 102

Brahe, Tycho, 35–36

brane, 104, 128

brane world, 128

break-up time, for galaxy clusters, 323

broken planet, 94, 152, 250

brown dwarf, 137, 141

Bruno, Giordano, 34

bulldozer, 260

Burbidge, Geoffrey, 134–135, 274, 280, 284–286

Burgess, Stuart, 174

Cain and Abel, 299

calibration of dating methods, 165

capture theory, of moon's origin, 157

captured asteroids, 158

carbon dating, 190–191, 196

carbon-14, 190–191, 196–197, 318

Carmeli, Moshe, 274, 289–291

Carmeli's CGR model, 289–291

cascade of creation events, 182

Casimir effect, 120

causality, 260

cause and effect, 16, 77, 131

c-decay, 174–175, 178

center of the universe, 21, 28, 36, 72, 127, 132, 135–136, 179, 184, 238

Cepheid variable stars, 40, 42

C-gravitons, 292–293

chance, 14, 61–63, 74–75, 77, 79, 82–86, 126, 140, 143, 150, 155, 234, 237, 244, 260, 277, 287, 296 chaotic early universe, 55, 130

chemical evolution, 14, 159–160

Chinese cosmology, 170, 249

Christ, 15, 63–64, 207–208, 217, 221–223, 225, 253, 257–258, 267, 296–298, 304, 306, 308–311

Christian universities, 34

chronometer, 188, 190

circularity of impact craters, 153

circumstellar disk, 151, 155

circumstellar material, 147

clay mineral surfaces, 160

clock problem, 185

closed universe, 108, 110

CMBR, 50–51, 111, 117, 123, 125, 127–128, 130, 134–135, 162, 226, 238, 254, 261, 266

coal, 191, 194, 196–197, 273, 283–284, 287, 291, 294, 316

cold accretion theory, 151, 158

cometesimals, 199

comets, 35–36, 93–95, 125, 128, 158, 180, 198–199, 240, 249–250, 252, 256–257, 291

competent cause, 260–261

compromise, 16–17, 53, 172, 202, 208, 259, 295, 297, 299–300, 306, 308–309

compromise positions on Genesis, 208, 259

computer models, 162

computer simulation, 140, 154–155, 157

condensation reaction, 159

confusion, Tower of Babel, 207, 310

consummation, return of Christ, 207, 267, 296, 301, 311

Copernican principle, 133

Copernicus, 34–36, 72, 296

core collapse, 142, 144

corruption and design go together, 248

corruption of human nature, 248

corruption in medieval church, 34

corruption, the Fall, 251, 253, 255

cosmic acceleration, 101

COsmic Background Explorer, 127, 287

cosmic deceleration, 70

Cosmic Designer, 74–75

cosmic expansion, 66, 74, 110, 119, 131–132, 137, 145, 162, 247, 251, 274–275, 277, 285

cosmic expansion accelerating, 108

cosmic expansion, biblical, 247, 251

cosmic history, 137, 173, 207, 232, 253, 295, 305

cosmic history, biblical, 295

cosmic history, creationist models173, 207

cosmic mass density, 137

Cosmic Microwave Background Radiation: see CMBR

cosmological constant, 47, 49, 87, 107, 110–113, 123, 290–291

cosmological constant problem, 112–113

cosmological models, 53, 70, 73, 100, 129, 132, 238, 266, 271, 273, 294

cosmological principle, 73, 100, 132–134, 136, 283, 294

Crab Nebula, 170, 182–183, 249

created light beams, 169

creation day 4, 66, 178–179, 181–182, 200–201, 255, 280

creation ex nihilo, 224, 297

creation week, 16, 170, 175, 251, 300

Creator, 15, 17, 20, 25, 27, 33, 43–44, 54, 59–60, 66, 72, 84, 105, 107, 120, 124, 132, 161, 170, 178, 203, 207–208, 212, 216–219, 222, 237, 241–246, 249, 252, 257, 281, 288, 299, 304–305, 309–310

creator spirits, 25

cricket, 81–82, 104

Crinum coal mine, 191

Cross, 17, 23, 103, 148, 207, 213, 223, 257, 311

cryptic clues in the Bible, 245–247

culture, crucial importance of, 223

Curse, 15, 207, 212, 218, 220–222, 232, 248–249, 251–253, 255–257, 298, 309–310

Dalrymple, G. Brent, 190–191

dark energy, 14, 110, 119, 128, 162, 290–291, 294, 327–328

dark matter, 14, 110, 125, 128, 136–139, 158, 162, 291, 294, 327

darkening of sun, moon, and stars, 248–249

Darwin, Charles, 16, 66, 75–76, 296, 298

daughter isotopes, 172

David, 207, 212, 301–302, 330

Davies, Paul, 56, 245

day, meaning of, 210, 227–231, 254

day-age theory, 167, 208, 259

De Duve, Christian, 158

Dead Sea Scrolls, 29, 31

death, 15, 64, 66, 207, 212, 218–219, 221–222, 232, 244, 255, 297–298, 301, 305–306, 310, 320

death, not a natural part of life, 298

deception, 63, 67, 168–169, 171–173, 208, 217, 219, 268, 295, 308–309

decoupling and the CMBR, 127

deep gravitational well, 178

deism, 295, 304–305

Dembski, William, 75

demon gods, 217

density fluctuations, 121, 130–132, 144–147, 149–150, 154, 284

density of the universe, 137, 290

destroying the gospel, 295, 297

destruction of a planet, 252

deuterium, 117, 125, 143, 146

devil, 63, 221, 232, 295, 299, 308

Dicke, Robert, 73

dimensions, 87, 102–105, 133

Dirac, Paul, 73, 288

dishonoring God, 295, 300

displacement behavior, 70

disrupted planet, 158, 167

distribution of star sizes, 150

divine nature shown in creation, 212, 242, 244, 249

DNA molecule, 161, 206, 245, 266, 320

doctrinal collapse, 295–296

dominion over God's creation, 63, 168, 217, 245, 253

Doppler effect, 48, 175

dust bunnies, 153, 316

dust grains, 156

early history of the universe, 266

earth a safe haven for life, 238–240, 249, 320

earth as center of the universe, 21, 28, 36, 72, 127, 132, 135–136, 179, 184, 238, 319, 322

earth clock, 178, 185, 200

earth suspended in space, 247

earth, circumference, 24, 165

earth, spherical shape, 23–24, 94–95, 107–108, 246

earth/moon system, 156

earth's magnetic field, decay of, 195, 199, 318

ecliptic, 25, 151

Eddington, Arthur, 97–98, 100, 125, 127, 226

Einstein, Albert, 44–49, 87–88, 91–93, 98, 100, 110–112, 124, 133, 138, 176–178, 274, 278, 289–290, 293–294

Einstein's Universe, 177

electricity, 89–90, 99, 106, 240

electromagnetic force, 89–90, 123

electromagnetic spectrum, 38, 42

electromagnetism, 87, 89, 91, 140, 193, 231

electron, 46–47, 88–90, 126

electron, quantum origin, 88

elliptical galaxies, 132, 139, 240, 281

embryonic star, 148

entropy, 107, 321

Enuma Elish, 30, 233

epicycle model, of Ptolemy, 28–29, 35, 328

equilibrium of isotope decay, 172–173

equilibrium universe, 106

Eratosthenes, 24, 165

erosion, 194

eternal power, evident in creation, 212, 240–242, 249, 253

Eudoxus, 28

event horizon, 96, 98–99, 101, 177, 179

evidence for a young earth, 193

exotic parameters, 291

explosion upon an explosion, 123–124

explosion, as big-bang origin, 49, 103, 109, 114, 116–124, 260

explosion, atomic bomb, 241

extra-terrestrial life, 159, 267

eyewitness account of creation, 54, 228, 300

faith in science, 71–72, 96, 121, 198, 263, 298

faith, defined, 71

faith, in everyday life, 71

fall of mankind, 15, 173–174, 192–193, 218–219, 250, 261, 297, 320–321

Ferris, James P., 160

fine tuning, 14, 123–124, 198

firmament, 29, 179, 229–231, 242, 250, 254

first generation of stars, 118, 143

first law of thermodynamics, 90, 106, 265, 288

fission products, 173

fission theory, of moon's origin, 157

fission tracks, 173

fission, nuclear, 141, 172–173

flat geometry of space, 87, 109, 134

flatness problem, 110, 113

flood of Noah, 176, 189, 196, 207, 241, 297, 310

flying machines, in the Bible, 246

Ford, Rev. Adam, 296, 298, 301, 309

forensic science, 68

Fornax supercluster, 273, 280–281

fossil record, 310, 189, 196, 297

fossil soils, 194

fountains of the deep, 247

four fundamental forces of physics, 74, 89–93, 193

Fourth Commandment, 15, 17, 20, 175, 224, 228, 306–307

fourth dimension, 133

fragmentation, 132, 150–151, 155, 282

fragmentation of gas clouds, 132, 150–151, 282

fragmentation problem, 150

frame of reference in time dilation, 176, 200, 289

framework hypothesis, 167, 208, 295

friction, 91–92, 157, 186

Friedmann, Alexander, 47, 101, 121

Friedmann equation, 101, 121

Friedmann-Lemaitre cosmology, 290

fundamental forces of physics, 74, 123

fusion power of the sun, 171

future trends in cosmology, 265

galactic neighborhood, 180, 229

galaxies, discovery of redshift, 273–275

galaxies, most distant, 48, 169, 202, 293

galaxies, origin of, 266, 272

galaxy clusters, 137, 139, 200–201, 276, 279, 287

galaxy collapse, 130–131

galaxy distribution, 328, 132

galaxy halo, 138

galaxy M51, 145

galaxy map, 134

galaxy, as milky nebulosity, 37

galaxy, necessary and sufficient universe, 77–79

Galileo, 34, 36–37, 72, 153, 296

Gallipoli, 109

gambling, 84–85

gamma rays, 42

Gamow, George, 49–50, 127

gap theory, 167, 208, 226, 259, 295, 327

Garden of Eden, 64, 168, 218, 296, 299

gas cloud dynamics, 143

gas giant planets, 141, 154–155, 239

general relativity theory, 16, 44, 87, 92, 100, 163, 176, 179, 274, 289

generations of the patriarchs, 215–216, 218

Genesis cosmogony, 181, 262–263

Genesis flood, 176, 194–195

Genesis, origin of heavenly bodies, 29–30, 167, 178, 226, 231

geochronologists, 190

geometry of space, 87, 108, 134

giant impacts, 157

giant molecular clouds, 144

giant planetesimal, 157

glass powder, 153

globular clusters, 111, 139, 148, 150

glory of God in creation, 15, 240, 304

glory of God in His word, 213, 240, 301, 303

God of the Bible, 57, 170, 252, 261, 305

God, as Designer, 75

God's judgment, 248, 297, 309–310

God's Word, the central dynamic of Christianity, 233

Goliath, 301–302

Grand Canyon, 191

gravitational attraction between molecules, 156, 278

gravitational collapse of gas cloud, 115, 130, 132, 141, 144, 154

gravitationally unstable disk, 155

gravity, 27, 37, 44, 74, 78, 87–101, 103, 107–108, 111, 119, 124, 132, 134, 138–140, 142–144, 149, 152, 154–156, 177–178, 193, 199–200, 205–206, 231–232, 253, 266, 274, 280, 289, 291–294

gravity wave detector, 124

gravity, discovery of law, 37

great mountain, burning with fire, 180, 257

Greenwich, 186

Halley's Comet, 33, 93

harmony of the spheres, 27

Harris model, 174

Hartnett's young solar system model, 180

Hawking, Stephen, 20, 59–60, 68, 74, 76, 99, 101–102, 111, 118, 120, 128–129, 183–184, 262

Hawking and Collins, 74

Hawking and Penrose, 101

heat clock, 187, 195

heat death, 107–108

heating by radioactive decay, 158

heaven, in Genesis, 29, 181, 224, 229–232, 247

heavy elements, 140, 151

heliocentric universe, 72

helium, 95, 115, 117, 125, 142–143, 146, 173, 192, 197, 284, 328

Herschel, William, 37

Hertzsprung-Russell diagram, 141, 200

Hillel, 32

Hindu *Suryasiddhanta*, 31

Hiroshima, 121

Holmes, Arthur, 188

honor of God in creation, 15, 304

honor of God in His Word, 213, 303, 307

honor, as cultural value, 301–302

honor, defined, 302–303

horizon problem, 123, 125

hot young stars, 147

Hoyle, Fred, 73, 269, 274, 280, 283–284, 286, 288

Hoyle, Burbidge, and Narlikar, 274, 280, 284

Hubble, Edwin, 41–42, 44, 47–51, 70, 73, 110–111, 119, 132–133, 148, 197–201, 247, 275–276, 285–287, 289–290, 293–294

Hubble age of universe, 50–51, 73, 199–200

Hubble constant, 70, 197, 200, 287, 289–290

Hubble expansion, 48, 50, 110–111, 119, 133, 200, 247, 285, 323

Hubble galaxy types, 148

Hubble law, 276, 287, 289, 294

Hubble redshifts in meta model, 293–294

Hubble Space Telescope, 132, 201, 286

Hubble-Carmeli time, 289–290, 317

Huber and Wächterhäuser, 160

human history, 212, 232, 272, 307

human history as cosmic history, 212, 232

Humphreys, Russell, 135, 176–181, 190, 192–193, 195–197, 199–200, 229–230, 247, 251, 262

Humphreys' white hole cosmology, 178, 200

hydrogen, 46–47, 95, 115, 117, 123, 125, 140, 142–143, 146, 155, 161, 179, 244, 278, 284

hydrolysis, 159–160

hyperspace, 133

hypersphere, 133–134

ice crystals, 155

ice planets, 154–155, 239

idolatry, 64, 218, 295, 304

impact craters, 152–153, 239, 250, 252

impossible events, 86

inflation, 14, 110, 117, 119, 121–125, 128, 130–131, 133, 145, 161–162, 184, 234, 327

information on DNA molecule, 161, 206

infrared, 42–43, 283

initial mass functions, 148

inner planets, 151–152

insect fossils, 71

intelligent design, 54, 75, 77, 79, 82, 114, 124, 140, 206, 244, 251, 266

intergalactic medium, 128

inverse square law, 96, 134, 138–139, 276

iron, 90, 115, 151–152, 157–158, 160, 250

iron sulphide, 160

irreducible complexity, 17, 234–235

isotope clocks, 167, 190, 196

isotope dates, creationist views, 189

Israelites, 15, 30, 215–218, 224, 228, 255, 306

Jansky, Carl, 43

Jastrow, Robert, 157

Jephthah, 301–303

Jesus, Alpha and Omega, 63, 237, 258

Jesus' Sermon on the Mount, 210, 307

Jesus' view of Genesis, 210

Jesus' view of sin, 299

Jewish calendar, 32

Jewish cosmology, 29

Job, 27, 221, 231, 247

Joly, John, 165, 187

Judgment Day, 63, 304

Jupiter, 27, 36, 90, 103, 141, 152, 154, 157, 169, 239, 250, 256

Jupiter, origin of, 151

Kepler, Johannes, 36–37

Kepler's laws of planetary motion, 36

Krauss, Lawrence, 113, 123

Kuhn, Thomas, 69

Kuiper belt, 198

Lada and Shu, 147

Large Magellanic Cloud, 170, 182–183

lava deposits, 191

laws of thermodynamics, 87, 90, 106–107, 187, 232, 265, 288, 321

Le Sage's theory of gravity, 293

lead isotope dating method, 172, 197

Leavitt, Henrietta, 40

Lemaître, Abbé Georges-Henri, 48–49

life, extra-terrestrial, 159, 267

life, origin of, 158–160, 266

Life, Tree of, 15, 218, 222

light cones, 183

lightning and thunder, 241

light-year, 40

limitations of science, 65

lithium, 117, 125, 143, 146, 328

local supercluster, 273, 281

Loeb, Abraham, 151

Lord Kelvin, 187–188, 195, 293

Lorentz, 176, 289–290

Lorentz and Einstein, 176, 289

luminosity, 40, 139–140, 274, 276–277

Lyell, Charles, 187

Mach, Ernst, 278, 282

Mach's principle, 278, 282

MACHOs, 138

magnetic field, as protective shield, 78, 239

magnetic field, decay of, 324

magnetic field, in vacuum, 90

magnetic field, of planets, 324

magnetic fields in gas clouds, 143–144, 150

magnetism, laws of, 87, 89, 140, 193, 231

main sequence stars, 140, 142–143

man, the cosmologist, 163, 257, 267

man's moral character, 67

man-centered universe, 238

Marduk, 30, 233

Mars, a barren wasteland, 239

Mars, as giant planetesimal, 157

Mars, journey to, 267

Mars, water on, 159

Masoretic text, 31, 214

mass density of the universe, 137, 290

mass/luminosity (ML) ratio, 139

matter era, 131

meaning of language, 209

meaning of the word day, 307–308

Mercury, lethal to life, 239

mergers, 132

meta model, 98, 274, 291–293

metallic elements, 118

metaphysical conjecture, 55

metaphysics, 49, 55–56, 58, 75

meteorites, 152–153, 157–158, 165–167, 189, 191, 240, 249–250, 252, 255–256

meteorites, isotopes in, 165–167

method and timing of creation, 205, 233, 252

microbes in the upper atmosphere, 160

Middle Ages, 32, 36

Milky Way, 40–41, 43, 47, 73, 94, 132, 138–139, 146, 169, 202, 238–239, 252

miracle, at Gallipoli, 109

miracles have causes, 77

miracles of Jesus confirm creation, 33, 261, 310, 321

miraculous cause of creation, 234

Mishnah, 31–32

missing mass problem, 136

missing mass problem solved, 292

MOdified Newtonian Dynamics, 138

molecular cloud core, 147

molecular hydrogen, 155

momentum, 46, 117, 154

MOND theory, 134, 139, 292

moon rocks, as meteorites, 157

moon, created on day 4, 181

moon, has no atmosphere, 156

moon, origin theories, 157

moons, origin of, 155, 157

Morris, Henry, 176, 212, 215, 226, 298–299

Morris, John, 190, 193

Moses' view of Genesis, 214

M-Theory, 104, 266

multiple universes, 75

multiverse, 74

Murder on the Orient Express, 65

myth of flat earth, 23–24

NASA, 60, 127, 129, 157, 159, 199, 267, 283

NASA Mission Statement, 159

natural selection, 62, 66, 76–77, 298

natural selection, of universes, 62

natural universe, concept of, 205

naturalistic assumptions in dating, 16, 166, 169

naturalistic materialism, 61, 265, 269

naturalistic models, 294

naturalistic starting assumptions, 169

navigation, 22

nebular hypothesis, 154

necessary and sufficient universe, 60, 77–78, 129, 238, 260, 262, 325

necessity, 72, 75, 82–83, 87, 140, 150, 288

negative pressure, 288, 291

Neptune, objects beyond, 254

Neptune, origin of, 155

neutrino, 88, 126, 172

neutrino, quantum origin, 126

neutron star, 96, 142, 170

neutrons, and nuclear forces, 142

neutrons, from big bang, 117

new cosmological theories, 268

new physics, 44, 49, 266

New Zealand, 191

Newton, Isaac, 37–38, 44, 83, 89, 91–93, 95–96, 102–103, 125, 134, 138, 171–172, 175, 198, 292, 296

Newton's first law of motion, 91–92

Newton's law of gravity, 89, 92, 96

Newton's laws, 37, 83, 92, 102–103

Newton's time convention model, 175

nickel, 151, 157, 250

Noah's flood, 63, 173, 176, 180, 189, 192–196, 207, 212, 217, 230, 241, 247, 250, 256, 297, 310, 318–319, 324

NOMA doctrine, 208

non-equilibrium, of universe, 106

non-relativistic models, 174

non-thermal motion, 144

Norman and Setterfield, 174

nuclear forces, 45, 87, 89–90, 99, 108, 123, 193, 231

nuclear fusion, 87, 95–96, 141–142, 171, 179

nuclear physics, 47, 113

nucleogenesis, 200

nucleosynthesis problem, 146

Occam, William of, 72

Occam's parsimony scoreboard, 126

Occam's Razor, 72, 125, 259

octopole, 136

Olbers, 158

one-particle universe, 225, 291

Oort cloud, 94, 198

open clusters, 148

open letter to scientific community, 327–330

open universe, 108, 110

operational science, 68–69

Opik, Ernst, 153

orbits, explained by gravity, 92–94

organic polymers, 159

origin of galaxies, 266, 272

origin of life, 158–160, 266

origin of man, Jesus' view, 211

origin of man, unique, 267

origin of meteorites and asteroids, 157

origin of moons, 155, 157

origin of planets, 151, 266

origin of stars, 140, 150, 266

origin of the universe, 19–20, 54, 59, 61, 66, 77, 79, 82, 105, 129, 131, 162–163, 205, 224, 260–261, 265, 288, 294, 300

origins science, 14, 68, 82

our choice, 271

out of nothing, creation, 16, 30, 63, 120, 175, 233–234

outer planets, 152, 199

outflow, as cause of star formation, 144–145

Oxford and Cambridge universities, 34, 112

ozone layer, as protective shield, 239

pale blue dot, 73, 257

panspermia, 160

Papua New Guinea, 81

paradigm, 69, 126, 131, 262, 269, 283

parallax method, 38–40

parsec, 39

parsimony scoreboard, 126, 132

particle accelerators, 47, 88, 124

paths of the sea, 245

Patterson, Claire, 165–166, 188–189

pear-shaped light cone, 184

pear-shaped time, 183–184

Peebles and Silk, 266

penal substitution theory of the atonement, 298

Pentateuch, 31, 214, 216

Pentateuch, central event of, 216

Pentateuch, defense of, 214

Penzias and Wilson, 50, 127

perfect cosmological principle, 73, 283

perfect original creation, 220, 297

perimeter of the earth's surface, 165

petrified forests, 194

phantom energy, 108

photosynthesis, 236

Pioneer 10, 92

plan of redemption, 15–16, 210, 218, 220, 222

Planck particle, 284

Planck time, 117

Planck, Max, 45

planetary magnetic fields, 199, 230

planetary rings, 199

planetesimal theory, 155

planetesimals, 115, 152–153, 157–158, 166, 250

plasma and radiation universe, 201, 328

plasma, defined, 99, 201

Plato, 27–28

Pleiades, 25, 148

Pluto, origin of, 155

Poirot, Hercule, 65

polarization of galaxy light, 134–135

polymer, a long molecule, 159–160

polystrate fossils, 194

Popper, Karl, 68–69

Population I stars, 143, 287

Population II stars, 143, 287

Population III stars, 143, 147

positron, 47, 88, 126

positron, quantum origin, 279

powers of heaven shaken, 250

prebiotic earth, 158

pressure, 78, 83, 95–96, 99, 123–124, 141, 144, 150, 172, 288, 291

pressure problem, 78, 144

pressure, of gas cloud, 78, 141, 144, 150

priming of gas clouds, 145–146, 148, 266

priming problem, 146, 148

primordial singularity, 99–102, 117–120

primordial surface of the earth, 227

probability of an event happening, 83–84, 86, 277

progressive creation, 167, 208, 211, 259, 295, 298, 304

progressive creation, 167, 208, 211, 259, 295, 298, 304

protein, naturalistic origin excluded, 160

proto-galactic clouds, 132

proton, 46–47, 88–90, 117, 126

proton, quantum origin, 126

protons, from big bang, 117

proto-planetesimal, 156

providence, 232

Ptolemy, 28–29, 35, 328

pulsars, 142, 170

Pythagoras, 27

QSS model, 284, 286–288

quadrupole, 136

quantization of galactic redshifts, 238

quantum era, 130–131

quantum fluctuation, 120

quantum mechanics, 47, 87–88, 103, 119

quantum pair production, 88, 126

quantum physics, 47, 120

quantum, defined, 45

quarks, 117, 284

quasar, 135, 273, 276, 279, 282, 285–286

quasar redshift plot, 134–135, 285

quasar, in meta model, 274, 293

quasar, source of new matter, 273

Quasi-Steady State theory, 73

radiation fog, 117

radio waves, 42–43, 134–135, 142, 202

radioactive decay, 90, 152, 158, 173, 189, 195

radioactive halos, 192, 197

radioactive isotopes, 172, 195

radioastronomy, 43

Radioisotopes and the age of the earth, 173, 189–190, 192, 195, 197

RATE group, 173, 192, 195–196

RATE project, 186

rationality paradox, 63

red giants, 141

redshift, 47–48, 273–274, 276–278, 285–288, 291, 293, 328

Reformation, 34, 296

relativistic time dilation, 163, 176, 183–185, 253, 261–262, 317, 323

relativity theory, 16, 44, 87, 91–92, 100, 133, 138, 163, 176, 179, 274, 278, 289

Renaissance, 34–35, 38

Resurrection, 15, 207, 210, 221, 253, 257, 272, 297, 311, 321

rocky planets, origin of, 151–152, 154

rogue gas scenario, 83, 86

Roman Empire, 28, 32

Ross, Hugh, 53–54, 84, 120, 124, 167, 202, 227, 245, 298

rotating cosmos, 135

rotation and turbulence, 87, 102

rotation rate of earth, 35, 181, 185–186, 227–229

rotation speeds in spiral galaxies, 137, 139, 292

rotational motion in universe, 103

ruler of this world, 63, 217

Sabbath and rhythm of life, 236–237, 253

Sabbath as sign of six-day creation, 15, 30, 228, 306

Sabbath commandment, 15, 30, 228, 255, 306

sacrifice of Christ, 15–16, 222

Sagan, Carl, 20, 24, 43, 53, 59–60, 68, 73, 101, 161

salt clock, 187–188, 196

salt lakes, 196

Sandage, Allan, 70, 285

Sarfati, Jonathan, 138, 159, 172, 202, 228

Satan deceives Adam and Eve, 217

Saturn, lethal to life, 239

Saturn, origin of, 154

Saturn, rings of, 199

scattering of light and redshift, 293

science and faith, 71, 96

scientific cosmology, 27–28, 32, 82

scientific method, 57–58, 61–62, 68, 271, 329

scientific naturalism, 271

scoreboard, 72, 126, 132, 259, 261, 265, 313, 321

scoreboard tables, 261, 313–325

scoreboard, biblical model, 317–320

scoreboard, big-bang theory, 313–316

scoreboard, common, 261, 321–325

Scripture cannot be broken, 210, 303

sea of gravitons, 292–293

Search for Extra-Terrestrial Intelligence, 60, 159

second law of thermodynamics, 106–107, 187, 232

sediment clock, 187, 194–195

sedimentary rocks, 187, 189, 230, 256

self-gravity, 150, 156

SETI program, 60, 159, 161, 257

Setterfield, Barry, 174

seven Cs of thelein history, 207, 310

Shadrach, Meshach, and Abednego, 220

Shammai, 32

Shapley, Harlow, 40–42, 44, 78

shock wave, 78, 142, 145–147

shock wave, as cause of star formation, 78, 142, 145–147

Silk, Joseph, 54–55, 101–102, 112, 116–117, 119, 129–132, 145, 266, 274

sin, 15–16, 63–64, 66, 212, 218–222, 248, 251–253, 295–301, 305, 309–310

sin dishonors God, 295, 300–301, 303

sin, and redemption, 301

sin, and stardust, 251

sin, and substitutionary death, 222–223, 298

sin, and suffering, 248

sin, and the Curse, 15, 212, 220–222, 248, 251–253

sin, in cosmic history, 248, 251–253

sin, original, 63–64, 299

sin, suffering, and death, 248, 297, 310

singularities, properties of, 99

singularity, 13, 48–50, 58, 66, 97–102, 107, 115–121, 128, 161, 184, 260, 283, 293

singularity, avoiding the primordial, 100, 120

singularity, false, 98

singularity, in Friedmann model, 101

singularity defined, 101

singularity, primordial, 99–102, 117–120

six-day creation, 14, 17, 20, 178, 211, 228, 255, 295, 300, 306–307

six-day creation and Sabbath, 30, 228, 306

six-day creation and time dilation, 181–185

six-day creation, compromise on, 16–17, 295, 306

six-day creation, in Judaism, 31

six-day creation, purpose of, 236–237, 307

six-day creation, written by God, 30, 306

six-day Creator, 203, 304

skies roll up like a scroll, 248, 251

Sloan Digital Sky Survey, 136

solar mass, unit in cosmology, 96

solar system, 36–38, 40–41, 45, 66, 73, 78–79, 89–90, 92–94, 118, 129–130, 136, 151–155, 157–158, 166–167, 180–183, 198–199, 202–203, 229–230, 235, 239, 242, 248, 250, 252, 254–256, 266–267

solar wind, defined, 239

source of light before the sun, 229

south celestial pole, 23, 170

space shuttle, 152–153

space travel, 267

spacetime and light cones, 183

spacetime in Carmeli model, 289

spacetime, and gravity, 44, 99

spacetime, and Newtonian physics, 44

spacetime, and relativity, 44, 274

spacetime, and world lines, 100–101

spacetime, in cosmic expansion, 119

spacetime, in Humphreys' model, 178–179, 181

spacevelocity, 274, 289

special relativity theory, 289

spectroscope, 38, 47

speed of light, 40, 44–46, 92, 125, 138, 174–176, 178, 183, 200, 203, 253, 276, 278, 289–290

speed of light and age of universe, 200, 203

speed of light and size of universe, 125

speed of light defines light cone, 183

speed of light in Harris model, 174

speed of light in Setterfield model, 174

speed of light in time dilation models, 176

speed of light, defined, 45

sphere, result of gravity, 95

spheres, harmony of, 27

spheres, in Greek cosmology, 28

spherical earth, Aristotle on, 28

spiral density waves, 145

spiral galaxies, 132, 137, 201, 240, 286, 292

spirit universe, 25–26

Spong, John Shelby, 296, 298, 301, 309

square kilometer array radio telescope, 288

standard model of particle physics, 87, 124

standard reference conditions for telling time, 164, 166, 185–186

star formation, 140, 144–151, 288, 322

star formation in gas clouds, 78, 144–151

star formation may never be explained, 241

star formation, goal of SKA, 288

star formation, in clusters, 148

star populations, 143

stardust, 118, 146, 151, 251–252

star-forming regions, 140, 147, 151

Starlight and Time, 170, 175–176, 183, 229, 247, 251

starlight and time problem, 170, 175, 183

starlight, observed in present only, 68

stars falling from the sky, 180, 252, 255, 257

stars, number of, 151, 247

starting assumptions, 56, 59–61, 65, 169, 262, 271, 283

starting point for origin of earth, 64

statistics, study of chance, 82–86

steady state theory, 73, 283

stellar evolution theory, 137, 142–143

sticking problem, 152, 154–155

stratigraphy, 189–191

stretched out the heavens, God, 178, 181, 247, 251, 255, 317, 323

string theory, 104, 107, 266

strong delusion, sent by God, 309

strong nuclear force, 89–90

suffering and death, 207, 248, 255, 297, 305, 310

summary of future trends, 269

summary of other cosmological models, 294

summary of star formation, 150

summary of the biblical model, 252

summary of the big-bang model, 161

summary of time scales, 203

sun darkening as heavenly sign, 248–249

sun, a Population I star, 143

sun, and momentum in solar system, 154

sun, as evidence of divine design, 243

sun, as sign of God's eternal power, 243

sun, created on day 4, 181

sun, powered by nuclear fusion, 171

sun, unit of mass in cosmology, 96

sun, unit of mass/luminosity ratio, 139

super-alien galaxy collector, 237–238, 252

superclusters, 137, 139, 200, 273, 276, 280–281

supernova, 78, 96, 114, 142–147, 149, 151–152, 166, 170–171, 182–183, 202, 249, 251–252, 261, 274, 290–291, 320

supernova remnants, 147, 149, 202, 274

supernova SN1987a, 171, 183

survey of galaxy models, 130

tables of probability, 84

Talmud, 31

Tegmark, 136

temperature of stars, 141, 155

theistic evolution, 17, 53, 167, 172, 208, 259, 295, 298

theistic world view, 75

thelein history, stronghold of faith, 207, 309–311

thelein universe, defined, 206

theological issues, 213, 295

theory of everything, 74, 89, 102, 128

theory of relativity, 91, 133, 138, 163, 176, 179, 278

thermodynamic dead end, 66, 99, 161

thermodynamics, laws of, 87, 106

thorium, 186, 197

Tiamat, 30, 233

Tifft, 135

time and age distinguished, 164

time dilation, 163, 176, 181–185, 200–203, 253, 255, 261–262

time dilation zone, 184

time is pear shaped, 183

timekeeping, 22–23

time machine, 14, 19, 56, 66, 118, 168, 190, 223, 262, 267–268, 300

time machine, and time tourists, 56

time machine, bicycle as, 262

time scale of creation, 211, 227, 307

time scale of creation, importance of, 307–308

time travel, apparently impossible, 56

time zones, 186

time-dilation models, 201

timing devices, modern are useless, 164

Torah, 29, 31

Tree of Life, 15, 218, 222

tree of the knowledge of good and evil, 219

tree rings, 168–170

triggering of gas cloud collapse, 145

turbulence, 87, 102–103, 143–144, 148–150, 171

UFOs, 268

ultraviolet radiation, 155

uncertainty principle, 46, 111, 120

uniformity of CMBR, and horizon problem, 125

universe is awash with life, 158

universe, what is it?, 72

unsolved problems in Hawking's cosmology, 262

uranium, 172–173, 186, 188, 197

Uranus, origin of, 155

Urey, Harold, 157

"use by" dates, 164

V838 Monocerotis, 242

vacuum of space and virtual particles, 111, 120

vacuum of space, and cosmological constant, 110–112

Van der Waal's forces, 152–153

Van Flandern, Tom, 98, 125, 127–128, 158, 274, 276, 291, 293–294

Van Flandern's meta model, 291, 98, 274

vapor canopy, 229

variable time scenario, 178

Venus, lethal to life, 239

Virgo supercluster, 273, 281

virtual particles, 111, 120

water molecule, finely tuned for life, 74, 123–124

water, as evidence of design, 123–124

water, in origin of life, 158–160, 227, 229–230

waters above, 179–181, 198, 229–230, 250, 254, 256–257

weak nuclear force, 89–90

weathering, 166, 194

Weinberg, 112–113

Wheeler, J.A., 97

white dwarfs, 97, 99, 141

white hole cosmology, 176, 178, 180, 200

Wilkinson Microwave Anisotropy Probe, 135

William of Occam, 72

WIMPs, 138

wind shear, 156

WMAP, 127, 135

world line, defined, 100

world views, 20, 53, 61, 75, 129, 166, 209, 238, 247, 271

Wright brothers, 184–185

X-rays, 42, 277

Yahweh, name of God, 216–217

young solar system (YSS) model, 198, 200, 201, 320

Zel'dovich and Novikov, 100–101

zircon crystals, 197

zodiac, 25